D1715602

The Many Faces of Weimar Cinema

Screen Cultures: German Film and the Visual

Series Editors:
Gerd Gemünden (*Dartmouth College*)
Johannes von Moltke (*University of Michigan*)

The Many Faces of Weimar Cinema

Rediscovering Germany's Filmic Legacy

Edited by
Christian Rogowski

CAMDEN HOUSE
Rochester, New York

First published 2010
by Camden House

Camden House is an imprint of Boydell & Brewer Inc.
668 Mt. Hope Avenue, Rochester, NY 14620, USA
www.camden-house.com
and of Boydell & Brewer Limited
PO Box 9, Woodbridge, Suffolk IP12 3DF, UK
www.boydellandbrewer.com

ISBN-13: 978-1-57113-429-5
ISBN-10: 1-57113-429-8

Library of Congress Cataloging-in-Publication Data

The many faces of Weimar cinema : rediscovering Germany's filmic
  legacy / edited by Christian Rogowski.
      p. cm. — (Screen Cultures)
Includes bibliographical references and index.
ISBN-13: 978-1-57113-429-5 (hardcover : alk. paper)
ISBN-10: 1-57113-429-8 (hardcover : alk. paper)
      1. Motion pictures—Germany—History—20th century. I. Rogowski,
Christian, 1956– II. Title. III. Series.

PN1993.5.G3M32 2010
791.430943'09042—dc22
                                                          2009048045

A catalogue record for this title is available from the British Library.

This publication is printed on acid-free paper.
Printed in the United States of America.

Contents

Illustrations

Preface

THESE ARE EXCITING TIMES for the study of Weimar Cinema: in the summer of 2008, the international press was abuzz with news that a nearly complete print of the original version of Fritz Lang's *Metropolis* (1927) had been found in Argentina, one that includes footage long thought to have been irretrievably lost.[1] Now we can look forward to the opportunity of experiencing Lang's legendary science-fiction epic as he originally imagined it both visually and aurally. In February 2010, a reconstructed version was unveiled at a lavish gala presentation at Berlin's Friedrichstadtpalast, complete with a live symphony orchestra performing the original score, and beamed to crowds at the Brandenburg Gate. This reconstruction, with some thirty minutes of recovered footage, may resolve many of the questions raised by the inconsistencies and omissions in the truncated version created in the 1920s for circulation in the United States, upon which much of the film's fame rests. While this may indeed be the most spectacular and the most significant rediscovery of Weimar film footage, it is only one instance in many. Over the past two decades, prints of many films from the period have resurfaced, primarily in European archives, sometimes in surprisingly good quality. Archives and research institutions in Europe and the United States have begun to collaborate on restoring rare films from the Weimar period, making them available to researchers and, increasingly, to interested audiences at large.

Today we can enjoy meticulous and intriguingly beautiful reconstructions not only of canonical masterpieces but also of many lesser-known, but no less important, Weimar German films. In the United States, Kino International has teamed up with the German Murnau-Foundation to release significant films on DVD, including some discussed in this volume, such as Ernst Lubitsch's early silent *Sumurun*, Robert Wiene's *Orlacs Hände* (The Hands of Orlac), and German "experimental" films. In Germany, Filmmuseum Munich has started an equally excellent series of DVD releases, among them Robert Reinert's *Nerven* (Nerves) highlighted in this volume. The Austrian Filmarchive in Vienna has made available other films, accompanied by extensive volumes of essays. It is to be hoped that such official releases of Weimar-era films will soon replace the numerous DVDs and videotapes of questionable quality (and often dubious origins) circulating in this country.

Outside academia, general audiences are now able to encounter films from the Weimar period in a variety of settings: summer festivals such as the "Internationale Stummfilmtage" (International Silent-Film Days) in Bonn draw tens of thousands to outdoor screenings of silent films; every fall, CineGraph Hamburg organizes an "International Film Festival of the German Filmic Heritage"; throughout the year, the Zeughauskino in Berlin shows a regular series, "Wiederentdeckt" (Rediscovered), in cooperation with Cinegraph Babelsberg; the Babylon Cinema in Berlin features "Stummfilmkonzerte" (Silent-Film Concerts) with superb live piano accompaniment; the film museums of Düsseldorf, Frankfurt am Main, Potsdam, Vienna, and the Filmpodium Zurich periodically screen Weimar German films as part of their public programming; the Kinothek Asta Nielsen (Frankfurt am Main) seeks to maintain the legacy of Germany's first movie superstar, Danish diva Asta Nielsen, with public screenings and scholarly symposia; the "Giornate del Cinema Muto" (Silent-Film Festival) at Pordenone, Northern Italy, regularly features films made in the Weimar period. And TV channels such as the Franco-German *arte* or Turner Classic Movies in the United States regularly broadcast reconstructed Weimar films as well. Thanks to the efforts of these institutions and initiatives, we now have unprecedented access to ever larger portions of the incredibly rich filmic legacy of the Weimar period. With every new discovery the history of Weimar Cinema has, in a sense, to be rewritten.

The present volume seeks to contribute to a reassessment of Weimar Cinema and to pay homage to its exciting richness and variety. The increased availability of Weimar films reminds us that the field is much more complex than had traditionally been assumed — and, to be sure, much larger than can be adequately covered in a single volume. In the roughly fourteen years that comprise the Weimar period, the German film industry produced more than 3,500 full-length feature films, that is, an average of around 250 films a year — a staggering number by any measure. True, the vast majority of these films have not been preserved. Yet most Weimar feature films were genre films, and we have more than enough samples from the hundreds of genre films that have survived to provide us with a general picture of the filmic output of Weimar Germany. All the same, I am painfully aware of a number of lacunae even in this sizeable overview of lesser-known films from the Weimar period. The essays here assembled may remind the reader that there are still many, many aspects of Weimar Cinema left to discover.

The present volume owes its existence to a large extent to the pioneering efforts of Eric Rentschler and Anton Kaes. Since the mid-1980s, in summer seminars and workshops, Rick and Tony have introduced generations of German Studies scholars in the United States to the study of German film in general, and to Weimar Cinema in particular. Many of the essays collected here owe their inspiration to the happy hours of screenings and discussions in German Film Institutes devoted to "Unknown Weimar Cinema" held at the University of Michigan in Ann Arbor during the summers of 2004 and 2006, with Johannes von Moltke as the gracious local host. I wish to dedicate this volume to Rick and Tony, as a gesture of my appreciation and gratitude for their scholarly expertise, their pedagogic acumen, their seemingly boundless energy, and the remarkable generosity with which they share their knowledge and love of the subject. The present volume will have succeeded if it can convey some of the fascination of the rich legacy of Weimar German film and make the reader hungry for more. These are, now more than ever, exciting times for the study of Weimar Cinema.

C. R.
Amherst, February 2010

Introduction: Images and Imaginaries

Christian Rogowski

WHAT IMAGES DOES THE NOTION "Weimar Cinema" conjure up? The twisted physiognomy of Conradt Veidt's somnabulist Cesare in Robert Wiene's *The Cabinet of Dr. Caligari* (1920), as he drags off damsel-in-distress Lil Dagover over the slanted nocturnal rooftops? The spooky shadow of Max Schreck's spidery vampire in F. W. Murnau's *Nosferatu* (1921), as he approaches his next innocent victim? The bulky presence of Emil Jannings as Mephisto in Murnau's *Faust* (1925), casting a furtively sinister look over his shoulders? The faceless hordes of despondent workers descending into the grimy futuristic underworld of Fritz Lang's *Metropolis* (1927)? Or Marlene Dietrich's shapely legs in Josef von Sternberg's *The Blue Angel* (1930) — as Lola Lola, the vamp, crooning seductively as she sits astride a barrel on the makeshift stage of a seedy nightclub?

The prevailing view of Weimar Cinema as sinister *auteurist* cinema is to a large extent the product of two accounts that came out in the aftermath of the Second World War: Siegfried Kracauer's provocatively titled *From Caligari to Hitler* (1947) established the view that the films produced during the Weimar period should be read as manifestations of a kind of collective unconscious, displaying a uniquely German preoccupation with authority and a desire for submission that foreshadows the willingness of Germans to submit to real-life dictator Adolf Hitler. Lotte H. Eisner's *The Haunted Screen* (first published in France in 1952 as *L'écran démoniaque* — literally, the "demonic screen") offers a complementing notion of a German predilection to brooding introspection by anchoring the artistic imagination of Weimar-period filmmakers in the tradition of early nineteenth-century German Romanticism, which found its way into film under the influence of legendary theater impresario Max Reinhardt.

These accounts, written by exiled German Jewish intellectuals in the aftermath of National Socialism, war, and the Holocaust, cast the Weimar Cinema as precursor to, or prophet of, the Third Reich and as heir to specifically German cultural traditions, suggesting a direct correlation, perhaps even a causal nexus, between cultural production and historical realities. Such theories appear to be predicated on a monolithic notion of national or cultural identity that supposedly finds its direct expression in films. To be fair to both Kracauer and Eisner, their own accounts provide much more nuance and complexity than the distillation that their ideas received in histories of international film, which only too often conflate Weimar Cinema with Weimar art film, and Weimar art film with "Expressionism." Yet Kracauer seems to essentialize a notion of German identity into the concept of the "German soul" (though restricting himself, at least rhetorically, to tendencies prevalent during a specific time and a distinct set of political circumstances), while Eisner more apodictically speaks of the "German mind" (Kracauer, 3; Eisner, 9). Both critics wrote for specific audiences under particular circumstances: Kracauer wrote for an American audience, aiming to explain to the general reader what it was about the Germans that led to the multiple civilizational catastrophe of National Socialism, genocide, and total war. Eisner addressed herself primarily to French *cinéastes*, salvaging a tainted national cultural heritage by highlighting the "good" German traditions that link Weimar Cinema with the fascinating legacy of German Romanticism. In ostensibly presenting the good, the bad, and the ugly about German culture, these accounts of Weimar German film gained much persuasive power, and their sustained influence rests on the possibility that there may be certain systems of values and beliefs that characterize a specifically German mentality and that such preoccupations manifest themselves in the filmic output of the Weimar period.

Kracauer's sociopsychological speculation about Germans' authoritarian leanings and Eisner's art-historical focus on Germans' soul-searching solipsism create what Thomas Elsaesser aptly calls a kind of theoretical "Moebius strip," a structure of thought that feeds upon itself, presupposing as given what it ostensibly seeks to explore (Elsaesser, 76). Giving the psychoanalytic theories of Jacques Lacan a socio-political twist, Elsaesser labels these closely related — but not identical — notions of a supposedly stable German identity a "historical imaginary," a term that highlights the constructedness of national identity as a product of projection and desire (rather than an expression of an inner essence or actuality) on the part of Weimar-era domestic and international audiences.

In recent years Kracauer and Eisner have been subjected to numerous critiques that focus on the gaps and omissions, the methodological flaws, the blind spots and distortions in their respective accounts of the cinema of the Weimar Republic. As Dietrich Scheunemann put it,

> while Kracauer's "realist" understanding of film as a mirror of the mentality of the nation misleads him in his assessment in particular of the meaning and significance of "non-realist" devices and approaches to film form, Lotte Eisner's predilection for expressionist art tends to eclipse other stylistic developments in the cinema of Weimar (Scheunemann, xi).

The present volume seeks to redress some of the shortcomings of these approaches by highlighting the tremendous diversity and variety of filmic productions of the period.[1] Weimar Cinema, as most of the essays assembled here indicate, was first and foremost a genre cinema, driven by commercial concerns. Much of it was centered on the marketability of recognizable stars: in this volume, Joseph Garncarz constructs a specifically German theory of movie stardom, which has similarities to the American model but is also significantly different from it; and Elizabeth Otto analyzes the multilayered persona of Conrad Veidt, perhaps the most popular actor of the period, in terms of its appeal to a wide variety of audiences. The importance of commercial considerations does not mean that the popular cinema of the Weimar Republic avoids contemporary social and political concerns. Anton Kaes was among the first to note that Weimar Cinema is more fruitfully approached in terms of the often unconscious legacies of a traumatic past rather than in Kracauer's terms as foreshadowing an authoritarian future: the experience of the First World War and of its aftermath — including the humiliation of defeat, the failed revolution, postwar political conflict, hyperinflation, and the collapse of traditional gender roles — and many other contemporary problems all left their mark on Weimar film (Kaes, "Der Film in der Weimarer Republik"; Kaes, *Shell Shock Cinema*). In fact, Weimar filmmakers often sought to exploit public interest in pressing issues of the day by presenting them in a popular format, such as the films that ostensibly combined "sexploitation" with public advocacy (see Jill Suzanne Smith's essay on Richard Oswald, and Christian Rogowski's essay on Wilhelm Dieterle), political melodramas (see the essays by Barbara Hales and Philipp Stiasny), horror films (see the essays by Anjeana Hans and Valerie Weinstein) or antiwar films (see the essays by Jaimey Fisher and Nancy P. Nenno).

We should also not underestimate the significance of technological innovation for the development of Weimar German film. The prominence of fantastic subject matter in early German film can be seen not only as a manifestation of specifically German predilections, as Lotte Eisner argued, but as a function of what Tom Gunning has labeled the "cinema of attractions" (Gunning, 56–62) a fascination with the specific possibilities offered by a new medium (which allowed and encouraged fantastic effects through the manipulation of the moving image). The fascination with the creative possibilities of the filmic medium finds perhaps its purest forms in the avant-garde "abstract films" of the 1920s (see Joel Westerdale's essay). Some of this innovative energy spilled over into the popular genre films of the period, for instance in the hallucinatory sequences in Robert Reinert's *Nerven* (Nerves, 1919), explored here by Barbara Hales. Focusing on the impact of the introduction of synchronous sound in the late 1920s, two essays in this volume explore the connection between aesthetic and technological innovation on the one hand, and political and social concerns on the other (see the essays by Ofer Ashkenazi and Jaimey Fisher).

The productivity of the Weimar German film industry is nothing short of astonishing: at the outset, in 1919, it produced no fewer than 470 films;

the next year, the number increased to a staggering 510 films (Prinzler, 44, 49). During the period of rising inflation following the war, with the German mark in steady decline, films were cheap to produce, especially if production companies had access to foreign, and thus more stable, currency. It was therefore important for German companies to make films that could be exported abroad. Yet German films were, for the most part, subject either to import embargos or to lingering anti-German sentiment after the war. In the face of such obstacles companies tended to produce genre films that often enough camouflaged their German origins. The Great War had drastically changed film markets all over the world, with Hollywood establishing a level of production against which all national film industries had to compete (Saunders, 51–83). The vast majority of fiction feature films produced in Weimar Germany sought to appeal to both domestic and foreign audiences. The choices of subject matter, casting, and visual style were dictated by marketing concerns, as was the drive toward technological innovation and experimentation.

The film boom of the immediate postwar period was short lived, with a decline in production coinciding with the increasingly volatile economic climate during the period of hyperinflation (1922–23). The initial advantage of access to foreign convertible currency quickly faded as the German mark plunged to several billion against a single US dollar (Widdig, 37). By 1923, at the height of hyperinflation, the yearly output had dropped to 253 films, declining further over the years to just 132 films in the last full year of the Weimar Republic, 1932 (Prinzler, 102). Ticket sales paint a similar picture: in 1926, the first year for which we have information, some 332 million tickets were sold in Germany (Prinzler, 73). With a population of around sixty-two million, this would mean that, statistically speaking, each German — from infant to old-age pensioner — made about five visits to a movie theater annually, attesting to the proverbial *Kinosucht* (cinema addiction) of Weimar German audiences (Rosenhaft).[2]

Weimar German interest in film was not restricted to feature-length narrative fiction film. Between 1918 and 1933, Germans encountered films in a wide variety of settings and formats. The most well-known non-fiction film genre of the period is that of the *Kulturfilme* (cultural films), usually short films about contemporary or historical topics that were shown in movie theaters before the main feature. They could cover anything from interesting locales or exotic flora and fauna to arts and crafts. The present volume includes an essay by Theodore F. Rippey on the most famous of such films, Wilhelm Prager's *Wege zu Kraft und Schönheit* (Paths to Strength and Beauty, 1926), a film both typical (in structure and style) and atypical (insofar as it assumed feature-film length) of that genre. A recent publication documents the astonishing richness and variety of this kind of filmic output — which often combined fictional and non-fictional elements — in a massive 700-page volume (Kreimeier/Ehmann/Goergen).

Another important aspect of cinema programs of the period is the inclusion of weekly newsreels, such as the *Messter-Woche* and the *Ufa-Wochenschau*, that provided audiences with visual information concerning current political and cultural events. In movie theaters, fiction features, then, were almost always shown in the context of a program that incorporated other sources of visual entertainment.

Outside the cinema, film was omnipresent as well: schools showed educational films; political organizations such as the pro-colonial lobby or the trade unions showed films advancing their respective political agendas, as did political parties, missionary organizations, and the churches; major companies pioneered industrial films for public relation purposes; and the period saw the beginning of advertising films, often featuring innovative animations, such as the charming short cartoon commercials produced by Julius Pinschewer. Just as many filmic techniques, such as stop-frame animation, the mobile camera, color, and synchronized sound, were developed both in fiction and in non-fiction film, many figures active in Weimar film, such as Walther Ruttmann, Ernö Metzner, Oskar Fischinger, and Lotte Reiniger, moved around between various arenas (commercial, industrial, or documentary films, artistic films, and narrative fiction features). The legacy of artistically ambitious "experimental" or "absolute" film has achieved international recognition (see Joel Westerdale's essay in this volume), while the vast output of non-fiction or "documentary" films (and their hybrids) is largely unknown outside the German-speaking countries.

Even if one restricts the focus to narrative feature films produced for commercial release in movie theaters, the essays assembled here show that Weimar Cinema was far from uniform. Rather, what characterizes Weimar Cinema is the impressive ingenuity and creativity displayed by filmmakers, constantly seeking to invent and reinvent new forms of storytelling and visual appeal. Moreover, the essays demonstrate that the cinema of the period was first and foremost a commercial cinema aimed at a mass audience, at home and abroad. Both Kracauer and Eisner display a certain mandarin disdain for products of mass culture, preferring to focus on a limited number of "quality films," while largely dismissing popular genre films as aesthetically weak and politically suspect. The most glaring lacuna in both critics' accounts is their neglect (or downright dismissal) of Ernst Lubitsch, who developed a distinctively German-Jewish style of satirical comedy during the war years and continued to produce a wide variety of genre films after 1919, including historical costume dramas and exotic fantasy films (see Richard W. McCormick's essay in this volume). The cheerfully anarchic subversiveness of Lubitsch's comedies, centered on recognizably Jewish male upstarts or *nebbishes* (initially played by Lubitsch himself) or feisty females (often played by Ossi Oswalda) is a far cry from either authoritarian leanings or high-brow Teutonic art. As Sabine Hake has shown, these comedies are distinguished by a child-like focus on easy wish-fulfillment, where social ascent and erotic gratification go hand in hand (Hake, 99). Lubitsch's charming comedies, no less than his other genre films, were tremendously popular in wartime and postwar Germany, casting doubts on the validity of many of Kracauer's and Eisner's claims.

Both Kracauer and Eisner, assimilated intellectuals with few, if any, ties to their own Jewish backgrounds, display an odd disregard for the fact that many, perhaps even most, of the important practitioners in Weimar Cinema were of German-Jewish or Austro-Hungarian-Jewish descent. For instance, the films that comprise a kind of canon of Weimar art film were created by a limited number of people, most of whom with a Jewish background. The sixteen films included in Noah Isenberg's *Weimar Cinema: An Essential Guide to Classic Films of the Era* (2009) were produced by Erich Pommer (six titles), Seymour Nebenzahl (two titles), and Paul Davidson, Albin Grau, Rudolf Meinert, Joe May, Michael Salkind, and Robert Siodmak/ Edgar G. Ulmer (one title each). Among directors we find Fritz Lang (whom the Nazis would later classify as a "half-Jew"), Joe May, Robert Siodmak/Edgar Ulmer, Josef von Sternberg, and Robert Wiene; among scriptwriters there are Karl Freund, Willy Haas, Hans Janowitz, Carl Mayer, and Billy Wilder/Robert Siodmak. It is estimated that of the around 10,000 people working in the German film industry during the Weimar period, some 2,000 were forced to emigrate to escape the racial and political persecution of the Nazi regime (Asper, 957). Likewise, most of the films discussed in this volume, the reader will note, were directed or produced by people of Jewish origin — from Germany (E. A. Dupont, Ernst Lubitsch, Erich Pommer, Kurt and Robert Siodmak, and Robert Wiene), from German-speaking Austria (Joseph Delmont, Richard Oswald, Robert Reinert, and Hanns Schwarz), or whose roots go back to other parts of the Austro-Hungarian Empire (Henrik Galeen, Heinrich and Seymour Nebenzahl) and eastern Europe (Victor Trivas) (see Stratenwerth/ Simon; Feld). Sometimes Weimar German films address specifically Jewish themes — such as issues of assimilation, acculturation, marginality, and identity — either directly (see the essays by Cynthia Walk and Nancy P. Nenno) or indirectly (see Richard W. McCormick's essay). And it will be remembered that legendary theater director Max Reinhardt, whom Eisner credits for introducing an unprecedented art of visual stylization into German film through his handling of crowds and his mastery at using the magic of lighting, had been born as Maximilian Goldmann to Jewish parents in a small town outside Vienna.

It is Eisner's focus on "Expressionist" film and its aesthetic lineage that is largely responsible for the fact that in the common imagination, at least outside Germany, "Weimar Cinema" and "German Expressionism" became nearly synonymous. Yet given the variety of styles and forms that can be found in the films of the period, it becomes clear that what can legitimately be labeled as "Expressionist" filmmaking constituted at best a small segment of the filmic output, and by no means the dominant one. Since Eisner's approach is primarily descriptive and does not claim the same kind of explanatory authority as does Kracauer, it is primarily Kracauer who has come under fire from various sides. Feminist critics like Patrice Petro noted that Kracauer's focus on authoritarianism leads him to neglect issues of gender and genre and questions of visual pleasure: more than half of film audiences in Weimar Germany were female, and the German film industry catered to them, their perceived needs and desires, by producing a wide variety of genre films such as domestic melodramas or romantic comedies. Likewise, film historian Heide Schlüpmann pointed out that Kracauer's dismissal of much of pre-Weimar German film as irrelevant "pre-history" neglects the emancipatory potential of Wilhelmine cinema: with its wide array of female explorers, adventurers, and detectives, the cinema of the *Kaiserreich* offered its female audiences plenty of role models whose agency and mobility challenged patriarchal authority and offered alternatives to traditional gender roles (Schlüpmann, 152).

The essays assembled here make it clear that Weimar Cinema was not primarily an *auteurist* art cinema that addressed (predominantly male) national preoccupations. Rather, it was a tremendously diverse popular cinema that developed a variety of genre forms, a commercial cinema that employed many different strategies to combine entertainment, edification, titillation, and visual pleasure to diverse audiences, male and female, lower and middle class, in Germany and abroad, of all sorts of political persuasions. Weimar films ranged from the brooding psychological dramas of males in crisis that address war trauma (see the essays by Barbara Hales and Anjeana Hans) to the cheerful exotic fairytales or romantic comedies that celebrate modernity, social mobility, and female agency (see the essays by Richard W. McCormick and Mihaela Petrescu). The vast majority of feature films produced in the Weimar republic were genre films that sought to be commercially viable in multiple arenas. They transported various ideological messages, appealed to diverse audiences in manifold ways, and sought to make use of new technologies (such as the mobile camera, sophisticated lighting techniques, and eventually sound) to enhance their marketability.

Weimar Cinema operated in a variety of transnational networks: the market for German films comprised not only the truncated German *Reich* in its post-Versailles borders but also the former Austro-Hungarian Empire and the rest of the Balkans. German film companies maintained strong ties with Soviet Russia and other parts of Eastern Europe, the Scandinavian countries, and various countries in South America. As Chris Wahl's essay in this volume shows, the German film industry scored significant successes in establishing a formidable presence in the French market and in other countries. There were joint business ventures with French and British companies. Various alliances were formed to combat the predominance of Hollywood in the European arena: the short-lived *Europäische Film-Allianz* (European Film Alliance; Efa) sought cooperation with American financiers in exchange for access to the American market; the various initiatives under the heading *Film-Europa* (Film Europe) sought to unify the different European markets under a joint heading; and, after the financial debacle of Fritz Lang's *Metropolis* (1927), Germany's biggest film company, Ufa, struggled to survive by entering into a complex production and distribution deal with the American studios Paramount and MGM, the *Parufamet* agreement. One of the more surprising, and intriguing, transnational projects was the involvement of German filmmakers in the birth of an indigenous film industry in India (the subject of Veronika Fuechtner's essay in this volume).

Weimar Germany and its film industry was a magnet for talent throughout the 1920s: aspiring artists flocked to Germany, not only from the Austro-Hungarian Empire and other parts of Eastern Europe but also from Scandinavia, and even France. The young Alfred Hitchcock went to Germany in the mid-1920s to perfect his craft as a director. Danish director Theodor Dryer made some of his most ambitious films in Germany. Swedish actress Greta Garbo appeared in German films before moving to the United States to launch her international career, as did many others. Just as such talent entered Germany across national boundaries from all directions, the German film industry after the First World War had to, and sought to, position itself both in a domestic market and in various international markets.

Many of the creative decisions of producers and directors working in the Weimar film industry cannot be viewed as reflections of particular ideological predispositions; they were primarily triggered by economic and technological concerns: innovative lighting and stylized acting could enhance a film's visual appeal and distinguish the film from the products of other countries. Conversely, streamlining a film to erase its German origins by providing well-crafted variations of established genres (such as the historical costume drama, the detective thriller, the action adventure film, the exotic fantasy film, and so on) could lower the resistance of international audiences to German products. The war had provided the German film industry with a unique form of protection: the embargo against foreign films had created tremendous demand for domestic product and the occupation of territories had vastly expanded the market. In response, dozens of film companies sprang up to profit from the increased business opportunities. After 1917, when three major film German companies were secretly consolidated into *Universum Film Aktiengesellschaft* (Ufa), at the behest of the German military command, the other, smaller, film companies found themselves pitted against a disproportionally large competitor. Later, with the artificial protection removed after military defeat, the German film industry encountered a disparity between the inflated production capabilities and a drastically shrunken market. After the war, the German film industry, with is many small, often under-capitalized production companies, found itself entangled in a complex tangle of infrastructural, economic, political, and cultural circumstances.

From this perspective, the "Germanness" of Weimar film emerges primarily as a function of a socio-economic double matrix, as the German film industry confronted two different sets of challenges: on the one hand, there was the problematic status of film within German culture, dominated by class-conscious, educated cultural elites hostile to a new medium viewed as lacking in *Bildung* — substance, sophistication, and depth. On the other hand was the peculiar position of German film in the international arena. In the wake of the Great War, German films faced anti-German hostility and import embargoes, as well as the increasing dominance of American film. In this dual context at home and abroad, even the thematic and stylistic characteristics of filmic Expressionism, for instance, had little to do with uniquely German predilections and preoccupations but rather with questions of domestic and international marketing. Given the political, cultural, and economic climate, what was called for was a kind of filmic product that could be recognized as "German" in a positive sense, both at home and abroad. For the domestic market, garnering cultural cachet involved an appeal to familiar cultural, largely middle-brow, traditions, such as German myths and fairy tales, and the ostensibly harmonic past of the Romantic and *Biedermeier* periods. In the international context it necessitated evoking prewar, primarily high-brow, traditions that had positive connotations, such as the boldly rebellious and innovative Expressionist movement.

"*Caligari* oder *Herrin der Welt*?" (*Caligari* or *Mistress of the World*?) is the headline that appeared on 9 March 1920 on the front page of the daily *Film-Kurier*, the most important trade journal for the German film industry. In his editorial, critic Robert Volz sums up what he sees as the two alternatives if German film wants to compete in an international arena: it could produce either high-brow quality films with a distinctively "German" touch, such as Robert Wiene's Expressionist film, *The Cabinet of Dr. Caligari*, or it could aim at popular adventure films, "Prunkfilme" (visual spectacles) such as Joe May's blockbuster adventure serial, *Die Herrin der Welt*, which appeal to a mass audience by flaunting high production values and superb entertainment value. Both films had premiered shortly before, and both had been greeted by the German press, with somewhat belligerent rhetoric, as potential "weapons" in the "fight for the world market" ("Kampf um den Weltmarkt"; Volz).

Where Kracauer and Eisner saw lone artists agonizing to give expression to, or collectives unconsciously falling prey to, specifically Teutonic preoccupations, we can see shrewd entrepreneurs at work cleverly assessing available economic options by adopting innovative strategies, what today we call product differentiation and niche marketing. Wiene's *The Cabinet of Dr. Caligari* of 1920, with its curious mixture of banal fantastic subject matter and quasi-avant-garde visual stylization, successfully fulfilled both roles as a self-consciously "artistic" film and as a marketable commodity. Films like *Caligari* helped expand its audience base at home by drawing on familiar cultural traditions that bestowed upon film a certain aura of respectability with middle-class audiences. Abroad, they presented a picture of Germany as a deeply conflicted nation in which striking artistic experiments sought to challenge the authoritarian traditions held responsible for starting the war.

Directors and producers like Joe May and Ernst Lubitsch adopted a different strategy: their adventure films, historical costume dramas, and exotic fantasies camouflaged their German origins: Joe May's *Die Herrin der Welt* features a Danish adventuress traveling all across the globe to seek vengeance on the man who ruined her family's life; his *Das indische Grabmal* (The Indian Tomb, 1921) centers on a British architect who gets called to India by a mysterious Maharaja to build a matchless mausoleum (Rogowski). Ernst Lubitsch successfully adapted Prosper Merimée's well-known novella (and Georges Bizet's popular opera) *Carmen* (1918), drew on oriental fantasies set in a mythical Baghdad in *Sumurun* (1920), and reinvented moments from European history, for instance Tudor England, in *Anna Boleyn* (1920). It was one of Lubitsch's lavish costume dramas, *Madame Dubarry* (released as *Passion*, 1919), set in pre-revolutionary France, that opened the doors for German film in the United States.

In economic terms, the central challenge for Weimar film was to produce a kind of brand identity for German film, to create a national cinema distinct from Hollywood products in which domestic audiences could see themselves mirrored (and which answered their desires in ways equal to or better than American films) and in which international audiences could recognize, accept, and come to appreciate what they thought they knew as distinctly "German" — or whose German origins they could forget, as they were swept away by interesting storylines, intriguing subject matter, or sheer visual splendor. This is exactly what they found in the exotic fairytales, action adventure films, costume dramas, and romantic comedies of well-known filmmakers like Ernst Lubitsch, Robert Wiene, and the early Fritz Lang, and lesser-known directors such as those covered in this volume — Joseph Delmont, E. A. Dupont, Henrik Galeen, Richard Oswald, Robert Reinert, and Hanns Schwarz — as well as countless others not included here, such as Ludwig Berger, Erik Charell, Richard Eichberg, Carl Froelich, Max Mack, Harry Piel, Otto Rippert, Reinhold Schünzel, and Wilhelm Thiele.

As the many films discussed in the essays assembled here demonstrate, the cinema of the Weimar Republic had many different faces: after the First World War, Germans did not necessarily crave dark and brooding tales of males in crisis, filmed with bizarre camera angles and high-contrast lighting. Instead, *pace* Kracauer and Eisner, Germans, like audiences elsewhere, voted with their feet — and with their pocket books — flocking to see exotic adventure tales, romantic comedies, detective thrillers, tearful melodramas, and other genre films that provided them with the fleeting vicarious pleasures of the silver screen.

Notes

[1] To single out a few of the most interesting "omissions" we cannot include here: there are the remarkable achievements of Lotte Reiniger, the German pioneer in stop-frame animations. Her *Die Abenteuer des Prinzen Achmed* (Prince Achmed's Adventures, 1926), combining thousands of cut-out silhouettes in an oriental fairy tale based on a story from *The Arabian Nights*, is a particularly astounding and charming piece of filmic innovation. Likewise, German daredevil superstar Harry Piel, still virtually unknown in the English-speaking world, who directed and starred in countless action adventure films and detective thrillers, has long been overdue for a rediscovery. Other possible but sadly absent topics include an assessment of the Weimar careers of the "dream couple" of Weimar German film, Lilian Harvey and Willy Fritsch. Not to mention the dazzling variety and charm of satirical musical comedies and sound film operettas produced in Germany during the Great Depression by people like Ludwig Berger, Erik Charell, Reinhold Schünzel, and Carl Froelich. The list goes on and on.

[2] To put these figures in perspective: in 1926, Germans were four to five times more likely to go to the cinema than in 2007. 1926: 332 million tickets sold, with a population of 62 million; 2007: 125.4 million tickets sold, with a population or around 83 million, according to the 2007 report of the *Filmförderungsanstalt* (German Federal Film Board), available online at http://www.ffa.de/index.php?page=publikationsuebersicht.

Works Cited

Asper, Helmut G. "Film." In *Handbuch der deutschsprachigen Emigration 1933–1945*, edited by Claus Dieter Krohn, Patrick von zur Mühlen, Gerhard Paul, and Lutz Winckler, 957–70. Darmstadt: Primus, 1998.

Eisner, Lotte H. *The Haunted Screen: Expressionism in the German Cinema and the Influence of Max Reinhardt.* Translated from the French by Roger Greaves. 1952. Reprinted, Berkeley and Los Angeles: U of California P, 1969.

Elsaesser, Thomas. *Weimar Cinema and After: Germany's Historical Imaginary.* London and New York: Routledge, 2000.

Feld, Hans. "The Jewish Contribution to the German Film Industry: Notes from the Recollections of a Berlin Film Critic." *Yearbook of the Leo Baeck Institute* 27(1982): 337–65.

Gunning, Tom. "The Cinema of Attractions: Early Film, Its Spectator, and the Avant-Garde." In *Early Cinema: Space, Frame, Narrative*, edited by Thomas Elsaesser, 56–62. London: BFI, 1990.

Hake, Sabine. *Passions and Deceptions: The Early Films of Ernst Lubitsch.* Princeton, NJ: Princeton UP, 1992.

Isenberg, Noah, ed. *Weimar Cinema: An Essential Guide to Classic Films of the Era.* New York: Columbia UP, 2009.

Kaes, Anton. "Der Film in der Weimarer Republik." In *Geschichte des deutschen Films*, edited by Wolfgang Jacobsen, Anton Kaes, and Hans Helmut Prinzler, 39–100. Stuttgart: Metzler, 1993.

——. *Shell Shock Cinema: Weimar Culture and the Wounds of War.* Princeton, NJ: Princeton UP, 2009.

Kracauer, Siegfried. *From Caligari to Hitler: A Psychological History of the German Film.* (1947). Princeton, NJ: Princeton UP, 1974.

Kreimeier, Klaus, Antje Ehmann, and Jeanpaul Goergen, eds. *Geschichte des dokumentarischen Films in Deutschland*, vol. 2: *Weimarer Republik, 1918–1933.* Stuttgart: Reclam, 2005.

Petro, Patrice. *Joyless Streets: Women and Melodramatic Representation in Weimar Germany.* Princeton, NJ: Princeton UP, 1989.

Prinzler, Helmut, ed. *Chronik des deutschen Films, 1895–1994.* Stuttgart and Weimar: Metzler, 1995.

Rogowski, Christian. "Movies, Money, and Mystique: Joe May's Early Weimar Blockbuster, *The Indian Tomb* (1921)." In Isenberg, 55–77.

Rosenhaft, Eve. "Lesewut, Kinosucht, Radiotismus: Zur (geschlechter-) politischen Relevanz neuer Massenmedien in den 1920er Jahren." In *Amerikanisierung: Traum und Alptraum im Deutschland des 20. Jahrhunderts*, edited by Alf Lüdtke, Inge Marßolek, and Adelheid von Saldern, 119–43. Stuttgart: Steiner, 1996.

Saunders, Thomas. *Hollywood in Berlin: American Cinema and Weimar Germany.* Berkeley: U of California P, 1994.

Scheunemann, Dietrich, ed. *Expressionist Film: New Perspectives.* Rochester, NY: Camden House, 2003.

Schlüpmann, Heide. *Der unheimliche Blick: Das Drama des frühen deutschen Kinos.* Basel and Frankfurt am Main: Stroemfeld/Roter Stern, 1990.

Stratenwerth, Irene, and Hermann Simon, eds. *Pioniere in Celluloid: Juden in der frühen Filmwelt.* Berlin: Henschel, 2004.

Volz, Robert. "*Caligari* oder *Herrin der Welt*?" *Film-Kurier* (9 March 1920).

Widdig, Bernd. *Culture and Inflation in Weimar Germany.* Berkeley: U of California P, 2001.

1: Richard Oswald and the Social Hygiene Film: Promoting Public Health or Promiscuity?

Jill Suzanne Smith

THERE ARE PLENTY OF REASONS to remember Richard Oswald in the context of Weimar film history. Born Richard W. Ornstein to a middle-class Viennese Jewish family in 1880, Oswald initially embarked upon a career in the theater. After fourteen years of acting, writing, and directing for the stage in Vienna, southern Germany, and Düsseldorf, he took up residence in Berlin in 1913 and began working as a director and screenwriter for Jules Greenbaum's film production company Vitascope. His first film script for Vitascope, a screen adaptation of the Sherlock Holmes detective drama *Der Hund von Baskerville* (The Hound of Baskerville, 1914), was immensely successful. Oswald spent the next twenty years of his life in Berlin and became one of the most popular and prolific filmmakers of his time. Between the years 1918 and 1933 he directed seventy feature films, most of which he also produced and wrote or co-wrote (Kasten/Loacker, 9, 12, 547–59; Bock, "Biographie"; Berger).

Employing strategies and business models that are traditionally associated with Hollywood cinema, Oswald measured the quality of his films by their popularity, and hence by their financial success (Belach/Jacobsen, 68). He recognized star power when he saw it, and in addition to working with already established film actresses such as Asta Nielsen, he is credited with kick-starting the film careers of controversial performance artists such as Anita Berber and the stage actors Conrad Veidt, Werner Krauß, and Reinhold Schünzel, all of whom became icons of Weimar Cinema. A savvy businessman, Oswald founded his own film production company, Richard-Oswald-Film GmbH (Ltd.) in 1916, which by 1921 he transformed into an *Aktiengesellschaft*, a public corporation with shareholders. The breadth of Oswald's body of cinematic work is staggering, including detective films, social melodramas, adaptations of crime, fantasy, and romance literature, epic historical dramas, and, after the transition to sound film, musical comedies and operettas. Film scholars in Germany who have recently rediscovered Oswald argue that his works offer us unrivaled insight into popular Weimar film and the tastes and whims of that era's mainstream audience (Kasten/Loacker, 12; Goergen, Introductory Essay, 3).

Despite the sheer number of films and range of genres attributed to Oswald, he is best remembered for one specific genre: the *Aufklärungsfilm* (social hygiene film).[1] Most often defined as "sex education films" that emerged amidst the chaos of the First World War to warn the German populace of the dangers of venereal diseases, the *Aufklärungsfilm* was a sensationalist filmic form already familiar to the Wilhelmine audience. The unique blend of titillation and education that is most often used to define *Aufklärungsfilme* of the early Weimar era could already be found in prewar films, such as the imported Danish film from 1910 entitled *The White Slave*, which, as cultural historian Peter Jelavich documents, "supposedly warned young women about pimps and prostitution but in reality were vehicles for depicting sexual violence and bondage" (243). While these early films drew the ire of conservative moral reformers, the fact that they were not set in contemporary German society but rather were "packaged in historical or exotic garb" made them palatable even to a bourgeois audience (Jelavich, 243). The first serious educational films, or *Lehrfilme*, represented a top-down form of enlightenment of the masses developed during the First World War by self-proclaimed public health experts, most of them doctors and politicians.

The use of film to educate the masses signaled a media shift within the public health, or social hygiene, movement, which before the war had limited itself to lectures and pamphlets. During the war organizations such as the *Deutsche Gesellschaft zur Bekämpfung der Geschlechtskrankheiten* (German Society to Combat Venereal Diseases; cited hereafter as DGBG) and institutions such as Karl August Lingner's *Deutsches Hygiene-Museum* (German Hygiene Museum) in Dresden sought to harness the power of the visual image by organizing traveling hygiene exhibits, staging theatrical productions, and making documentary films (Schmidt, 29–32). While the public was initially both fascinated and repulsed by the images of diseased bodies presented in such works, they were quickly bored by the dry, factual, scientific tone of the *Lehrfilme* (Kasten/Loacker, 83; Schweisheimer, 8). It was Richard Oswald who realized that hygiene films first had to *appeal* to the viewing public before they could *educate* them, and in 1917 he teamed up with the DGBG to make the first social melodrama on venereal disease, *Es werde Licht!* (Let There Be Light!).[2] The film's title, with its blatant call for illumination, directly links Oswald's project with the enlightenment, or *Aufklärung*, of its audience.

Es werde Licht! became the prototype for a new symbiosis of science and film, of public health advocacy and entertainment, which Oswald himself called the "social hygiene film" ("sozialhygienisches Filmwerk"). It remains unclear to this day, however, what the exact relationship was between the DGBG and Oswald's production company. In addition to acting as scientific consultants during the film's production, the DGBG likely lobbied to protect the film from censorship and may even have helped Oswald to secure partial state funding for the project; in turn, the health organization benefited from the publicity generated by the film and may have shared in the profits (Kasten/Loacker, 84). The film was a hit with both audiences and reformers; the latter praised Oswald for his tasteful and sensitive treatment of such a delicate subject. Oswald took this praise and ran with it, making three sequels to *Es werde Licht!* before the end of the war, a move that was interpreted by many as motivated more by financial greed than by an altruistic compulsion to educate the masses. While the DGBG retreated from him, Oswald kept the support of other prominent sex reformers. Iwan Bloch, the pioneer of sexology, served as the medical advisor for sequels 2 and 3, and the Berlin sexologist Magnus Hirschfeld worked with Oswald on the fourth sequel, entitled *Sündige Mütter (Strafgesetz, §218)* (Sinful Mothers [Penal Code §218], 1918), which warned its viewers of the perils of illegal abortion. Other members of the medical establishment maligned the latter two sequels for their lack of scientific clarity and for their sensationalism (Schweisheimer, 68).

With the end of the war in November 1918, German censorship laws that had been in effect since 1906 were abolished. Within six months of the lifting of censorship, Oswald and Hirschfeld raised eyebrows and tempers again by collaborating on two controversial hygiene films, *Die Prostitution* (Prostitution, 1919) and *Anders als die Andern* (Different from the Others, 1919).[3] With prostitution and homosexuality as their respective topics, both films challenged the German state's right to legislate sexual behavior. Medical professionals, intellectuals, and politicians spanning the range of the political spectrum accused Oswald and Hirschfeld of creating films that encouraged rather than discouraged sexually permissive behavior among audience members. The popularity of the Oswald/ Hirschfeld films, particularly with urban audiences, spawned an entire crop of films by lesser-known directors with titles meant to both allure and horrify — *Das Gift im Weibe* (The Poison in Woman, 1919), *Hyänen der Lust* (Hyenas of Lust, 1919), and *Im Rausche der Sinne* (Intoxicated with Sensuality, 1920) — that appealed to the public's prurient desires (Hagener, 170–74; Steakley, 190). Unwittingly targeted as the cause of this proliferation in "sexploitation" films, Oswald tried valiantly to defend his films from slander.[4] As much as current scholars of Oswald's work may lament the narrow association of such a versatile director with this controversial genre, it is important to acknowledge the central role that Oswald, his *Aufklärungsfilme*, and their reception played in the first years of the Weimar Republic, particularly in the political debates concerning the reinstatement of artistic censorship, in aesthetic discussions of the competing media of film and theater, and in social discourses on prostitution and female sexuality.

Quite understandably, *Anders als die Andern* has been widely discussed and analyzed in recent scholarship for the crucial role it played in
the formation and assertion of homosexual identity in Weimar Germany
and in the movement led by Hirschfeld to abolish §175 of the penal code,
a law that outlawed male homosexuality. However, only scant attention has
been paid to *Die Prostitution* and the myriad social and aesthetic issues it
raises. This is likely due in part to the fact that the film was destroyed in
1922 and can only be reconstructed — or excavated — through a careful
analysis of promotional materials, reviews in the press, notes from censorship proceedings, and written reactions by politicians, medical professionals, and cultural critics. *Die Prostitution* was just as important to the
debates surrounding film censorship and the legal control of the body
politic as *Anders als die Andern,* and possibly more so. Indeed, when we
examine texts from across the political and cultural spectrum, we find that
it was the subject of prostitution — rather than homosexuality — that
provoked the greatest outrage and anxiety from all camps over the spread
of venereal diseases and the moral laxity of the German public, particularly
its female citizens.

Although most film critics of the day raved about Oswald's film *Die
Prostitution*, public officials excoriated it as the prototype for the multi-
tude of sex-themed films that followed its release, works that members of
the leftist USPD (Independent Socialist Party of Germany) simply labeled
as exploitative "Prostitutionsfilme" and defined as a "cultural disgrace of
the highest order" ("Kulturschande ersten Ranges," quoted in Sturm,
64). In her investigation of the parliamentary debates on film censorship,
Eva Sturm documents how, in order to express his support of censorship,
the liberal representative of the DDP (German Democratic Party), Paul
Ende, cited an anonymous literary critic who compared the permissive
atmosphere of German cinemas with brothels (72). This conflation of
cinema and brothel, of film and prostitution, is symptomatic of how
criticism of specific films such as Richard Oswald's *Die Prostitution*
became unhinged from the individual works themselves to form a larger
discourse, in which representatives from the political, scientific, and cultural fields vied for control over both the body politic and the new cinematic medium.

Education or Seduction? *Die Prostitution* and the Female Audience

One of the most common criticisms leveled against *Die Prostitution* at the
time of its release was that it presents prostitution not as dangerous and
demeaning but as glamorous and inviting. In his 1920 study, which offers
guidelines for the proper use of film in the social hygienic education of the

masses, the medical doctor Waldemar Schweisheimer expresses his incredulity about the fact that Oswald's film makes no mention of the connection between prostitution and venereal diseases (Schweisheimer, 71). Before Schweisheimer's study even appeared, however, cultural critics including the young playwright Bertolt Brecht and the satirist Kurt Tucholsky had already voiced their concerns about the film, claiming that the scenes set in the brothel "do not deter, but rather, at the very least, excite" ("schrecken nicht ab, sondern reizen höchstens an," Tucholsky, 404). The glamorized image of the prostitute was indeed used to promote social hygiene films such as the Oswald/Hirschfeld production, as one can see from the film poster for *Die Prostitution* (fig. 1.1). The poster shows a slim, attractive woman in a low-cut yet tasteful gown placed in front of throngs of admiring gentlemen. Her heavy makeup and sunken eyes are the only physical markers that betray her profession and imply her possible sickness. The only other clue to her potential deadliness is the skeleton-like face in the lower far right corner of the poster, yet this is nearly hidden in the crowd of adoring men's faces. The prostitute herself looks not at her admirers but at the poster's viewer, beckoning with a seductive look. Viewing this poster, one could see why Brecht and Tucholsky accuse the film of promoting prostitution. However, today's scholars of the *Aufklärungsfilme* remind us that, while the films' sensationalistic advertising materials (titles, posters) may fit the popular appeal of sex in the Weimar Republic, they rarely have anything to do with the actual plot of the films they represent (Hagener/Hans, 17–19). Indeed, a brief review of *Die Prostitution* in one of Berlin's daily newspapers praises the film, its director, and its actors for treating this potentially sensational topic with "tact and taste."[5] The narrative constructed by Oswald seems to do little to entice its viewers into prostitution, especially when one considers the fates of the main female protagonists.

The film tells the tale of two sisters who live with their good-for-nothing father in a working-class neighborhood in Berlin. Oswald depicts the sisters as clear opposites in both appearance and character; Hedwig (Gussy Holl) is the good sister — a sweet, demure, and hardworking secretary — while Lona (Anita Berber) is the bad sister who seduces her sister's boss, the intellectual Alfred Werner (Conrad Veidt) and then leaves him for a career as a prostitute in a luxury brothel. When Alfred goes to the brothel to retrieve Lona, to his shock and dismay he finds Hedwig there instead, who was, through the complicity of her own father, drugged, abducted, and brought to the brothel against her will. Struggling against the advances of her first potential "John," Hedwig is aided by Alfred, who fights off the man and rescues her. A contemporary film review describes the fight scene thus: "There was nothing like it in German cinemas before. This scene is extraordinarily impressive."[6] Hedwig and Alfred find happiness together and get married, while Lona slides further into ruin. She

Fig. 1.1. Poster for Die Prostitution *(1919), designed by Josef Fenneker. Courtesy of the Bundesarchiv-Filmarchiv Berlin.*

works in the brothel until the madam casts her out, and once she is back on the street, she turns to her former lover Karl Döring (Reinhold Schünzel), who promptly becomes her pimp. Lona prostitutes herself willingly for Döring until she meets her grim end at the hands of a *Lustmörder* (sexual murderer), played by Werner Krauß (fig. 1.2).

By organizing the plot around the fates of an opposing pair of sisters, one of whom finds marital bliss, and one of whom is murdered, Oswald relies on a tried and true narrative formula: in the end, good is rewarded and evil is punished (Oswald, "Der Film als Kulturfaktor," 104). As scholars of Oswald's work have noted, the filmmaker used this formula with repeated success, for example in *Es werde Licht!* in which the good brother is the doctor and hero of the film, while the bad brother is a decadent painter who dies of venereal disease (Kasten/Loacker 86, 126). The familiar paradigm of good versus evil, Oswald himself argued, was crucial to educating the general public, which would be more apt to follow the path of the good character and read the punishment of the evil character as a clear warning against similar behavior. He wrote specifically about how filmmakers should portray prostitutes in a way that would strike fear into the hearts of female viewers and actively deter them from following the same path (Oswald, "Der Film als Kulturfaktor," 104).

The figure of the *Lustmörder* is instrumental to Oswald's goal of deterrence. With a nod to his own beginnings in the theater, Oswald finishes off the prostitute Lona in the same way that the modernist dramatist Frank Wedekind offs the notorious social-climbing whore Lulu in his 1892 play *Die Büchse der Pandora* (Pandora's Box) — with the knife of a Jack-the-Ripper character. The *Lustmörder*, who, incidentally, always goes free, can be read as the ultimate vigilante, who enacts justice by removing the dangerous erotic woman from society (Tatar, 54). However, Oswald's film remains ambivalent in regard to the question of the causes of prostitution. Is Lona, like Lulu, driven by an innately corrupt sexuality, or is she a victim of the social ills of prostitution? Is *she* the dangerous woman, or does the danger lie in the institution of prostitution itself? The arrest of Karl Döring, Lona's lover and pimp, at the end of the main narrative suggests that gender and economic relations are somehow culpable, yet the film leaves these questions open (see also Hirschfeld, 295). Still, its ominous message seems clear: prostitution is an ill-fated enterprise.

Despite *Die Prostitution's* grim ending, critics of the film such as Schweisheimer claim that even Lona's brutal death does not trump the film's glamorous (he uses the word "glänzend") depiction of her life in the brothel (72). Conflating the "shimmering nightclubs" depicted in the films with the bourgeois *Lichtspielpaläste* (film palaces) of the Weimar Republic, Bertolt Brecht also imagines how the on-screen action will translate into the real-life seduction of the women in the audience. Paying no

Fig. 1.2. Promotional postcard showing Anita Berber and Werner Krauß in Die Prostitution *(1919). Courtesy of the Bundesarchiv-Filmarchiv Berlin.*

attention to the on-screen secretary Hedwig, who successfully resists the sexual advances of the men in the brothel, Brecht is more concerned with the secretaries in the audience. He comments: "The young girls sitting in the cinema, most often next to the young man who bought their ticket, are instructed that refusal is pointless. All the bosses are infused with male desire and pour their secretaries wine; there are no objections allowed."[7] In Brecht's view, the message conveyed to women by the *Aufklärungsfilm* is one of nonresistance: it is best to accept the movie ticket from one's boyfriend or the glass of wine from one's boss and give him what he expects in return. In other words, Brecht blurs the line between the fictional prostitute in the film and those women he imagines as her viewers, for both allow themselves not simply to be seduced but to be *bought*. Brecht's "concern" for the young women's personal welfare is echoed by Tucholsky, who suggests that if sex education is truly the goal, then the most appropriate filmic genre is the dry, empirical *Lehrfilm*, shown separately to same-sex audiences (406). But it is Schweisheimer who argues the point in the clearest terms: *Aufklärungsfilme* have become "pornographic films" (*Animierfilme*) that encourage extra-marital copulation and accelerate the spread of venereal disease (74).

Reading these men's arguments, we can see that their critique of Oswald's film has less to do with the film itself and more to do with their views on its female spectators and with social anxiety over female sexuality. In fact, Schweisheimer and Brecht's scant or inaccurate mention of *Die Prostitution*'s plot insinuates that they probably had not even seen the film but rather based their accounts of it on hearsay. Schweisheimer even takes recourse to an urban legend that appeared in a September 1919 issue of *Die Weltbühne* concerning a man boasting about how easily he seduced a sixteen-year-old girl after noticing that the *Aufklärungsfilm* had aroused her (Schweisheimer, 76). This anecdote was one that also circulated on the floor of the German parliament during the debates on film censorship (Sturm, 72, 78–79; see also Moreck, 200–201). Oswald's particular film on prostitution functioned, then, as a springboard for a more general critique of an entire filmic genre, the *Aufklärungsfilm*, and its presumably negative social effects on women. The concern expressed by Brecht, Tucholsky, Schweisheimer, and Weimar politicians alike for the well-being of young women only thinly veils their anxiety about an active form of female sexuality that falls outside the social institutions of marriage and prostitution.

Such anxiety was emblematic of the early Weimar years, in which "women's uncontrolled sexuality" was linked "to the specter of profound social disorder" (Roos, 63). The First World War dealt a devastating blow to the bourgeois family and its gendered division of labor. Two million German men, half of whom were married, lost their lives to the war (Domansky, 442). The war caused a proliferation of public roles for women, and the drafting of the Weimar constitution in 1919 granted them suffrage and full rights as citizens. They took on roles other than those of daughters, wives, and mothers; they were also co-workers and comrades in leisure. Concurrent with this proliferation of public roles for women came the public outcry against a perceived increase in prostitution among the young women of the new republic (Roos, 73–74; Usborne, 75). Regardless of whether or not women really were prostituting themselves in order to survive the economic chaos of the inflation years, the fact that they were *perceived* to be doing so demonstrates how the lack of a social code for distinguishing sexually active, working women from paid prostitutes caused *all* single, non-monogamous women simply to be marked as prostitutes.

The increased visibility of single, working women met with two — not necessarily separate — reactions in the social and cultural discourse of the time. The first reaction, present in all the essays analyzed thus far, is to depict these women in explicitly sexual terms — as sexual objects that are passive, easily seduced. The second reaction, quite evident in the essay by Brecht, presents women as dimwitted dupes easily manipulated from above by their male bosses, lovers, or even cultural institutions like film studios. This is an argument that resurfaced later in the 1920s in one of the seminal essays on female film spectatorship in the Weimar Republic, Siegfried Kracauer's "The Little Shopgirls Go to the Movies" (Die kleinen Ladenmädchen gehen ins Kino, 1927). Here the moviegoers are young, single women whose designation as shopgirls signifies their limited education. Like the typists in Brecht's text, Kracauer's shop workers are naive girls who confuse film with reality, perceiving adventure films as true getaways or believing in fairy-tale endings filled with riches and romance ("Shopgirls," 288, 291). Film represents a temporary escape from the drudgery of their lives tending shop, an escape that allows them to dream or cry for a few hours without critical thought or reflection. As the shopgirls dab the tears from their cheeks, Kracauer observes: "Weeping is sometimes easier than thinking."[8] Their rapt attention betrays their inaction.

Anticipating Kracauer's explication of the shopgirls' passivity is pivotal to an understanding of how Brecht and Tucholsky depart from Schweisheimer in their critique of the *Aufklärungsfilme*. The real crux of Brecht's and Tucholsky's respective arguments is *not* that hygiene films should indeed be indicting prostitution as a danger to public health, as Schweisheimer maintained. Their concerns are more of a cultural and political nature; put simply, they chastise both the film audience and the filmmakers for choosing sex and profits over politics. When artistic censorship was lifted in November 1918, leftist intellectuals such as Brecht and Tucholsky hoped that the cinema would become a platform for diverse political voices, yet these hopes were dashed by the immense popularity of the *Aufklärungsfilme* and the financial success they brought to their creators. As Brecht ironically states in the final sentence of his essay, "Business is booming, *Prostitution* is extended by 'popular demand,' and freedom is the best of all circumstances."[9] Tucholsky, too, laments that the people have been duped, while "the false friends of the people make money."[10] In their respective essays, prostitution takes on a double meaning: it is both the title of Oswald's film and a cipher for the mass medium of film, whose existence is based upon selling sex for money. Freedom, certainly not the kind that Brecht or Tucholsky envisioned, is defined not in political terms but rather in sexual and financial ones.

These arguments foreshadow how Kracauer would evaluate the phenomenon of the *Aufklärungsfilm* nearly three decades later in *From Caligari to Hitler*:

> They were just vulgar films selling sex to the public. That the public demanded them rather indicated a general unwillingness to be involved in revolutionary activities; otherwise interest in sex would have been absorbed by interest in the political aims to be attained. (. . .) It was as if [Germans] felt paralyzed in view of the freedom

offered them, and instinctively withdrew into the unproblematic pleasures of the flesh. (46)

The *Aufklärungsfilm*, according to Kracauer, was just the tip of the iceberg of Weimar culture's "sexual decadence," a decadence that prevented political action.

Indeed Tucholsky implies in his essay that Magnus Hirschfeld made a Faustian bargain by teaming up with Richard Oswald and using the medium of film to further the sex-reform agenda. He equates Hirschfeld with Faust by quoting and slightly altering the passage from Johann Wolfgang von Goethe's canonical play "Mit euch, Herr Doktor, zu spazieren, ist ehrenvoll und *ist Gewinn*" ("Doctor, to walk with you is ever an honor and *is profit*") to "Mit euch, Herr Doktor, zu spazieren, ist ehrenvoll und *bringt Gewinn*" ("Doctor, to walk with you is ever an honor and *brings profit*," 406, emphasis added) to underscore his depiction of the making of the *Aufklärungsfilm* as a purely financial enterprise. Both Brecht and Tucholsky were gravely concerned about the commercial success of film and its implications for the theater. Tucholsky argued that filmmakers such as Oswald are "sellouts" who lack the talent to produce true art — theater (405). Brecht reveals his mandarin genre bias, as well as his own economically motivated envy, in the very first line of his essay, when he writes, "If the cinemas keep showing such filth as they are currently allowed to do, then soon no one will go to the theater anymore."[11] Lines such as this show us where these intellectuals' true concerns lay; perhaps more important than the sexual mores and political action or inaction of the film audience was its supposed fickleness: film's prurient allure could mean the demise of politically engaged culture.

What gets lost in these critiques is the fact that sex and sexuality was in fact highly politicized during the Weimar Republic, particularly through the work of the sex reform movement, in which Magnus Hirschfeld was a prominent activist. As we will see, *Die Prostitution*, especially when viewed in the context of Hirschfeld and Oswald's other two collaborative projects, proves to be a vehicle for a sex-reform agenda that had already been articulated before the First World War but sought, in the last years of the war and the first years of the republic, to challenge draconian laws that governed sexuality and thereby personal freedom.

Profits and Politics: *Die Prostitution* and the Sex Reform Agenda

When the *Bund für Mutterschutz und Sexualreform* (BfMS; League for the Protection of Mothers and Sex Reform) formed in 1911, its members, who included, among others, the feminist activist Helene Stöcker, the psychoanalyst Sigmund Freud, the writer Frank Wedekind, and sexologists Iwan

Bloch and Magnus Hirschfeld, defined the following three goals as central to their socio-political agenda: the increase in women's reproductive rights through access to birth control and the reform of the abortion law, §218; the abolition of §175, which declared male homosexuality punishable by law; and the end of state-regulated prostitution under §361, 9 (Stöcker, 202–4). Although this organization and the *Wissenschaftlich-humanitäres Komitee* (Scientific-Humanitarian Committee) led by Hirschfeld remained active during the First World War, the politicization of sexuality intensified dramatically in 1918, when the prospect of a new democratic constitution presented the perfect opportunity for change in the sections of the penal code that regulated sexual behavior (Grossmann, 16).

The topics of the three film projects undertaken by Oswald and Hirschfeld in 1918 and 1919 are clearly aligned with the goals of the sex-reform movement: the fourth installment of *Es werde Licht! Sündige Mütter (§218)* criticized anti-abortion law by implying that it drives women to have back-alley abortions; *Anders als die Andern* boldly called for the removal of laws penalizing homosexuals by concluding with a scene in which Hirschfeld's hand crosses §175 out of the law book for the new republic (Kasten/Loacker, 109; Steakley, 187); and the narrative frame of *Die Prostitution* also symbolically attacks the state control over prostitution by staging a fictional trial. Here, the defendant, an erotic woman with long, tousled hair and wearing a tightly-fitting dress personifies the institution of prostitution. Instead of casting Anita Berber (who played the prostitute in the film's main narrative) in the role of "die Prostitution," Oswald shrewdly chose the more innocent looking Kissa von Sievers. At the end of the trial, she sinks to her knees in relief, and the final words of the film read, "Prostitution is acquitted. We want to help to relieve need, to create humane laws, for we have no right to judge."[12] It comes as no surprise to learn that the trial scene was one of the first to be removed by local censors in Munich in 1919, where the lifting of national censorship seemed to be of little consequence (Birett, 561).

The disassociation of prostitution in Oswald's film from the realm of the court can be read as a plea against the system of state regulation, a system that was instituted in 1871 and involved the mandatory registration of prostitutes with the *Sittenpolizei*, or vice squad. Sexual contact between prostitutes and their clients was to take place within the confines of a brothel, not on the street, and this contact was sanctioned and controlled by the state. Subject to the arbitrary control of the vice squad, prostitutes "lacked basic personal rights"; their bodies were subject to compulsory medical exams, and their homes could be invaded by the police at any time (Roos, 55). Feminists and socialists in Wilhelmine Germany were the first to call for the abolition of regulations, and their protests against the system only intensified in the wake of the First World War. Oswald's film signifies an important moment in this anti-regulation discourse. An advertisement for the film that appeared several months before its premiere shows that its critique of regulated prostitution is intentional. After announcing the film's title and featuring the names of Hirschfeld and Oswald, the ad promises that the film will deal with the themes of prostitution, public health, and the dangers of "free" prostitution, while posing the question, "is garrisoned prostitution any less dangerous?"[13] The choice of the word "kaserniert" has particular resonance in light of the German military's use of the brothel system during the war as a way of maintaining soldiers' morale and keeping them ready for battle, a practice that was partially responsible for the wartime rise in venereal diseases (Domansky, 449).

The release of *Die Prostitution* coincided with a number of public debates on the issue of prostitutes' rights and the abolition of state regulation. In the spring of 1919 in Berlin, for example, feminists petitioned the city government to disband the vice squad and place prostitutes under the protection of a Municipal Welfare and Rescue Center (Roos, 196). Sex reformers envisioned an alternative to legal regulation that would decriminalize prostitution, outlaw brothels, and allow prostitutes access to private health care, provisions that were later included in the Law for Combating Venereal Diseases, passed in 1927 (Roos, 130–31). The most marked contributors to this discussion, however, were prostitutes themselves. During the years of 1919 and 1920 prostitutes in Berlin and Hamburg organized to form unions and discuss "issues such as prices, competition, the conduct of the police and physicians, professional hazards and effective countermeasures" (Roos, 105). Among the supporters whom the prostitutes elected to the executive council of the *Hilfsbund der Berliner Prostitutierten* (Auxiliary Association of Berlin Prostitutes) was none other than sexologist Magnus Hirschfeld himself (Hirschfeld, 358).

The social hygiene films Hirschfeld made with Richard Oswald, then, were not merely part of a publicity stunt that conveniently coincided with the opening of Hirschfeld's Institute for Sexual Research in 1919. They were projects true to Hirschfeld's own sexual-political activism and his support of human rights. In stark contrast to Kracauer's assessment of *Die Prostitution* as an apolitical, exploitative sex film (44), it is more appropriate to place the film in the broader context of sexual activism and the hope for democratic reform. Looking back at the chaotic first months of the Weimar Republic from the relative stability of the year 1928, the film critic Walter Kaul waxes enthusiastic about the "*Sturm-und-Drang* era of German film," when filmmakers were finally free to put the struggles and issues of the time onto the silver screen. During that exciting time, he writes, it was Richard Oswald who "had . . . the right eye" for timely topics, and without a trace of scorn Kaul exclaims: "He [Oswald] created the *Aufklärungsfilm!*"[14] Hence Richard Oswald's *Aufklärungsfilme* must not be seen as products of the alleged commercialization of sexuality for belittled prurient masses but rather as genuine and influential contributions to the sexual-policy discourses in the nascent democratic culture of the Weimar Republic.

Notes

[1] For examples of film scholarship that connect Richard Oswald almost exclusively with the hygiene film, see Kracauer, *From Caligari to Hitler,* 43–47; Kreimeier, 9–18; Kaes, 42–44; and Hake, 31, 37. Kasten and Loacker's book, in contrast, examines Oswald's entire oeuvre and is critical of gestures that judge him through the narrow lens of the hygiene film; see also Goergen, "Ein ganzer Kerl," 247–315.

[2] *Es werde Licht!* which had five acts and was 2,055 meters long, was produced and directed by Richard Oswald and based on a screenplay by Oswald and Lupu Pick. Professor Alfred Blaschko of the DGBG served as the medical consultant. The first screening of the film took place on 2 March 1917 in Berlin, with Bernd Aldor in the starring role of Dr. Georg Mauthner. The plot is as follows: Paul Mauthner, an unfaithful husband (portrayed as a decadent artist) contracts syphilis from a disreputable woman and spreads the disease to his wife, who unknowingly spreads it to their unborn daughter. The wife dies while giving birth, and Paul's brother Georg, a doctor, cures the daughter of her illness and raises her in Paul's absence. Years later Georg is called to the deathbed of his dying brother, who regrets his own negligence and wishes to be reunited and reconciled with his daughter. The film was placed under "Jugendverbot," which forbade youths under the age of eighteen from viewing it. Its censorship number is B.40377 (Kasten/Loacker, 86, 546; Bock, "Filmographie," in Belach & Jacobsen, 144).

[3] *Die Prostitution,* later renamed *Das gelbe Haus* (The Yellow House) and then *Im Sumpfe der Großstadt* (In the Swamp of the Metropolis) to appease the censor, premiered on 1 May 1919 in Berlin. Richard Oswald wrote, directed, and produced the film in consultation with Magnus Hirschfeld. Anita Berber, Gussy Holl, Conrad Veidt, and Reinhold Schünzel starred in the film, which was 2,566 m long (in Austria 2,700 m); it was banned in Bavaria soon after its release (censor number B.42921). The film was destroyed in 1922. See Birett, 564; Bock, "Filmographie," in Kasten/Loacker, 549; Bock in Belach/Jacobsen, 152. Unlike *Die Prostitution, Anders als die Andern* has been, at least in part, recovered, and a DVD version can be purchased through the film distributor Kino International (2003). Although there is some confusion about which film premiered first, the latest filmographies (and an examination of contemporary sources) show that *Anders als die Andern* premiered to the general public on 30 May 1919 at the Prinzess-Theater in Berlin, nearly one month after *Die Prostitution.* The press screening on 24 May 1919 at the Apollo-Theater in Berlin included introductory remarks by Hirschfeld (Kasten/Loacker, 549; Steakley, 188). Oswald produced and directed, and he and Hirschfeld cowrote the screenplay. The film was originally between 2,115 and 2,280 m long, and the surviving fragment used for its restoration was only 871 m (Steakley, 197). For an excellent discussion of this film as well as its censorship history and reception both in Germany and by gay audiences in the United States, see Steakley.

[4] Using the well-known film trade journal *Film-Kurier* as his venue, Oswald distanced himself from the string of sexual films in his article "Zensur oder Selbstzucht?" ("Censorship or Self-Control?" 19 Jun. 1919), and he threatened to

file lawsuits against those who dared to slander his name and his films in an "Offener Brief an die Mitglieder der Nationalversammlung und an alle, welche meine Filme nicht gesehen haben" ("Open Letter to the Members of the National Assembly and to All Those Who Have Not Seen My Films," 9 July 1919).

[5] "Takt und Geschmack"; "Die Films der Woche," *Berliner Tageblatt,* 4 May 1919.

[6] "Bislang sah man in Deutschland noch nie etwas derartiges im Film. Diese Szene ist von einer ungewöhnlichen Eindrucksfähigkeit." Quote taken from an anonymous review, "Aus der Tiefe der Weltstadt," in *Bühne und Film* 3 (1919). Courtesy of the Bundesarchiv-Filmarchiv, Berlin.

[7] "Die jungen Mädchen, die im Kino sitzen, meistens den jungen Mann neben sich, der das Billett bezahlt hat, werden darüber aufgeklärt, daß jedes Sträuben [. . .] nutzlos ist [. . .]. Alle Chefs sind mit der männlichen Begierde behaftet und schenken ihren Stenotypistinnen Wein ein; es *gibt* keine Widerrede" (Brecht, 41; emphasis in original).

[8] "Weinen [ist] manchmal leichter als Nachdenken" (Kracauer, "Shopgirls," 292). It is interesting to note that both Brecht and Tucholsky portray sniffling, sobbing women in the audience of the *Aufklärungsfilm* (Brecht, 41; Tucholsky, 405).

[9] "Die Geschäfte blühen, die *Prostitution* wird vielfach 'auf Wunsch' verlängert, und die Freiheit ist der beste aller Zustände" (Brecht, 41).

[10] "Die falschen Volksfreunde verdienen Geld" (Tucholsky, 406).

[11] "Wenn die Kinos weiterhin solche Schweinereien wie eben jetzt spielen dürfen, dann geht bald kein Mensch mehr in die Theater rein" (Brecht, 40).

[12] "Die Prostitution wird freigesprochen. Wir wollen helfen, die Not lindern, menschliche Gesetze schaffen, denn wir haben kein Recht zu richten" (Kasten/ Loaker, 128; Fischer, 35).

[13] "Das soziale Filmwerk *Die Prostitution.*"

[14] The entire passage from Kaul's essay, from which I took excerpts, reads: "Richard Oswald hatte damals den richtigen Blick und den richtigen Griff. Es war die Sturm- und Drangperiode des deutschen Films. Krieg, Revolution und Inflation hatten die Zeit aufgerührt und aufgewühlt. In der neuen Freiheit wurde jeder Stoff gepackt, den die Zeitströmung zutrug. Der deutsche Film war damals aktuell. Opium und Kokain, Prostitution und sexuelle Abnormitäten . . . das waren die Themen, die Oswald aufgriff. Er schuf den Aufklärungsfilm!" (Kaul, "Richard Oswald — Henny Porten," 456; also quoted in Goergen, "Ein ganzer Kerl," 288–89).

Works Cited

Anon. "Aus der Tiefe der Weltstadt." *Bühne und Film* 3 (1919).

———. "Die Films der Woche" (Review of *Die Prostitution*). *Berliner Tageblatt,* 4 May 1919.

———. "Das soziale Filmwerk *Die Prostitution.*" *Der Film* 50 (1919).

Belach, Helga, and Wolfgang Jacobsen, eds. *Richard Oswald: Regisseur und Produzent*. Munich: edition text + kritik, 1990.

Berger, Michael. "Richard Oswald: Kitschkönig und Volksaufklärer." In *Pioniere in Celluloid: Juden in der frühen Filmwelt*, edited by Irene Stratenwerth and Hermann Simon, 201–5. Berlin: Henschel, 2004.

Beyfuss, Edgar, and I. Kossowsky, eds. *Das Kulturfilmbuch*. Berlin: Cryselius & Schulz, 1924.

Birett, Herbert, ed. *Verzeichnis in Deutschland gelaufener Filme: Entscheidungen der Filmzensur, 1911–1920; Berlin, Hamburg, München, Stuttgart*. Munich and New York: K. G. Saur, 1980.

Bock, Hans-Michael. "Biographie." In Belach and Jacobsen, 119–32.

———. "Filmographie." In Belach and Jacobsen, 136–80.

———. "Filmographie." In Kasten and Loacker, 542–61.

Brecht, Bertolt. "Aus dem Theaterleben." *Der Volkswille*, Augsburg, Nov. 1919. Repr. in *Werke: Große, kommentierte Berliner und Frankfurter Ausgabe*, vol. 21, 40–42. Berlin and Frankfurt am Main: Aufbau & Suhrkamp, 1989–97.

Domansky, Elisabeth. "Militarization and Reproduction in World War I Germany." In *Society, Culture, and the State in Germany, 1870–1930*, edited by Geoff Eley, 427–63. Ann Arbor: U of Michigan P, 1996.

Fischer, Lothar. *Tanz zwischen Rausch und Tod: Anita Berber, 1918–1929 in Berlin*. Berlin: Haude & Spener, 1996.

Goergen, Jeanpaul. "Ein ganzer Kerl: Richard Oswald im Spiegel der Kritik, 1914–1929." In Kasten & Loacker, 247–315.

———. Introductory essay on Richard Oswald. *Filmblatt* 12.34 (Summer 2007): 3–4.

Grossmann, Atina. *Reforming Sex: The German Movement for Birth Control and Abortion Reform, 1920–1950*. New York and Oxford: Oxford UP, 1995.

Hagener, Malte, ed. *Geschlecht in Fesseln: Sexualität zwischen Aufklärung und Ausbeutung im Weimarer Kino, 1918–1933*. Munich: edition text + kritik, 2000.

Hagener, Malte, and Jan Hans. "Von Wilhelm zu Weimar: Der Aufklärungs- und Sittenfilm zwischen Zensur und Markt." In Hagener, 7–22.

Hake, Sabine. *German National Cinema*. London and New York: Routledge, 2002.

Hirschfeld, Magnus. *Geschlechtskunde*. Vol. 3. Stuttgart: Julius Püttmann, 1930.

Jelavich, Peter. "'Am I Allowed to Amuse Myself Here?' The German Bourgeoisie Confronts Early Film." In *Germany at the Fin de Siècle: Culture,*

Politics, and Ideas, edited by Suzanne Marchand and David Lindenfeld, 227–49. Baton Rouge: Louisiana State UP, 2004.

Kaes, Anton. "Film in der Weimarer Republik: Motor der Moderne." In *Geschichte des deutschen Films,* edited by Wolfgang Jacobsen, Anton Kaes, and Hans Helmut Prinzler, 38–98. Stuttgart and Weimar: Metzler, 2004.

Kasten, Jürgen, and Armin Loacker, eds. *Richard Oswald: Kino zwischen Spektakel, Aufklärung und Unterhaltung.* Vienna: Verlag Filmarchiv Austria, 2005.

Kaul, Walter. "Richard Oswald — Henny Porten." *Berliner Börsen-Courier,* 28 September 1928.

Kracauer, Siegfried. *From Caligari to Hitler: A Psychological History of the German Film.* 1947. Revised & expanded edition, Princeton, NJ: Princeton UP, 2004.

———. "Die kleinen Ladenmädchen gehen ins Kino." 1927. Reprinted in *Das Ornament der Masse: Essays,* 279–94. Frankfurt am Main: Suhrkamp, 1977.

———. "The Little Shopgirls Go to the Movies." In *The Mass Ornament,* edited and translated by Thomas Y. Levin, 291–304. Cambridge, MA: Harvard UP, 1995.

Kreimeier, Klaus. "Aufklärung, Kommerzialismus und Demokratie oder: Der Bankrott des deutschen Mannes." In Belach & Jacobsen, 9–18.

Moreck, Curt (a.k.a. Konrad Haemmerling). *Sittengeschichte des Kinos.* Dresden: Paul Aretz Verlag, 1926.

Oswald, Richard. "Der Film als Kulturfaktor." In Beyfuss and Kossowsky, 103–6.

———. "Offener Brief an die Mitglieder der Nationalversammlung und an alle, welche meine Filme nicht gesehen haben." *Film-Kurier,* 9 July 1919.

———. "Zensur oder Selbstzucht?" *Film-Kurier,* 19 June 1919.

Roos, Julia. *Weimar's Crisis through the Lens of Gender: The Case of Prostitution.* PhD diss., Carnegie Mellon U, 2001. Ann Arbor: UMI, 2001.

Schmidt, Ulf. "'Der Blick auf den Körper': Sozialhygienische Filme, Sexualaufklärung und Propaganda in der Weimarer Republik." In Hagener, 23–46.

Schweisheimer, Waldemar. *Die Bedeutung des Films für soziale Hygiene und Medizin.* Munich: Georg Müller, 1920.

Steakley, James D. "Cinema and Censorship in the Weimar Republic: The Case of *Anders als die Andern*." *Film History* 11 (1999): 181–203.

Stöcker, Helene. "Aufruf der Internationalen Vereinigung für Mutterschutz und Sexualreform." 1911. Reprinted in *Frauen und Sexualmoral,* edited by Marielouise Janssen-Jurreit, 202–4. Frankfurt am Main: Fischer, 1986.

Sturm, Eva. "Von der Zensurfreiheit zum Zensurgesetz: Das erste deutsche Lichtspielgesetz (1920)." In Hagener, 63–79.

Tatar, Maria. *Lustmord: Sexual Murder in Weimar Germany.* Princeton, NJ: Princeton UP, 1995.

Tucholsky, Kurt. "Die Prostitution mit der Maske." In *Gesammelte Werke,* vol.1: *1907–1924,* edited by Mary Gerold-Tucholsky and Fritz J. Raddatz, 404–6. Reinbek bei Hamburg: Rowohlt, 1960.

Usborne, Cornelie. *The Politics of the Body in Weimar Germany.* Ann Arbor: U of Michigan P, 1992.

Wedekind, Frank. *Die Büchse der Pandora: Stücke.* 2 vols. Munich: Langen & Müller, 1970.

2: Unsettling Nerves: Investigating War Trauma in Robert Reinert's *Nerven* (1919)

Barbara Hales

> *Hysteria is an infectious disease.*
> — Julius von Wagner-Jauregg

Hysteria and *Nerven*

IN THE WAKE OF THE FIRST WORLD WAR, an entire generation was saddled with the psychological trauma resulting from the mass death of 10 million soldiers on the battlefield (Winter, 15–53; Keegan, 3). This psychic trauma was particularly felt in Germany, where 2 million soldiers were killed and another 4 million disabled ("The Legacy of War," 5). In conflicts such as Verdun for the French, Somme and Flanders for the British, and the retreat of 1915 for the Russians (Ferro, 85), soldiers were trapped in the trenches and subjected to shelling from guns, projectiles, and air attacks (Ferro, 85–97). German playwright Carl Zuckmayer commented on the understandable trauma of a generation subjected to this sort of physical and emotional onslaught: "how it lives, along with its dead, how it raises its head, gathers its scattered limbs, slowly, gropingly, unsteadily, stumbling" (24). The shell-shocked soldier who returned to the home front also had to reconstruct his mental space. Physician Ernst Simmel, working in a neurosis station in 1918, concluded that returning soldiers had to confront a world changed by war, a situation with which the personality had to struggle (Simmel, *Kriegs-Neurosen*, 5).

Anton Kaes notes that Weimar's early Expressionist cinema replicates the "physical and mental desert the first technological war left behind" (Kaes, "War," 128). For example, in F. W. Murnau's famous *Nosferatu* (1922), the character Hutter — echoing the trek of millions of World War One soldiers — travels to the East and returns home in a neurotic state. In *Nosferatu*, a small nineteenth-century German town symbolically experiences the mass death felt on the battlefield as a plague ravages the city (Kaes, "Weimar Cinema," 64). Similarly, in Robert Wiene's *The Cabinet of Dr. Caligari* (1920), the inmate of an insane asylum captures the medical community's attempts to treat the war neurotic as he recounts a disjointed story about a sadistic psychiatrist and a hypnotized patient (Kaes, "War," 128). Cultural historian Modris Eksteins argues that only the cinema was able to capture the extreme psychic crisis of this age: "Only the *son et lumière* effects of the cinema seemed capable of anything like an appropriate evocation of the new age, its horror, anxieties, and pleading" (Eksteins, 209).

Often considered the first German Expressionist film, Robert Reinert's largely unknown *Nerven* is notable for its role in recording the frenzy of illness following the First World War.[1] The film's narrative depicts the German postwar preoccupation with war neuroses and mass infection, which both the medical community and the popular press believed to be factors that incited revolution. The mise-en-scène (the visual design, the staging, and editing of the film) further emphasizes the dynamic of psychic uneasiness as characters dart in and out of the frame, interrupting the viewer's sense of proportionality.[2] In contrast to later war films, such as G. W. Pabst's *Westfront 1918* (1930), that depict accounts on the battlefield (see Jaimey Fisher's essay in this volume), Expressionist films such as *Nerven* present the viewer with a firsthand encounter with the psychic unconscious affected by the ravages of war.

Nerven's first act, its main narrative, begins with factory owner Roloff (Eduard von Winterstein) and his wife Elisabeth (Lya Borré) at the 500th anniversary celebration of their family business. Roloff promises that he has an invention that will make the wealthy gentlemen in attendance "masters of the world"; the explosion of machines, however, destroys the factory and signals the rising up of workers on the street. While Johannes (Paul Bender), the teacher, preaches the end of "greed and power" to the mob, a young gardener flees into the streets and senselessly murders a random man in the crowd. The gardener is then placed up against a wall and shot in retaliation. In this same sequence, a hysterical Marja (Erna Morena) is preparing for her wedding day. She palpably feels the fervor of the revolutionary upheaval and takes to the streets to observe the turmoil. The frenetic movement of the characters in this scene is underscored by the intertitle: "Do you not feel the mysterious electricity charging the air?"

Madness is not only exhibited by the revolutionaries; it is evident in all of the film's characters. Roloff believes that Johannes has raped his sister Marja, and she confirms this fantasy, sending Johannes to jail for the alleged crime; she later admits to Roloff that Johannes did not rape her. Roloff then strangles Marja, only to realize that he has been hallucinating. Descending into madness, Roloff seeks help from a psychiatrist and befriends Johannes; yet in spite of these efforts to regain his sanity, Roloff's strange delusions persist with visions of the ghost of Johannes, vengeful revolutionaries, and a haunting depiction of his own double. He finally requests and receives a lethal dose of poison from Johannes, who pities him.

Madness, hallucination, and suicide are themes that run throughout *Nerven*'s disjointed narrative. Roloff projects his mental illness onto an overarching view of the world, stating: "My own nerves mirror the nerves of the world." The causes of mental illness are revealed by the psychiatrist: "the progression of civilization, the struggle for existence, anxiety and the terrors of the war, [and the] sins of the parents." Roloff suggests that only when the horrors of the war are no longer felt — when the "frenzy" ends — can humankind recover. The psychiatrist pronounces Roloff hopelessly lost on account of the overwhelming nature of his hallucinations. Roloff cannot outrun the "ghosts of the dead" who are rising up to seek vengeance on him. As David Bordwell notes, "Roloff is haunted by bodies in death throes, twisted landscapes, and contorted imagery of murderous hands" (Bordwell, 6). In a frenzied scene, Roloff calls up the images of writhing bodies, and then of men fighting. Even as he climbs the steps of his villa, agitated men move around him, providing a symbolic marker that the effects of mental illness are felt on the home front. The burden of illness, presented in Roloff's dreams, is illustrative of a German public burdened by the trauma of war neurosis.[3]

Mental instability on the home front is also evident in *Nerven*'s frenetic mise-en-scène. Characters appear to leap at the viewer, and hallucinatory imagery emphasizes the instability of reality. The viewer is overwhelmed by the nervousness of the characters darting in and out of the frame and by the disorienting close-ups, in which face shots blot out the background (Bordwell, 16–17). In one of Roloff's hallucinations, the screen is filled with enormous claw-like hands, then with the close-up image of the dead gardener from the film's beginning, only to be replaced by what looks like the head of a camel (fig. 2.1). Roloff's mental instability is further intimated as the viewer is left confused about Johannes's suicide. As a ghostly Johannes moves towards Roloff, stating "You killed me, Roloff," we find that Roloff has in fact imagined Johannes's death.

The Medical Diagnosis of War Neurosis

Nerven's depiction of Roloff's mental instability echoes the early twentieth century medical community's understanding of the war hysteric. Early on in the war, German doctors and psychologists argued that symptoms such as deafness, muteness, paralysis, and other motor disturbances exhibited by soldiers might be caused by psychological trauma rather than being the result of a biological condition.[4] Sigmund Freud and others working in the area of psychoanalysis were instrumental in formulating early theories of war neurosis. According to Freud, when the state demands that the individual fight in war, there is an end to the suppression of passions and "men perpetrate deeds of cruelty, fraud, treachery, and barbarity so incompatible

Fig. 2.1. The hallucinations of Roloff (Eduard von Winterstein). Screenshot.

with their level of civilization that one would have thought them impossible" ("Thoughts," 280).

Freud notes that civilization's peacetime prohibition of killing keeps powerful instinctual urges in check; however, when individuals are forced into a wartime environment, the individual must release these urges or become a casualty himself. If the individual unconsciously refuses to allow the primitive side of his psyche to come to the surface, then a mental breakdown in the form of war neurosis is inevitable. War neurosis is thus caused by the traumatized soldier's internal struggle between the desire to continue fighting and his apprehension or incapacity preventing him from fighting ("Memorandum," 213). Freud's understanding of war neurosis suggests that the condition is caused by the conflict between the individual's concern for his own survival and his duty to the state (213).

As the war progressed, psychologists and psychiatrists debated whether this form of mental illness was, in reality, a malingering condition. Doctors had diagnosed soldiers who were refusing to fight as "hysterical" and lacking a "will to fight."[5] In his 1916 address to the War Congress of the German Association for Psychiatry, Robert Gaupp breaks down war neurosis into neurasthenia, with symptoms of chronic fatigue resulting from service on the frontlines, and male hysteria, resulting from a predisposition to illness (Gaupp, "Kriegsneurosen," 360). On the one hand, the causes of neurasthenia are found in the fatigue of body and spirit, resulting from the constant tension of trench life (363). Hysteria, on the other hand, is a psychopathological reaction to a psychologically stressful situation. In short, the illness of the hysteric lies in the man himself and not in wartime conditions (369). While the neurasthenic's fatigue can be treated by simple rest, the hysteric's fits, tremors, and paralysis cannot be easily treated (370–71). For psychiatrist Armin Steyerthal, hysteria yields a plethora of negative associations, including "psychopathic inferiority complex, degeneration, born criminality, pathological lies, simulation, exaggeration, conscious fraud, and female feebleness."[6]

The medical understanding of war neuroses thus considers the war hysteric as a weak-willed individual prone to shirking and malingering rather than a casualty of war. In contrast to the neurasthenic, who has the will but not the stamina, the hysteric possesses a faulty genetic make-up, resulting in the rejection of the will to fight (Bonhoeffer, 58). The war hysteric's lack of "nerve" was an issue seen in the very method of treatment deemed acceptable by the psychiatric community. Eric Leed suggests that the harsh treatment of war neurotics, evident through faradization, solitary confinement, and other methods of coercion therapy, was an acknowledgement that neurosis was considered an illegitimate exit from the war (Leed, 165).

The trial of Viennese psychiatrist Julius von Wagner-Jauregg provides evidence of the disciplinary nature of treatment given to hysterical soldiers during the First World War. In 1918 Professor Wagner-Jauregg was charged with the torturous use of both electric shock and solitary confinement in his treatment of Lieutenant Walter Kauders.[7] While Wagner-Jauregg testified that Kauders was a malingerer with a tendency to whine,[8] Kauders offered a quite different account as he described the procedure of administering electric shock treatments:

> The operator takes the metal brush, which is connected to the apparatus by a lead; and now the candidate is brought in. He is greeted by shouts of "Miserable malingerer," "You're in for it," and so on . . . I saw through the spy-hole of my isolation room a man being stretched out undressed on the bed. Seven men were holding him still . . . Kozlowski now began as usual to apply the brush to the particularly sensitive spots at the tips of the toes. The man screamed with pain as though possessed. (Kauders quoted in Eissler, 203–4)

According to the Wagner-Jauregg trial transcripts, doctors treated soldiers using intense electric shock in hope that the hysteric's symptoms would disappear and that he could then be sent back to the front. Freud noted, in his testimony during the trial, that the soldier's inclination to escape the war was lodged in the unconscious. The intention of electric-shock therapy was designed to create an unbearable situation for the soldier, giving him a reason to desire a return to the front: "Just as [the soldier] had fled from the war into illness, means were now adopted that compelled him to flee back from illness into health" (Freud, "Memorandum," 213).

Only in the years following the war would these treatments of the neurotic be regarded as improper. Faradization and other cruel treatments of neurosis were denounced in Weimar newspapers. Alfred Polgar wrote for *Die Weltbühne* in 1920 that a world accustomed to the torture of electric shock was no world at all (Polgar, 589). Neurologist R. Hirschfeld criticized faradization and its possible future damage to patients, noting that some individuals had already died during electric-shock treatment (Hirschfeld, 687). Ernst Simmel spoke against forcible and restrictive methods, such as the indiscriminate use of hypnosis (*Psycho-Analysis,* 30). Notwithstanding the postwar critique of unethical medical practices, the medical discourse concerning war neuroses made it clear that the neurotic himself was to blame for his illness.

Contagion

Robert Gaupp was not alone in considering the sheer number of hysterics in the war to be a threat for Germany: the best men were dying on the battlefield, while the unhealthy hysterics were left behind and declared unfit to serve in the war ("Kriegsneurosen," 389). During and after the First World War the German medical community came to express concern that the neurotic soldier would contaminate the home front with his alleged weakness of will. War doctors and psychiatrists feared that neurotic symptoms such as shaking could spread from soldier to soldier on the front, but also from the neurotic soldier to the community.

In a 1918 article entitled "Die Kriegsneurasthenie" (War Neurasthenia), for instance, psychiatrist Willy Hellpach notes that neurosis can befall both soldiers at the front and those on the home front (Hellpach, 180). He underscores the threat that the German people face after the war, questioning whether soldiers and front neurotics will carry their neuroses into peacetime. Neurosis thus could be passed on like a plague by soldiers returning from the front. In a similar manner, in 1920 psychiatrist Erwin Stransky wrote that the "physical and psychological cripples and degenerates" ("körperlichen und seelischen Krüppeln und Entarteten") present a danger of infection not only for the German community but also for the entire world (Stransky, 273). In Germany, this contagion would ultimately be associated with the socialist uprising that ushered in the new political system of 1919.

The opening scenes of *Nerven* convey this contagious sense of hysteria. The main plot is preceded by a prologue that uses crosscutting to juxtapose

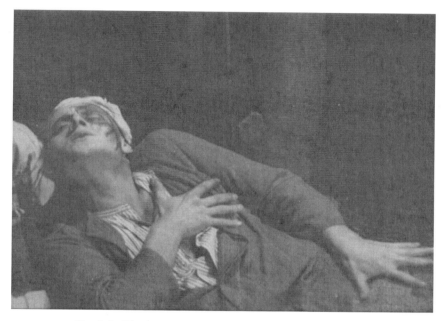

Fig. 2.2. The dying soldier in the film's prologue. Screenshot.

dead soldiers on the battlefield with a peasant mother looking anxiously into the distance. The bodies heaped upon one another signify the randomness of death. The depersonalized character of death shifts as a single wounded soldier is carried by his comrades. This is followed by a returning image of the forlorn mother, whose association with the battlefield is revealed by the intertitle: "Mother! Thousands of miles from home your son is dying." In desperation, the mother flails her arms in the air. In contrast, the son's final movements become increasingly sexualized — he places his fist on his heart and grabs his throat; finally he runs his hand down his leg as if in a state of ecstasy (fig. 2.2).

Nerven's initial montage sets up a correspondence between the battlefield and the home front. The mother feels the son's death even though they may be hundreds of miles apart. The dying soldier's agony is matched by the mother's pain, evident in her raised arms and frantic facial expression. The symmetry of this montage is, however, disrupted by faulty eyeline matches. While the mother looks to the left beckoning her son, we see the son also looking left — away from the mother — suggestive of his mental confusion. Mental illness is further emphasized in this scene by the stylized treatment of war and death. The Romantic setting of the killing field adds to the scene's disturbing unreality — the dreamy image of the tree trunk and the mass of corpses evoke artistic creations such as those of Francisco Goya and other Romantics. The feminized nature of the soldier is also unsettling — his final pose is reminiscent of French nineteenth-century neurologist Jean-Martin Charcot's famously sexualized female hysterics (Showalter).

In the second part of the prologue we see the shadow of an unidentified man, who enters from the right of the frame. The image of a reclining woman then appears at the bottom left-hand corner. The "murderer" grasps the woman's throat as she struggles to break free. Finally, the man's mad expression changes to one of serenity as the camera pans up to a bird-cage — at this point, the man benevolently fills the bird's bowl with water.

Throughout this scene, the viewer is only presented with small frag-ments of the room and denied an adequate sense of spatial relations. This confusion deepens when the images of the woman and the birdcage appear unexpectedly. The discordance of the man's brutality toward the woman and subsequent care for the bird is explained by his contorted facial expres-sions, suggesting he suffers from a form of mental illness. The film's nar-rative progression implies that the mental illness exhibited by the dying soldier is the same malady that infects the murderer of this scene. The infectious nature of neurosis is thus represented visually, as war neurosis in the film moves from the battlefield to the home front.

Revolution

At the same time that Weimar psychiatrists were attempting to treat the epi-demic of war neuroses, they blamed the war neurotics for instigating the revolution that brought the German monarchy to an end (Eissler, 47). According to psychiatrist Emil Kraepelin, the German people turned their attention away from the enemy of the First World War and moved instead to a life of inner feelings: they became sleepwalkers, moving through postwar life without conscious action (Kraepelin, 177). In this state, the masses were susceptible to revolution, incited by hysterical personalities: "In all mass movements, we encounter traits that without question point to a deeper affinity with hysterical phenomena."[9] Likewise, physician Helenefriderike Stelzner argues that it is the war neurotic who stimulates the masses on the home front (Stelzner, 409). The psychotic revolutionary preys on the disen-franchised who are unable to integrate into the social order (Stelzner, 393).

In both the medical journals and the popular press of the period, returning war neurotics were regarded as potential revolutionaries and thus as a serious threat to political stability.[10] Psychiatrist Robert Wollenberg confirms the relationship between war neurosis and revolution in his 1931 memoirs, noting that the neurotic patients in his hospital all left to join the revolution: The "lame" and the "shakers," who had once walked with canes, now found their strength and took to the streets, he writes, joining "men in field-grey uniform who waved a red flag."[11] On a similar note, neurologist Kurt Singer sees the revolution as a potential cure for war hysterics. The conclusion of the war had removed the threat of the trenches; the thrill of street fighting had allowed hysterics to compensate for their feelings of inferiority (Singer, 331).

Numerous doctors and psychiatrists listed the supposed hysterical characteristics of participants of the revolution. Neurologist Hermann Oppenheim, for example, divides the leaders of the German revolution into three groups: the mentally disabled, the manic-depressives, and the psychopaths (Oppenheim, 1). Likewise, in a 1919 article entitled "Forensische Begutachtung eines Spartakisten" (Forensic Assessment of a Spartacist), psychiatrist Kurt Hildebrandt describes two types of psychopaths involved in the revolution — the "Gesellschaftsfeind" (antisocial individual) who is driven by his ego, and the "Hochstapler" (con man) who is a war neurotic (Hildebrandt, 479). The latter category of revolutionary is not interested in politics but only in monetary gain. Hildebrandt provides a psychological profile of Kunstmaler M. as war hysteric, swindler, and revolutionary, all tendencies he claims were evident at an early age. And in a 1919 study that examined fifteen revolutionary leaders in detail, psychiatrist Eugen Kahn found the following characteristics: "ethically challenged psychopaths," "hysterical personalities," "fanatical psychopaths," and "manic depressives."[12] According to Kahn, these left-wing individuals are psychologically deficient just like the German masses of the period: the masses have become mentally unstable after the war, allowing the revolutionary element to gain a foothold (Kahn, 105).

Film historian Jan-Christopher Horak argues that Reinert's film represents the "conservative interpretation of the civil war" that erupted around the German revolution of 1918–19 (Horak, 185). In his reading, *Nerven* depicts the struggle between the socialist leader and the industrialist over who will wield power over the community (183). Teacher Johannes, the workers' leader, tells the crowd that "great unrest and discontent are marching across the world" (fig. 2.3). While Johannes is preaching the "end of greed and power" to the masses, the demented gardener runs through the streets with an ax and kills the first man he meets. The gardener's insanity is revealed in his odd physical movements and facial tics. His association with the soldier in the prologue (they turn out to be brothers) again underscores the relationship between war neurosis and the home front: the lower-class family has lost two sons, namely a son in the war and one in the revolution. Mental illness, brought on by war, is ultimately played out on the home front.

The mise-en-scène of the film also supports the relationship between battlefield and home front. The stylized tableau of death on the battlefield

Fig. 2.3. Johannes (Paul Bender) tries to calm the unruly masses. Screenshot.

that opened the film is associated with the surreal nature of the city streets. The clouds, symbolizing mental instability, are present both in the battle-field scenes and in the street fighting; the implied guns of war in the bat-tlefield scenes are explicit in the street scenes of the revolution. The common practice of tinting film stock for emotional effect is employed here: neuroses and death are carried home like the plague, infecting the city with the color of blood-red.

These initial images of revolution are repeated in Roloff's dreamscape after he has visited the psychiatrist. In his hallucination, Roloff replaces the hysterical gardener in the streets, as he imagines himself put up against the wall and shot. This is followed by a close-up of the ghostly gardener, who expresses a look of revenge and hatred. Madness as the cause of revolution is again suggested in Roloff's persecution mania as his ghostly double — who stands in for the gardener — follows him and ensures his destruction. Finally, Roloff and his double are perched in the clouds, recalling the sym-bolic representation of hysteria present in the first part of the film.

The film's anti-revolutionary tendency is epitomized at its outset. Roloff the industrialist calls together the gentlemen of the city in order to celebrate his company's anniversary and to open an industrial complex.

According to Roloff, new machines and tools will mean that the upper class is in a position to "take over the world." But Roloff's plans end when the factories explode. Amid the burning factories and marching workers, Roloff advises the upper-crust businessmen to remain cool ("Don't lose your nerve, keep calm like me. Otherwise everything is lost"). He then pledges to continue the fight, even as armed workers flood the streets threatening mob violence. It is at this point that Roloff begins to shake, just like a war neurotic: his nerves were "made of steel" before the destruction of the factories, but afterward they are shot. With a cinematic cut to the factories blowing up, we are led to believe that the revolutionary acts of the workers are the cause of Roloff's mental instability.[13]

Just as the traumatized "shakers" — who had lost control over their bodies on account of war trauma — were in the real world released from psychiatrist Robert Wollenberg's hospital into the community, so too is Roloff's shaking in the film representative of a contagion passed on to the home front. The double that plagues Roloff in his fantasies is evocative of the returning neurotic, bringing illness to the home front and reminding the German populace of a war that was not won. Likewise, the revolutionary leader Johannes comes to represent mental instability. This can be seen both in his role as relentless avenger in Roloff's hallucinations, as well as in his identification with the imagery of men tied to the battlefield.[14] There is the implication that Roloff, as the representative of the home front, eschews responsibility for the returning neurotic Johannes's fate. Roloff states, "I am not a murderer . . . [Johannes] committed suicide." One might also understand that the erratic Johannes as war neurotic represents the downfall of Roloff, and in a wider sense the German populace: it is Johannes who gives Roloff the poison to take his own life. We are left with two ideas about war neurosis: individuals on the home front are not culpable, and the war neurotic is the culprit.

The nervous scenario reflected in the first part is tempered by the film's coda: the two survivors, Johannes and Elisabeth, forming a new couple, are shown in a pristine mountain landscape tilling the soil as progenitors of a new Germany; they display movement in nature as a remedy for a previously depicted nervous (urban) environment (fig. 2.4). Placed next to the film's images of healthy nude bodies, found in the prologue and epilogue, *Nerven's* answer to shattered nerves could be seen as a course of healthy living. Michael Cowan has argued that the early-twentieth-century practice of *Willenstherapie* (found for example in Émile Jaques-Dalcroze's school of rhythmical gymnastics) was an attempt to address the condition of abulia (loss of willpower) by retraining the will through movement aimed at producing a moderating effect (Cowan, 183).[15] The positive emphasis on body culture is evident in *Nerven's* healthy bodies, as well as with slogans such as "Back to Nature! Work!" and "New Nerves, New Human Beings!"

Fig. 2.4. Survivors Johannes (Paul Bender) and Elisabeth (Lya Borré) begin a new life. Screenshot.

The film seems to offer a spurious solution to a political and psychic crisis in suggesting that mental and physical health can be regained through a return to "nature," through unalienated labor in a rural setting. The film's healthy bodies provide a counterbalance to the film's presentation of psychic trauma: the stress on physical conditioning is a feeble attempt to fix Germany's infirmity. Throughout the film the viewer is constantly reminded of mental illness through repeated images of writhing, hysterical bodies. The preponderance of frenetic sexualized bodies in *Nerven*, in both the fantasy sequences depicting debauchery and the famous "living intertitles" that show tableau-like arrangements of near-nude bodies (fig. 2.5), brings to mind Joachim Radkau's notion that the discourse on nervousness was, in fact, a hidden conversation about sexuality: "The bed is the actual battlefield of the neurasthenic" (Radkau, 144).[16] In sum, it is the twisted, hysterical body seen throughout Reinert's *Nerven* that suggests that a cure for nerves is not so easily found. Roloff, the central character in the film, succumbs to nerves; the film's narrative focuses primarily on his illness and downfall, outweighing any emphasis on the healthy body as an answer to nervousness.[17] The cinematic portrayal of

Fig. 2.5. Innovative "living intertitle" in the American version of Robert Reinert's Nerven. *Screenshot.*

nervous energy through the frenetic mise-en-scène further confirms the emphasis on illness.

Conclusion: Unnerved by Defeat

Weimar psychiatrist Robert Gaupp states that never in the history of the German people had there been such a state of psychic emergency as in 1918: the masses are sick and stand under the threat of complete collapse (Gaupp, *Die künftige Stellung*, 4). This sentiment is echoed by Reinert's character Roloff in *Nerven*, who states that "the world's nerves are ill." *Nerven* evokes Weimar Germany's social crisis both in its depictions of hysterical and hallucinating characters and its fragmented narrative. If blame could be heaped on the returning soldier, then society would be able to distance itself from the war and the subsequent revolution. Films like *Nerven*, as well as *Caligari* and *Nosferatu*, in which the soldier is symbolically depicted as madman, must be read in the context of the cultural milieu of an unsettled Weimar Germany. The vilification of the war neurotic, both in the medical discourse and in films of the period, was indicative of Germany's overall inability to accept defeat.

Notes

All translations not otherwise noted are my own. I would like to acknowledge the many valuable comments on *Nerven* by the participants in the 2004 German Film Institute, led by Anton Kaes and Eric Rentschler, as well as by this volume's editor, Christian Rogowski.

The epigraph to this chapter is drawn from K. R. Eissler, *Freud as an Expert Witness: The Discussion of War Neuroses between Freud and Wagner-Jauregg.* trans. Christine Trollope (Madison, WI: International UP, 1986). Julius von Wagner-Jauregg is speaking here.

[1] In 1918, Reinert formed his own production company, Monumental-Film GmbH, and shortly thereafter directed the film *Opium*, which opened in February of 1919. *Nerven* opened soon afterward at Munich's Kammer-Lichtspiele Theater in December 1919. Reinert's cameraman for both *Opium* and *Nerven* was Helmar Lerski. For more information on Reinert's career see Horak. The Munich Filmmuseum recently acquired *Nerven* from Gosfilmofond (Moscow) and has restored and released the film on DVD: www. edition-filmmuseum.com.

[2] For an extensive coverage of Reinert's expressionist revision of depth staging in *Opium* (1919) and *Nerven* (1919), see Bordwell.

[3] Women are not only the victims of male "nervousness" but also the perpetrators of neurotic behavior, seen in Marja's leveling of false rape charges, as well as Elisabeth's commission of arson.

[4] Neuropathologist Hermann Oppenheim believed that neurotic symptoms in war were caused by physical injury to the brain or nervous system. For the understanding of war neurosis in the disciplines of psychology and physiognomy, see Lerner, 61–85.

[5] Physicians and psychiatrists discussed the neurotic soldier's desire to recover or his "will to health." See Hellpach, 212. Hellpach notes that the soldier reacts hysterically because of a fear of the front: "If there isn't at least an aversion to being at the front, there is no war hysteria" ("Wo nicht mindestens Frontscheu vorhanden ist, dort gibt es keine Kriegshysterie," 179).

[6] "Psychopathische Minderwertigkeit, Degeneration, geborenes Verbrechertum, pathologische Lüge, Simulation, Übertreibung, bewußten Schwindel, [und] weibische Schwäche" (Steyerthal, quoted in Nonne/Wachsner 271).

[7] In 1918 Wagner-Jauregg was charged by the Austrian Commission for the Investigation of Derelictions of Military Duty with medical misconduct for his unethical practices during the war.

[8] Wagner-Jauregg in K. R. Eissler, *Freud as an Expert Witness: The Discussion of War Neuroses between Freud and Wagner-Jauregg*, trans. Christine Trollope (Madison, WI: International UP, 1986), 39–45. Eissler's text covers Freud's and

Wagner-Jauregg's testimony before the 1920 commission charging Wagner-Jauregg.

[9] "In allen Massenbewegungen begegnen uns Züge, die ohne weiteres auf eine tiefere Verwandtschaft mit hysterischen Erscheinungen hinweisen" (Kraepelin, 176–77).

[10] The fear of destabilization and political upheaval is reflected in the genre of anti-Bolshevist films of the early Weimar period; see Philipp Stiasny's essay in this volume.

[11] "Männer in feldgrauer Uniform [, die] eine rote Fahne schwangen" (Wollenberg, 142–43).

[12] "Ethisch defekte Psychopathen," "hysterische Persönlichkeiten," "fanatische Psychopathen," and "Manisch-Depressive" (Kahn, 93–102).

[13] We may assume that the workers, in fact, sabotaged Roloff's new industrial complex.

[14] David Bordwell asserts that it is the Johannes figure who is strangling his wife at the beginning of the prologue. This interpretation would bolster the contention that Johannes is mentally unstable, with this instability linked to the battlefield at the start of the film (6).

[15] In Cowan's reading of Wilhelm Prager's film, *Wege zu Kraft und Schönheit* (1924/25), jumping bodies, namely the Germanic *Königssprung* ("royal leap") emerge as a representation of "ancient" body culture (164–70). See also Theodore F. Rippey's essay on Prager's film in this volume.

[16] "Das Bett ist der eigentliche Kampfplatz des Neurasthenikers" (Radkau, 144).

[17] The relationship between Johannes and Elisabeth represents the last part of *Nerven's* narrative, which is also fueled by nervous affliction. Elisabeth, a "nervous wreck," burns down the family villa, resulting in the death of Johannes's sister. After spending time at a convent, Elisabeth is finally united with Johannes.

Works Cited

Bonhoeffer, Karl. "Granatfernwirkung und Kriegshysterie." *Monatsschrift für Psychiatrie und Neurologie* 42 (1917): 51–58.

Bordwell, David. "Taking Things to Extremes: Hallucinations Courtesy of Robert Reinert." *Aura* 6.2 (2000): 4–19.

Cowan, Michael. *Cult of the Will: Nervousness and German Modernity.* University Park: Pennsylvania State UP, 2008.

Eissler, K. R. *Freud as an Expert Witness: The Discussion of War Neuroses between Freud and Wagner-Jauregg.* Translated by Christine Trollope. Madison, WI: International UP, 1986.

Eksteins, Modris. "The Cultural Impact of the Great War." In *Film and the First World War,* edited by Karel Dibbets and Bert Hogenkamp, 201–12. Amsterdam: Amsterdam UP, 1995.

Ferro, Marc. *The Great War, 1914–1918.* London: Routledge 1993.

Freud, Sigmund. "Memorandum on the Electrical Treatment of War Neurotics." In *The Standard Edition of the Complete Psychological Works of Sigmund Freud,* edited by James Strachey, 17:211–15. London: Hogarth, 1959.

———. "Thoughts for the Times on War and Death." In *The Standard Edition of the Complete Psychological Works of Sigmund Freud,* edited by James Strachey, 14:275–300. London: Hogarth, 1959.

Gaupp, Robert. "Kriegsneurosen." *Zeitschrift für die gesamte Neurologie und Psychiatrie* 34 (1916): 357–90.

———. *Die künftige Stellung des Arztes im Volke.* Tübingen: Laupp, 1919.

Hellpach, Willy. "Die Kriegsneurasthenie." *Zeitschrift für die gesamte Neurologie und Psychiatrie* 45 (1919): 177–229.

Hildebrandt, Kurt. "Forensische Begutachtung eines Spartakisten." *Allgemeine Zeitschrift für Psychiatrie und psychisch-gerichtliche Medizin* 76 (1919): 479–518.

Hirschfeld, R. "Aus der Praxis der sogenannten aktiven Psychotherapie." *Medizinische Klinik* 28 (14 July 1918): 687–88.

Horak, Jan-Christopher. "Robert Reinert: Film as Metaphor." *Griffithiana* 60/61 (October 1997): 181–89.

Kaes, Anton. "War — Film — Trauma." In *Modernität und Trauma: Beiträge zum Zeitenbruch des Ersten Weltkrieges,* edited by Inka Mülder-Bach, 121–30. Vienna: WUV, 2000.

———. "Weimar Cinema: The Predicament of Modernity." In *European Cinema,* edited by Elizabeth Ezra, 59–77. Oxford and New York: Oxford UP, 2004.

Kahn, Eugen. "Psychopathen als revolutionäre Führer." *Zeitschrift für die gesamte Neurologie und Psychiatrie* 52 (1919): 90–106.

Keegan, John. *The First World War.* New York: Vintage Books, 2000.

Kraepelin, Emil. "Psychiatrische Randbemerkungen zur Zeitgeschichte." *Süddeutsche Monatshefte* 16 (1919): 171–83.

Leed, Eric J. *No Man's Land: Combat and Identity in World War I.* Cambridge: Cambridge UP, 1979.

"The Legacy of War." In *The Weimar Republic Sourcebook,* edited by Anton Kaes, Martin Jay, and Edward Dimendberg, 5–6. Berkeley: U of California P, 1994.

Lerner, Paul. *Hysterical Men: War, Psychiatry, and the Politics of Trauma in Germany, 1890–1930.* Ithaca, NY: Cornell UP, 2003.

Nonne, Max, and F. Wachsner. "Therapeutische Erfahrungen in der Behandlung sogenannter Neurosen." *Zeitschrift für die gesamte Neurologie und Psychiatrie: Referate und Ergebisse* 15 (1918): 271–73.

Oppenheim, Hermann. "Seelenstörung und Volksbewegung." *Berliner Tageblatt*, 16 April 1919, 1–2.

Polgar, Alfred. "Faradische Ströme." *Die Weltbühne* 16 (1920): 587–89.

Radkau, Joachim. *Das Zeitalter der Nervosität: Deutschland zwischen Bismarck und Hitler.* Munich: Carl Hanser Verlag, 1998.

Showalter, Elaine. *The Female Malady: Women, Madness, and English Culture, 1830–1980.* New York: Pantheon Books, 1985.

Simmel, Ernst. *Kriegs-Neurosen und "Psychisches Trauma."* Leipzig and Munich: Verlag von Otto Nemnich, 1918.

———. *Psycho-Analysis and the War Neuroses.* International Psycho-Analytical Library No. 2. London: International Psycho-Analytical, 1921.

Singer, Kurt. "Das Kriegsende und die Neurosenfrage." *Neurologisches Zentralblatt* 38 (1919): 330–34.

Stelzner, Helenefriderike. "Psychopathologisches in der Revolution." *Zeitschrift für die gesamte Neurologie und Psychiatrie* 49 (1919): 393–408.

Stransky, Erwin. "Der seelische Wiederaufbau des deutschen Volkes und die Aufgaben der Psychiatrie." *Zeitschrift für die gesamte Neurologie und Psychiatrie* 60 (1920): 271–80.

Winter, Jay. *Sites of Memory, Sites of Mourning: The Great War in European Cultural History.* Cambridge: Cambridge UP, 1995.

Wollenberg, Robert. *Erinnerungen eines alten Psychiaters.* Stuttgart: Ferdinand Enke, 1931.

Zuckmayer, Carl. "Erich Maria Remarque's *All Quiet on the Western Front.*" In *The Weimar Republic Sourcebook*, edited by Anton Kaes, Martin Jay, and Edward Dimendberg, 23–24. Berkeley: U of California P, 1994.

3: Humanity Unleashed: Anti-Bolshevism as Popular Culture in Early Weimar Cinema

Philipp Stiasny

"DON'T SHOOT ME!" the director yelled. Then he gave the order to attack: an infernal noise started, machine guns firing, spotlights flooding the ground, and soldiers in army uniform began to climb the barricades of the Spartacist rebels. On 13 March 1920, under the guidance of Joseph Delmont, *Die entfesselte Menschheit* (Humanity Unleashed) was being filmed in the studios at the Zoo in Berlin.[1] At the very same time, not far outside, another insurrection was taking place, a real one: an ultraright-wing military group led by Wolfgang Kapp seized control of strategic buildings in the German capital and forced the democratically elected government to leave the city. Yet this effort to restore the monarchy failed to garner the support of the civil service and the population: after only four days, the so-called Kapp-Putsch collapsed.

The two incidents — the shooting of Delmont's film and the attempted *coup d'état* — reflect both the imaginary and the real threat to the young Weimar Republic. For years, extreme groups on both ends of the political spectrum sought to undermine the stability of the state through acts of political violence: in January 1919 the Spartacists had staged an unsuccessful attempt at fomenting a Communist uprising; throughout 1919 and 1920 violent clashes between revolutionary workers and the authorities occurred in different parts of Germany; right-wing militias committed politically motivated murders, and civil war seemed imminent.

Delmont's *Die entfesselte Menschheit* clearly reflects a growing fear of political radicalization, here associated with violence from the Left. For the broad majority of the German public, dominated by the mainstream bourgeois press, Bolshevism (and its near-synonym, Spartacism) embodied the danger of total collapse of the German Reich, symbolizing civil war, chaos, and anarchy. Anti-Bolshevism ran across a broad spectrum, ranging from Social Democrats, Liberals, and *Zentrum* Catholics to the political Right, including groups of militarists, monarchists, anti-Socialists, and former representatives of annexation. The uneasy alliance of these disparate groups mirrored the *Burgfrieden* (political truce) of the war years, shifting the focus from the wartime fight against enemies on the outside to a postwar fight against the perceived enemies within. Similar to the "red scare" that grabbed the United States after the First World War, this ideology in defense of the state can be described as "radical anti-radicalism" (Murray, 279).

In explicit or allegorical ways, many German films from the early post-war years deal with the revolution and the civil war in Russia, and with the collapse of the German Empire and the uprisings after 1918. These anti-Bolshevist films are important cultural-historical documents in that they show how burning issues of the time, such as the Spartacus uprising, were integrated into popular culture. In what follows, I wish to give a short overview of anti-Bolshevist films to set the stage for a closer analysis of Delmont's *Die entfesselte Menschheit*, as a film paradigmatic of this now largely forgotten genre.[2]

Performing Violence: From *Unsühnbar* to *Der Tod aus Osten*

The first fiction film showing clearly anti-Bolshevist tendencies emerged during the war itself, in the context of a propaganda campaign against the strikes of grumbling, war-weary workers: the plot of *Unsühnbar* (What Cannot Be Atoned For, 1917, directed by Georg Jacoby) revolves around two brothers. The older one serves on the front, while the younger one works in an ammunition factory in their hometown.[3] A mysterious stranger inflames the young, radical factory workers against their older and respectable colleagues. He instigates a strike to protest reductions in the already small food portions. Because of the strike the soldiers at the front run out of munitions supplies and the older brother is killed in an enemy attack. Only now does the younger brother realize the disastrous consequences of the strike and his own guilt. He seeks atonement by volunteering for the army.

In terms of narrative and form, *Unsühnbar* displays key elements that would return in many anti-Bolshevist films later on: a political, moralizing story centered on the conflict between "ideal" (Social Democratic) workers and "evil" (Communist) ones; key motifs such as the dissimilar brothers, crowds that are easy to manipulate, and the figure of an enemy provocateur whose seductive power relies on his strong erotic charisma. Until 1917, German film propaganda had concentrated on non-fiction films. *Unsühnbar* marks a decisive turning point, in that it is a fiction film that seeks to boost the fighting morale of the audience by resorting to exciting and emotionally gripping elements derived from crime film and melodrama.

The revolution of November 1918 created considerable unrest among German film producers. Representatives of the film industry were quick to declare their sympathy with the new government, aligning themselves with the moderate politics of Social Democracy, producing many anti-Bolshevist and history films as well as those aiming for international reconciliation.[4] Directors were asked to make films that would "support the spirit of democracy" and that would help prevent the emergence of "a dictatorship of the proletariat in the very place of the former, fortuitously overthrown dictatorship of the military."[5] Not a single company produced fiction films in favor of Bolshevism and proletarian dictatorship. Producers were eager to appeal to both working-class and middle-class audiences, including the educated bourgeoisie, who traditionally regarded the cinema and mass culture with a certain reserved disdain.

The Danish film *Folkets Ven* (The Friend of the People, 1918, directed by Forrest Holger-Madsen) was released in Germany as *Söhne des Volkes* (Sons of the People) and subsequently became a box-office success, exerting a profound effect on cinematic anti-Bolshevism in Germany. As the advertisements announced, *Söhne des Volkes* promoted "the fusion of socialist groups against Bolshevism."[6] The three brothers at the center of the story represent well-known stereotypes: Hellmuth, an intellectual newspaper editor who seeks political reform along moderate, Social Democratic lines; Waldo, an impulsive blacksmith who advocates violent revolution; and Oskar, a crippled, weak, and introverted watchmaker, who is a loner without fixed political conviction but is easy to manipulate. Hellmuth marries the daughter of the rich leader of the Conservative Party against her father's will. Acting on behalf of Waldo, Oskar attempts to murder the leader of the Conservatives. Spurred on by a Russian revolutionary, Waldo leads armed radicals to start an insurrection. As Oskar commits suicide in his prison cell, Waldo suddenly renounces the use of violence and asks Hellmuth, now himself a member of the government, for forgiveness. Standing in front of the rubble of his own house, Hellmuth warns the crowds of the dangers of civil war and "Bruderkrieg" — war among brothers.

In the German version of the film this civil war is described as a direct consequence of the First World War.[7] Here Hellmuth appears as the politically and morally perfect mediator between radicals from the Left and the Conservative establishment, resembling a savior and religious leader. Alongside its political message of moderation, *Söhne des Volkes* offers a huge spectacle. The viewer witnesses mass scenes with furious crowds, street fights over barricades, heated debates in parliament, the attack on a house, and its complete destruction in an explosion. Drawing on elements of the sensation film genre, *Söhne des Volkes* has a more dramatic pace and higher production values than *Unsühnbar*.

The Danish film's formula of a social parable disguised as a sensation film would become paradigmatic for the German anti-Bolshevist films in subsequent years. Key narrative clichés are used time and again: the hero's mediation between the extremes; the conspiracy led by a Russian revolu-

tionary; the romance that crosses divisions of class and politics; the manipulation of the masses; and the final plea to overcome the division of society
through collective labor and a respect for law and order (a pattern that can
be found in Robert Reinert's *Nerven* as well; see the essay by Barbara
Hales in this volume). Contemporary audiences, it would seem, were
attracted less by the moral values conveyed by such films than by the
excitement associated with the elements of sex, violence, crime, melodrama, and lavishly staged sensations.[8]

Although riddled with clichés, these films took a stand against radicalism from both the Left and the Right: reactionary, anti-democratic, and
unfeeling capitalism is embodied by arrogant manufacturers who either go
down dying or change their minds for the better; the conversion of a
cynical capitalist into a tolerant follower of democratic ideas symbolizes the
success of antiradicalism. Alongside young newspaper editors and progressive factory owners, engineers and doctors frequently played the hero; with
the help of new groundbreaking inventions they manage to ease hardship
for the people and heal the social split.[9]

A few films refer directly to the contemporary situation in revolutionary Russia, drawing a frightening picture of a cruel Communist regime
built upon anarchy, terror, moral downfall, and the brutal elimination of
its enemies.[10] In *Der Tod aus Osten* (Death from the East, 1919, directed
by Martin Hartwig), for instance, two lovers fight against the new
Communist rulers and their despotism in one of the Baltic states. Finally,
the couple is put against a wall and shot. This film in particular divided
critical opinion. Some critics explicitly praised the realistic, frightening
depiction of a violent regime and saw the love story as a necessary concession to the taste of the audience. Other reviewers sharply rejected the
chosen form of realism as highly problematic. For them the "enormous
number of atrocities, murders, looting, rape, execution of hostages, and
other horrible scenes of all sorts" bore the risk that "the audience will
reject the film for its excess of ugliness" (Lewandowski, "Der Tod"). This
view was shared by the Berlin Board of Censorship, which banned *Der Tod
aus Osten* after the introduction of centralized censorship in the summer
of 1920. The censors conceded that the film was doubtlessly intended as a
warning. Still, they were not sure whether the film would not have the
opposite effect — by inciting rebellious behavior in the viewer.[11]

"A Document of Recent History": *Die entfesselte Menschheit* and the Staging of the Spartacus Uprising

Joseph Delmont's film *Die entfesselte Menschheit* of 1920 deserves a special
place among the anti-Bolshevist films.[12] It represents an adaptation of the

first fictional account of the so-called Spartacus uprising of January 1919 in Berlin, the novel *Die entfesselte Menschheit* by Max Glass. Published in the fall of 1919, the novel offers a panorama of a world gone mad, a world full of disease and violence in which the war has not really come to an end. The allegory centers on a dialogue between, on the one side, the followers of evolutionary constructive labor — like the German chemical engineer Clarenbach — and advocates of a radical new beginning on the other — represented by the Russian revolutionary Karenow, who appears as a mysterious, almost contagious figure with hypnotic power and the ability to manipulate the masses (indeed, the novel depicts Karenow also as a vampire). A reviewer of this "*Seelengeschichte* (psycho-history) of the wild days in Berlin" states: "This is not a realistic novel; its figures are symbols of spiritual conditions of many kinds which — clashing against each other — cause explosive inflammation during the period" (Reuter; see also Hahnemann). Borrowing from contemporary discourses about war, revolution, and nervous disease, the novel suggestively highlights an undercurrent of dangerous and uncontrollable sexuality. With its fragmentation into many episodes, it creates the sense of rushed disorientation. Delmont's film, by way of contrast, reduces the number of the protagonists and uses a continuous narration instead.

The film's story starts in 1917: German engineer Michael Clarenbach (Paul Hartmann) and Bernhard Winterstein (Carl de Vogt), a former officer demoted for insubordination, find themselves prisoners of war in a Russian camp. Far away from home, Clarenbach longs for his faithful wife, Rita (Trude Hoffmann), and Winterstein for his not-quite-so-faithful mistress, Camilla (Marion Illing). Winterstein escapes and joins the charismatic Russian agitator Karenow (Eugen Klöpfer), who preaches the complete destruction of the existing order as a precondition of World Revolution. After their seizure of power the Bolshevists release the German prisoners of war. Clarenbach returns to Berlin, is happily reunited with Rita, and then enthusiastically gets back to his work as director of a chemical factory. Shortly afterward, the German Republic is declared and the war comes to an end. Clarenbach meets Winterstein, who spreads Karenow's revolutionary ideas in Berlin. With Winterstein's help, Karenow has gathered a group of conspirators willing to use violence.

Karenow seeks to win Clarenbach over. He explains: "Poverty is our plough and misery our fertilizer. Out of blood and distress the New will rise! [. . .] The whole fabric of the world has to be destroyed and broken into pieces in order that we shall construct a more beautiful and brighter building upon the rubble." Unlike Karenow, Clarenbach believes that constructive labor is the only cure for a society that is ill at its core. He successfully appeals to the striking workers in his factory to work collectively for a better future. But Karenow, driven by hatred of Clarenbach, undermines the front of his enemies. He exercises his mysterious powers on Clarenbach's wife, Rita, who is emotionally neglected by her husband and becomes fascinated with revolutionary ideals. Also, at the behest of Karenow, Winterstein's mistress Camilla seduces the young and innocent Turenius (Arthur Bergen), whose father owns a large ammunitions factory. Through Camilla, the conspirators get hold of the keys for the ammunitions depot and blow up the whole factory. Clarenbach suspects Karenow, but as he enters the latter's apartment he finds his wife instead of the fugitive. In fact, Rita has warned off Karenow.

The conspirators further provoke the workers and their sympathizers and initiate strikes and mass meetings, which culminate in an uprising. The followers of Karenow, with prostitutes and criminals amongst them, open their secret depots and arm themselves. They set up barricades and occupy houses. Street fights start. The rebels angrily resist the intervention of government troops and the new auxiliary forces that Clarenbach has established. But the rebels are defeated. Winterstein dies, while Karenow escapes. Yet as he passes Clarenbach's factory, Karenow witnesses a crowd of furious workers threatening Rita. Karenow saves the woman but is himself killed. Over Karenow's dead body Clarenbach and Rita reconcile as Clarenbach declares: "His will was pure. But his way was wrong. When he died he must have been horrified by the effects of his own propaganda." Then Clarenbach declares the new philosophy: "The time has come to start working."

The production company Nivo-Film started shooting *Die entfesselte Menschheit* at the end of February 1920, with Joseph Delmont as director and author Max Glass as scriptwriter and artistic adviser. In the context of the political turmoil created by the abortive Kapp-Putsch that March, newspaper articles about the filming drew the attention of the Foreign Office to *Die entfesselte Menschheit* (fig. 3.1). Nivo-Film was asked to allow a member of the Foreign Office to see the film before its release, clearly in an effort to exert influence over the final version of a potentially worrisome film that would be exported and would have an impact on Germany's image abroad.[13] On 23 April 1920, *Die entfesselte Menschheit* was first screened in front of the press and received a generally positive feedback.

"This film is a document of recent history, and this alone makes it immensely valuable," critic Herbert Lewandowski wrote. "For the first time, a German film of such huge dimensions has not been dressed up in a foreign style. This film is completely German, and that is why it will arouse excitement abroad. It will also function as an unbeatable tool of propaganda for the majority of the German people who still have higher ideals than strikes, revolution, and war among brothers!" ("Die entfesselte Menschheit"). Other reviewers agree in ascribing a positive propaganda value to *Die entfesselte Menschheit*. In a testimony to the film section of the Foreign Office, which had to decide whether the distribution of the film should be supported by the state, the official in charge praises the film's

Fig. 3.1. During the filming of Die entfesselte Menschheit, *Berlin, 1920. Photo by Willy Römer. Agentur für Bilder zur Zeitgeschichte, Berlin.*

moral intentions and its antirevolutionary stance. Yet he also notes, somewhat ambivalently, that the film could provoke a dangerous side-effect, in that it "not only frightens but also allures" the viewer.[14]

In June 1920 the censors gave their permission to release *Die entfesselte Menschheit*. Perhaps because of the politically still volatile situation Nivo-Film did not distribute the film straight away. Instead, the official premiere only took place in November. Now the Social Democratic newspaper *Vorwärts* disapproved of the depiction of the workers as too negative; it emphasized that in reality the majority of the workers fought in defense of law and order.[15] For parts of the conservative press the opposite held true. They blamed the film for painting an all-too-positive picture of the workers (Olimsky). The bourgeois liberal newspapers, however, were mainly in favor of *Die entfesselte Menschheit*. The well-established *Vossische Zeitung* of Berlin praised the filmmakers for their courage: "Nobody likes it when his wounds, whose scars are hardly healed, are touched. It is of no consequence whether he wears such scars with pride or shame. [. . .] Very effectively, without any exaggeration or diminution, the images of the uprising still fresh in our memory are presented. They are skillfully connected with the destiny of several individuals who drown in the current of brutal events, not seeing the light of the morning sun that brings the liberation of the people."[16]

The Homecoming Soldier, the Vampire, and Their New Battleground

Die entfesselte Menschheit shows civil war as a consequence of the First World War, for instance, through Karenow's extremely martial language in the intertitles. Indeed, a war of words predates the street fights. Karenow's radical doctrine legitimizes destruction as a necessary means of purification and recovery; it demands pitilessness, cruelty, and terror. On the level of the plot, Clarenbach and Winterstein, both returning prisoners of war, bridge the gap between war and postwar. They come back to their loved ones believing that nothing has changed, clinging to an idealized, patriarchal concept of love and partnership. For them the metropolis is no longer the home they dreamed of but a battleground of gender relations.

The returnees have to rethink their own ostensibly outdated concepts of masculinity. Most of the time, Clarenbach treats his wife Rita more as a saint than as a woman. He completely neglects her in order to search for salvation and harmony in his laboratory. Only when he learns that Rita is intellectually and sexually attracted to his political opponent Karenow does Clarenbach react. Stimulated by a somewhat archaic erotic rivalry for Rita, he is forced back into a traditional male role. The former war victim, sentenced to passivity, now regains his strength.

Winterstein, on the other hand, learns more quickly that the woman he longed for in captivity no longer matches his ideal. Camilla's sexual activity is not limited to him alone. From this perspective, Winterstein's commitment to the revolution reflects his desire to compensate for humiliation, degradation, and sexual frustration. His personal crisis is exacerbated when Karenow begins to exploit Camilla for the revolutionary cause. Playing Winterstein, Carl de Vogt gives a virile, determined, and dashing performance in line with his well-known screen persona, familiar for instance from Fritz Lang's adventure thriller, *Die Spinnen* (The Spiders, 1919/1920). *Die entfesselte Menschheit* adds a new aspect to de Vogt's film personality: he plays a lonely, broken man hardly able to suppress his strong sexual desire, which bursts out from time to time.

The central figure in the battle of the sexes is Karenow himself. His screen image follows the pattern of depicting revolutionaries and Communists as "villainous criminals" — a convention that would later be sharply criticized by Béla Balázs (Balázs, 147–49). Karenow, played by Eugen Klöpfer, develops an intensive, scintillating presence, sporting a shaggy full beard and a fur cap, his eyes surrounded by dark makeup (fig. 3.2). Karenow, both in his persona and in his appearance, is modeled on a real predecessor, the well-known Soviet agitator Karl Radek (1885–1939), whose sinister image had by 1919/20 become synonymous with the negative stereotype of a Jewish Bolshevist for some segments of the German public.

Fig. 3.2. Russian Bolshevist agitator Karenow (Eugen Klöpfer) stirs up the crowd in
Die entfesselte Menschheit. Illustrierter Film-Kurier *2.16 (1920): 5. Courtesy of*
Deutsche Kinemathek, Berlin.

In Karenow's presence both his fellow conspirators and his opponents
feel nervous and insecure. His penetrating, hypnotic look was compared
by a reviewer to "a snake's paralyzing gaze."[17] A scene in which Karenow
visits Clarenbach's factory illustrates the agitator's demonic power.
Clarenbach enters the balcony of his laboratory and peers down on the
factory's courtyard to discover Karenow waiting there — as if the intruder
had announced himself telepathically. Looking down on the courtyard in
a long shot, reflecting Clarenbach's point of view, the camera moves down

and approaches Karenow's face very closely. Just before his eyes finally fill the whole frame, a reverse shot from Karenow's perspective is cut in and shows Clarenbach staring down, completely captivated. The camera movement has a zoom-like effect: Karenow's gaze works like suction, and even Clarenbach is unable to resist. The criminal, enigmatic leader of the conspiracy displays the seductive qualities of a vampire. Unlike his relative, Murnau's Nosferatu, the true hero of *Die entfesselte Menschheit* does not need long teeth — his eyes suffice to bite, suck, and infect his victims.

Among Karenow's opponents, young Turenius, too, falls victim to the battle of the sexes initiated by the Bolshevik. Camilla, seductive and herself seduced, functions as Karenow's weapon. During their first encounter Turenius is bewildered by Camilla: not only does she flirt without restraint, but she also downs schnapps like a sailor. With the upper part of her body dressed like a man, wearing a waistcoat and a tie, Camilla symbolically stakes a claim in the male arena. When she later enters a reception in Turenius's home in elegant, feminine dress, however, Camilla's appearance fully matches the clichéd looks of a rich, spoiled, and bored society lady. In both incarnations, as androgynous provocateur and as trophy mistress, Camilla evokes the metaphor of bloodsucking also used in conjunction with Karenow. Whether the vamp appears in masculine or feminine guise is unimportant; the effect is the same: gender relations have become confused, and old notions of masculinity are in danger.

The clash of gender relations finds its climax in a scene during the uprising in which a group of prostitutes — the so-called "Flintenweiber" (rifle women) — slaughter a helpless captive. Although the existing film material does not contain this particular scene, a set photograph offers a vivid impression: Rosa Valetti, in the role of a prostitute fighting for revolution, grimly threatens a wounded soldier with a long knife (fig. 3.3).[18] Writing about the actual film, one reviewer describes in detail how her character "slowly and deliberately spits in the face of a captured, defenseless, blood covered soldier of the *Reichswehr*, before finally killing him."[19] Here, more than anywhere else, the thesis of a close relationship between the civil war and the war of the sexes is pushed to the foreground. The film's moral message concerning "humanity unleashed" is clear: the (male) bourgeois, patriarchal order of society is threatened by (feminized) terror and extermination.

Iconography, Style, Genre

With its extremely violent, often repulsive images, the novel by Max Glass tested the limits of representation, that is, the limits of what was then, in 1920, allowable. In fact, the novel contains apocalyptic scenes akin to those found in a modern splatter movie. To a certain extent Delmont's

Fig. 3.3. A prostitute (Rosa Valetti) and her "rifle women" attack a wounded soldier. Illustrierter Film-Kurier 2.16 (1920): 7. *Courtesy of Deutsche Kinemathek, Berlin.*

version translates this aesthetic of horror and terror into film (within the narrow constraints imposed by the reintroduction of film censorship in May 1920). Moreover, the film reduces the novel's allegorical and apocalyptic elements for the sake of a stronger realistic appeal. The film's plot is temporally and topographically more closely attached to its contemporary context than is the case in the novel.

The uprising is presented in half-documentary style as a great spectacle. The film draws on a contemporary iconography that had already been established through postcards, photographs in the illustrated press, and documentary films.[20] Berlin, in *Die entfesselte Menschheit*, becomes a veritable battleground. Automobiles packed with armed men race toward the camera at breakneck speed; a crowd of strikers completely fills the frame; the rebels take cover behind barricades made of huge packets of newspaper; they tear out stones from the pavement and fire shots from freshly dug trenches; machine guns are placed on rooftops; civilians rush into the basement to find shelter from heavy firearms; a house is hit, and the people in the basement are swallowed by a cloud of smoke. Big spotlights, furnishing the whole scenery with an almost picturesque mood, search the ground of the no-man's-land between the enemy lines. The muzzles of the guns are aimed directly at the viewer. Then the government forces attack the rebels. We see soldiers running forward; we see them conquer the barricades. Finally a group of rebels, held at gunpoint and with raised arms, pass a crowd. Warned by Rita, Karenow escapes over the rooftops of the metropolis, vanishing in the urban jungle. All this is depicted in quick succession, and only a few intertitles interrupt the film's feverish pace. The editing helps enhance excitement: Rita is shown waiting in her flat. Although for her the civil war is to an extent invisible, she is nevertheless haunted by its noise in her living room. Bewildered, she covers her ears with her hands. Thus the noise of combat, as a visual sign, is present even in this silent film.

The climactic street fights shot in the studio and on location in Berlin found praise with the critics. Compared with the short combat scenes in the fictional German war films from the years 1914 to 1918, such as *Unsühnbar*, the battle scenes in *Die entfesselte Menschheit* are markedly different: they are staged with much greater financial, technical, and human effort, and the pseudo-documentary mise-en-scène also marks a major and easily detectable stylistic difference. This "docu-aesthetic" applies to only half the narration; the remainder of the film follows the usual patterns of popular genre film, with borrowed motifs such as the mysterious stranger, the super-criminal, the seductive vamp, and the conspiracy. Here too, an agitator from Russia leads a conspiracy.[21] As in other films this seductive conspirator possesses a strong erotic charisma that inscribes a sexual layer to the cause he fights for. The revolution of the political order becomes a sexual revolution as well.

Die entfesselte Menschheit is the only surviving fiction feature film that depicts the Spartacus uprising in Berlin. It is both a typical example of the subgenre of anti-Bolshevist films and an exception. It differs from most of the other films in that it is based on a novel that elicited respect and attention from serious literary critics, rather than being dismissed as pulp fiction. In addition, its production values are unusually high — throughout, the considerable financial investment in technology, design, direction, and acting is evident.

From the point of view of genre history, the anti-Bolshevist films use varying motifs from detective and spy films and from serial crime melodramas. Among them are the vamps and *femmes fatales* — all those Tatjanas, Ilkas, Sonjas, and Marjas — the seductive and seduced women in the service of revolution who confuse so many male characters in the films. There is a direct line between the foreign agitator in *Unsühnbar* to Karenow as an *homme fatal*, men and women alike falling victim to his power — similar to Count Orlok, the pale hero of *Nosferatu* (1921, directed by F. W. Murnau). Several other well-worn motifs are found in *Die entfesselte Menschheit*, such as the images of the furious crowd of manipulated workers, and the idealistic scientist who wants to save the world. The film uses the motif of the

"Bruderkrieg," which in *Unsühnbar* and *Söhne des Volkes* appears literally as a conflict among brothers and also stands in as a metaphor for the civil war, in a figurative way: Clarenbach and Winterstein at first suffer together as prisoners of war and then develop into enemies who fight each other.

Attractions, Messages, and Guilty Pleasures

What kind of image of revolution and civil war is supported by the anti-Bolshevist films? While most of the anti-Bolshevist films can generally be labeled as political problem films, they also belong to the genre of the sensation film. Their production values — the "Schauwert" (visual appeal) — depend heavily on action and spectacle, often combined with a melo-dramatic plot. This mixture is, as suggested before, indebted to the formu-lae of genre film. Images of agitated masses, street fights, and spectacular destruction address the audience's appetite for sensation and excitement, evoking feelings of desire and fear alike. Fiction and reality merge, as an old iconography based on earlier products of popular culture combines with a new iconography derived from a contemporary political and cultural discourse and its representation in other media.

It may feel strange that the stories told in these popular quasi-genre films again and again culminate in the defeat of the rebels and the victory of the moderate party. How can visual pleasure and curiosity be maintained if the outcome is always more or less the same and if the message tends to be conciliatory or even defeatist? Taking the history of the sensation or action film into account, it would seem that outcome and message are not central to the audience appeal of a film. The form of the film's narration, its mise-en-scène, and its sophisticated and expensive production values seem to be much more important. For this *Die entfesselte Menschheit* is a good example, not least because the film offers another relevant feature: in terms of screen time, the activities of the villains attract far more attention than the good guys. Interest is focused less on the exemplary, "normal" people and more on the outsiders — the violent, the jealous, the evil, and the mentally ill. The representation of the civil war resembles the represen-tation of evil and often ambivalent negative heroes in popular culture as the super-criminal and the vamp, since both aim to satisfy the guilty pleas-ures and the wish to be thrilled on the part of the viewer.

Among contemporary critics the prevailing opinion was that anti-Bolshevist films should be applauded for their message. And perhaps some of the film producers even had in mind to cause a cathartic effect in the audience. However, some critics also expressed their worries about the opposite effect: that the films might draw attention and sympathy to the rebels and thus work in favor of Bolshevism. Probably for this reason the censors banned the anti-Bolshevist films, without exception, for children and youths. This meant, in effect, a significant state intervention into the film business and its finances. Even worse, from the summer of 1920 onward the new central Board of Censorship frequently demanded that scenes of upheaval and street fights be cut. The censors clearly sought to reduce the possibility of ambivalent political effects. Yet by reducing the sensational aspects of these films — their "Schauwert" — the censors also considerably limited the potential of their commercial success.

By the mid-1920s, revolution and civil war had become the subject of the famous Russian Revolution films of Sergei Eisenstein and Vsevolod Pudovkin, which were also distributed and debated in Germany. Here the Bolshevist's seizure of power is presented as the precondition for ending the World War and overcoming an unjust social order. German films from this period hardly ever touch on the subject of revolution and civil war. And when they do, these films no longer express an anti-Bolshevist position. They tend to romanticize the subject and lack any overt political ambition. Ultimately, they reflect a view both melancholic and melodramatic on a past that has just gone by.

The Rebel and the Gambler

Today the anti-Bolshevist films made in the years immediately following the First World War are forgotten. Still, scholars of Weimar Cinema will feel familiar with many of the narrative and visual clichés and the desires and fears reflected in these films, as they reappear in altered form in other and more canonical films of that period. The super-criminal with his threatening gaze, and the manipulated masses, stubborn employers, idealistic scientists, and enemy agents, strike and anarchy, street fighting and class conflict, final understanding and reconciliation; all these figures, themes, and motifs are not limited to anti-Bolshevist films but instead have found their way into the collective imagination. As the ideology of anti-Bolshevism loses its discursive dominance and its relevance for bourgeois cohesion in the early and mid 1920s, the figures and motifs used by this ideology start to float around independently. Thus, sometimes quietly, sometimes loudly, an echo of the anti-Bolshevist discourse can be traced in the cinema of the 1920s.

Fritz Lang's *Dr. Mabuse, der Spieler* (Dr. Mabuse, the Gambler, 1922) is an example that shows how clichés used in anti-Bolshevist films live on in later times, even if the films have nothing to do with Bolshevism at all. Lang's two-part film presents a whole arsenal of familiar images and motifs. Central to the narration is the complex of a carefully planned conspiracy and profound infiltration. The visual references to earlier anti-Bolshevist films can be best observed in the second part. In one scene, Mabuse, a protean con-man and mass hypnotist, acts as an agent provocateur and agitates a working-class audience in a proletarian tavern to take action against the police. Soon the crowd rushes onto the street in fury, like an uncontrollable flood.[22] Later, at the climax, a veritable war between Mabuse and the authorities breaks out. When the gangsters take cover in a house and start a shoot-out with the police, the film presents images of fierce street fights, hidden gunmen, policemen who get shot and collapse in the street, and soldiers of the *Reichswehr* with steel helmets, firearms, and hand grenades. These images not only anticipate the iconography of future gangster movies such as *Underworld* (1927, directed by Josef von Sternberg) and *Scarface* (1932, directed by Howard Hawks). They also refer back to the images of the civil war that in 1919 to 1920 could be found in newspapers, illustrated journals, and documentary films as well as the anti-Bolshevist fiction films. While Fritz Lang later claimed that the first version of *Dr. Mabuse, der Spieler* started with "a brief, breathless montage of scenes of the Spartacus Uprising, the murder of Rathenau, the Kapp Putsch, and other violent moments of recent history," this seems to be a myth (Eisner, 59; see also Kracauer, 82). Lang's Mabuse inherits the features of both the super-criminal and the screen-Bolshevik. In every situation he is able to mask himself and show his hypnotic powers; he is equally able to seduce masses and individuals, men and women, the poor and the rich. Lang used an existing iconography by removing its political context: the film strips familiar images of their ideological meaning and focuses on emotional appeal, turning sociopolitical conflicts into a war against organized crime. It is no surprise then that few contemporaries saw the film as an attempt to "mentally act out the horrors of the war."[23] Although masterfully condensed by Fritz Lang, a once ubiquitous popular culture has lost its memory and the sense of its own historicity.

Even so, the contemporary censors felt uncomfortable with the political resonances of Lang's film, focusing their criticism on the battle scenes and especially the images of fallen policemen: "The street fights remind us of nervous times in which those fights took place, though they had different roots. In this regard, the population has calmed down. However, if such fights are now presented in great detail and in an exaggerated manner to a mass audience, they will produce the nervous atmosphere of those past times anew."[24] Although the higher appeal Board of Censorship would later reinstate a number of cuts, the censors initially demanded several cuts in the fighting scenes.[25] The censors, who in their writings carefully avoid the term revolution, invoke the notion of a wound still fresh and not yet healed. They hold that an injunction against certain depictions is necessary for the process of healing not to be disturbed: instead of collective memory they recommend a collective silencing with regard to the civil war and its effects. In their decisions on *Doktor Mabuse, der Spieler*, the censors drew from the same argument as in 1920 when they did not allow the re-release of *Der Tod aus Osten*.[26] Touching on such a painful memory still seemed to be dangerous in May of 1922, and the Berlin censors felt that public order needed to be protected.

Lang himself continued in highly eclectic ways to rework the stereotypes of anti-Bolshevist films. In *Metropolis* (1927), for instance, futuristic architecture and the apparent emphasis on science fiction are balanced against older motifs such as the destructive class struggle and its resolution in a final appeal to collective labor. *Metropolis* may fail as a message movie but is unprecedented in terms of spectacle. In *Spione* (Spies, 1928) a banker, who looks like Lenin and who is bound to a wheel chair, wants to rule over the world with the help of a spy organization and his female Russian top agent, Sonja. Again, one spectacular sensation follows the other. And again, Lang has drained the political subtext from the anti-Bolshevist iconography he employs. In his German films Lang always maintained a distance from straightforwardly political film genres such as the war film. Instead, in Lang's films the modern city appears as a battleground.

The visual traditions and points of reference that Lang drew upon and that were latently familiar to a contemporary viewer are obscure today. The body of anti-Bolshevist films that have survived is relatively small and makes a conclusive judgment difficult. Nevertheless, compared with the cinematographic images of the First World War from before and after 1918 the anti-Bolshevist films present images of revolution and civil war whose emphasis on their sensational character stands out. Contemporaries often complained that documentary films made in wartime were boring, while fictional films almost completely left out the spectacular aspect of the war. Such films generally lacked mass scenes and the martial depiction of violence. For example, in a film like *Unsühnbar* the war at the home front is presented in the formula of a spy film. Significantly, the few scenes at the front lines are restaged with little effort, and the figure of the enemy soldier is unimportant. By way of contrast, in the anti-Bolshevist films of the early 1920s the protagonists of aggression, violence, and threat play the leading roles. In the anti-Bolshevist scenarios, formerly anonymous aggressors attain a distinct physiognomy. *Die entfesselte Menschheit* represents the civil war as a continuation of the First World War, displaced inside the nation. In doing so, the film anticipates later war films, predicated on the "realist paradigm" that dominated the aesthetics of the second half of the 1920s.

Notes

I wish to thank Edward McGarrell and Rainer Schlautmann for their generous help. I also thank Barbara Schütz (Bundesarchiv-Filmarchiv) for supporting my research on *Einigkeit und Recht und Freiheit*.
[1] -ll-. "Technische Evolution im Revolutionsfilm."

[2] I owe many thanks to Kevin Brownlow's pioneering study on the "Red Scare" in American films in his *Behind the Mask of Innocence*, 442–62.

[3] For a detailed discussion of *Unsühnbar* see Stiasny. A film copy of *Unsühnbar* is held by the Bundesarchiv-Filmarchiv, Berlin.

[4] Anon. "Sozialistische Konjunktur."

[5] Anon. "Die Aufgaben der Filmindustrie im politischen Kampf."

[6] Advertisement in *Der Film* 47 (23 November 1918). For a more detailed discussion of the film see Tybjerg, 254–61. A film copy of *Folkets Ven* is held by the Danske Filmmuseum, Copenhagen.

[7] Program leaflet for *Söhne des Volkes*, 1918, Paper collection of the Deutsche Kinemathek, Berlin.

[8] Examples are *Irrwahn* (Delusion, 1919, directed by Hans Werckmeister), *Desperados* (1919, directed by Toni Attenberger), *Satanas* (1919, directed by F. W. Murnau), and *Wirbel des Verderbens* (Maelstrom of Doom, 1919, directed by Siegfried Dessauer).

[9] Engineers and doctors as heroes can be found in *Zwischen zwei Welten* (Between two Worlds, 1919, directed by Adolf Gärtner), *Retter der Menschheit* (Savior of Humankind, 1919, directed by Carl Neißer and Franz Mehlitz), *Hungernde Millionäre* (Starving Millionaires, 1920, directed by William Wauer), *Die Welt ohne Hunger* (World without Hunger, 1920, directed by Artur Wellin), and *Am Webstuhl der Zeit* (At the Loom of Time, 1921, directed by Joe May).

[10] See *I.N.R.I. — Die Katastrophe eines Volkes* (I.N.R.I. — Catastrophe of a People, 1920, directed by Ludwig Beck) and *Der Todesreigen* (The Round Dance of Death, 1922, directed by William Karfiol).

[11] See censorship decision B.43693, 21 August 1920, and B.264, 25 October 1920. Published at http://www.deutsches-filminstitut.de/zengut/ df2tb812zb. pdf.

[12] A complete copy of *Die entfesselte Menschheit* has not survived. However, most of the film was reused in *Einigkeit und Recht und Freiheit* (Unity and Law and Freedom, 1926, directed by Joseph Delmont). A nitrate copy of this film is held by the Bundesarchiv-Filmarchiv, Berlin. A relatively precise idea of the lost film can be obtained through the combination of the surviving film material, the censorship card, and other written sources. The intertitles are quoted from the censorship card B.20, 29 June 1920, Bundesarchiv-Filmarchiv, Berlin.

[13] The correspondence between the Foreign Office and Nivo-Film can be found in the Bundesarchiv Berlin Lichterfelde, file R 901/72086–72088.

[14] Expert opinion by Dr. Robert Volz commissioned by the Foreign Office, 15 June 1920. Bundesarchiv Berlin Lichterfelde, R 901/72088, 297.

[15] ef. "Die entfesselte Menschheit."

[16] lp. "Die entfesselte Menschheit." *Vossische Zeitung*, 23 Nov. 1920. See also articles under the same title in the *Berliner Tageblatt* 533 (21 Nov. 1920) and *B.Z. am Mittag* 272 (22 Nov. 1920), and the collected reviews in *Der Film* 48 (27 Nov. 1920): 5.

[17] cr. "Die entfesselte Menschheit."

[18] See *Illustrierter Film-Kurier* 2.16 (1920): 7.

[19] cr. "Die entfesselte Menschheit."

[20] See the press photos in *Revolution und Fotografie*. For a comparison of fiction and documentary film see *Stürmische Tage in Berlin* (Stormy Days in Berlin, 1919, produced by Deulig). A copy of this documentary film is held by the Bundesarchiv-Filmarchiv, Berlin.

[21] This is also the case in *Satanas, Wirbel des Verderbens,* and *Am Webstuhl der Zeit.* In *Söhne des Volkes* the character of the Russian remains in the background, while in *Unsühnbar* there appears a hostile foreigner whose origin is not further explained.

[22] On Lang's artistic sources see Schönemann, 44–50.

[23] "[S]eelischen 'Abreagierung' des Kriegsentsetzens." Anon. "Die Erscheinungen der Nachkriegszeit im Film." *Berliner Illustrirte Zeitung,* 30 April 1922. Quoted from Jacques, *Dr. Mabuse* 1:303.

[24] Censorship decision B.5827, 17 May 1922, 2. Published at http://www.deutsches-filminstitut.de/zengut/df2tbdub+069z.pdf.

[25] See censorship decision O.27.22, 18 May 1922, 7. Published at http://www.deutsches-filminstitut.de/zengut/df2tb069z.pdf.

[26] See censorship decision B.264, 25 Oct. 1920, 4–5.

Works Cited

Anon. "Die Aufgaben der Filmindustrie im politischen Kampf." *LichtBildBühne* 47 (23 November 1918): 37–42.

———. "Die entfesselte Menschheit." *Berliner Tageblatt,* 21 November 1920.

———. "Die entfesselte Menschheit." *B.Z. am Mittag,* 22 November 1920.

———. "Die Erscheinungen der Nachkriegszeit im Film." *Berliner Illustrirte Zeitung,* 30 April 1922.

———. "Sozialistische Konjunktur." *Der Film* 47 (23 November 1918): 1.

Balázs, Béla. "Der revolutionäre Film." *Die Rote Fahne,* 10 October 1922. Reprinted in Béla Balázs, *Schriften zum Film,* 2 vols., edited by Helmut H. Diederichs, Wolfgang Gersch, and Magda Nagy, 1:147–49. Berlin: Henschel, 1982.

Brownlow, Kevin. *Behind the Mask of Innocence: Sex, Violence, Prejudice, Crime; Films of Social Conscience in the Silent Era.* Berkeley and Los Angeles: U of California P, 1990.

cr. "Die entfesselte Menschheit." *Berliner Börsen-Courier,* 21 November 1920.

ef. "Die entfesselte Menschheit." *Vorwärts,* 21 November 1920.

Eisner, Lotte H. *Fritz Lang.* London: Seeker & Warburg, 1976.

Hahnemann, Andy. "'Der Tod jagt durch die Straßen . . .': Zur Psychopathologisierung der Revolution in Max Glass' *Die entfesselte Menschheit*." In *"Friede, Freiheit, Brot!" Romane zur deutschen Novemberrevolution*, edited by Ulrich Kittstein and Regine Zeller, 41–58. Amsterdam and New York: Rodopi, 2009.

Jacques, Norbert. *Dr. Mabuse: Medium des Bösen*. Edited by Michael Farin and Günter Scholdt. Hamburg: Rogner & Bernhard, 1994.

Kracauer, Siegfried. *From Caligari to Hitler: A Psychological History of the German Film*. Princeton, NJ: Princeton UP, 1947.

Lewandowski, Herbert. "Die entfesselte Menschheit." *Der Film* 18 (1 May 1920): 47.

———. "Der Tod aus Osten." *Der Film* 49 (7 December 1919): 51.

-ll-. "Technische Evolution im Revolutionsfilm." *Berliner Börsen-Courier*, 28 March 1920.

lp. "Die entfesselte Menschheit." *Vossische Zeitung*, 23 November 1920.

Murray, Robert K. *Red Scare: A Study in National Hysteria, 1919–1920*. Westport, CT: Greenwood, 1980.

Olimsky, Fritz. "Die entfesselte Menschheit." *Berliner Börsen-Zeitung*, 21 November 1920. Quoted in *Film und Presse* 21 (4 December 1920): 491.

Reuter, Gabriele. "Die entfesselte Menschheit." *Vossische Zeitung*, 1 February 1920.

Revolution und Fotografie: Berlin 1918/19. Edited by the Neue Gesellschaft für bildende Kunst. Berlin: Dirk Nishen, 1990.

Schönemann, Heide. *Fritz Lang: Filmbilder, Vorbilder*. Berlin: Edition Hentrich, 1992.

Stiasny, Philipp. *Das Kino und der Krieg, Deutschland 1914–1929*. Munich: edition text + kritik, 2009.

Tybjerg, Casper. *An Art of Silence and Light: The Development of the Danish Film Drama to 1920*. PhD diss., U of Copenhagen, 1996.

4: Desire versus Despotism: The Politics of *Sumurun* (1920), Ernst Lubitsch's "Oriental" Fantasy

Richard W. McCormick

MANY CRITICS HAVE ATTACKED Lubitsch's historical costume films for their distortion of history, among others Siegfried Kracauer (48) and Lotte Eisner (82) in their canonical books on Weimar Cinema. In Lubitsch's defense, arguments have been made that these films are escapist fantasies made by a director who was relatively oblivious to politics (even the revolutionary turmoil on the streets of Berlin in the aftermath of the First World War). For instance, Hans Helmut Prinzler, one of the film historians interviewed in Robert Fischer's documentary film *Ernst Lubitsch in Berlin*, argues that Lubitsch simply didn't pay attention to politics. Pola Negri, the famous female actor who starred in a number of Lubitsch's films of this period, explained the success of the first of Lubitsch's costume films, *Die Augen der Mumie Ma* (The Eyes of the Mummy Ma, 1918), as a product of "its intensely romantic oriental fatalism," which was "precisely the kind of escapism that a war-weary people craved for" (140). No one would claim that Lubitsch's primary agenda as a filmmaker was political — although much later in Hollywood he did start production of an overtly anti-Nazi film, *To Be or Not To Be*, in the fall of 1941, while the United States was still officially neutral.

It is true that throughout his career Lubitsch primarily made comedies and "escapist fantasies." But even "escapist fantasies" have politics; that is, they can be read politically, and the aim of this essay is to explore the politics of his "oriental" costume film, *Sumurun*. The film is clearly a fantasy without any clear historical referent other than a vague connection to the tales in *Arabian Nights* (as implied in the film's American release title, *One Arabian Night*). Thus historical "distortion" is not at issue here in the same way it is for Lubitsch's historical films about the mistress of France's Louis XV, *Madame Dubarry* (1919; American release title *Passion*) and the second wife of England's Henry VIII, *Anna Boleyn* (1920; American release title *Deception*).[1] This does not make Kracauer any kinder to *Sumurun*, which he accuses of "melodramatic sentimentality" (52). Nonetheless, I would maintain that the politics of Lubitsch's "ahistorical" and "apolitical" films — the comedies as well as the costume films —always involve a very frank portrayal of conflicts around sex, gender, class, and power. And they are always informed by a sympathy for the underdog and the outsider that is not unrelated to his own background as a German Jew.

Sumurun & Lubitsch's Early Career

Sumurun is an adaptation of Friedrich Freska's pantomime *Sumurun* (1910). The title page of Friedrich Freska's script claims that the play is based on "oriental fairy-tale motifs" ("orientalischen Märchenmotiven"). Its first stage production was directed by Max Reinhardt in 1911. In the same year the nineteen-year-old Ernst Lubitsch joined the Reinhardt troupe; it seems he played a slave in *Sumurun* that year and would continue to play various roles in it during the many Reinhardt productions of the pantomime (Spaich, 123).[2] Lubitsch would remain a member of the Reinhardt ensemble until 1918.

As early as 1913 Lubitsch began acting in short films, farces in which he frequently played Jewish characters (often employees in retail shops). In 1915 he began to direct these films as well. Up through 1918 he often acted in the films he directed, stopping only when he had become so successful that he began making longer comedies such as *Ich möchte kein Mann sein* (I Don't Want to Be a Man, 1918) and exotic historical melodramas such as *Die Augen der Mumie Ma* (The Eyes of the Mummy Ma, 1918) and *Carmen* (1918). In 1919 his career really took off with comedies such as *Die Austernprinzessin* (The Oyster Princess) and *Die Puppe* (The Doll) and the big-budget historical epic *Madame Dubarry* (*Passion*), which not only made him internationally famous but also led ultimately to the offer from Hollywood that lured him to America in 1922, where he would remain until his death in 1947.

In 1920, when he directed *Sumurun*, Lubitsch was at the peak of his German career, directing several films in that same year, including another big-budget historical film, *Anna Boleyn* (*Deception*) and successful comedies such as *Kohlhiesels Töchter* (Kohlhiesel's Daughters). The production team for *Sumurun* was filled with regular collaborators of Lubitsch's: the screenplay was written by Lubitsch and his cowriter, Hanns Kräly; Theodor Sparkuhl was the cinematographer; Kurt Richter designed the exotic sets, which impressed contemporaries like the critic Fritz Olimsky, who visited the set in April of 1920; and Ali Hubert designed the all-important costumes. The film had an impressive international cast, including the Polish Pola Negri, the Swede Jenny Hasselqvist, and the Norwegian Aud Egede Nissen, as well as famous German actors such as Paul Wegener, Harry Liedtke, and of course Lubitsch himself. Paul Davidson's Union Film produced the film; shooting began in Berlin on 13 March 1920, and the film premiered on September 1 of the same year. In 1947, near the end of his life, Lubitsch would write that the film, which he called a "playful fantasy," achieved only moderate success when compared to his three most successful historical costume films, *Carmen, Madame Dubarry,* and *Anna Boleyn* (cited in Prinzler/Patalas, 107).[3]

The plot of the film is somewhat complicated, but it is probably best explained as two interwoven subplots focusing on two female roles, the dancer (played by Negri) and the harem favorite, Sumurun (Hasselqvist). This film, like so many of Lubitsch's films, is addressed primarily to women spectators, for the narrative is driven in large part by female desire — the dancer's promiscuous desire for men but also for riches and "upward mobility," and Sumurun's desire for Nur Al-Din, the garment merchant (Liedtke, clearly the male "heartthrob" of the film). The dancer is part of a ragged troupe of wandering entertainers that includes the old hunchback clown (Lubitsch), whose love for her is unrequited. She eagerly leaves the troupe after her first performance in the city ruled by the old sheik (Wegener), having enchanted him (and his son the young sheik as well). A slave merchant (Paul Biensfeldt) buys her for the old sheik, much to the dancer's delight and the hunchback's despair.

The hunchback then ingests magic pills that induce a death-like sleep. The old woman of the troupe (Margarete Kupfer) believes him to be dead, until she finds the written instructions for the pills; she hides his body in a sack, which is then stolen by "Mutti" and "Putti," the two comic slaves of the garment merchant. Through a series of comic ploys the hunchback's body ends up at the palace of the sheik, where the old woman is able finally to revive him. Upon waking, however, he witnesses the dancer arrive at the palace and entice the old sheik to take her immediately to his chambers. Seeing this, the hunchback refuses to leave, waiting at the gate for a chance to enter the palace to search for the dancer.

Meanwhile the other subplot has unfolded in the sheik's harem. His favorite consort Sumurun has been obsessed with her love for Nur Al-Din and cold to the old sheik, who, after having heard someone whistling at her window, orders that she be killed, sure that she is encouraging this man in the courtyard below. Sumurun had only minutes earlier thrown a flower down to Nur Al-Din, but at the moment the old sheik hears the whistle, the man below is not Nur Al-Din but the young sheik (Carl Clewing), the old sheik's son. Upon learning that it was his son who had beckoned to Sumurun, the old sheik decides to spare her.

But being spared does not make Sumurun warm up to the old sheik; rather she is colder than ever to him. Thus he wants to find a new favorite for his harem, and at the slave merchant's suggestion he goes in disguise into the city to watch the dancer perform. Meanwhile Sumurun and the harem women, accompanied by the palace eunuchs, leave the palace to buy fabrics at the shop of Nur Al-Din, where her servant (Nissen) distracts the eunuchs and arranges for Sumurun and her beloved to meet alone. The servant also hatches a scheme to have Nur Al-Din carried secretly into the palace in a trunk full of garments; the body of the seemingly-dead hunch-back has already been hidden in this same container, and this is how he, too, ends up at the palace.

Sumurun's servant and the other harem women arrange for Nur Al-Din and Sumurun to be alone together in a chamber of the palace. Meanwhile, in the old sheik's bedchamber, the dancer makes the old man chase her for awhile before she allows him to carry her to his bed. The next time we cut back to the two, the old man is asleep on the bed, and the dancer is awake. A true "vamp" of the sort Negri would so often play, she goes to the window and beckons to the young sheik to come up to her. The hunchback, still outside the gate, witnesses this, and, enraged, he climbs up to the window in which the dancer had been, only to peer inside to see her in the embrace of the young sheik, with the old sheik asleep on the bed. Seeing the hunchback in the window, the dancer, who thinks he has died, screams. This wakes the old sheik, who quickly rises to stab the dancer and then chases after his son, whom he slays with his sword. Unable to find the palace guards, he goes through the palace, only to find Sumurun in the arms of Nur Al-Din. The old sheik attacks the two lovers, but they are saved when the hunchback runs up from behind and stabs the sheik, thus avenging the murder of his beloved dancer.

Germans, Jews, and "Orientalism"

Lubitsch was born in Berlin, but his father had come from Russia to Berlin, where he achieved success in the retail garment trade. Lotte H. Eisner, herself an assimilated German Jew, arguably betrays in her negative verdicts on many of the films of Ernst Lubitsch a certain "Mandarin" disdain for the latter that seems to be related to his roots among the *Ostjuden*, the Jews of Eastern Europe — "Lubitsch was too Jewish for her" (Grafe, 82). Eisner writes of the "rather cynical humour" of the "Jewish lower-middle class" engaged in the garment trade in Berlin and claims to note even in Lubitsch's sophisticated American comedies a trace of "the vainglory of the *nouveau-riche*" (79).[4] In her discussion of Lubitsch's historical cos-tume films, Eisner states, "For Lubitsch, one-time shop assistant, History was never to be more than a pretext for telling love stories in sumptuous period costumes . . ." (82).

In any case, when discussing the film *Sumurun*, a reference to the gar-ment trade makes perfect sense, given the importance of the garment merchant and the fabrics he sells for both the narrative and spectacle in this "oriental" film. But the most direct connection to Lubitsch's biography is of course not to his work in his father's shop but rather to his work with Max Reinhardt's ensemble and specifically his appearances in Max Reinhardt's theatrical productions of *Sumurun*. And of course the film adaptation that Lubitsch directed was also one in which he himself again took a role as an actor after not having acted in any of his films for about two years. It is the last film in which Lubitsch would ever appear as an actor.

Siegfried Kracauer, too, sees an autobiographical and (an unwittingly) self-reflexive aspect to Lubitsch's performance in the role of the hunchback juggler in *Sumurun*: "Through his identification with a juggler who drowns horror in jokes, Lubitsch involuntarily deepens the impression that the vogue he helped create originated in a blend of cynicism and melodramatic sentimentality" (52). The "vogue" Kracauer accuses Lubitsch of helping to create consisted of the historical costume films at the beginning of the Weimar Republic. *Sumurun*, however, is really something of a hybrid between such historical pageants and the expensive, exotic adventure films of the early Weimar Republic, such as Fritz Lang's *Die Spinnen* (The Spiders, 1919) and Joe May's *Das indische Grabmal* (The Indian Tomb, 1921). *Sumurun* is not really an action/adventure epic like those films, but it is an exotic "oriental" fantasy.

We cannot look at an "oriental" fantasy set in the Middle East without taking Edward Said's famous study *Orientalism* into account, even if, as Fritz Göttler has written, *Sumurun* is "more Jewish-Germanic than Arabian nights" (140). What did it mean for German (and Austrian) Jews such as Max Reinhardt or Ernst Lubitsch — or poet Else Lasker-Schüler, for that matter — to indulge in "Orientalism"? It isn't quite the same thing as it would be for non-Jewish Germans, I would submit. In fact, in the late Wilhelminian era or the early Weimar Republic, "Orientalism" would most aptly refer not to negative depictions of the Middle East or Islam but rather to those of Eastern European Jewry. We should also remember that in 1920, the same year that Paul Wegener appeared as an oriental despot in *Sumurun*, he also played an Eastern European, Jewish "monster," in the title role of *Der Golem* (The Golem), the famous film he directed (Isenberg).

If it seems inappropriate to equate anti-Semitism in Germany with Orientalism, allow me to cite Said himself: ". . . I have found myself writing the history of a strange, secret sharer of Western anti-Semitism. That anti-Semitism and, as I have discussed it in its Islamic branch, Orientalism resemble each other very closely is a historical, cultural, and political truth . . ." (27–28). Orientalism, of course, as Said has taught us, is always a European projection onto the Middle Eastern "Other"; it produces discourses that always reveal much more about Europe than anything else. I would argue therefore that the politics of Lubitsch's *Sumurun* — clearly a fantasy, a fairy tale — are to be found in what the film tells us about

Europe and more specifically, Weimar Germany, a new republic that had so recently been an authoritarian monarchy.

Indeed, it is an "orientalist" prejudice against *Ostjuden* that we find in Eisner's (and, latently, in Kracauer's) attitude toward Lubitsch — ultimately a form of "self-hatred" or internalized anti-Semitism on the part of more assimilated, "Western" or "German" Jews who found the presence of less assimilated "Eastern" Jews so embarrassing. Lubitsch himself has been accused of a similar "self-hatred" because of his "Jewish comedies," the farcical films of the 1910s that seem to exploit anti-Semitic stereotypes — but, as Valerie Weinstein argues, these films should rather be interpreted as examples of an appropriation of those stereotypes that is different from "self-hatred" and is instead comparable to the kind of "camp" appropriation associated with another oppressed minority — gay men. Such an appropriation exaggerates a stereotype in such a way that implies critique. This linkage between Jewish and gay strategies for dealing with oppressive stereotypes points to a potential alliance among many groups considered less than fully human by the gender and racial politics of the dominant European culture in the early twentieth century, including gay men, "feminized" Jewish men, "sexually aggressive" Jewish women, and ultimately all women. And these groups have a lot in common with the marginalized groups who can be seen as ultimately triumphant over a despotic patriarchy in *Sumurun*: the vagabond artists, the enslaved women of the harem, the eunuchs, and the black slaves.

Joel Rosenberg counts the hunchback juggler Lubitsch plays in *Sumurun* among what he calls "implicit Jews" (212). Visually, the association is suggested by how Lubitsch jokingly foregrounds the anti-Semitic stereotype of his prominent — "Jewish" — nose in the film: in a slapstick scene in which the old woman finally revives the comatose hunchback she inserts a straw in his nose, making him sneeze (fig. 4.1). On the thematic level, S. S. Prawer notes that Lubitsch's character in *Sumurun* is closely related to the brash, arrogant young male characters he had played in his early Jewish comedies: the tragic hunchback is just the other side of the coin. In the ugly old entertainer who desperately tries and continually fails to win the heart of the woman he loves, we see exposed all the insecurities that lie beneath the overcompensating self-assertion of all the "Pinkuses, Lachmanns, and Meyers" of the farces. While the latter characters are often compared to Lubitsch's own past as an ambitious young man who had worked in his father's retail shop, Prawer points out that none of them shared Lubitsch's own "striving away from the rag trade" to art (52), whereas in *Sumurun*, Lubitsch's final screen role is as an entertainer. True, he plays an impoverished old hunchback clown who is rejected by the woman he loves, and then who, as a "corpse," is dragged about, placed in a sack, and carried about in a trunk, hidden again and again but always "returning," like the repressed. Finally, upon waking from the "dead" he finds his love in the arms of another man and then watches powerlessly as she is murdered.

Fig. 4.1. The hunchback (Ernst Lubitsch) being revived by a straw stuck up his nose. Screenshot.

And yet it is this marginalized character who slays the despot and frees everyone else. The "rag merchant" may get the girl (although not the dancer loved by the hunchback, but rather the sheik's favorite, Sumurun), but it is Lubitsch's hunchback clown who is the hero of the narrative. By stabbing the old sheik, who has already killed his son, the hunchback has eliminated the hierarchy, at least for the time being, and it would seem that although his personal motivation is anger and despair at the loss of the dancer whom he loved in vain, he nonetheless takes action on behalf of all those whom the hierarchy has oppressed — the garment merchant, the ragged troupe of entertainers, the eunuchs and the slaves, and especially the enslaved women of the harem.

Female Desire: Transgression and Rebellion

The *Illustrierter Film-Kurier* (Illustrated Film-Courier) that accompanied the film's premiere in September 1920 contained a synopsis of the film by scriptwriter Hanns Kräly that ends as follows: "The tyrant has fallen. The oppressed women can now breathe free again — the hunch-back opens the gates of the harem, leads them toward freedom. He himself, however, takes up his instrument and plays the strings. He must dance and gambol again — for the public wants to laugh." The end of the film clearly celebrates the liberation of the women from the harem. Here we may be reminded of Thomas Brandlmeier's characterization of Lubitsch's comic films before the end of the First World War: "The cin-ema of Lubitsch is corrosive, caustic, and pre-revolutionary" (112). Yet of course his big-budget films in the early republic definitely come "after" the German Revolution, and they are not as anarchistic as the earlier comedies — somewhat analogous, perhaps, to the manner in which the German Revolution of 1918 was not as radical as the Russian one of 1917.

But women do triumph at the end of *Sumurun*. In fact it is not the hunchback but rather a woman, Sumurun's servant, who, as the morning dawns, opens the gates and bids her mistress and Nur Al-Din farewell as they leave the palace, heading toward the camera — and toward freedom, it would seem. Above all it is Sumurun who benefits most from the events at the end of the film. One way to interpret this ending would be that a woman's "pure," monogamous love for a middle-class merchant triumphs over a decadent feudal autocracy — alluding to an old trope in bourgeois ideology that dates back to the "bourgeois tragedies" of the late eight-eenth century in Germany. Sumurun's "pure love" is contrasted with the dancer's promiscuity; at the film's end, then, the "bad girl" is punished, and the "good girl" is rewarded.

This reading, however, overlooks how often Sumurun has risked death over the course of the film by persisting in her stubborn love for the mer-chant and her cold rejection of the powerful, abusive old sheik. One never sees Sumurun react to the sheik with anything but coldness, anger, or fear. At one point she displays resigned submission — but not to the sheik, only to her impending death early on in the film as she is ready to kneel at the chopping block to be beheaded, just before being spared at the very last moment. Even after this close call she rebuffs the old sheik's advances, and indeed she will soon meet the merchant in his shop. The agency and power of Sumurun's desire is clearly portrayed — when she is alone with the merchant in his shop, it is she who extends her leg to have him put on the anklet he shows her. In doing so he is overcome with desire and bends down to kiss her ankle. Sumurun swoons, but nonetheless it is she who stands up, pulling *him* up to her so that she can kiss him, her head posi-tioned *above* his, her hands holding *his* face (fig. 4.2). *She* is the subject, and he the object, of desire.

Nonetheless, the most transgressive female character of the film is surely the dancer, and it is the hunchback's love for her that motivates the slaying of the sheik, which overturns the autocratic order at the end

Fig. 4.2. Sumurun (Jenny Hasselqvist) pulls Nur Al-Din (Harry Liedtke) up to her so that she can kiss him. Screenshot.

of the film. Pola Negri's dancer is a character very similar to most of the other roles she played in Lubitsch's films, but this role is especially comparable to her role as Jeanne, who becomes Madame Dubarry in the film of the same name. In both films she plays a character who exploits her sexual attractiveness to "sleep her way to the top" of the social hierarchy — in *Madame Dubarry* (*Passion*) becoming the mistress of Louis XV, and in *Sumurun* making her way to the bedchamber of the all-powerful sheik. Negri's dancer, it seems to me, belongs among what Sabine Hake has termed the "wayward women" of German early silent cinema, personified primarily by actress Ossi Oswalda in Lubitsch's early comedies. If Oswalda functioned as "Lubitsch's female alter-ego" in the comedies from 1917 on (Brandlmeier, 111), I would submit that Pola Negri plays a similar role in the costume films in which she stars. After all, Lubitsch, who as the son of a prosperous Eastern European Jew was considered "nouveau-riche" by the likes of Eisner, certainly had an understanding of the transgressive nature of "upward mobility" in imperial Germany. And the male characters in his early Jewish comedies were not only quite aggressive in their pursuit of women but also quite willing to use a sexual

Fig. 4.3. Sumurun's servant (Aud Egede Nissen) distracts the head eunuch (Jakob Tiedtke, on the right) and the other eunuchs so that she can smuggle Nur Al-Din into the palace. Screenshot.

liaison to ensure economic and social success (usually by marrying the boss's daughter).

The importance of female desire in the film is clear: Sumurun's single-minded desire for Nur Al-Din drives the plot, as does the even more transgressive desire of the dancer for a number of men, for clothes, and for power — although we should not forget that the dancer, too, desires Nur Al-Din, and she is quite devastated and disoriented by his rejection of her; he is the only man who rebuffs her advances. Again, Nur Al-Din is the narrative's "object of desire," and the acquisition of that "object" is accomplished not just by the intensity of Sumurun's desire for him but also by the clever agency of another woman, Sumurun's servant. It is she who through her manipulation of the palace eunuchs manages to create time for Sumurun and Nur Al-Din to meet alone in his shop, then to smuggle him into the palace, and finally to allow them to be alone together in a chamber of the harem (fig. 4.3). Meanwhile, the eunuchs sleep in a drunken stupor, having been induced to drink by the women of the harem, with Sumurun's servant in charge.

Eunuchs, Slaves, and Vagabond Entertainers

The dancer and all the women of the harem are slaves, and the palace eunuchs are their guards, but this does not make them appear powerful — any power they hold in the palace of the sheik is the result of literal castration, and much of the film's comedy is at their expense. They are but one group among many others of oppressed and/or marginalized figures in the film, for whom the slaying of the despot at the end of the film would also be a liberation. Like the eunuchs, these other marginalized figures are, for the most part, comic characters: the two look-alike (twin?) slaves of Nur Al-Din, Mutti and Putti; the black slaves, male and female; and of course the "professional" comedians, the motley troupe of entertainers, above all the hunchback clown, but also the old woman who dances with the snakes and who drinks so much in celebration of the money earned through the sale of the dancer to the slave merchant.

Mutti and Putti are the two dark-haired slaves of Nur Al-Din who dress alike, cause mischief, and frolic about in ways that seem inappropriate for adult heterosexual males. Perhaps they are simply childish clowns, but they don't appear to be very young at all. The very names they are given in the credits may lead viewers today to suspect something a bit queer about them: Mutti and Putti don't seem to be Arabic names, and in German of course they mean "Mommy" and the plural form (from Italian) of "cherub" — again, not especially masculine designations. Their major plot function is to run off with the bag containing the hunchback's "corpse" from the entertainer's tent, where they have gone to steal things (during the performance we have already seen them function as pickpockets). Mischievous petty thieves who hide their shenanigans from their virtuous but lovesick (and rather melancholic and passive) master, they mainly provide a slapstick, comic relief, as in their exaggerated fright at finding a body in the sack and their panicked, bumbling effort to hide the body in their master's shop, or when they fight over a coin tossed to them later by the head eunuch. They might be twins, and their dark looks are such that they might be read as Jewish. During the dancer's performance in the tent we do get a reaction shot of them looking at her with desire — one of a few reaction shots of various men (including a black slave) that seem to imply that desire for the dancer unites men of all classes and races. Nonetheless there seems to be something sexually ambiguous about them.

There is no doubt that there is something sexually "different" about the eunuchs, of course. They are fat, bald, easily exhausted and easily fooled, and they are the butt of many jokes, starting with their first appearance, all wearing the same type of hat and costume, lined up in a row, sitting outside the palace gate under the windows of the harem, looking bored. Up above, the women of the harem have been learning to juggle

Fig. 4.4. The head eunuch in the center, his hat having been knocked off by one of the apples dropped by the women of the harem. Screenshot.

fruit, and then the head of the harem, Sumurun's servant, decides that they should all drop the apples onto the heads of the eunuchs below. One apple knocks the hat off the eunuch in the center. It is the head eunuch (Jakob Tiedtke); without a hat he is thus distinguished from the rest and in effect introduced to us (fig. 4.4). The eunuchs are comic figures but also endearing ones, especially the head eunuch, who seems to have a special bond with the harem women, especially with Sumurun and her servant. Compared with the violent and arbitrary despotism and the bullying masculinity of the old sheik and his son, the eunuchs are clearly more like the harem women they "guard."

Gender politics are clearly invoked when Sumurun's servant tries to persuade the head eunuch to save Sumurun from being beheaded. She wants him to appeal to the young sheik to confess to his father that it was he at the harem window. When he seems fearful about intervening, she appeals to his "masculine" pride, and this persuades him to act. It is perhaps a cruel joke to invoke the "masculinity" of a eunuch, yet in the context of this narrative it seems at the same time to be an example of an appeal for humane solidarity among the oppressed, for whom courage is especially dangerous. And in the end, of course, courage has nothing to do with the status of one's genitals.

Considering the function of the black slaves in the film, that is, the roles portrayed by actors who were of African heritage, we move into a realm in which Weimar Cinema was often guilty of egregiously racist stereotyping (American cinema was of course much worse). Lubitsch's comedy of the previous year, *Die Austernprinzessin* (The Oyster Princess, 1919) opens with the American capitalist, Mr. Quaker, the "oyster king," being pampered by a number of black servants, in a way that makes us uncomfortable today. There are not many jokes at the expense of the black slaves in *Sumurun*. Rather it is through laughter that their oppression by the old sheik and other authority figures — and their discontent with that oppression — is made clear. Early in the film, there is a scene very reminiscent of *Oyster Princess*: the sheik wakes in his bedchamber, and there are a number of male black slaves there to attend to him. Still sleepy and grumpy, he kicks one of the slaves who is trying to help him put on his shoes. The slave is knocked down and is hurt, and the sheik then laughs sadistically; the other slaves join in the laughter, but they stop as soon as the sheik glares at them — his sadism is not for their enjoyment. Any one of them could become his next victim.

Later in the film it is the slave merchant who represents the hierarchy; the dancer has just been brought to his house to be dressed and groomed to be taken to the palace and presented to the old sheik. Female black slaves have been massaging her and attending to her (again comparable to the scene in *Oyster Princess* in which the title character is being bathed, massaged, powdered, and dressed by a bevy of female servants — albeit women who are not black). The slave merchant is shown in close-up giving the dancer advice about how to comport herself with the mighty sheik; his mouth keeps chattering on and on, and in annoyance the dancer finally slaps him so that he will shut up. Immediately there is a cut to the black women laughing in glee at their master's come-uppance, and then there is a cut back to the dancer, who also laughs. There is a bond between these slaves and the dancer, who is herself a slave — and the character whose transgressions will overturn the hierarchy.

As for the entertainers, the dancer's importance is clear, and the role of the hunchback in eliminating the despot is of course crucial. The old woman is a comic character whose drunkenness is emphasized along with her greed — shown in her delight at the money earned by the sale of the dancer to the sheik. Nonetheless she also turns out to be sympathetic through her true devotion to and concern for the comatose hunchback: she insists on keeping track of his "corpse" and eventually she is able to revive him. As a group, this dishevelled group of entertainers is disruptive from their first entrance into the city, unleashing a "carnivalesque" disruption. News of their arrival causes the unruly masses to stream through the streets in a manner reminiscent of many other films of the era, but whereas in a film such as Paul Wegener's *The Golem*, the (Jewish) urban masses seem threatening, here their representation is much more sympathetic, especially in contrast to the portrayal of the autocratic order that oppresses them. Taking to the streets in their eagerness for a bit of entertainment that relieves the monotony of their lives, they create a public obstacle to the social hierarchy represented by the young sheik on horseback. The latter, wearing a spiked helmet oddly reminiscent of a *Pickelhaube* (a "pimpled helmet," the slang term for the distinctive Prussian helmet), orders his mounted guards to charge the mob and rid the city of the entertainers. He is then confronted by the dancer, who seductively persuades him to allow the entertainers to stay.

Send in the Clown

In a 1985 article feminist filmmaker and theorist Laura Mulvey reconsidered some of the positions she had taken in her famous essay "Visual Pleasure and Narrative Cinema" (1975).[5] In doing so, she explored the concept of the "carnival," especially as developed by Mikhail Bakhtin, whom she quotes: "As opposed to the official feast, one might say that carnival celebrated temporary liberation from the prevailing truth and from the established order; it marked the suspension of all hierarchical rank, privilege, norms, and prohibitions" (Bakhtin, 10; cf. Mulvey, "Changes," 174). Mulvey notes how carnival relates to the "tripartite narrative of ritual structure," that is, the idea that narrative opens with the status quo, and then the status quo is overturned — as in the carnival — in the middle or "liminal" phase of the narrative, only to have the status quo restored in the third phase, the closure of the narrative (174).

Sumurun's carnivalesque disruption of authority is initiated as the entertainers enter the city. Almost simultaneously, Sumurun's rebellious desires add to the disruption, which is advanced even more radically by the transgressive dancer. But this disruption is not overturned in the closure of the film, those two shots after the hunchback clown has stabbed the despotic old sheik. The first shot shows us that, as a new day dawns, Sumurun's servant opens the gates of the palace to free the lovers, who walk not toward the horizon but toward the camera, toward us, the viewers. The final shot is of the hunchback clown playing his stringed instrument again; he seems sad, for he is in fact mourning the dancer's death. He is not, *pace* Kracauer, "drowning horror in jokes" (52). Nor is this final shot a restoration of the despotic status quo; rather it is a return of the hunchback to his role as an entertainer. Despotism is vanquished, love triumphs, and art endures.

The perhaps naive belief in the power of art and entertainment embodied in this ending is arguably typical of the German avant-garde before the First World War, the milieu in which Friedrich Freska's "oriental" pantomime and Max Reinhardt's famous theatrical productions of it emerged. Like any "orientalist" fantasy, *Sumurun* tells us more about Europe than it does about any fantasized "Orient," and thus its utopian portrayal of a despotic, autocratic order overturned by a revolt of women, slaves, and entertainers most likely reveals revolutionary fantasies, albeit naive, about imperial Germany.

In post-revolutionary Germany, Lubitsch's fantasy, in which the favorite consort of the monarch ends up with a garment merchant, is not revolutionary in the Marxist sense, but it can be interpreted as a celebration of a new democratic order in which aristocratic — and Christian — origins were no longer supposed to be prerequisites for full participation in German society, now reincarnated as a republic in which citizens of all classes — and both genders — had an equal vote. The importance of female desire in Lubitsch's film might of course be seen as purely market-driven, but I would argue that it can also be understood as consistent with his affinity for the oppressed and the marginalized. This is evident in the groups with whom he seems to sympathize within *Sumurun* and from the transgressive upward mobility of Pola Negri's character. The fact that Lubitsch chose to make his final screen appearance in the role of the hunchback clown who avenges the death of the character played by Negri is also significant. The idea that a band of second-rate entertainers could foil despotic oppression is one that would emerge again many years later in his most political comedy: *To Be or Not to Be* (1942).

Notes

[1] As Thomas Elsaesser maintains in his discussion of Lubitsch's *Madame Dubarry* (1919), which has long been criticized as a "travesty" of the French Revolution, the political analysis of any "historical" film is by no means exhausted by the attempt to judge its historical accuracy (196–97). In any event, *Sumurun*, according to the filmography in Prinzler/Patalas (209), is set in Baghdad of the ninth century C.E., and its supposed basis in "oriental fairy-tale motifs" makes historical accuracy not very relevant.

[2] Weinberg (see also p. 83), citing Alfred Hitchcock (7), asserted that Lubitsch played the hunchback juggler in a Reinhardt production of *Sumurun* (see also Prawer, 52, and Hake, *Passions*, 25). However, this is not verified in Prinzler/Patalas or Spaich. Eyman writes that exactly if and when this occurred is open to dispute; Lubitsch certainly did not play the role in 1911, when Hitchcock saw the play (69).

[3] Eyman considers the film to have been unsuccessful (69–70), but Hake points out that it was included with *Deception* on the "Top Ten List" by the National Board of Review for the United States in 1921 (*Passions*, 58). Petrie reports that in June 1922 an article in the US journal *Photoplay* classified *Sumurun* (*One*

Arabian Night) as only "mediocrely successful" in financial terms (16). The film earned attention as much for Lubitsch's acting as for his direction of the film, with *Variety* and the *New York Times* enthusiastic about his acting, but the latter critical of his directing (20; Petrie himself considers Lubitsch to have "atrociously over-played" his role as the hunchback; 64).
⁴ In fairness to Eisner, she ascribes the cynical humor of the Jewish lower middle-class to "that sense of comic fatalism peculiar to people used to enduring pogroms and persecutions" (79).
⁵ Mulvey, Laura. "Changes."

Works Cited

Bakhtin, Mikhail. *Rabelais and His World*. 1965. Translated by Helene Iswolsky. Bloomington: Indiana UP, 1984.

Brandlmeier, Thomas. "Early German Film Comedy, 1895–1917." In *A Second Life: German Cinema's First Decades*, edited by Thomas Elsaesser and Michael Wedel, 103–13. Amsterdam: Amsterdam UP, 1996.

Eisner, Lotte H. *The Haunted Screen: Expressionism in the German Cinema and the Influence of Max Reinhardt*. 1952. Translated by Roger Greaves. Berkeley: U California P, 1969.

Elsaesser, Thomas. *Weimar Cinema and After: Germany's Historical Imaginary*. London: Routledge, 2000.

Eyman, Scott. *Ernst Lubitsch: Laughter in Paradise*. New York: Simon & Schuster, 1993.

Fischer, Robert. *Ernst Lubitsch in Berlin*. 110 min. Munich: Transit Film, 2006.

Freska, Friedrich. *Sumurun: Eine Pantomime in 9 Bildern*. 1910. 10th ed., Berlin: Erich Riess, 1911.

Göttler, Fritz. "Commentary on *Sumurun*." In Prinzler and Patalas, 139–40.

Grafe, Frieda. "Was Lubitsch berührt." In Prinzler and Patalas, 81–87.

Hake, Sabine. "The Oyster Princess and The Doll: Wayward Women of the Early Silent Cinema." In *Gender and German Cinema: Feminist Interventions*, edited by Sandra Frieden, Richard W. McCormick, Vibeke R. Petersen, and Laurie Melissa Vogelsang, 2:13–32. Providence, RI: Berg, 1993.

———. *Passions and Deceptions: The Early Films of Ernst Lubitsch*. Princeton, NJ: Princeton UP, 1992.

Illustrierter Film-Kurier. Program material for *Sumurun*. 1920: No. 24.

Isenberg, Noah. *Between Redemption and Doom: The Strains of German-Jewish Modernism*. Lincoln: U of Nebraska P, 1999.

Kracauer, Siegfried. *From "Caligari" to Hitler: A Psychological History of the German Film*. Princeton, NJ: Princeton UP, 1947.

Mulvey, Laura. "Changes: Thoughts on Myth, Narrative and Historical Experience." 1985. Reprinted in Mulvey, *Visual and Other Pleasures,* 159–76.

————. *Visual and Other Pleasures.* Bloomington: Indiana UP, 1989.

————. "Visual Pleasure and Narrative Cinema." 1975. Reprinted in Mulvey, *Visual and Other Pleasures,* 14–26.

Negri, Pola. *Memoirs of a Star.* Garden City, NY: Doubleday, 1970.

Olimsky, Fritz. "Kurt Richter." *Berliner Börsen-Zeitung,* 4 April 1920. Reprinted in program, "*Sumurun*: Stummfilmkonzerte zu Gast in babylon berlin:mitte," 18 April 2006.

Petrie, Graham. *Hollywood Destinies: European Directors in America, 1922–1931.* London: Routledge, 1985.

Prawer, S. S. *Between Two Worlds: The Jewish Presence in German and Austrian Film, 1910–1933.* New York: Berghahn Books, 2005.

Prinzler, Hans Helmut, and Enno Patalas, eds. *Lubitsch.* Munich: C. J. Bucher, 1984.

Rosenberg, Joel. "Shylock's Revenge: The Doubly Vanished Jew in Ernst Lubitsch's *To Be or Not to Be*." *Prooftexts* 16 (1996): 209–44.

Said, Edward W. *Orientalism.* 1978. Reprint, New York: Vintage Books, 1979.

Spaich, Herbert. *Ernst Lubitsch und seine Filme.* Munich: Wilhelm Heyne, 1992.

Weinberg, Herman G. *The Lubitsch Touch: A Critical Study.* Third revised, enlarged edition. New York: Dover Publications, 1977.

Weinstein, Valerie. "Anti-Semitism or Jewish 'Camp'? Ernst Lubitsch's *Schuhpalast Pinkus* (1916) and *Meyer aus Berlin* (1918)." *German Life and Letters* 59.1 (January 2006): 101–21.

5: Romeo with Sidelocks: Jewish-Gentile Romance in E. A. Dupont's *Das alte Gesetz* (1923) and Other Early Weimar Assimilation Films

Cynthia Walk

THE FIRST WORLD WAR and its aftermath saw an increase in the mass migration of Eastern Jews to the cities of Western Europe, triggering a rise in anti-Semitism. If earlier generations had fled persecution in Tsarist Russia and the border provinces of the Hapsburg Empire, these new migrants were now trying to escape the chaos engendered by the Russian Revolution and the collapse of the Austro-Hungarian Empire. Mostly Orthodox Jews with distinctive dress, beliefs, and customs, they became a visible foreign presence on the streets in the West. Traditional and unmodernized, they also represented "brothers and strangers" to assimilated urban Jews in places such as Berlin and Vienna, who received them with ambivalence.[1]

Released in 1923, *Das alte Gesetz* (Ancient Law), by director Ewald André Dupont, reenacts the migration of Jews from Eastern Europe to the capital of the Austrian Empire in the 1860s through the journey of Baruch Mayer, an Orthodox Jew and aspiring actor, from a shtetl in Galicia to the stage of Vienna's preeminent theater, the *Burgtheater*.[2] There his career is promoted by a benefactor at the imperial court, whose interest in the young actor is not just artistic but also romantic. Archduchess Elisabeth Theresia is smitten by his performance in Shakespeare's *Romeo and Juliet*, despite the signature Orthodox sidelocks that tumble out of his cap, creating a scandal in the court audience.

I propose to examine *Das alte Gesetz* along with three other feature films made in Germany and Austria between 1919 and 1924 — *Der Ritualmord* (Ritual Murder, directed by Joseph Delmont, 1919), *Der Golem, wie er in die Welt kam* (The Golem, How He Came into the World, directed by Paul Wegener, 1920), and *Die Stadt ohne Juden* (The City without Jews, directed by Hans Karl Breslauer, 1924) — where a potential romantic relationship between Jew and Gentile functions as a metaphor for the possibilities and limits of assimilation. Responding to waves of Jewish refugees fleeing Eastern Europe in the wake of the First World War, these films represent cinematic interventions in the ongoing German debate about *die Judenfrage* (the Jewish question) during a period of escalating anti-Semitism that fomented xenophobia about immigration and fear of miscegenation. In this environment sexual relations between Jews and Gentiles became charged with taboo (if only for a vocal minority as yet), and inter-ethnic intimacy potentially signified transgressive interracial romance.

My analysis focuses on how *Das alte Gesetz* engages and negotiates this minefield for the Weimar film audience along a spectrum of views on both sides. On the one hand are Gentile German (respectively, Austrian) anxieties over ethnic difference and Jewish otherness in light of the influx of refugees from Eastern Europe — anti-Semitism. On the other hand are Orthodox and Zionist Jewish anxieties over the loss of tradition and community in the modern, urban, secular culture of Western Europe, as well as concerns among acculturated Jews about the destabilizing impact of newcomers on their own status along with the integration of the new arrivals — assimilation. I argue that Dupont's film addresses these issues through a historical plot with a double-coded message that resolves them — filmically at least — for both Jewish and non-Jewish German audiences.[3] Focusing on the relationship between the central character, an immigrant from Galicia, and his patroness in Vienna, I will analyze the function of Jewish-Gentile romance in *Das alte Gesetz* and as a recursive motif in other Jewish-themed films of the early Weimar era. While Dupont's film is at the center of my argument, I situate it within a field of films by minority and mainstream German and Austrian directors concerned with the urgency of the Jewish question in postwar Europe.

In the chaotic climate following the collapse of both the German and the Austro-Hungarian empires, immigrant *Ostjuden*, as they were called, became a target of anti-Semitic rhetoric from politicians throughout Germany and Austria. While the Jewish communities in Berlin and Vienna increased overall between 1910 and 1925, Eastern Jews comprised little more than 1 percent of either city's overall population.[4] Despite their relatively modest presence, the immigration of Eastern Jews provoked the disproportionate and exaggerated perception that they were a serious civic problem, described as a drain on municipal resources and an invasion of foreigners whose different physiognomy, religion, and culture resisted acculturation. The reaction against *Ostjuden* quickly escalated from demagoguery to political agitation and government-sponsored legislation, such as a November 1919 Berlin edict authorizing the expulsion of any Eastern Jews who had committed a crime.

Against this background, *Der Ritualmord*, directed by Joseph Delmont (1919) was marketed as an "enlightenment film" (*Aufklärungsfilm*) to educate the public on the dangers of anti-Semitic propaganda, in this case to dispel the myth of blood libel, the sensationalized claim that Jews engage in human sacrifice. Though the film has been lost, its plot can be reconstructed from contemporary reviews.[5] Set in a rural village in Tsarist Russia, where Jews and Gentiles live together in a peasant culture, the film features a pogrom, showing violence done to innocent Jewish villagers over unfounded rumors that they practice ritual murder. A young Russian student, Sasha, steps in to rescue the head of the Jewish community from being stoned to death by the angry mob and falls for his daughter. Disaster is averted in a dramatic confrontation, where false accusations in a plot to discredit the Jews are exposed and the myth is debunked, making possible a return to peaceful coexistence between the villagers. While the extant reviews do not reveal much detail about Sasha's relationship with the daughter of the Jewish leader, social harmony is restored through the intervention of an exemplary Gentile, whose enlightened engagement across ethnic boundaries includes a rudimentary romance.

The following year the issues of anti-Semitism and assimilation were explored from a different perspective, again in part through the mixed-couple motif. Adapted from an old Hebrew legend, *Der Golem*, directed by Paul Wegener, is a mythical narrative set in sixteenth-century Prague about a giant warrior sculpted out of clay, who is called into being by the Rabbi of the Jewish ghetto to protect his people from the emperor's decree of banishment from the realm.[6] The inhabitants of the ghetto city, visually modeled after *Ostjuden*, are characterized as unruly and dangerous and a threat to the stability of the German Empire through recursive crowd scenes with dark figures swarming the streets. The subplot concerns a secret affair between the Rabbi's daughter Miriam and Florian, a Gentile messenger who delivers the edict from the imperial court. Miriam embodies the anti-Semitic stereotype of *die schöne Jüdin*, the beautiful but lethal seductress. Her alluring gaze — in a female version of the more common trope of the male Jew as sexual predator — entices Florian into an illicit relationship, which ends badly when a jealous rival in the Rabbi's house discovers them in her bedroom and rouses the Golem to violence, killing Florian and setting a fire that nearly destroys the ghetto city. *Der Golem* represents an assimilation narrative with boundaries defined by racial anti-Semitism, promoting the fear that miscegenation leads to catastrophe.[7] At the end, as Miriam sinks into the arms of the Rabbi's young assistant, the endogamous Jewish couple is reestablished, consistent with the main plot that promotes Jewish separatism with an anti-Semitic twist: Jews here remain an unwelcome presence in the German Empire. Although the emperor withdraws his decree to banish them, the final shot of the film emphasizes the segregation of the Jewish community within the host country behind the massive closed gates of the ghetto. The impossibility of the mixed couple in *Golem* presents a view that assimilation beyond separate social coexistence will not be tolerated by either side.

Moving the mixed couple scenario from the medieval East to the Enlightenment West of the mid-nineteenth century, E. A. Dupont's *Das alte Gesetz* subsequently resets the boundaries of assimilation. In this film, the director commemorates the journey of his grandparents' generation from the Eastern border to the capital of the Austrian Empire in the 1860s, another period known for the mass migration of Jews from the provinces to Vienna, drawn by the promise of economic and social advancement. The historical setting places the film in the context of the legal emancipation of Jews in the German-speaking countries, where they had achieved full civil status in 1862 (Baden), 1867 (Austria), and 1869 (in the North German Confederation). Although the North German regulations carried over in 1871 into the constitution of the Second Reich, it took until 1874 for a civil law to take effect permitting mixed marriage.[8] Set in the context of the gradual emancipation of Jews into German-speaking society, the potential romance between Baruch and his patroness illustrates the shifting boundaries of assimilation advocated by various segments of the Gentile and Jewish communities prior to and during the Weimar Republic.

For the Gentile audience of the 1920s with a protective view of class privilege and social hierarchy, casual affairs might be tolerated, but the archduchess's repeated advances toward Baruch provoke concerns about more serious romantic involvement between aristocrats and commoners. In Baruch's four private audiences with her, the archduchess asks him each time to make a wish, hoping that her desire for him will be reciprocated. Following his successful premiere in the title role of Hamlet — one of many professional opportunities she has facilitated — Elisabeth invites Baruch to meet her outside in the palace garden (fig. 5.1).

Though the scene is clearly framed as a romantic tryst through the garden-in-the-moonlight setting, the couple remains separated by the shadow of an enormous tree falling between them, a broad dark line down the center of the image here that forms a barrier they do not cross. Exiting to the side, Baruch will not see the fan she drops for him, a missed cue whose significance does not escape her court minder. For the Gentile audience it is particularly significant that all the initiative for a romantic relationship comes from the archduchess. Baruch's body language consistently emphasizes his restrained and deferential posture in a way that counters fears of Jewish subversiveness as well as anti-Semitic sexual clichés of the Jewish male aggressor circulating in right-wing popular culture.[9] When the romance succumbs to what is quaintly called "court etiquette," the threat of an inter-ethnic liaison — representing a misalliance to social conservatives and transgressive miscegenation to racial anti-Semites — is averted.

For Gentile and Jewish spectators alike, the farewell scene signifies mutual acceptance of institutional prohibitions in the pre-emancipation era against disruptive social and sexual boundary crossing. Under pressure at the Hapsburg court to break off the inappropriate relationship, the arch-

*Fig. 5.1. The rendezvous between the Archduchess (Henny Porten) and Baruch
(Ernst Deutsch). Screenshot.*

duchess explains that this must be their last meeting and reaches out ten-
derly toward Baruch, as if to embrace him (fig. 5.2).

But Baruch demurs. Pulling her hands down and folding them
together, he steps back. This farewell scene pantomime in effect overturns
the anti-Semitic scenario of Jewish-Gentile rape; the sequence of gestures
shows that she seeks and indeed offers intimacy, which he discreetly
declines. In the background of the shot here, a strategically placed pure
white statue parallels the figure of the archduchess. The impact of actress
Henny Porten's screen persona in this role cannot be overestimated. One
of Germany's first national film stars, she was celebrated in the industry
press as an embodiment of the ideal German woman (see the essay by
Joseph Garncarz in this volume).[10] Her iconic status and putative
Germanness helped to validate the philosemitic tendency of this film for
contemporaries.

Like their Gentile counterparts, but for different reasons, Jewish spectators in the Weimar film audience also may be anxious about whether
Baruch will succumb to the entreaties of the archduchess. Interfaith
romance represents a threat to Jewish identity among Orthodox and

Fig. 5.2. The Archduchess bids Baruch farewell. Screenshot.

Zionist Jews, if it leads to out-marriage. To them the film offers a sympathetic portrait of the shtetl as the home of authentic *Urjuden,* a corrective to the prevailing negative view of East European Jewry.[11] While Baruch has left the shtetl, he has internalized the rule of endogamy, that "ancient law" of Jewish tradition. Expressing gratitude to Archduchess Elisabeth for enabling him to penetrate the hierarchy of the court theater, he nonetheless refuses her advances and remains faithful instead to Esther, his childhood sweetheart from Galicia, who eventually joins him in Vienna, where they are married. The kiss withheld from the archduchess in the farewell scene in due course is bestowed on Esther, consummating the engagement of the endogamous Jewish couple in a full embrace, framed within an oval mask as a tableau shot (fig. 5.3).

Beyond the limits of social assimilation demarcated by the prohibition and disruption of the mixed couple, *Das alte Gesetz* offers a model for the successful cultural integration of immigrant *Ostjuden,* here through the performing arts as a promising venue for talented and ambitious young artists. Ernst Deutsch as Baruch recuperates his own biography in the central role of the professional actor, who can be seen as a representative figure for many assimilated Jews in Weimar theater and film.[12] Significantly, the

Fig. 5.3. Baruch's betrothal with his childhood sweetheart Esther (Margarete Schlegel). Screenshot.

embedded stage productions in the film all involve non-Jewish characters in the classical repertory of high-culture Western theater (Romeo, Hamlet, Don Carlos).[13] In this respect Baruch's career reproduces the path of pre-emancipation Jews in Germany and Austria who embraced *Bildung*, the ideal of learning, as a vehicle of social mobility and condition of entry to the bourgeoisie, if not the highest social circles. Yet in *Das alte Gesetz* cultural assimilation has its limits too. In a scene that challenges the Orthodox migrant from Galicia to redefine his identity in Europe, Baruch Mayer stands in front of a mirror to prepare for his audition at the *Burgtheater* (fig. 5.4).[14] While he contemplates changes in dress and appearance, retaining his distinctively Jewish name will be a key signifier of the broader but still limited assimilationist agenda in this film.[15] Baruch Mayer: the fictional moniker combines a biblical reference to the Old Testament with a popular surname among Jews in South Germany.

The central character in *Das alte Gesetz* never alters his given or family name,[16] but he does cut off his sidelocks. Large tailor shears in the mirror scene shot reproduced here warn of self-mutilation in the impending gesture. However the film forges a compromise that avoids

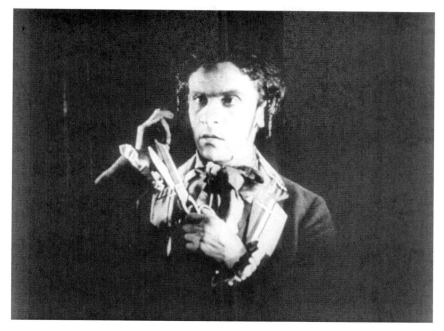

Fig. 5.4. Standing in front of a mirror, Baruch cuts off his sidelocks. Screenshot.

or at least moderates the ominous implications of this act, tantamount to castration and later practiced by Nazi soldiers upon their victims in occupied territories as a sadistic form of *Entjudung* (de-Judaization). Though Baruch removes these conspicuous markers of Jewish orthodoxy, he remains observant in private. Later in the film he will commemorate Yom Kippur on the opening night of *Hamlet*, reading the ritual prayers in his backstage dressing room before going onstage for the performance with the prayer book under his costume.[17] Thus Baruch symbolically reconciles religious observance with the demands of his secular career. *Das alte Gesetz* stops short of full integration in its qualified view of assimilation, promoting acculturation within limits that preserve Jewish distinctiveness and loyalty to ethnic heritage, while avoiding apostasy and betrayal.

Contemporary reviews of the premiere at the Marmorhaus theater in Berlin on 29 October 1923 indicate that *Das alte Gesetz* was well received. One reviewer acknowledged its finesse with tricky subject matter ("die Heikligkeit des Themas"). Another conceded that while the scenario ventured into dangerous territory, it managed to navigate successfully the competing interests of different factions in the audience.[18] However, events outside the theater soon showed that Dupont's film had overplayed the possibilities of assimilation.

Some ten days later, on 9 November 1923, the headline of the Zionist newspaper, *Jüdische Rundschau,* somberly proclaimed what it called "the fateful hour of German Jewry" ("Die Schicksalsstunde des deutschen Judentums").[19] The lead article reported anti-Semitic agitation and mob violence on a scale unknown in modern Germany up to that time, noting that as many as ten thousand people had swarmed the streets of Berlin over several days, plundering and looting Jewish businesses, and beating and robbing anyone who looked like a Jew. The background of the Berlin pogrom was the government's sudden and unexplained decision to rescind the distribution of relief money at the height of postwar hyperinflation, with increasing unemployment and rising prices (on 5 November 1923 a loaf of bread cost 78 billion marks).[20] Right-wing agitators seized the opportunity to spread the rumor that speculators had taken advantage of the situation. According to the reports, the specific target of the pogrom were the "Galicians" — here a generic code word for all Jewish migrants from Eastern Europe living in Berlin — portrayed as spongers profiting from the hardships of Weimar Germany's inflation economy. The nationalist press defended the riots as justified retaliation.[21] By contrast, in its 9 November editorial the *Jüdische Rundschau* used this occasion to challenge the inherited politics of assimilation — implicitly even the qualified version advocated in *Das alte Gesetz* — as an outdated and bankrupt strategy for Germany's Jews:

> Anti-Semitism has spread like a plague throughout Germany. After having recently become official government policy in Bavaria, it has now also claimed victims in Berlin. Do the Jews comprehend what is happening today? The fruits of Jewish emancipation are in disarray. The politics of assimilation has shipwrecked. Today German Jewry confronts the fact that its politics of the last century is completely bankrupt.[22]

For some (not only Zionist critics who were ideologically opposed to assimilation) the Berlin pogrom along with incidents elsewhere throughout Germany and Austria demonstrated the failure of assimilation, reigniting the issue of whether Jews belonged in these countries at all. To the extent that Eastern Jews became conflated with the general Jewish question, the animus against *Ostjuden* concealed hostility toward Jews at large.

The political initiative to expel the Jews as unwanted inhabitants is taken up after *Der Golem,* once again together with a mixed couple motif, in the 1924 *Die Stadt ohne Juden.*[23] This topical *Zeitfilm,* made in Austria, addresses the Jewish question, along with inflation and unemployment, as a critical issue of the day, by imagining what might happen if an anti-

Semitic slogan in contemporary Viennese politics were implemented. "Out with the Jews!" ("Hinaus mit den Juden!"): what would the consequences be, if the Jews were in fact expelled, not just some and not just those seg-regated in ghettos or internment camps, but all of them actually deported? Though Hans Karl Breslauer's adaptation of the best-selling satirical novel by Hugo Bettauer fictionalizes the setting with the ironic name Utopia, the film was partly shot on location in Vienna, and that city's politicians also serve as a model for the composite figure of the chancellor.[24] His par-liamentary speech exposes the expedient logic of racial anti-Semitism ("Something must be done — therefore I propose the expulsion of the Jews") along with its arbitrary categorization (". . . and that also includes baptized Jews . . . as well as children of mixed marriages . . . however, second-generation baptized children will be pronounced Aryans").[25]

Die Stadt ohne Juden distinguishes between Eastern Jews, who live in segregated communities, and acculturated Western Jews, who pass as part-ners in as many as five mixed-couple relationships. Among them, it is the triumphant romance between a Jewish man and a Gentile woman that drives the plot and eventually leads to a repeal of the parliamentary law: Leo Strakosch intervenes to claim his prospective bride and ends up saving the entire Jewish community. While the successful intermarriage scenario seems to celebrate a view of Jewish identity that privileges full assimilation, the construction of Eastern Jewish separatism resonates with problematic patterns.[26] The film's portrayal of how the hero manages to reverse the expulsion law may also suggest anti-Semitic clichés about scheming Jews and so compromises a positive view of their assimilation. Leo returns from exile abroad in disguise, masquerading as a Catholic. Acting surrepti-tiously, he first distributes pamphlets on behalf of the Jews in the name of a bogus *Bund wahrhaftiger Christen* (League of True Christians). Later, when the measure to repeal the expulsion law threatens to be short by one vote in parliament, Leo contrives to make an especially recalcitrant anti-Semitic legislator, Councillor Bernart, so drunk that he will miss the vot-ing session. Then, after paying a cab driver to drive Bernart "to Zion, for all I care," he winks at the camera and smirks with satisfaction over the success of his clever ruse. On the one hand, this masquerade turns the main character into a *Doppelgänger* with a comic spin on one of the central motifs of Weimar Cinema. On the other hand, it promotes troubling notions of Jewish duplicity and subversion. The putative threat posed by an assimilated Jew who can blend in and pass without detection is also reinforced by the casting of a Gentile actor (Johannes Riemann) as the protagonist.

Throughout 1924 the Jewish newspaper in Vienna, the *Wiener Morgenzeitung*, followed the production of *Die Stadt ohne Juden* with eager anticipation, yet never published a review after its release. The film's many unsettling ambiguities suggest the uncertain prospects of any resolution. While Leo rescues the Jewish community so he can consummate his marriage with Lotte, his Gentile fiancée, the expulsion decree is over-turned by single vote — and then only because of a trick to sabotage the opposition — illustrating just how precarious and elusive even social assimilation had become.

The early Weimar assimilation films between 1919 and 1924 emerged in response to a backlash of racial anti-Semitism against immigrant *Ostjuden* during the postwar era, addressing the vexed topic of assimilation through a mixed-couple scenario. While the dynamic of the mixed couple here cuts across gender and ethnicity in a variety of ways,[27] in each case Jewish-Gentile romance initiates a discourse on the boundaries of assimila-tion, with different answers to that question. *Das alte Gesetz* seeks to defuse mutual anxieties around ethnic difference for Jewish minority and dominant Gentile elites in postwar Weimar Germany, by offering a con-ciliatory Enlightenment model, set in mid-nineteenth-century Vienna, that allows both groups to maintain their integrity. Social and cultural integration is affirmed, provided there is no compromise to dominant class hierarchy or minority ethnic identity. Here the boundaries of assimilation are symbiotic collaboration short of intermarriage.[28] While the mixed-couple plot achieves stability on mutual terms in *Das alte Gesetz*, the other films reveal the enduring power of Gentiles, as the dominant majority in European societies, to dispose and set the limits. In *Ritualmord*, bare sur-vival of the rural Jewish villagers in Russia in a brutal pogrom depends on the intervention of an educated and romantically engaged Gentile leader. Its vision of tenuous coexistence is amplified in *Der Golem*, where the fail-ure of the mixed couple affirms a policy of ghettoization within the medi-eval German Empire. By contrast, *Die Stadt ohne Juden* offers an empowering triumph on behalf of the modern urban Jewish community in a Western utopia that is nonetheless illusory. Leo and Lotte may wed, but the flip-flop parliamentary vote empties mixed marriage of any real power to secure the collective status of the Jews, who are more or less only toler-ated within the civil order for their usefulness to the economic self-interest of the Gentile majority.

The plight of the *Ostjuden* is dramatized repeatedly in different his-torical settings, challenging discrimination against them. A pogrom is halted and expulsion decrees are rescinded, while racist clichés are exposed and in some cases effectively overturned. There is even one attempt to de-exoticize the foreignness of the shtetl milieu. Yet in all these assimilation films — with the exception of *Das alte Gesetz* — underlying anxieties around the Jewish question ultimately remain unresolved and the specter of government-sponsored anti-Semitic violence looms. Its director, E. A. Dupont, himself retreated to a more pessimistic view of the prospects in a later film near the end of the Weimar era, where the mixed-romance for-mula leads to tragedy and the possibility of any form of assimilation bridging the gulf of ethnic difference seems remote. *Zwei Welten* (Two Worlds, 1930) — the title says it all.[29]

Notes

[1] See Aschheim, ch. 3; Wertheimer, ch. 2; and Volkov, ch. 13.

[2] *Das alte Gesetz*, directed by Ewald André Dupont, premiered on 29 October 1923 at the Marmorhaus theater in Berlin. A restored 35mm print is available at the Deutsche Kinemathek in Berlin. I am grateful to Martin Koerber and the staff in the film archive for their assistance with the frame enlargements in this essay. The images are based on digital photographs of the film print prepared by Marian Stefanowski. Full credit information for all German films under discussion here is available on the internet at www.filmportal.de. On Dupont's career in Germany, Britain, and America, see Bretschneider.

[3] The concept of double coding here builds on an approach recently proposed by Henry Bial that theorizes the varied appeal of Jewish minority cinema in terms of imaginary subject positions that coalesce around minority and mainstream, Jewish and non-Jewish spectators (Bial, 16–19). While Bial's focus is contemporary American culture, in which Jewishness is no longer the contentious issue it once was, in the difficult climate of postwar Weimar Germany the idea of a spectrum on each side is useful to accommodate multiple views that may not only supplement but also contradict one another.

[4] The number of refugees fluctuated sharply during the war and decreased somewhat with repatriation afterwards. In 1925 Berlin there were approximately 44,000 *Ostjuden* among 173,000 Jews in a city population of 4 million inhabitants (Maurer, 78). After 1918 in Vienna there were approximately 30,000 *Ostjuden* in a city population of some 2.5 million inhabitants (Hoffmann-Holter).

[5] *Der Ritualmord*, directed by Joseph Delmont, had an initial viewing for the press in 1919 and was publicly released 1921. For reviews of the 1921 premiere, see Stratenwerth and Simon, 234–37.

[6] *Der Golem, wie er in die Welt kam*, directed by Paul Wegener, for Universum Film A.G. (Ufa), was released in 1920. The restored version is available on DVD (Kino International, 2002).

[7] Prawer (39–41) tries to rescue *Der Golem* from what he regards as "anti-Semitic innuendoes" in this reading of the film, which he suggests is anachronistic. However Isenberg (77–104) has effectively contextualized the iconography of *Golem* and its repertoire of Jewish figures among many debates and writings on the Jewish question in the years surrounding the film's production, including the German edition of the *Protocols of the Elders of Zion*, which appeared the same year, 1920. More recently see Bartov (1–6).

[8] On the political and social history of Christian-Jewish mixed marriage in Germany, see Meiring.

Fig. 5.5. Anti-Semitic cartoon from Deutschvölkische Monatshefte *(May 1923).*

⁹ The image of the male Jew as sexual predator had become a cliché of *völkisch* literature, for example in the popular novel of Artur Dinter, *Die Sünde wider das Blut* (The Sin against Blood, 1917), and in salacious caricatures circulated by journals such as the nationalist periodical *Deutschvölkische Monatshefte*. Its May 1923 issue features a rape fantasy in which a sprawling female nude is despoiled by a male aggressor with Jewish features depicted as a monstrous bloodsucker (fig. 5.5). Note the helmet and shield with the imperial eagle on the ground. These emblems define the figure as Germania, now a disarmed warrior, in an allegorical representation of national vulnerability to a Jewish takeover (von Braun, 192–93).
¹⁰ "Henny Porten is not only a great artist, she is the prototype of a *German* artist" ("Henny Porten ist nicht nur eine grosse Künstlerin, sie ist der Typus einer d e u t s c h e n Künstlerin"; Holberg, 5). See also Knut Hickethier on the "national physiognomy" of Porten's star image (Belach, 160–61). Note: all translations in this essay are my own.

[11] Avrom Morewski, a leading actor with the Vilna Jewish Theater from Warsaw, played Rabbi Mayer in *Das alte Gesetz* and also served as an ethnographic consultant for the scenes in the ghetto milieu. Reviewers often comment on the careful attention to Jewish ritual in the synagogue and home. In this respect Dupont's film parallels a trend among Weimar-era German-Jewish writers to recover and affirm their ethnic heritage in the East in what Michael Brenner calls a search for authenticity. Compare *Das ostjüdische Antlitz* (The Face of East European Jewry, 1920) by Arnold Zweig; Brenner, 142–46.

[12] One historical model for Baruch seems to have been the nineteenth-century virtuoso actor, Bogumil Dawison (1818–72), a Polish Jew who migrated from Lemberg (Galicia), joined the *Burgtheater* ensemble in 1849 under the director Heinrich Laube, and became widely known for his performance of Hamlet, among other roles in the classical repertory. Laube's memoirs (ch. 18, 184–87) actually offer a profile of Dawison that is quite critical and biased, suggesting obstacles confronting Jewish actors before emancipation in 1871 that were glossed over in the idealized fictional career of Baruch Mayer (see discussion in Prawer, 22–26). About Ernst Deutsch, Kurt Pinthus reported: "Twelve years ago [1911] I introduced Ernst Deutsch, then a young actor right out of acting school, to [Max] Martersteig, director of the Leipzig theater, for whom he auditioned — alternately halting and passionate — with Romeo. In this film the same Deutsch plays the same Romeo, now as a young renegade from the ghetto, for *Burgtheater* director Laube." ("Vor zwölf Jahren [1911], führte ich dem damaligen Leipziger Intendanten Martersteig den eben von der Theaterschule kommenden jungen Schauspieler Ernst Deutsch aus Prag zu, der ihm halb zaghaft, halb ungezügelt den Romeo hinlegte. In diesem Film spricht diesen selben Romeo dieser selbe Deutsch als entlaufenes Ghettojüngelchen dem Burgtheaterdirektor Laube vor.") A number of Jewish actors with successful careers in Weimar theater and film subsequently wrote autobiographies that address their own experience of assimilation. See especially Kortner; Granach.

[13] By contrast *The Jazz Singer* (1927), a Hollywood film of the same period with a comparable theme (assimilation in a scenario with a mixed-couple relationship), focuses on popular rather than high culture as the main venue of acculturation for Jewish entertainers in twentieth-century America.

[14] The *Zensurkarte*, the official censorship report for *Das alte Gesetz* issued by the *Film-Prüfstelle* Berlin before the premiere (B.07801, 18 October 1923), was not rediscovered until after the restored version was completed in 1985. It shows that the mirror scene in the original version of the film came *after* the audition rather than before. The different placement of this scene affects the argument about assimilation in a subtle but powerful way. It is framed as Baruch's response to a fait accompli, rather than the projection of an unfulfilled wish. As a character, Baruch appears more self-assured and secure in his Jewish identity. Cutting off his sidelocks is not an impulsive move in advance of the audition in a rush to please, but a deliberate and even reluctant accommodation to the circumstances of his new position.

[15] Compare the audition of yet another famous migrant actor from Galicia, who was coached to change his given name, because "it sounds too Jewish for the

Deutsches Theater." So Jessaja Gronach became Alexander Granach (1890–1945). See Granach, 225. The pressure to conceal or erase the conspicuous markers of Jewish difference was particularly strong in visible public careers, in this case for an actor at Berlin's leading nationally identified German theater. Granach's experience in 1912 provides historical context for a concession that Baruch Mayer was not willing to make.

16 Weinstein's comparative analysis of two major assimilation films, *Das alte Gesetz* and *Jud Süss*, provides valuable insight into the genre (the theme of dissolving boundaries and the use of dissolves as an editing technique to render it visually) as well as the continuities between Weimar and Nazi cinema. However the argument posits a structural model (Jewish penetration into Gentile society across permeable boundaries) that assumes the process of assimilation goes in one direction only and is always linear. That misses the two-way dynamics of *Das alte Gesetz* in several important ways. On the one hand, as I have shown, the initiative in romance here comes entirely from the Gentile partner, and the boundaries that emerge are mutual. On the other hand, Baruch's trajectory negotiates competing impulses (often rendered through parallel montage) in what might be described as a tension between assimilation and dissimilation. In the mirror scene he crosses one boundary but pulls back from another. By not changing his name (Weinstein misreads the intertitle here; 504), Baruch retains the primary signifier of his ethnic identity and strongly affirms his Jewishness.

17 In her presentation on "Affect in History: Weimar, Jews, and Spectatorship" at the German Studies Association conference in 2006, Darcy Buerkle identified the affective appeal of *Das alte Gesetz* for assimilated Jews in the Weimar film audience in "the anticipatory anxiety of being rendered visible." Baruch's acting career, premised on visibility, exemplifies their main problem. To fashion an acceptable self-presentation and pass as a Jew in secular society, he relinquishes the sidelocks that expose him to mockery in his first performance as Romeo, but carries the hidden *sidur* (prayer book) on his body for Hamlet.

18 del, "Das alte Gesetz" (available online at www.filmportal.de); and Aschau.

19 November 9 is known as a day on which a number of pivotal events in twentieth-century German history took place: in 1918 the proclamation of the Weimar Republic; 1923 Hitler's Beer Hall Putsch; 1938 the *Kristallnacht* (Night of Broken Glass) pogrom; and 1989 the fall of the Berlin Wall. Adding to the list, the newspaper report of Germany's first twentieth-century pogrom on this day in 1923 actually refers to events that took place on 5–8 November.

20 For the impact of inflation on the rise of anti-Semitism, see Widdig. The documentation includes a table that tracks retail prices for bread in Berlin throughout 1923 (46).

21 Deploying the rhetoric of racial anti-Semitism, the *völkisch* nationalist newspaper, *Deutsche Zeitung*, called the *Scheunenviertel* riots self-defense against parasites on the body of the German *Volk*: "The Jew-baiting [was] . . . really revenge that the deceived people took on its bloodsuckers." ("Die Judenhetze [war] . . . in Wahrheit die Rache, die das betrogene Volk an seinen Aussaugern nahm.")

[22] "Der Anti-Semitismus, der in ganz Deutschland wie eine Pest um sich gegriffen hat, hat nachdem er in der letzten Zeit vor allem in Bayern zur offiziellen Regierungsmaxime geworden ist, nun auch in Berlin seine Opfer gefordert. . . . Verstehen die deutschen Juden was heute vor sich geht? . . . Die Früchte der Juden-Emanzipation sind ins Wanken geraten. Die Politik der Assimilation . . . hat Schiffbruch gelitten. Das deutsche Judentum steht heute vor der Tatsache, dass seine Politik des letzten Jahrhunderts völlig bankrottiert. hat."

[23] *Die Stadt ohne Juden*, dir. Hans Karl Breslauer, H. K. Breslauer-Film, 1924, videocassette, Filmarchiv Austria, 2000. Published together with an anthology of critical essays (Geser/Loacker).

[24] For example, the chancellor's speech justifying expulsion as a necessary measure to root out the may beetle (*Maikäfer*) that is destroying the roses satirizes the biological metaphor used by Vienna's mayor, Leopold Kunschak, in his notorious parliamentary address of 1920, when he compared the Eastern Jews to an infestation of locusts that needs to be exterminated. Pest control was a common trope in anti-Semitic politics.

[25] "Es muss gehandelt werden — daher schlage ich die Ausweisung der Juden vor . . . und es kommen auch getaufte Juden in Betracht . . . und auch Kinder aus Mischehen . . . Getaufte Kinder in der 2. Generation werden zu Ariern erklärt."

[26] As in *Der Golem*, the *Ostjuden* here are portrayed as mostly poor, old, devout, and foreign. Shown in groups, often from the distance of a long shot, they remain anonymous figures whose religious symbols emphasize their cultural and ethnic difference, strangers whose alien ghetto markings make them objects of curiosity and pity (Kitzberger, 434–39).

[27] Contrast Judith Doneson's paradigm for the mixed couple in later American Holocaust films, in which an (active and masculinized) Christian always rescues the (passive and feminized) Jewish mate (Doneson, 163–65).

[28] If these limits in *Das alte Gesetz* were reassuring to many on both sides of the film audience, they created a quandary for some — notably Henny Porten, whose mixed marriage to Wilhelm von Kaufmann put the actress at odds with her role as archduchess in the resolution of the film. Otherwise, this role, in which she was the Gentile sponsor of Baruch's rise to stardom in a fabulously successful career, must have been gratifying for Porten to play. After all *Das alte Gesetz* was produced by Comedia-Film, a company she owned.

[29] See Prawer's informative commentary on the German version of this multilingual project, along with many other lesser-known Jewish-themed films of the era.

Works Cited

Anon. "Die Schicksalsstunde des deutschen Judentums." *Jüdische Rundschau*, 9 November 1923.

Aschau, Frank. "Das alte Gesetz." *Die Weltbühne*, 27 March 1924.

Aschheim, Steven E. *Brothers and Strangers: The East European Jew in German and German-Jewish Consciousness.* Madison: U of Wisconsin P, 1982.

Bartov, Omer. *The "Jew" in Cinema: From "The Golem" to "Don't Touch My Holocaust."* Bloomington: Indiana UP, 2005.

Belach, Helga. *Henny Porten: Der erste deutsche Filmstar, 1890–1960.* Berlin: Haude & Spensersche, 1986.

Bial, Henry. *Acting Jewish: Negotiating Ethnicity on the American Stage and Screen.* Ann Arbor: Michigan UP. 2005.

Brenner, Michael. *The Renaissance of Jewish Culture in Weimar Germany.* New Haven, CN, and London: Yale UP, 1996.

Bretschneider, Jürgen, ed. *Ewald André Dupont, Autor und Regisseur.* Munich: edition text + kritik, 2002.

del. "Das alte Gesetz." *LichtBildBühne,* 3 November 1923.

Doneson, Judith. *The Holocaust in American Film.* Philadelphia: Jewish Publication Society, 1987.

Geser, Guntram, and Armin Loacker, eds. *Die Stadt ohne Juden.* Edition Film + Text 3. Vienna: Filmarchiv Austria, 2000.

Granach, Alexander. *Da geht ein Mensch: Ein autobiographischer Roman.* Augsburg: Ölbaum, 2003.

Hoffmann-Holter, Beatrix. "'Ostjuden hinaus!' Jüdische Kriegsflüchtlinge in Wien 1914–1924." In Geser & Loacker, 314–18.

Holberg, Gustav. *Henny Porten: Eine Biographie unserer beliebten Filmkünstlerin.* Berlin: Verlag der LichtBildBühne, 1920.

Isenberg, Noah. *Between Redemption and Doom: The Strains of German-Jewish Modernism.* Lincoln and London: U of Nebraska P, 1999.

Kitzberger, Michael. "Bild-Störung: Repräsentationen des Jüdischen in 'Die Stadt ohne Juden'." In Geser & Loacker, 415–44.

Kortner, Fritz. *Aller Tage Abend: Autobiographie.* Berlin: Alexander Verlag, 2005.

Laube, Heinrich. *Erinnerungen, 1841–1881.* Leipzig: Max Hesses Verlag, 1909.

Maurer, Trude. *Ostjuden in Deutschland, 1918–1933.* Hamburg: Christians, 1986.

Meiring, Kerstin. *Die Christlich-Jüdische Mischehe in Deutschland, 1840–1933.* Hamburg: Dölling & Gallitz, 1998.

Pinthus, Kurt. "Ernst Deutsch." *Das Tagebuch,* 10 November 1923.

Prawer, S. S. *Between Two Worlds: The Jewish Presence in German and Austrian Film.* New York & Oxford: Berghahn, 2005.

Stratenwerth, Irene, and Hermann Simon, eds. *Pioniere in Celluloid: Juden in der frühen Filmwelt.* Berlin: Centrum Judaicum, 2004.

Volkov, Shulamit. *Germans, Jews and Antisemites: Trials in Emancipation.* Cambridge: Cambridge UP, 2006.

von Braun, Christina. "Und der Feind ist Fleisch geworden: Der rassistische Anti-Semitismus." In *Der ewige Judenhass,* edited by Christina von Braun and Ludger Heid, 149–213. Berlin and Vienna: Philo, 2000.

Weinstein, Valerie. "Dissolving Boundaries: Assimilation and Allosemitism in E. A. Dupont's *Das alte Gesetz* (1923) and Veit Harlan's *Jud Süss* (1940)." *The German Quarterly* 78 (2005): 496–516.

Wertheimer, Jack. *Unwelcome Strangers: East European Jews in Imperial Germany.* New York & Oxford: Oxford UP, 1987.

Widdig, Bernd. *Culture and Inflation in Weimar Germany.* Berkeley: U of California P, 2001.

Zweig, Arnold. *The Face of East European Jewry.* Translated by Noah Isenberg. Berkeley: U of California P, 2004.

6: "These Hands Are Not My Hands": War Trauma and Masculinity in Crisis in Robert Wiene's *Orlacs Hände* (1924)

Anjeana Hans

A WOMAN RECLINES ON A BED in a shadowy room. She holds a letter, raises her hand and begins to read. The film cuts to the hand-written letter: "My beloved! One more night and a day and then I will again be with you. I will take you in my arms . . . My hands will caress your hair . . . and I will feel your body trembling beneath my hands."[1] The camera cuts back and lingers on her as she stares into space, smiling, chest heaving as she begins to clasp the letter to her chest.[2]

This sequence, the opening scene of Robert Wiene's silent film *Orlacs Hände* (The Hands of Orlac, 1924), carried particular resonance for German audiences after the First World War, evoking the anxieties of soldiers eager to return from the front lines as well as those of the women at home reading their missives with equal longing.[3] Yet *Orlacs Hände* is no overt war film and does not directly address a soldier's return. Instead, it is a horror film, the story of a pianist who is the victim of a train accident, and whose experimental treatment — consisting of the transplantation of the hands of a convicted murderer to replace his own mutilated hands — leads to his increasing instability and delusion. The horror revolves around a common motif — that of "possession" contingent upon hybrid bodies, seemingly a continuation of the great Frankensteinian fantasy of the nineteenth century: the recreation of life from death, the animation of the mortified object. While Dr Frankenstein's monster is composed entirely of foreign parts, resistant to forming a whole and violently acting out the mood of its inception, here we see the fantasy of an estranged part that transforms the body as a whole. Cinematically, the fantasy takes shape both in remakes of *Orlacs Hände*, such as Karl Freund's *Mad Love* of 1935 and Edmond T. Greville's *Les mains d'Orlac* of 1960, as well as in modern B-horror films such as Eric Red's *Body Parts* of 1991. In Wiene's film, however, this near-universal image of horror evokes a direct connection between the traumatic reality of war and a home front irrevocably changed, where previously stable hierarchies and social positions were no more.

German culture and society were deeply and permanently marked by the Great War, and peace had done little to heal the psychological and physical wounds, instead exacerbating them. As Richard W. McCormick notes, the massive casualties at the front (2.4 million) and at home (300,000) were only the most obvious effects of the war on the populace; hand in hand with the loss of lives went the collapse of "Germany's dominant order," the end of the empire and the inauguration of a "chaotic period of revolution, counter-revolution, and hyperinflation that would take four years to 'stabilize'" (McCormick, 61). The war had torn apart not only individual bodies and lives but also the very fabric of existing social structures. And there were visual reminders of both elements of destruction: the absence of those men who did not return and the presence of those who returned as amputees or otherwise mutilated. Maria Tatar argues that, against the backdrop of the mutilated bodies of returning soldiers and the collapse of previous social hierarchies, women — whose bodies seemed to have escaped unscathed — came to represent a direct threat to male subjectivity (Tatar, 12). On the one hand, women posed a threat to traditional models of masculinity, embodied in the idea of the "New Woman" — educated, emancipated, employed in the workforce, and generally opposed to conventional feminine roles. On the other, they became "a covert enemy" who had "cheered on" the soldiers (Tatar, 12), only to become agents of the "betrayal" — a notion propagated by military leaders such as Erich Ludendorff as the *Dolchstoßlegende* (legend of the stab in the back), according to which defeat was a result not of military failure but of a failure on the part of the civilian Germans on the home front (McCormick, 20).

In addition to facing changed social and gender dynamics as well as physical and financial challenges, returning soldiers also had to come to terms with a sense that their own identity was forever changed, that they were no longer the same men they had once been: having faced the need to kill or be killed, how were they to reintegrate into a peace-time society? Many soldiers experienced physical and psychological symptoms of what was termed *Kriegsneurose*, war neurosis — from "shaking and paralyses" ("Zittern und Lähmungen") to nightmares and flashbacks (Freud, "Gutachten," 707). The loss of control over one's own body exacerbated a profound identity crisis: the soldiers not only returned to a changed world, but they did so as men irrevocably changed by their traumatic experiences of combat, injury, and death.

That the collective trauma of war and of a fundamentally changed society should find its expression in the cinematic medium is not surprising. Siegfried Kracauer argues that "what films reflect are not so much explicit credos as psychological dispositions — those deep layers of collective mentality which extend more or less below the dimensions of consciousness" (Kracauer, 6), and poses, in a sense, the question that motivates this reading of *Orlacs Hände*: "What fears and hopes swept Germany immediately after World War I"? (Kracauer, 8). Anton Kaes notes, in connection with Robert Wiene's earlier film *The Cabinet of Dr. Caligari*, that all of Weimar culture — and particularly Expressionist cinema — was marked by the experience of war; combat and death "returned after 1918 as stories of madness and mass murder" (Kaes, 62). Though not an Expressionist film in the narrow sense, *Orlacs Hände* focuses on the protagonist's declining state of mind and depicts the murder of his father, symbolically evoking the mayhem of war and the sense "of an entire world gone mad" (Kaes, 62). The story of the maimed pianist stages this crisis on multiple levels: in terms of physical disability, mental anguish, social rejection, and gender politics. Perhaps the true element of horror in the film lies in the fact that this rather far-fetched story, with its somewhat implausible plot, actually reenacts a common experience of men in Germany after the First World War.

Based on Maurice Renard's novel *Les mains d'Orlac*, published in 1920 and translated into German in 1922 (Jung/Schatzberg, 116), Wiene's film tells the story of Paul Orlac, a world-famous pianist who, returning from his final concert tour, is involved in a train accident. Though Paul survives the accident, his hands do not. At the urging of his wife, Yvonne, Paul's doctor replaces the pianist's mutilated hands with those of a man recently executed for murder. Paul's recovery is fraught with distress: he becomes convinced that his newly attached hands maintain a life of their own, combating him for their control and inclining him to violence. Wrestling with his body and struggling for mental stability, Paul also strives to preserve his social status and to save his marriage. Events escalate when his estranged father is found murdered and Paul is implicated. His despair grows further when he is blackmailed by a man claiming to be the executed murderer, Vasseur, ostensibly revived by having his head reattached (much like Paul his hands). Unlike most Expressionist films, *Orlacs Hände* does not deny the audience a happy ending: the police discover that the plot to frame Paul and to drive him to madness was masterminded by this blackmailer, who is in fact not only an imposter named Nera but also the perpetrator of both the murder for which Vasseur was executed and that of Paul's father. Paul's hands are thus not those of a murderer after all, and, with his name cleared and his mind put at ease, Paul can reconcile with his wife.

Wiene's film premiered in Germany in 1924 and was applauded as "one of the most important German-language films" of the time (Jung/Schatzberg, 116). However, contemporary critics read the film primarily as a "simple" Gothic tale, with Paul in one reviewer's view "a human being devastated by a mystical fate" (Michaelis). Conrad Veidt, who plays Paul Orlac, was already famous for his depictions of tortured characters, most notably the somnambulist Cesare in Wiene's *The Cabinet of Dr. Caligari*

(1920). Veidt's stunning performance dominated *Orlacs Hände* to such a degree that an early American review noted: "Were it not for Veidt's masterly characterization, 'The Hands of Orlac' would be an absurd fantasy in the old-time mystery-thriller class."[4] Contemporary reviews often displayed a tangible reluctance to address a complex of fantasies and anxieties apparently too disturbing to be acknowledged.

Evoking the original notion of trauma as a somatic wound, the hands of Orlac, which are both attached to and estranged from him, become a multilayered signifier of physical, psychological, moral, and social trauma. The film, as Klaus Kreimeier argues, focuses on "the dissolution of the unity of body and psyche, body and soul" (Kreimeier, 74; translation by author). In the fantasy of the film, the hands, not Paul, act out a murder — a split mirroring that of soldiers who return home as both heroes and killers, praised for their deeds and tormented by their guilt. This ambivalence in returning soldiers' minds triggers what Freud calls an "ego conflict" ("Ichkonflikt") in that it represents a confrontation between the formerly unified "peace-ego" ("Friedensich") and the newly emerged "warlike ego" ("neues kriegerisches Ich"; Freud, "Kriegsneurosen," 323); the return from the war-front results in just such a fractured subjectivity as we see in Paul. The physical symptoms associated with this internal conflict — particularly shaking and paralysis — are the very symptoms we see in Veidt's performance as Paul.

The question of moral guilt finds an easy answer in the tale of betrayal that the film offers in form of the mystery plot. Paul apparently maintains his innocence: not only because the hands are retroactively found innocent of committing murder in the past, but also because his present violent inclinations turn out to be based on the whispering of a blackmailer and murderer, the man who calls himself "Vasseur," but is actually Nera (played by Fritz Kortner). Nera's plan to frame Paul echoes the *Dolchstoßlegende*, the conspiracy theories of the postwar period mentioned above. Filmic fantasies allow for simultaneous staging of conflicting concepts. On the one hand, the film takes up the legend of exculpation, put forth by the prewar ruling class, and, on the other hand, it acts out fantasies of revenge against this class, which had cold-heartedly thrown millions of soldiers into lost battles before it finally abandoned them altogether. In the framework of the film, we might interpret the murder of Paul's estranged father — who, through his depiction in a setting dominated by Gothic architecture, is associated with the past social order — as an act of revenge against this premodern order. While the struggle of malevolent fathers and forsaken sons is, of course, a widespread motif in German Expressionism, in the postwar environment this generational conflict takes on new significance.

Germany's prewar society was predicated on a strict separation between social and domestic spheres, spheres it marked as masculine and

Fig. 6.1. Yvonne (Alexandra Sorina) reads her husband's letter. Screenshot.

feminine respectively. It comes as no surprise, then, that blurring the boundaries between these spheres and challenging prewar gender roles and power relations appeared as a threat and provoked a hostile response. In the film, gender trouble translates into a troubled marriage. Significantly, Yvonne (played by Alexandra Sorina) is the active partner: she procures the transplant for Paul after the railroad accident and she manages the couple's increasing financial difficulties. In doing so, she comes to function as a competitor rather than a submissive partner, and, as such, becomes the focus of Paul's hostility. If Paul symbolically represents the soldier who returns from the war-front irrevocably changed, Yvonne, in turn, embodies the homeland that is no longer *Heimat*, a safe haven, but rather home-front, a site of struggle, a location of deep-rooted tension. Her French name, "Yvonne," may even denote that the enemy has indeed entered the family. Measured against the fantasies and anxieties as well as the real-world concerns and considerations that inform postwar Germany, the film clearly pits a mutilated man against a "New Woman."

Orlacs Hände begins by showing us Yvonne, anticipating her husband's return, reading a letter in which he expresses his desire to once again hold her in his arms (fig. 6.1). Only after witnessing Yvonne's preparations do we see Paul, performing in his final concert. It is significant that Paul is presented in a slightly high-angle medium close-up, seated at the piano, looking down at his hands. The equation of his hands with his identity is emphasized by fading from this shot to a close-up of his hands moving across the piano keys. We next see a sequence in which shots of Yvonne preparing for Paul's return are crosscut with shots of a train speeding down the tracks, before suddenly derailing. The accident unfolds with terrifying speed: initially, we see a single shot of a passing train, before cutting to Yvonne, waiting for her husband's arrival. The film then cuts back to a shot of train tracks, then to one of a train moving toward the camera, before showing a switch operator. Immediately after this, we cut to two trains passing each other; one suddenly, rapidly, runs off the tracks. The accident itself takes only a few seconds; it is the aftermath that dominates this scene, with short shots of the wreckage, of men pulling bodies from the cars, and of the victims, many of them women and children, rapidly crosscut with shots of Yvonne hearing of the accident and commanding her driver to take her to the site. Once there, Yvonne quickly takes action, searching in the wreckage until she locates Paul and has him transported from the site.

In his discussion of the treatment of war neurosis, Freud drew an explicit connection between the traumatic effects of war and that of railroad accidents.[5] The sheer chaos of the cinematic moment is emphasized by the mise-en-scène and cinematography: frames are cluttered, angles are askew, and the smoke, spotlights, and torches suggest confusion.[6] The chaos is further underlined by the rapid cuts — some shots are so short as to become virtually subliminal. The shots of the casualties of the accident — a woman's body swinging down into the frame, a crying child accompanied, significantly, by a young man in a military-style uniform — bring to mind the casualties of the recent war. The train accident, then, reads much as one might imagine the aftermath of battle. Yvonne's actions — her immediate, active response to news of the accident, and her determined search for Paul once at the site — introduce the crucial conflict that coalesces around gender roles: with Paul incapacitated, Yvonne sheds her previous passivity and takes control. The train wreck becomes a source both of physical and psychic trauma: through it, Paul's hands are mutilated; at the same time, it marks the moment from which his hitherto stable role as provider is threatened by Yvonne's new-found activity.

Even before receiving a mysterious letter telling him that the hands are those of Vasseur, the executed murderer, Paul is haunted by the sense that something is amiss. Immediately after he wakes up to find himself surrounded by Yvonne and the doctors, he sees what appears to be a disembodied head watching him through a window above the door to his room. His reaction makes it clear that his fears stem not only from the external events but also from an internal awareness that, somehow, he is no longer identical to the man he was before the accident, the man whose subjectivity was inextricably bound up with his hands. As yet unaware of the newly attached appendages, Paul states: "There . . . the head . . . isn't it looking at my hands?" ("Dort . . . der Kopf . . . Sieht er nicht auf meine Hände?").

After he receives the letter informing him of the origin of his "new" hands, Paul continues to deteriorate. Paul confronts his doctor, asking whether his hands will ever again be able to play. His identity has hitherto been founded on his status as pianist. His sense of self is destabilized by his inability to continue in his profession. Later, Paul prepares to return home to Yvonne. He raises his hands and studies them carefully, then lowers them, saying that "these hands" shall never again touch another human being. The significance of this moment is emphasized by a cut to Yvonne preparing for his arrival, after which we cut back to Paul, attempting to put his wedding ring on his finger. Unable to do so — his new hands are far too large for the band — he puts the ring in his pocket, suggesting that the emotional and sexual bond with his wife is irrevocably severed: Paul is literally no longer the man who married Yvonne.

The connection between his roles as pianist and husband is reaffirmed when Paul arrives at their home. The sequence begins with a wide interior shot of Yvonne awaiting his arrival. Paul enters on the left, yet does not move towards her. When Yvonne approaches him, he moves as though to embrace her, but then stops and remains immobile. We then see Paul in another room, approaching his piano. In a medium shot, we see Paul caress, then kiss the lid of the piano before sitting down and raising the hinged cover to reveal the keys as Yvonne enters (fig. 6.2). As in the initial concert scene, we cut to a close-up of Paul's hands on the keys as he begins to play, then immediately see a medium reaction shot of Yvonne as she looks away from him, indicating that he no longer plays with his previous skill. Paul stops playing and closes the keyboard cover. We then, as in the previous scene, return to a long shot of the two, as Yvonne moves toward him and embraces him; as before, Paul raises his hands as though to caress her, then lowers them again, remaining immobile. The fact that he caresses and kisses the piano eroticizes the moment;[7] indeed, we might read his failure in the attempt to play as symbolic of his failure with Yvonne — recall his letter, in which he anticipated caressing and kissing her. Her response to his failure to play as before — her physical turn away from him — signals her rejection of the man he has become.

And what is initially figured as reluctance to touch Yvonne with these hands, which he so acutely perceives as alien, escalates into aggression in a later scene, in which Paul discovers in his home the dagger he knows to

Fig. 6.2. Paul Orlac (Conrad Veidt) embraces his piano. Screenshot.

be Vasseur's murder weapon. In response to his mounting suspicions regarding the origin of his new hands, Paul has sought out more information in the newspaper. One article makes note of Paul's own difficulty in recovering and his inability to play the piano, while the second provides grisly details of Vasseur's murderous act, including a description of the dagger, the hilt of which was marked by an "X." When Paul returns home, we see him enter, then stop and recoil, as the film cuts to a close-up of a dagger lodged in an interior door, its hilt clearly marked with an "X." Paul stumbles back, then moves toward the dagger and grabs it. We then cut to a shot of the piano-room, as Paul lifts the piano's lid and puts the dagger inside. Looking at his hands, he raises and addresses them, stating that he feels a "coldness" rising from them into his soul. Shortly after this scene, we return to the image of Paul in the room, this time moving with his arms outstretched, as though being pulled by his hands, toward the piano. He removes the dagger and closes the lid of the piano. Here, we cut to a shot of Yvonne in bed, sitting up as though startled. Cut back to a shot of Paul holding the dagger, moving into the shadows at the rear of the shot, before we again see Yvonne, first getting out of bed, then listening at the door. Again, we cut back to Paul, who is now raising the dagger and making stabbing motions. As Yvonne enters the room and witnesses his actions, Paul attempts to conceal the dagger behind his back, then backs away from her as she moves towards him, and finally orders her out: "Don't come near me . . . go!" ("Komm mir nicht nahe . . . geh!").

Within the narrative of the film, the scene acts out Paul's perception of his hands: as alien appendages that control him, that literally lead his helpless body to actions that he would otherwise not take. Yet the scene might also be read in another way. Consider two other seminal horror films from the era: F. W. Murnau's *Nosferatu* (1922), the first of many cinematic retellings of Bram Stoker's *Dracula* (1897), and Fritz Lang's slightly later *M* (1931), which focuses on a child murderer. In the former, as the vampire leaves his home to enter the room of his victim, we see a similar focus on his hands, as though they, like Paul's, are pulling him toward his victim. In the latter, as the child molester and murderer, whom the urban underworld has hunted down, cowers before the kangaroo court and attempts to explain his actions, he uses his hands similarly as he states: "But I, can I do any different? Don't I have this damned thing in me? The fire, the voice, the torture? I always feel it, someone is chasing me, it's I myself, following myself." In both films the hands come to represent not an external will being imposed on the monstrous figures but rather an internal compulsion towards violence, a compulsion that might, as in the case of *M*'s murderer, be at odds with conscious drives and desires, but nevertheless stems from within. Similarly, we can interpret this scene in *Orlacs Hände* as enacting not an external force acting on Paul through his "alien" hands, but rather an internal urge, pushing him to act out a murder — an interpretation that is supported by the revelation at the end of the film that the hands Paul has been given are in fact not the hands of a murderer.

Paul's hostility toward Yvonne is rooted in her social and sexual transgression. With Paul incapacitated by the accident, Yvonne takes on the role of primary provider, thereby transgressing the boundaries of her former identity as his wife. Her move from the domestic spaces in which she is situated before the train accident into a public space signified by her interaction with the doctor, the creditors, and Paul's father suggests a second transgression: she is no longer the object exclusively of Paul's desires but rather that of the desires of these other men. While pleading with the doctor to save Paul's hands, she approaches and virtually embraces him; in their subsequent interaction, he repeatedly takes her hand in his. Yvonne, in other words, has escaped the domestic sphere, functioning as an erotic object not only for her husband but also for the other men whom she encounters. Paul, metaphorically doubly castrated through the loss of his former social and financial status as well as through his marital impotence, exhibits hostility towards her, not because of an external will embodied by

Fig. 6.3. Regine, the maid (Carmen Cartellieri), is scared of Paul's hands. Screenshot.

the alien hands, but rather because she represents a threat to his social and sexual superiority.

The sexual nature of his hostility is further suggested through his interaction with the maid. Acting on Nera's orders that she should "seduce his hands" ("Verführe seine Hände"), the maid approaches Paul as he is seated on a sofa. In a sequence of medium shots we see her approach him, kneeling next to him on the ground, then crawling closer before grasping his hand and kissing it. We then see a sequence of close-ups: first, Paul starts and pulls his hand out of her grip, then he pauses, reaches towards her, and caresses her head, first with one, then with both hands. A close-up of Paul's smiling face demonstrates that he is experiencing pleasure in this interaction with the maid. We then see a close-up of the maid, who begins to look worried as his hands caress her more roughly, before pushing his hands away, telling him that they hurt her, "like the hands of a murderer" ("wie Mörderhände") (fig. 6.3). Paul, unable to caress or even approach his wife, is quite happily able to do so to the maid. The latter, by virtue of her social position, is of course figured as socially inferior to Paul — a fact emphasized by the spatial positioning, as she kneels and crawls towards him. With the maid, then, Paul feels secure in his superiority, and is thus able to react towards her "as a man." Significantly, however, here too his initial caress turns to aggression. Nera and the maid — as well as the narrative of the film as a whole — conspire to convince both Paul and the viewer that the alien appendages are guiding his immoral behavior.

Superficially, the resolution of the film seems to restabilize Paul's identity. The supposed "Vasseur" demands money in return for not accusing Paul of his father's murder. Paul, at Yvonne's urging, goes to the police, then agrees to bring the money to his blackmailer. The police enter and unveil "Vasseur" as the imposter, Nera, yet might still have arrested Paul were it not for the intervention of the maid, who arrives and explains that Nera in fact planted Vasseur's (and now Paul's) fingerprints using special gloves. Paul, recalling the doctor's assertion that mind and spirit are in control of the body, seems to be "healed" of his identity crisis. His subsequent actions seem to confirm that he has reassumed his former role: Yvonne faints, and it is Paul who guides her out of the bar in which the resolution occurs. The next shot — an exterior shot, in which Yvonne swoons and Paul catches and carries her to a bench — suggests that all is now well: former gender and social positions are reaffirmed, now it is Paul who is dominant within the public sphere and who functions as the protector for his wife when her body fails her. This next-to-final moment in the film, combined with the final shot — a close-up of Paul and Yvonne's faces, with Paul's hands first caressing and then covering Yvonne's face — presents the notion that, once again, he will take the lead in their relationship, with the reaffirmed man literally effacing the "New Woman" (fig. 6.4).

And yet the ostensible resolution to Paul's crisis of subjectivity certainly does not put an end to all of the questions raised. The hands, after all, we find out, were not in fact those of a murderer; the murderous urges that so unsettled Paul and that found expression in the rejection of and hostility towards Yvonne, then, are rooted not in the alien appendages but rather in his own self.[8] And, regardless of the "innocence" of the "new" hands he has been given, Paul's identity, after all, has been irrevocably changed: his body is still a hybrid one, his hands — symbols of his livelihood and of his will — are still those of another man. In other words, we might still read the final shot as an expression of some level of continued aggression towards Yvonne. In this reading, then, the "solution" to the crisis of masculine identity precipitated by changing social and gender norms would be tied to a return to prewar mores; the aggression Paul exhibits towards the (temporarily) emancipated Yvonne is an innate part of his new identity that emerges in response to female empowerment. At the same time, we might interpret the murder of Paul's estranged father as suggesting that the past, rigidly patriarchal, social mores must be

Fig. 6.4. Paul, healed of his affliction, embraces his wife Yvonne. Screenshot.

destroyed in order to enable Paul to move forward and overcome his trauma.

The film suggests that the crisis of male identity precipitated by the changed social arena with which returning soldiers were confronted after the war inevitably surfaced as aggression directed towards the women who appeared to be usurping social roles formerly reserved for men. At the same time, while acknowledging that a return to previous power hierarchies might seem to represent a solution to this crisis, it hints that such a rigidly patriarchal hierarchy is an obsolete relic of the past. Though Paul's crisis is superficially resolved in the end, the resolution remains incomplete, suggesting that this crisis is an inevitable response to the traumatic experience of war and the changing social and cultural norms. Wiene's *Orlacs Hände* is thus much more than a simple horror film, for it depicts the manner in which the experience of the First World War and the changed social and cultural norms and hierarchies of the postwar period struck at the foundation of notions of male identity and subjectivity, and represents the difficulties faced by men and women as they renegotiated gender hierarchies and identities in Germany after the First World War.

Notes

1 "Liebste! noch eine Nacht und ein Tag und dann bin ich wieder bei Dir. Ich werde Dich in meine Arme schliessen . . . Meine Hände werden über Dein Haar gleiten . . . und ich werde fühlen, wie Dein Körper unter meinen Händen erzittert."

2 I am indebted to the organizers of and participants in the German Film Institute's symposium "Unknown Weimar II: International Connections," held at the University of Michigan at Ann Arbor (6–12 August 2006), where I was first able to view *Orlacs Hände*. The discussion of the film at the symposium was invaluable to my analysis. I also want to thank Patrick Fortmann and Joel Westerdale for reading this article at various stages and offering many valuable comments and suggestions.

3 *Orlacs Hände* is available for purchase on DVD from www.kino.com; a 35mm print of the film, as well as of a version on video that differs slightly from the former, can be rented from the Friedrich-Wilhelm-Murnau Stiftung in Wiesbaden, Germany. I have been able to view all three of these versions, as well as a version that aired on *arte* TV in Germany. I base my analysis primarily on the 35mm print, as this is the most complete version of the film. However, I have used the original German intertitles that were included on the Murnau Stiftung's video version of the film.

4 "The Hands of Orlac," *Variety* [New York], 20 Jun. 1928.

5 Freud, "Gutachten," 706. Eric Rentschler also noted the symbolic function of train accidents as representative of war in this period during the German Film Institute symposium at the University of Michigan, Ann Arbor, 6–12 August 2006.

6 As John D. Barlow notes in his discussion of this scene: "The train wreck, although staged entirely with a naturalistic set, is shot to highlight its disorder. As in the set of *Raskolnikow*, there are no parallel lines. We find instead an emphasis on crisscrossings and oblique angles, all shot in a shadowy atmosphere, with steam from the rescue train floating through the transecting searchlight beams" (Barlow, 59).

7 Ursula von Keitz suggests that this moment constructs Orlac's musical virtuosity as specifically erotic (von Keitz, 63).

8 Ursula von Keitz reads this element of the film in a similar manner in her analysis of *Orlacs Hände*, though she focuses on Orlac's psychosis not as a representation of a response to the trauma of the First World War and to postwar social change but rather as a result of a problematic relationship to his fragmented body (von Keitz, 61).

Works Cited

Anon. "The Hands of Orlac." *Variety* [New York], 28 June 1928.

Barlow, John D. *German Expressionist Film*. Boston: Twayne Publishers, 1982.

Freud, Siegmund. "Einleitung zu *Zur Psychoanalyse der Kriegsneurosen.*" 1919. Reprinted in *Gesammelte Werke 12: Werke aus den Jahren 1917–1920,* 321–24. Frankfurt am Main: Fischer, 1999.

———. "Gutachten über die elektrische Behandlung der Kriegsneurotiker." 1920. Reprinted in *Gesammelte Werke: Nachtragsband; Texte aus den Jahren 1885–1938,* 706–10. Frankfurt am Main: Fischer, 1999.

Jung, Uli, and Walter Schatzberg. *Beyond Caligari: The Films of Robert Wiene.* Providence, RI: Berghahn, 1999.

Kaes, Anton. "Weimar Cinema: The Predicament of Modernity." In *European Cinema,* edited by Elizabeth Ezra, 59–77. New York: Oxford UP, 2004.

Kracauer, Siegfried. *From Caligari to Hitler: A Psychological History of the German Film.* Princeton, NJ: Princeton UP, 2004.

Kreimeier, Klaus. "Notorisch anders: Conrad Veidt; Zur schauspielerischen Repräsentation der Devianz." In Rüffert et al., 69–76.

McCormick, Richard W. *Gender and Sexuality in Weimar Modernity: Film, Literature, and "New Objectivity."* New York: Palgrave, 2001.

Michaelis, Heinz. "Orlacs Hände." *Film-Kurier,* 2 February 1925.

Rüffert, Christine, Irmbert Schenk, Karl-Heinz Schmid, Alfred Tews, and Bremer Symposium zum Film, eds. *Unheimlich anders: Doppelgänger, Monster, Schattenwesen im Kino.* Berlin: Bertz + Fischer, 2005.

Tatar, Maria. *Lustmord: Sexual Murder in Weimar Germany.* Princeton, NJ: Princeton UP, 1995.

von Keitz, Ursula. "Prothese und Transplantat: *Orlacs Hände* und die Körperfragment-Topik nach dem Ersten Weltkrieg." In Rüffert, 53–68.

7: The Star System in Weimar Cinema

Joseph Garncarz

WHEN WE THINK OF WEIMAR CINEMA, great directors like Friedrich Wilhelm Murnau, Fritz Lang, or Georg Wilhelm Pabst come to mind, but not star performers such as Harry Liedtke, Alphons Fryland, Henny Porten, or Claire Rommer. Their names are largely forgotten today, because their films have not become part of the canon that shapes our image of Weimar Cinema. Stars are often identified with the medium of film, and film stars with the Hollywood film industry.[1] If the US film-star system is taken as the standard model, one might mistakenly conclude that star systems never existed in European countries. In opposition to this view, I argue that star systems did indeed exist in Europe, but that they functioned differently from the US system in some respects. As I hope to show, Weimar Cinema had a well-developed star system, and cultural specificity is the most important condition for a star system to function efficiently.

To conceptualize and analyze culturally specific star systems, we cannot simply use a theory of stardom developed for a specific region or period, namely the star system of the classical Hollywood cinema; instead, we must devise a new theory that is flexible enough to encompass the entire range of possible variations in the phenomenon of stardom. Furthermore, we not only need to analyze the cultural specificity of star systems but must also explain their particular mode of existence. In the European case, it is useful to take into account two culturally specific contexts: first, the star system of the theater, which was established before cinema, and second, long-standing religious traditions that profoundly shaped the cultural identities of different countries — including institutions such as the theater and the cinema.

A Theory of Stardom, Revisited

An analysis of stars and star systems of different cultural contexts, it would seem, requires a clear concept of what stardom means beyond the boundaries of different countries or media. However, there is as yet no generally applicable theory of stardom. Most studies, such as the ground breaking one by Richard Dyer, take a particular definition for granted without making it explicit (Dyer). None of the existing star theories grasp the multiplicity of the phenomenon across various cultures, because their definitions generalize from the Hollywood case and neglect the individual historic, cultural, or media-specific characteristics. The influential theory of Richard de Cordova, for example, assumes that the availability of and public interest in information on the private lives of stars is a necessary condition for the phenomenon of stardom (de Cordova). Furthermore, most star studies consider only actors as stars. As we will see, in Weimar Germany, actors' stardom was defined differently than in the United States (especially with regard to information about private lives), and film directors were often regarded as stars. The German case, then, shows that theories that make general claims are in fact limited to their respective historic object of examination.

In what follows, I will draw on sociological and cultural approaches, such as those used by Francesco Alberoni and Richard Sennett, that are helpful for developing a general theory of stardom (Alberoni; Sennett). For my purposes, it will be sufficient to point out two of the most salient features of the phenomenon by focusing on the significance that stars have for their audiences: film stars are unique personalities who arouse a special interest in their audiences.[2] In principle, persons of almost any function in entertainment media can become stars — for example, actors, directors, or musicians. "Unique" means that stars are readily distinguishable from one another, and a "special interest" simply means that some actors or directors are preferred over others. A "star image" not only comprises a star's visual and discursive presentation (the customary definition) but also involves the audience's selection and interpretation of this presentation, on which success depends (Ligensa). Instead of assuming a homogeneous single "audience," it makes more sense to talk about specific audiences that favor specific actors or directors. Since a specific audience chooses its stars at a specific historical time and place, star status is usually limited by certain historical-temporal and spatial-cultural boundaries. Thus we find that international stars or stars who are popular over several generations are the exception. Given that popularity is the basic condition for the phenomenon of stardom, an analysis of images is not sufficient; it must always be complemented by empirical evidence that indicates a given star's popularity with his or her audience (Dyer, 182). Stars differ from one another not only in visual-discursive terms (with regard to their public image) but also in economic-financial terms (with regard to their market value). A star's market share can be measured, for example, by box-office receipt figures or by the proportion of votes in contemporary popularity polls.

A film industry cannot make stars; all it can do, as it were, is to nominate the candidates for election by its audience (Alberoni).[3] For the film industry, the advantage of a star's popularity with his or her audience is that a new film becomes a kind of calculable commodity, because the involvement of a star in a particular film already presents a potential selling point, independent of the film in which he or she appears (Sedgwick/

Pokorny; Pokorny/Sedgwick). We may speak of a "star system" when stars are systematically built up and successful images are commercially exploited in a purposeful manner. The phenomenon of star systems presupposes a society that allows media representations to be widely circulated among the public.

A national star system may change dramatically during its history. The Hollywood star system itself is an example, because, for instance, the discourse on stars' private lives has changed over time, as has the manner in which images are created and controlled. Similarly, star systems in different countries may differ significantly; the Weimar star system functioned differently than Hollywood's star system did during the same period. If we accept the basic theory of stardom proposed here, namely that audience choices are determined by a preference for clearly identifiable performers with whom moviegoers developed a special relationship, it can be shown that Weimar Cinema did indeed have a highly developed star system.

Analyzing Weimar's Film-Star System

Weimar Cinema was primarily a commercial cinema. The star system was the Weimar film industry's most important means to attain extraordinary financial and economic success in the national market. The primary indicator of the popular success of a given national cinema is to be found in attendance and box-office-revenue figures. On the basis of supply data, such as the sheer number of American films supplied and distributed in Germany, Kristin Thompson argued that Weimar Cinema had trouble finding a foothold in the German film market (Thompson, 107). Yet if one analyzes demand data from the period, that is, revenue figures and box-office surveys, it becomes evident that Weimar Cinema was in fact an extremely popular national cinema: throughout the 1920s two thirds of the market revenues were earned by German films, as opposed to only one third earned by all foreign films taken together, including those from the United States.[4]

In Hollywood, star directors, such as Cecile B. de Mille, were an exception, whereas in Weimar Germany, directors such as Fritz Lang, F. W. Murnau, and G. W. Pabst were commonly regarded as stars. Many films of famous directors such as Fritz Lang did not have star actors in their casts but were marketed solely on the drawing power of the director's name and his reputation for artistic quality and versatility. For instance, some of the posters for his films *Die Nibelungen* (The Nibelungs, 1924), *Metropolis* (1927), and *M* (1931) display solely his name rather than those of the actors. The exclusive focus on the director's name, however, was the exception: for example, for the Ufa production *Ein Walzertraum* (The Waltz Dream, 1925), advertisements used not only the name of director Ludwig Berger but also those of the star performers, Willy Fritsch, Xenia Desni, and Mady Christians.[5]

The marketing strategy of making the director the focal point of advertising was no guarantee for success with audiences at large. The strategy tended to work well with Fritz Lang, because his name stood for a certain type of film, that is, films of monumental scale with striking production values, such as the science fiction films *Metropolis* (1927) and *Frau im Mond* (Woman in the Moon, 1929). But as a rule, star performers proved to be bigger draws at the box office than directors, as an analysis of the top films in 1925/26 and 1926/27 shows. This indicates that using the director's prestige as a marketing tool was not a response to audience demand but rather reflected, as a contemporary put it, "the great significance . . . for a film's production process" that German film elites attributed to the director's role (Mühsam, 36).

Surveys conducted among readers of fan magazines, which form the basis of contemporary popularity rankings, show how strong the German audience's interest in star performers actually was. Such popularity polls exist for the years between 1923 and 1926. They show a marked concentration on a very small number of stars: more than 80 percent of the readers' votes were cast for the top ten male and female stars, respectively. The top five female stars were Henny Porten, Claire Rommer, Lil Dagover, Lya Mara, and Lya de Putti; the five most popular male stars were Harry Piel, Otto Gebühr, Harry Liedtke, Conrad Veidt, and Charles Willi Kayser.[6] In the United States, by contrast, the top ten stars received only 20 to 40 percent of all votes.[7] This difference reveals a cultural specificity, namely that German audiences were culturally much more homogeneous than audiences in the United States, with a much greater consensus among the German moviegoers as to whom they liked. These popularity polls also show a significant preference for domestic stars: in fact, all the top stars (while not all of German descent) made a career primarily in German films. The German film industry valued these lists highly in its planning of film projects, suggesting that such surveys can be regarded as fairly representative.[8] The strategy of banking on audience polls reaped its significant rewards: nine out of fourteen of the greatest box office hits in Germany during the 1925/26 and 1926/27 seasons used the most popular performers as their leads.[9]

Not only did the stars hold center stage in their films, but they also dominated the extra-filmic discourse. As a rule, a film's marketing revolved around its star. On posters, lobby cards, advertisements, and program booklets the star was always the primary focus of publicity. The star's name and face dominated the visual design of advertising campaigns, with specific selections and variations to provide a recognition effect — but also a certain element of surprise — for the moviegoers. In a system of intertextually related advertising materials, the star became a special guarantor of a film's quality and therefore an important incentive for the moviegoer to choose a certain film. Print media such as cinema magazines (for example, *Die Filmwoche*, with a weekly print run of 35,000 to 40,000 copies), collectible picture postcards (circulated in tens of thousands), and billboard posters presented and circulated star images everywhere.

Through these media, clearly differentiated star images were disseminated: heart-throb Harry Liedtke (1882–1945) was the "hero of every young girl's dreams," as one of his film titles read (*Der Held aller Mädchenträume*; directed by Robert Land, 1929); debonair Alphons Fryland (1889–1953) was the aristocratic *bon vivant*; stately Henny Porten (1890–1960) represented the ideal of German womanhood (fig. 7.1); suave Claire Rommer (1904–?) was the attractive, fun-loving girl; and impish Lya de Putti (1899–1931) projected the image of the "naughty child." These images were reinforced by various means, often by typecasting. The most famous case of such typecasting, perhaps, is that of Otto Gebühr (1877–1954), who essentially made a living from his remarkable physical resemblance to Frederick the Great by playing the legendary eighteenth-century Prussian king in numerous so-called *Preußenfilme* that sought to recapture a supposedly glorious national past.

Weimar film studios primarily produced star vehicles: in the words of a contemporary commentator, films were "wrapped around their stars like custom-made clothing" (Pordes, 61). For example, Harry Liedtke appeared alongside the young Marlene Dietrich in Robert Land's *Ich küsse Ihre Hand, Madame* (I Kiss Your Hand, Madam, 1929) as a former Russian guard officer who now has to make his living as a waiter in a restaurant, where he is a great success with the ladies. Lya de Putti played trapeze artist Berta-Marie in E. A. Dupont's *Varieté* (1925), a young, vivacious, beautiful, and sexually attractive woman, a role that closely corresponded to her public persona. Star postcards, with posed portraits that made stars "physically" accessible to the private sphere of their fans, show how a uniform image was created through clothing, hairstyles, and make-up. Harry Liedtke projected the air of the consummate ladies' man by way of his luxuriously elegant clothes and his meticulous grooming; his intense gaze, his flawless complexion, and the unusual shape of his eyebrows gave him a special appeal (fig. 7.2). Lya de Putti was presented as a youthfully innocent, but at the same time a provocatively erotic, modern woman; she appeared in casual clothes with a certain eccentric flair and wore up-to-the-minute hairstyles, fashionably bobbed or with curls.

The actor-star system of Weimar Germany differed from that of Hollywood, not only in terms of culturally specific star images, but also in terms of structure. As is well known, the Hollywood film industry was controlled by a small number of studios, which bound stars with long-term contracts and took care of the creation and maintenance of their images. All the same, a few American stars such as Mary Pickford, Douglas Fairbanks, and Charles Chaplin owned their own companies and thus were able to control their own images (Koszarski, 260–341). In Weimar Germany, by contrast, a large number of small studios competed fiercely for market shares;[10]

Fig. 7.1. Henny Porten (1890–1960), Germany's top female silent film star. Collectible fan post card. Garncarz collection.

4031/4

Fig. 7.2. Harry Liedtke (1882–1945), heartthrob of the silent screen. Collectible fan post card. Garncarz collection.

Ufa and Emelka were the only studios with somewhat greater power.[11] In 1926, for instance, eighty-one German companies produced 185 feature-length films, and forty-two of these companies produced only a single film (Jason, 41). Even the two largest German film companies of the 1920s, Ufa and Emelka, only produced a relatively small number of films; in 1926, Ufa made twelve and Emelka made nine films. Unlike other German film companies of the period, these two companies were vertically integrated just like the US majors, that is, they produced, distributed, and exhibited their films.

In contrast to their Hollywood counterparts, Weimar star performers largely maintained personal control of their public images, sometimes seeking the help of agents, and they often received large shares of the profits from publicity materials. For instance, the stars' share of the profits from the postcard series published by Ross was twice as high as that of the respective film production company (Hens/Neeb, 41–42). Not beholden to a particular studio or company, they could decide which projects to accept and what kind of information about them would be disseminated to the public. For the most part, German stars usually worked as freelancers, committed themselves to a particular studio for a short period only, or even founded their own production companies. Perhaps the best-known example of this practice, daredevil Harry Piel (1892–1963), produced, directed, and starred in dozens of his own action adventure films between 1919 and 1933. Audiences in the Weimar Republic knew exactly what to expect from a movie advertised as a "Harry Piel film" — a thrilling crime story with surprising plot twists, exciting physical stunts, and state-of-the-art special effects (fig. 7.3). Likewise, Asta Nielsen (1881–1972), possibly the most popular actress of pre-Weimar German cinema, headed her own production company in Germany after 1921.

A further structural difference lies in the kind of information that was disseminated on film stars by the press. In Hollywood, stars were differentiated mainly through their private lives — that is, stories about family, spouses, children, divorces, love-lives, scandals, and so forth (de Cordova) — whereas in Germany publicity did not reveal anything more than basic biographical data (such as birthdays or weddings), but never information on families, marital problems, love-lives, divorces, or scandals. The German stars, being in control of their images, by and large refused to disclose information on their private lives. "Whenever a German film reporter wants to do something for a film star's popularity, the German film artist usually resists with all his might," notes a contemporary observer.[12] The press, on the whole, cooperated in the endeavor to protect the privacy of stars, as in these responses by a popular film magazine to fans' inquiries: "[Fryland] does not want to reveal the name of his wife to the public"; "Alphons Fryland, dear Inge, does not at all approve of having his private affairs exposed to the public; can you blame him for that?"[13] Likewise, the German association of movie theater owners was also opposed to reports

Fig. 7.3. Harry Piel (1892–1963), action adventure star famous for his daring stunts, on the cover of the fan magazine Die Filmwoche *8 (20 February 1929). Garncarz collection.*

on the stars' private lives: its trade paper, *Film-Kurier*, voiced disapproval of the practice of reporting scandals (on the occasion of Lya de Putti's fall from a window)[14] and devoted only a few ironic remarks to the reactions of Harry Liedtke's female teenage fans ("die kleinen Mädchen") to his wedding, rather than exploiting the event.[15] This indicates a strong general cultural consensus within the Weimar German film industry that the private lives of stars were to be kept separate from their public personae.

Weimar film stars differentiated their images by a discourse on art rather than on their private lives. Instead of reports on the stars' personal affairs, much was written on their professional activities, such as their backgrounds in the theater, their approaches to acting, their favorite roles, and their latest film projects. German stars primarily defined themselves as artists; they did not call themselves *Filmsterne* or *Filmstars* but *Filmlieblinge* (literally, "film darlings"), indicating the direct emotional relationship between performers and their admirers (Delmont). Weimar performers preferred the term *Filmliebling* over that of star, because of the associations connected with the Hollywood phenomenon and the English word — to them, stardom connoted a lack of talent, sensational advertising, and a pathological craving for recognition. Actors in the United States were proud when they became stars, whereas German actors did not want to be categorized as stars and even felt insulted if they were.

The star as artist was the main concept of Weimar film publicity, and the legitimate theater, from which the star system originated, was still the culturally dominant medium. Books on single stars and entries in reference books were constructed as biographies of artists, which followed the career of a person who discovered his artistic vocation early in life and found his or her fulfillment in films (Porten; Holberg; Liedtke; Lohmeyer). For most stars, a direct connection with theater was established: Claire Rommer, Mady Christians, Otto Gebühr, Conrad Veidt, Willy Fritsch, Ernst Hofmann, and Emil Jannings were all said to have worked for Max Reinhardt, the famous Austro-German theater director. Alternatively, a career in film was shown not to fall short of standards set in high culture: Henny Porten came from a family of theater people, Lee Parry from a family of artists, and Lil Dagover was married to a theater actor. Eighty-one percent of all 300 biographical entries from the *Lexikon des Films* (Encylopedia of Film) of 1926 refer to an artistic background, with 73 percent of the actors stating that they were based in "legitimate" theater (that is, that they had either had theatrical training or had begun their career in theater); 8 percent stated that they had started out in ballet or opera. After subtracting those who did not give any information, this leaves only 9 percent who had begun their career in films directly (Mühsam/Jacobsohn). Whether these claims are true or not is of no importance; rather, the important conclusion to be drawn from these biographies is that being connected to the legitimate theater was an essential part of an actor's image, even when he or she was a top star in films. This discourse on film stars as artists functioned, among other things, as a means of legitimatizing the actors who worked in a medium that was not yet fully accepted socially in Germany in the 1920s.

Within this discourse on art, the success of stars with their audience was usually explained by their artistic merits, namely their skill in portraying their roles: "Harry Liedtke's popularity is not only due to his masculine appearance and his artistic versatility; it is primarily due to the fact that he is one of those actors who internalize their parts. He studies his roles in minute detail, because he is simply a consummate artist" (*Das Harry Liedtke Buch*, 46). However, with the audiences at large, these artistic merits were not really the primary reasons for a Weimar film star's popularity; rather, they were smitten with personal characteristics such as elegance and charm. A survey conducted in 1927 by the *Deutsche Filmwoche*, which asked respondents to name not only the actors they liked most but also those they thought to be the most accomplished performers, shows that the number of actors named in both categories is relatively small: only six of the most popular female actors and two of the most popular male actors also appear in the category of best actors. For example, Harry Liedtke made the top ten in both categories, but in the category of "most popular" he received 1,556 votes, whereas in the category of "best actor" he received only 400 votes.[16]

The German film industry's unwillingness to engage in a discourse on the stars' private lives did not completely correspond to the audience's demand. In the readers' sections of popular cinema magazines (for example, *Die Filmwoche, Neue Illustrierte Filmwoche, Film-Magazin,* or *Filmfreund*), fans asked at least as many questions about their stars' private lives as about their professional activities. The questions asked most often concerned personal characteristics (such as eye or hair color or off-screen personality), whether the star was married or single, or what the name and profession of his or her spouse was. In contrast to the editorial parts of the magazines, in which only the films and professional lives of the stars were discussed, the readers' sections were set in very small type and thus already marginalized by their visual layout. The readers' sections not only show the audience's curiosity concerning the private lives of their stars but also reveal that this demand was not always satisfied, because not all of the printed questions received an answer (which incidentally implies that the questions themselves were probably not manipulated and thus give a fairly accurate representation of readers' interests). Editors seemed willing to give answers only when the private information requested was in some way part of the stars' professional life. For example, the spouse's name and profession were only revealed if he or she was also connected with film or theater: "Dear film fan Erika [. . .], in answer to your request I regret that I may not tell you the names of Alphons Fryland's and Harry Piel's wives. But since neither of them has anything to do with films, the names could not really be of any interest to you anyway."[17]

Art films, which are often identified with German films of the 1920s, only make up a small part of the total German film output during this decade. Since larger companies had greater capacities for innovation, and since Erich Pommer, Ufa's head of production between 1923 and 1926, was dedicated to furthering film art, Ufa became the center of creative filmmaking. Due to uncompromising artistic ideals, overly extravagant production methods, and misjudgments in marketing Ufa almost went bankrupt. In March 1927, media mogul Alfred Hugenberg's group took over Ufa, and the company was completely reorganized by Ludwig Klitzsch. The aim was to consistently orient films toward audience demand and to make production processes economically efficient. Around 1928/29, Ufa, in accordance with its new market orientation, adapted the presentation of its stars more to the audience's wishes.[18] Compared with other publications, magazines that were connected with Ufa in one way or another began to reveal more information about the stars' private lives. The new postulate was: "Film stars do not have any 'private affairs.' They must not be allowed to have any. To whom they are engaged, to whom they are married, whom they divorced and why, and why there are no children — all this must be openly discussed in public" (Roth, 635, 638). Beginning in 1929, information on spouses can be found in greater frequency, even when they were not artists by profession. For example, the interested reader could learn that Henny Porten was married to Dr. Wilhelm von Kaufmann, a medical doctor, and Claire Rommer was the wife of Adolf Strenger, a businessman. Nevertheless, the discourse remained centered on the star as artist, and scandals were still taboo.

Interestingly enough, in contrast to German stars, the private lives of US stars, such as Mary Pickford and Norma Talmadge, were indeed discussed at some length in the editorial parts of German film magazines.[19] However, even though information on the private exploits of film stars was important to fans, it was not important enough to make German fans turn to US stars. The favorite performers of the period all shared their German audience's culture. Even the new form of reporting about stars' private lives in the late 1920s remained true to the basic cultural consensus between producers and audiences, which was the condition for stars to be accepted in Germany, but it closed the gap between supply and demand that had existed before.

The Cultural Specificity of Weimar's Star System

In many ways, the contours of the Weimar film-star system were already established earlier, during the Wilhelmine period. The film-star system emerged around 1910 in connection with the multiple-reel narrative feature film, which became a cornerstone of film programs in permanent cinemas. Prior to and during the First World War, film series featuring prominent actors were the primary marketing device for popular films.

Films were launched as part of a series bearing the name of the star performer, for example, Danish actress Asta Nielsen headed her own "Asta Nielsen-Serie," directed by Urban Gad. Some popular performers even established their own production companies, such as Ellen Richter (1893–1969), who starred in her own exotic adventure films, known as the "Ellen Richter Serie," from around 1913 until the mid-1920s.

In addition, it can be shown that the film-star system followed the model of the already established and very successful nineteenth-century theater-star system. At that time, a theater-star system developed in Germany, based on what contemporaries called *Virtuosentum*, that is, an elite of virtuoso performers (Berns; Stettner). Neither the play nor the playwright, but rather the star actor was the main attraction for the audience. These celebrated star performers traveled, working with different theater companies, and appeared in classical plays as well as in contemporary entertainment.

The German film-star system of directors followed the model of the *Regietheater*, the theater tradition emerging in the early twentieth century that gave the stage director primary artistic and managerial control (Hays; Girshausen). It fell to the directors to interpret and stage a given play according to their particular artistic vision. In addition, just as German film stars were to do later, German theater star performers distinguished themselves through artistic merit and their ability to deliver brilliant performances in different character roles. Theater stars were regarded as the more talented and proficient actors, the virtuosi of their art, as a contemporary observer noted in 1881 (Friedmann). In order to differentiate themselves from other actors, stars often developed idiosyncratic styles of performance, for example Charlotte Wolter's famous scream. This is not to say that American theater stars did not develop their own idiosyncratic styles of performance, but in the United States performers were primarily differentiated by the individual personal characteristics that they displayed in their private lives (McArthur). The respective theater systems, then, can be said to prefigure and to contribute to the different dynamics of movie stardom that were to emerge later in Germany and the United States.

If we ask why such a nationally specific — German — film-star system came to exist, then we also need to consider a central difference in the basic mentalities of German and United States audiences by analyzing the discourses and social institutions that were a driving force for building dominant national and cultural identities. The US film-star system's culturally specific moral discourse on the stars' private lives is based in the Puritan tradition. According to the predestination doctrine of Calvinist Protestantism, secular success is a sign of election by God. A successful person is therefore, or should be, a good person who has nothing to hide. If such an elected person fails to behave morally, he or she will be punished more strongly than anyone else. In the United States, as sociologist Max Weber noted, this punishment is exerted not by the church but by the public, because the

Puritan sects abolished the church as a centralized institution (Weber, 279–317). Thus, the public became the central controlling power of morally upright and virtuous behavior, especially in terms of monitoring successful members of society. Like other Europeans, most Germans were not subject to the need to prove themselves incessantly in everyday life, because even though the two dominant religious denominations — Lutheran Protestantism as well as Roman Catholicism — maintain the notion of Original Sin, there was always the option of receiving absolution or to atone for sins by routine church practices. Sins were considered a private matter, and it was not the public but the church that sanctioned behavior. The severest punishment in US sects was to exclude sinners from their communities, but European churches would rarely excommunicate members. The persistence of such religious and cultural traditions explains how and why Weimar Germany's film elites refused to publicize their private affairs, because the culture in which they operated regarded such affairs as a private matter.

In the United States, then, the art discourse was subordinated to the moral discourse, whereas in Germany, the art discourse was relatively independent of moral demands. Due to the high status of art within the bourgeois system of German culture, all German actors — whether they were stars or not — always sought to define themselves as artists. The high status of art in German culture was in turn also deeply rooted in religious traditions. While American Puritanism condemned art, the two dominant religious traditions in Germany took a different stance: Roman Catholicism supported it, and Lutheran Protestantism never managed to suppress its importance in German culture. In addition, beholden to the German tradition of *Bildung* — the value placed on the cultivation of aesthetic refinement through education — Weimar Germany's film elites in their self-fashioning placed higher value on artistic achievement than on mass popularity. As shown above, actors, directors, and producers sought to validate their status as artists by laying claim to the cultural cache of legitimate theater.

Often enough, this tendency created a somewhat odd asymmetry between supply and demand: since they defined themselves as artists and refused to publicize their private affairs, it appears that the stars — who exercised a great deal of control over the production and dissemination of their public images — did not completely satisfy their audience's demand for intimacy. Whereas German audiences showed a keen interest in the personal and private lives of their "film darlings" — without, however, making stars test cases and role models of moral norms — the performers themselves sought to be appreciated and admired primarily for their artistic merits. We thus find an interesting contradiction at the core of Weimar film culture: the film industry catered to a mass audience with a great deal of economic and financial success, while at the same time refusing to yield completely to the demands of the marketplace. Even though Weimar Cinema operated under the laws of a market economy, its star system indicates that for the key players profit was not the sole — or even the primary — motivation.

— Translated by Annemone Ligensa

Notes

[1] Not much work has been done on nationally specific star systems. See Fischer/Landy and Redmond/Holmes.

[2] See my theory on stardom; Garncarz, "Die Schauspielerin wird Star: Ingrid Bergman — eine öffentliche Kunstfigur."

[3] For a case study see Garncarz, "Playing Garbo: How Marlene Dietrich Conquered Hollywood."

[4] Anon. "1138 Kinos gaben 4702 Stimmen."; see also Garncarz, "Hollywood in Germany."

[5] See the advertisements for the premiere of this film in *LichtBildBühne,* 12 December 1925, 7; and 19 December 1925, 17.

[6] The list of the top ten Weimar film stars is reprinted in full in Garncarz, "Made in Germany." 264.

[7] Cf. Anon. "Movies and Movie Stars." I am indebted to Annemone Ligensa for this information.

[8] Anon. "Wer ist der beliebteste Filmstar?"

[9] Compare the top ten stars, in Garncarz, "Made in Germany," 264, with the list of the top ten films reprinted in Garncarz, "Hollywood in Germany," 122.

[10] See Garncarz, "Art & Industry."

[11] On Ufa, see Lipschütz, 33–44, Bock/Töteberg, and Kreimeier; on Emelka, see Putz.

[12] "Von glücklichen Ehen und unglücklicher Reklame."

[13] "Pazzo's Briefe," *Filmwoche* 44 and 28.

[14] "Große Sensation gefällig?"

[15] "Harry heiratet."

[16] "Das Resultat unserer Rundfrage," 14.

[17] "Pazzo's Briefe," 652.

[18] See the Minutes of Ufa Board Meetings on 29 May 1928 and 10 August 1928 (in the Bundesarchiv-Filmarchiv, Berlin).

[19] "Von glücklichen Ehen und unglücklicher Reklame," 334–35.

Works Cited

Anon. "1138 Kinos gaben 4702 Stimmen." *Film-Kurier,* 2 June 1930.

———. "Große Sensation gefällig?" *Film-Kurier,* 19 December 1925.

———. "Harry heiratet." *Film-Kurier,* 27 March 1928.

———. *Das Harry Liedtke Buch.* Vienna: Film-Buch und Zeitungsverlag der Illustrierten Film- und Kinorundschau *Mein Film,* 1928.

———. "Movies and Movie Stars." *Fortune,* July 1937.

———. "Pazzo's Briefe." *Filmwoche* 28 (1925): 652.

———. "Pazzo's Briefe." *Filmwoche* 44 (1925): 1046.

———. "Das Resultat unserer Rundfrage." *Deutsche Filmwoche* 11 (18 March 1927): 14.

———. "Von glücklichen Ehen und unglücklicher Reklame." *Filmwoche* 17 (1924): 334–35.

———."Wer ist der beliebteste Filmstar?" *Film-Kurier,* 18 July 1923.

Alberoni, Francesco. "The Powerless 'Elite': Theory and Sociological Research on the Phenomenon of the Stars." In *Sociology of Mass Communications,* edited by Dennis McQuail, 75–98. Middlesex, NY: Penguin, 1976.

Berns, Ulrich. *Das Virtuosengastspiel auf der deutschen Bühne.* Cologne: Selbstverlag, 1959.

Bock, Hans-Michael, and Michael Töteberg, eds. *Das Ufa-Buch.* Frankfurt am Main: Zweitausendeins, 1992.

de Cordova, Richard. *Picture Personalities: The Emergence of the Star System in America.* Urbana and Chicago: U of Illinois P, 2000.

Delmont, Joseph. "Filmlieblinge." *Neue Illustrierte Filmwoche* 23 (1924).

Dyer, Richard. *Stars.* London: British Film Institute, 1982.

Fischer, Lucy, and Marcia Landy, eds. *Stars: The Film Reader.* New York and London: Routledge, 2004.

Friedmann, Siegwart: "Über das Virtuosentum in der Schauspielkunst." In *Vor den Coulissen: Originalblätter von Celebritäten des deutschen Theaters,* edited by Josef Lewinsky, 43–47. Berlin: Hofmann & Comp., 1881.

Garncarz, Joseph. "Art & Industry: Germany Cinema of the 1920s." In *The Silent Cinema Reader,* edited by Lee Grieveson and Peter Krämer, 389–400. New York and London: Routledge, 2004.

———. "Hollywood in Germany: The Role of American Films in Germany, 1925–1990." In *Hollywood in Europe: Experiences of a Cultural Hegemony,* edited by David W. Ellwood and Rob Kroes, 94–135. Amsterdam: VU UP, 1994.

———. "Made in Germany: Multiple-Language Versions and the Early German Sound Cinema." In *"Film Europe" and "Film America": Cinema, Commerce, and Cultural Exchange, 1920–1939,* edited by Andrew Higson and Richard Maltby, 49–73. Exeter, UK: U of Exeter P, 1999.

———. "Playing Garbo: How Marlene Dietrich Conquered Hollywood." In *Dietrich Icon,* edited by Gerd Gemünden and Mary R. Desjardins, 103–18. Durham, NC: Duke U P, 2007.

———. "Die Schauspielerin wird Star: Ingrid Bergman — eine öffentliche Kunstfigur." In *Die Schauspielerin: Zur Kulturgeschichte der weiblichen Bühnenkunst,* edited by Renate Möhrmann, 321–44. Frankfurt am Main: Insel, 1989.

Girshausen, Theo. "Regietheater." In *Theaterlexikon,* vol. 2: *Epochen, Ensembles, Figuren, Spielformen, Begriffe, Theorien,* edited by C. B. Sucher, 348–52. Munich: dtv, 1996.

Hays, Michael. "Theater and Mass Culture: The Case of the Director." *New German Critique* 29 (1983): 133–46.

Hens, Gerold, and Ursula Neeb. "Auf Wiedersehen im nächsten Film: Filmstars auf Bildpostkarten." *Fotogeschichte: Beiträge zur Geschichte und Ästhetik der Fotografie* 67 (1998): 39–50.

Holberg, Gustav. *Henny Porten: Eine Biographie unserer beliebten Filmkünstlerin.* Berlin: Verlag der LichtBildBühne, n.d. [1920].

Jason, Alexander. *Handbuch der Filmwirtschaft.* Berlin: Verlag für Presse, Wirtschaft und Politik, 1930.

Koszarski, Richard. *An Evening's Entertainment: The Age of the Silent Feature Picture, 1915–1928.* Berkeley, Los Angeles, and London: U of California P, 1994.

Kreimeier, Klaus. *The Ufa Story: A History of Germany's Greatest Film Company, 1918–1945.* New York: Hill & Wang, 1996.

Liedtke, Harry. *Vergeßt mich nicht.* Berlin: Der Buchladen Kurfürstendamm, 1927.

Ligensa, Annemone. "Stardom after the Event." In *Louise Brooks: Rebellin, Ikone, Legende,* edited by Günter Krenn and Karin Moser, 172–211. Munich: edition text + kritik, 2006.

Lipschütz, Rahel. *Der Ufa-Konzern: Geschichte, Aufbau und Bedeutung im Rahmen des deutschen Filmgewerbes.* Berlin: Energiadruck, 1932.

Lohmeyer, Walter Gottfried. *Das Otto Gebühr-Buch.* Berlin: Scherl, 1927.

McArthur, Benjamin. *Actors and American Culture, 1880–1920.* Iowa City: U of Iowa P, 2000.

Minutes of Ufa Board Meetings on 29 May 1928 and 10 August 1928, Bundesarchiv-Filmarchiv, Berlin.

Mühsam, Kurt. *Film und Kino.* Dessau: Dünnhaupt, 1927.

Mühsam, Kurt, and Egon Jacobsohn. *Lexikon des Films.* Berlin: Verlag der LichtBildBühne, 1926.

Pokorny, Michael, and John Sedgwick. "Stardom and the Profitability of Film Making: Warner Bros. in the 1930s." *Journal of Cultural Economics* 25 (2001): 157–84.

Pordes, Victor E. *Das Lichtspiel: Wesen, Dramaturgie, Regie.* Vienna: Lechner, 1919.

Porten, Henny. *Wie ich wurde.* Berlin: Volkskraft, 1919.

Putz, Petra. *Waterloo in Geiselgasteig: Die Geschichte des Münchner Filmkonzerns Emelka (1919–1933) im Antagonismus zwischen Bayern und dem Reich.* Trier: WVT, 1996.

Redmond, Sean, and Su Holmes, eds. *Stardom and Celebrity: A Reader.* London: Sage, 2007.

Roth, Dr. R. "Sind Stars Privatpersonen?" *Filmwoche* 27 (1929): 635 and 638.

Sedgwick, John, and Michael Pokorny. "Movie Stars and the Distribution of Financially Successful Films in the Motion Picture Industry." *Journal of Cultural Economics* 23 (1999): 319–23.

Sennett, Richard. *The Fall of Public Man.* New York: Knopf, 1976.

Stettner, Anna. *"Wer ist ein Virtuose der Schauspielkunst?" Das Phänomen des Virtuosentums im deutschen Sprechtheater des 19. Jahrhunderts.* Munich: microfiche edition, 1998.

Thompson, Kristin. *Exporting Entertainment: America in the World Film Market, 1907–34.* London: British Film Institute, 1985.

Weber, Max. "Die protestantischen Sekten und der Geist des Kapitalismus." 1919/20. Reprinted in *Die protestantische Ethik I: Eine Aufsatzsammlung,* 279–317. Gütersloh: Mohn, 1984.

8: *Schaulust*: Sexuality and Trauma in Conrad Veidt's Masculine Masquerades

Elizabeth Otto

*Something apparently in between star and character type. The ador-
ing young girls want to see him as a star; a certain type of mature
woman as the above mentioned something in between; but we only
want to see him as a character type, for that's where the slim, sinewy
ascetic is totally at home. He is the personified spirit of the third
dimension, thus the fourth dimension. When he wants to, his eyes look
into the fourth realm, his visage becomes transparent and seems as if
it has been eaten away by all his passions. His dark soul is visible on
his face! And then he even plays upon this soul, as if it were a tortured,
screeching violin. He is an indispensable enrichment, a type all his
own!*

— Heinz Salmon, "Charaktertyp" 1919[1]

CONTEMPORARY COMMENTATORS RHAPSODIZED about Conrad Veidt's
unusual appeal to his public, and Erika and Klaus Mann would later
write that almost no actor was as popular as Veidt in interwar Germany
(95). As we see in the above quotation, as early as 1919 film critic Heinz
Salmon emphasized Veidt's multiple attractions for his fans, who saw him
as a standard love object, as spiritual and an artist, and as an otherworldly
ascetic. Writing three years later, critic Fritz Scharf discussed Veidt as a
cultural phenomenon with wide-reaching influence: "Damsels from ages
eight through eighty who are even mildly infected by the hysteria have
each made HIM an altar in their more or less roomy bosoms; for pale looking lads, HE is their life's goal personified" (43).[2]

In *Hinter den Kulissen* (Behind the Scenes), a 1927 photomontage by
Bauhaus artist Marianne Brandt, Conrad Veidt's face emerges out of an
inky darkness to nuzzle the head of a dreaming New Woman (fig. 8.1).
Veidt seems both alluring and — with his gaunt features, sleepy eyes, and
almost leering smile — somehow sinister. He presents a stark contrast to
his pendant figure on the New Woman's right, Douglas Fairbanks as a
grinning allegory of Hollywood's superficial appeal. Veidt's face is served
up on a crescent-moon strip of white to frame it as a figment of the New
Woman's imagination and the subject of her fantasy. The theater-like darkness of this photomontage frames Veidt and Fairbanks as opposing poles

Fig. 8.1. Marianne Brandt, Hinter den Kulissen *(Behind the Scenes), 1927.*
Collection Stiftung Bauhaus Dessau.

of masculine allure on display for a desiring, modern female viewer. Significantly, Brandt's work uses the visual to evoke the tactile. The female figure floats with closed eyes in a mysterious space, surrounded by men she cannot see but upon whom she mentally focuses as she feels the stroking of a disembodied hand upon her back. Brandt's photomontage suggests how, for Germany's interwar viewing public, Veidt's appearance could evoke an array of emotional content, including sensuality and mystery. Indeed, his face alone could conjure a particularly visceral and embodied response, which was a powerful imprint of his screen presence.

Thomas Elsaesser has pointed out how Siegfried Kracauer "rightly recognized how many of the films from the early 1920s dealt with specifically *male* anxieties centered on vision, perception, and fear of symbolic castration" (39). Brandt's montage and Kracauer's analysis both highlight the focus on masculinity that was so essential to Weimar Cinema. What fascinated audiences was the power and the mutability of Veidt's performances as wounded, dangerous, and sexualized.

While many of the characters that Veidt played might have seemed unappealing on the surface — evil rulers, crazed killers, outcasts, and even Death, in *Unheimliche Geschichten* (Eerie Tales; Richard Oswald, 1919) — Veidt's desirability also formed a persistent subtext in many of his films. Veidt's fans saw him as tremendously handsome and sexually attractive, "quite a heart-throb," according to film historian Richard Dyer ("Less," 14). Veidt was also considered by his public to be a paradigmatic masculine ideal. A 1930 essay in the culture and literary magazine *Uhu* posits Veidt as a male type who was being copied by nearly all young men of the day (von Hollander, 223–26). The accompanying cartoon by Erich Godal shows a menacing Conrad Veidt double as a darkly brooding, discontented, and dangerous-looking barber about to lather up a corpulent customer (fig. 8.2). Veidt appeared in Germany's first gay-rights film, *Anders als die Andern* (Different from the Others; Richard Oswald, 1919), and thus became a hero of Weimar's burgeoning gay culture and a symbol of the sexual openness that flourished despite continued repression in the new democracy. At the same time, the gender bending aspects of his star sign — the collection of ideas and desires associated with a star through his film roles and media coverage, and even in gossip about him — were important in the way that they offered heterosexual female viewers a lust object who might not be marriageable and thus not threatening to women's newfound freedoms. Not only was Veidt one of the most popular stars of the Weimar period, but in many ways he seems to have embodied essential aspects of it. He often appeared to epitomize a new masculinity; in other roles he seemed feminized. This duplicity also came out in his frequent representations of duality and forms of the *Doppelgänger* or double. These complexities in Veidt's public persona, as Dyer has pointed out, made him the quintessential Weimar star ("Less," 15; Eisner, 109).

Fig. 8.2. Erich Godal, "The role model of Conrad Veidt lives in thousands of lads' hearts and is copied and empathized with as much as possible." Uhu, January 1930.

As this essay and my exploration of Veidt's films will show, it was precisely the fact that Veidt could be so many different things to different fans that made him one of the best-loved stars of the Weimar period. I explore what exactly it was that appealed to Veidt's many and vastly varied fan groups by considering his star sign as a semiotic and cultural text, following Dyer's work on the culture of stars (*Stars*, 10, 18). Dyer has himself pointed to ambiguities in Veidt's star sign that made him both widely appealing and disturbing, or even repulsive ("Less," 14–15). Above all, essential to Veidt's star sign was the fact that it functioned in multiple ways, allowing him to be a wounded man with a past, a gay icon, a dangerous temptation for heterosexual women, and a point of identification for both hetero- and homosexual male viewers. Before turning to close analyses of key examples of Veidt's films, I want to situate his star sign in relation to issues in war, representation, and the construction of masculinity.

The First World War was the most powerful referent for Veidt's interwar roles. His own experience of war was short-lived. He served briefly on the Eastern Front and participated in the Battle of Warsaw, before returning to acting full-time because of his health (Battle, 9–10). While his participation was short, in some of his film roles he became a cipher for aspects of others' war trauma, as Anjeana Hans notes in her essay in this volume. Veidt's portrayals in a wide range of films offered a representation of types who, like the ex-soldiers in interwar society, had killed on the orders of others and were haunted by their past crimes. And many of the roles Veidt played involved exposing a wounded nature and exploring newfound vulnerability, problems that many soldiers had to deal with when they returned home. Thus his acting enabled mourning for the losses of the war, a response to aggressive, militarized masculinity, and reflection on new forms of modern manhood.

A master of Expressionist acting, Veidt was able to turn silent film's primary limitation — that actors could not use their voices to express themselves as they could on the stage — to his advantage in order to create gripping performances. But perhaps even more important for Veidt's acting than his body were his strong facial expressions, and his face was often praised for being mask-like. The Veidt phenomenon in Weimar Cinema can best be understood as a response to a crisis in masculinity, which revealed manliness as a form of masquerade. This crisis arose as a response to the First World War and the resulting loss of belief in an essential manhood.

While artifice, superficiality, and the masquerade have traditionally been viewed as the unique purview of women, the conventions of masculinity are as much constructions as their feminine counterparts (Brod, 13). Interwar masculinity can fruitfully be understood in terms of tools such as Joan Rivier's concept of masquerade or Judith Butler's theory of gender as performance; these have been essential for examining constructions of womanhood and homosexuality, identity positions that are considered as culturally marked categories. There is considerable evidence that events of the First World War, including the mass conscription of men, the total mobilization of culture and society, the unprecedented number of wounded, and Germany's defeat, led to an unhinging of the construction of reified masculinity in the war's wake. Weimar manhood existed in a never-before-seen damaged and complex state. In Veidt's foregrounding of a performative, wildly varied, and shifting masculinity — one that often suggested a wounded nature and evoked alternatives to male heterosexuality — he epitomized the interwar attempt to come to grips with the past and the search for new ways of being a man.

Veidt performed in over seventy films during the interwar period (Soister, ix–xii), but the depth and breadth of his Weimar roles has been lost to history. In order to analyze his wide-ranging and complex appeal, I will discuss a few of his surviving films from the interwar period, with a particular focus on four of them. While Veidt's traits often carry over from one film and film genre to another, two of these foreground his desirability, *Anders als die Andern* (Different from the Others; Richard Oswald, 1919) and the remake of *Der Student von Prag* (The Student of Prague; Henrik Galeen, 1926).[3] The other two explore potentially violent characters: *Das Cabinet des Dr. Caligari* (The Cabinet of Dr. Caligari; Robert Wiene, 1920) and *Orlacs Hände* (The Hands of Orlac; Robert Wiene, 1924). The notion of *Schaulust*, which appears in the title of this essay — denoting curiosity or, literally, the desire to look — embraces two essential aspects of Veidt's star appeal. It conveys the drive to view things that are horrible or frightening; these are often references to traumas of the past. But the term *Schaulust* also suggests the idea of sexually charged looking and erotic spectacle. Both of these aspects are essential to what made Veidt one of the most successful and compelling stars of the Weimar period.

Richard Oswald's 1919 *Anders als die Andern*, which survives only in fragmentary form, has often been seen as the paradigmatic *Aufklärungsfilm* or "enlightenment film," a genre of educational cinema that most often treated social aspects of sexuality (see Jill Smith's essay in this volume). Between 1918 and 1922 Veidt acted in a number of Oswald's *Aufkärungsfilme* on such themes as §218, Germany's anti-abortion law (*Es werde Licht!* [Let There Be Light! 1917/1918]), and prostitution (*Die Prostitution* [Prostitution, 1919]), films made specifically to advocate legal and moral change. In general, Veidt's participation in these films linked his star sign to leftist politics and the sexual counterculture of the Weimar Republic, and it encouraged the public to see him through a sexualized lens. As Dyer points out, because *Aufklärungsfilme* presented educational material that many felt to be out-and-out pornography, audiences were already primed to see relatively tame scenes as titillating ("Less," 13).

Anders als die Andern was a successful film in its day, and it had a major impact because of the controversy it caused (Dyer, "Less," 9; Steakley,

Anders, 86–158). While its theme is tragic love between two men, the focus of the film is Germany's §175, an anti-homosexuality law that led to the common practice of blackmailing men who were even suspected of being gay. Sexologist Magnus Hirschfeld cowrote, coproduced, and appeared in the film; by 1904 he estimated that at least two thousand homosexuals were the victims of blackmail annually (Steakley, "Cinema," 186).

In addition to exploring personal tragedies caused by §175, *Anders als die Andern* provides an early template for a repeating theme in Veidt's work: the guilty man who must atone for past crimes. In the film, Veidt plays the concert violinist Paul Körner, typical of the many skilled, artistic types he would continue to play in the future. These artistic attributes also correspond with Veidt's reputation as a gifted stage actor, which he had earned as a member of Max Reinhardt's famed theater ensemble. The film combines elements of a melodramatic love story, a classical *Bildungsroman* — a story focused on the education and development of a young protagonist — and the didacticism typical of the *Aufklärungsfilm*. This didacticism is visible principally in Hirschfeld's appearances in the film as an expert witness explaining homosexuality as a natural phenomenon and arguing for its decriminalization.

As Dyer asserts, much of *Anders als die Andern* is at pains to emphasize ideal love, embodied by Paul's protégé Kurt Sivers (Fritz Schulz), over the base sexuality exuded by Franz Bolleck (Reinhold Schünzel) ("Less," 14). This structure reveals Paul as a man with a past. After only the briefest of flirtations at a gay dance, Paul invites Franz home with him. But instead of finally being able to fulfill the homosexual desires with which we have seen him struggle from a young age, Paul finds himself the victim of Franz's plot to blackmail him using §175. These events haunt Paul once he meets and seems to find happiness with Kurt; Franz lurks in the bushes and materializes like a figment of Paul's own guilty conscience. As time goes on, Franz's demands for money increase until Paul goes to the authorities. Franz then officially accuses him of homosexuality; Paul is publically tried, convicted, and humiliated. After serving his time in prison, he finds his career as a pianist ruined, and he kills himself. In death, however, the broken body of Veidt's character displayed in his casket inspires love, new understanding, and regret on the part of his family and friends.

In *Anders als die Andern*, key characters of both sexes are smitten with Paul, and they seem to model and reflect the admiration and desire felt by many of Veidt's fans. But most important was the film's status as a touchstone of Weimar's gay liberation movement. Letters received and published by Hirschfeld attest to the public's perception of the film and Veidt's performance as providing a documentary-like look at the tragic contradictions of contemporary gay life. Many of these letters expressed profound gratitude to Hirschfeld for having revealed the painful reality of §175 to the public (quoted in Steakley, *Anders*, 72, 74–75).

Subculture gossip would have made Veidt's own sexuality an important intertext for this film. Most historians assume Veidt's heterosexuality, probably because of his three well-publicized marriages. Others state that he was gay, but they do so without elaborating on any evidence or complicating notions of identity (Doty, 26). Christopher Isherwood's memory of Veidt's regal presence at a gay costume ball provides a clear connection to Weimar homosexual culture (21). Veidt's participation in such events helped secure his place as one of the patron saints of Weimar's gay community, even as the mainstream press continued to focus on his life as husband and father.

At the same time, *Anders als die Andern* need not have disrupted his female fans' sexual fantasies; the film presented Veidt in what was already becoming a standard role for him: the ardent lover. Women in the audience seem to have looked past the fact that the object of his affections in this case was male. But the film also reached out directly to female fans in different ways: according to some of the letters received by Hirschfeld, many women saw in Paul their sons, brothers, and friends who were potential victims of § 175 (quoted in Steakley, *Anders*, 74–75). Thus, near the start of Veidt's film career, his viewers seemed to enjoy seeing him represent sensitive and wounded masculinity. This trend, along with themes of guilt and redemption, plays out in subsequent roles.

Robert Wiene's *Das Cabinet des Dr. Caligari* of the following year made Veidt famous as a ghostly, malevolent, supernatural force and a sleepwalking menace who is controlled by another. It was around this film that many aspects of Veidt's star sign coalesced. In *Caligari*, Veidt's slim, jersey-clad body becomes a linear work of art interacting with the film's dizzying and claustrophobic mise-en-scène. In the film Francis (Friedrich Fehér) and his friend Alan (Hans Heinrich von Twardowski) go to the local fair and see the sideshow of Dr. Caligari (Werner Krauß) and his somnambulist Cesare (Veidt). Cesare predicts the imminent death of Alan, and, indeed, he is found dead the next morning. The chaos deepens when Cesare kidnaps Jane (Lil Dagover), the woman with whom both Francis and Alan are in love. It is ultimately revealed that Dr. Caligari is the assumed name of the head of a local insane asylum. He has become fixated on a medieval story of a man named Caligari who was able to make a somnambulist murder at his command, and the modern Caligari has been compelling Cesare to do just that. When, at the end of the film, Dr. Caligari is shown the body of the dead Cesare, the malevolent doctor goes insane. As in *Anders als die Andern*, the sight of Veidt's body laid out is a turning point near the end of the film.

Caligari is one of the most often discussed films of the Weimar period, for which it has been taken to be paradigmatic (Scheunemann, "Double," 125). At the end, the film returns to the situation that opened it, and it is revealed to us that Francis is actually a patient in the asylum and that Dr.

Caligari is in fact the kindly director of the "real" institution. Thus the entire story is presented as the figment of Francis's diseased mind. Because of this frame, *Caligari* has been the subject of an influential critique by Kracauer since, he argues, the film brackets off and ultimately dismisses its own criticism of authoritarianism (43). Recently several scholars have offered more nuanced interpretations. Stefan Andriopoulos situates *Caligari* in relation to early twentieth-century viewing habits and contemporaneous medical debates on hypnosis and the power of criminal suggestion. He finds that ". . . the paradoxical narrative structure of Wiene's film can also be read as a self-reference to the 'peculiar oscillation' in which, according to [psychologist Hugo] Münsterberg, the spectators of early cinema alternated between the insight into the mediality of the filmic projections and an intermittent suspension of disbelief" (102). Julia Walker writes of *Caligari* as reflecting on a conflict in changing models of the self. She finds that "by bracketing this story inside the story of Francis's delusion, the film creates an endless displacement of certainty" (621). Identity is in flux, and, in the end, Frances — and we, as viewers — are haunted by Cesare, even as we are left to wonder if he too was only a helpless inmate in the asylum.

In a postwar world in which many women did not understand the men who came back to them, the figure of Veidt's Cesare made overt the imagery of a ghostly shadow of a man who lives among normal humans but is himself barely alive. Veidt's character murders at Caligari's command and appears to act only in response to the doctor's impulses. One of the film's authors, Hans Janowitz, later wrote that with hindsight he and coauthor Carl Mayer came to see the film as treating "the corresponding connection between our Doctor Caligari and the great authoritative power of a government that we hated, and which had subdued us into an oath, forcing conscription on those in opposition to its official war aims, compelling us to murder and to be murdered" (Janowitz, 224–25). Viewed through the lens of his role in a tyrannical system, the figure of Cesare becomes an object of pity as much as fear. He commits horrible deeds, but through no will of his own. Veidt's character is an allegory of the postwar, traumatized male.

In his now classic study of proto-fascist masculinities, *Male Fantasies*, Klaus Theweleit — like Kracauer before him — explores the roots of Nazi ideology in post-First World War representations. Theweleit argues that for the men who became members of *Freikorps* (right wing paramilitary groups) a maintenance of control over the body's wholeness and its boundaries was psychologically essential (40). Through this they held on to their identities as soldiers, identities that were developed in the recently lost war. More importantly they stave off what Theweleit refers to as "the mass," a term that covers filth, animal nature, the enemy, and women, all of which the soldier male must avoid at all costs in order to maintain himself (3–7). Theweleit asserts that such organizations as the army and certain concepts, including culture, race, nation, and wholeness, aid in the

Fascist male's defense against the mass (43). Relying on psychoanalytic theory, Theweleit argues that a man who "heaves himself out of the mass" (he is quoting one Captain Berthold) becomes the phallus, or the phallic German (50–52).

But what happens to a soldier male who is drawn into the mass by, for example, embracing his darker nature, or associating with or falling for a woman? A look at Walter Benjamin's 1928 text, *The Origin of German Tragic Drama,* suggests an answer to this dilemma. For Benjamin, breaking down the boundaries of the self and opening it up to that which is the most loathed can be the basis for making new meaning and for reinventing an older form of representation: allegory, in which the discarded fragments of the past can be brought together to create new meaning. For Benjamin, these fragments are akin to Baroque representations of gruesome death that ultimately point to resurrection and everlasting life. "And this is the essence of melancholy immersion: that its ultimate objects, in which it believes it can most fully secure for itself that which is vile, turn into allegories, and that these allegories fill out and deny the void in which they are represented" (232–33). Following on Benjamin's argument, we may theorize that the creation of masculine representations that evoke the war and do not maintain control over the body's boundaries might serve as a strategy to allegorize and explode militarized and potentially fascist constructions of manhood inherited by men of the post–First World War period, and to turn the war's wounded into allegories of future resurrection.

Thus, contrary to Kracauer's critique, and especially *because* of *Caligari*'s ambiguity, the film allows for an investigation of the underside of militarized masculinity. This occurs most powerfully in the foregrounding of Veidt's representation of a figure who is not able to take control of himself or to shore up his independent identity. Following on co-scriptwriter Janowitz's recollections, we may think of Cesare as a stand in for the millions of young men who, when the film premiered, had only recently returned from the war front. Thus framed, in the action of the film Cesare seems unable to regain a civilian identity, for he inappropriately continues to obey orders and kill once he has returned home from the front. Further, his abduction of Jane suggests that, like a rapist — another kind of war criminal — he cannot hold his sexual desires in check. And Cesare's physical appearance and movements suggest the actual dissolution of his bodily boundaries through his interaction with the film's disorienting sets (fig. 8.3). Kracauer later wrote that "when Conrad Veidt's Cesare prowled along a wall, it was as if the wall had exuded him" (70).

Perhaps most importantly, Veidt's Cesare is ambiguously gendered through an unusual mixture of masculine and feminine traits. His heterosexual masculinity is evinced through his murderous power and his desire for Jane, yet his clingy clothing and slender body correspond more to the

Fig. 8.3. Cesare (Conrad Veidt) and Jane (Lil Dagover) become part of the nightmarish décor in Robert Wiene's expressionist classic, The Cabinet of Dr. Caligari *(1920). Screenshot.*

interwar female bodily ideal of the "New Woman," later ambiguously idealized in Otto Dix's famous 1926 *Portrait of the Journalist Sylvia von Harden*. Other traits suggest Cesare's femininity or emasculation. In his pairing with Dr. Caligari, he is subservient. Alexander Doty reads the film as having a strong gay subtext, an interpretation that makes sense, given the fact that *Caligari* followed so closely on the heels of *Anders als die Andern*.[4] Further, Cesare is a seer, an ability most often linked to female witchcraft. We are told that he "knows all things" and that he can look into the future. Finally, Cesare is reduced to a child-like state by Dr. Caligari in scenes where we see him tending to Cesare's sleeping and waking and even spoon-feeding him. The character of Cesare is a powerful mixture: dangerously masculine, feminized, and infantilized, and this mixture spoke obliquely to the situation of returning veterans and the women around them. If *Anders als die Andern* dwells on Paul's guilty past, *Caligari* represents a Cesare who is unable to successfully integrate into the present.

Themes of past guilt and a present inability to be a part of society are revisited in another Robert Wiene film, *Orlacs Hände* of 1924, one of the

Fig. 8.4. Conrad Veidt acting out the trauma of loss of control over the body in Robert Wiene's Orlac's Hände *(1924). Screenshot.*

best examples of Veidt's expressive work. In this film, however, these themes are given an added twist: the man whose body is driven to kill is still in possession of his conscience. *Orlacs Hände* shows Veidt as a man who seems to be disintegrating before our eyes. Orlac, a concert pianist, comes to possess what he believes are the hands of a murderer through a train wreck and the magic of imaginary transplant science. In his virtuoso performance, Veidt creates a traumatic unity of disparate parts, and the film deepens key aspects of Veidt's star sign (fig. 8.4). He appears as the sensitive artist, a passionate husband, and a dangerous monster who is a threat to those he loves.

The film evokes the memory of the recent war as a crisis in creative production, as Orlac's hands go from being the site of his artistry to — through their jerking movements and ability to lead his body — signs of his wounded fracture and criminal potential. Where Orlac's hands were once his most prized appendages and his creative instruments, they become horrible prosthetics and grotesque, unwanted additions to his innocent body, which they render suspicious. Scenes of Orlac running through his mansion at the mercy of his hands show him controlled by their evil intent. Lotte Eisner commented on the complexity of Veidt's movements in this film, saying that he "dances a kind of Expressionistic ballet, bending and twisting extravagantly, simultaneously drawn and repelled by the murderous dagger held by hands which do not seem to belong to him" (144–45). When his father is found strangled, Orlac is unsure whether or not he has killed him, as are we. Orlac thus has hands which seem compelled to murder, even though his body and mind say he must not.[5] The doubling that is made literal in many of Veidt's films is here transposed directly onto Veidt's body.

As in *Caligari*, Veidt's character is shown in some part emasculated. For Orlac, this too occurs through his hands. Whereas he initially has a close relationship with his wife — we are told in an intertitle that he loves his piano as he does his wife's body, for example — after the accident, operation, and apparent revolt of his new hands, he vows that he will never again touch anyone, including his wife. The end of his marital intimacy is made overt in a scene in which Orlac lovingly strokes his piano and tells his wife Yvonne (Alexandra Sorina) how he longs to touch her but never will. The scene also relies on heavy symbolism to suggest his impotence: Orlac begins to play the piano, and he is no longer able to hit a single true note. One of the central questions of the film is whether the body or the mind will rule Orlac; this seems settled here, when the pianist's hands are shown to no longer be subject to his will. Veidt embodies mental and corporeal fragmentation through his expressive acting to reveal the heart of a man who cannot tell if he is being haunted by a murderer within or if he is simply going insane.

An evil double, a devil's bargain, a warrior's past, and themes of passion and attraction form the heart of one of Veidt's richest performances, the 1926 *Der Student von Prag*, a remake of Stellan Rye's famous 1913 film, directed by Henrik Galeen. The film is set in early nineteenth-century Bohemia and stars Veidt as Balduin, a student who, though he is the best fencer in all of Prague, is penniless. Through the enchantments of the Mephisto-like Scapinelli (Werner Krauß), he meets and falls in love with Countess Marguerite (Agnes Esterhazy), who is equally smitten but is out of his reach because of his poverty. Scapinelli offers Balduin a fortune in exchange for an item of his choice in Balduin's pitiful student room. The offer, of course, proves too good to be true; Scapinelli takes Balduin's reflection from the room's large mirror, and the story is thus a complex reworking of the classic *Doppelgänger* motif in which Veidt's characters so often find themselves enmeshed. Soon Balduin lives in a palace, performs good works, and has befriended the countess and her circle. But his reflection begins to make disturbing appearances and, worse yet, to commit crimes that eventually lead to Balduin's expulsion from the university and make him a social outcast among the aristocracy. Haunted and eventually hounded by his double, Balduin returns to his humble student room with its large mirror, where he confronts and shoots his reflection in the chest. The bullet lodges in his own heart, and he slowly collapses, gazing at his restored reflection a happy man.

Of the four films I address in this essay, Veidt's appeal as a conventional heartthrob is shown most clearly in *Der Student von Prag*. Here Veidt's character is a magical combination: he is attractive, strong, and masculine yet soulful and haunted (fig. 8.5). Through his skills at fencing, he evokes a gentlemanly soldier or warrior; yet he is also to be pitied since, initially, these skills do not help him out of poverty and subsequently they cannot protect him from his double. His desirability and soldierly iconography both function in a complex manner. Veidt's Balduin is introduced to us as the most admired of his fellow students for his legendary fencing abilities. And he is shown to be attractive to all the women who appear in the film: the countess, Lyduschka the peasant flower girl (Elizza La Porta), and even an older noblewoman at a ball. Together, these female characters' admiring gazes model a response to Veidt for female viewers. He is presented as a lust object to be looked at and as enviable for his physical prowess and status as a bit of a bad boy. Veidt appears as sexy but brooding and even — because of his double — dangerous. He is far from the marriageable type, and thus, as in previous roles, he offers the stuff of fantasy without compromising the newfound freedoms of New Woman viewers.

Despite Lyduschka's persistent mooning, Veidt plays a type of desirable man who is much deeper than such conventional film flames as Harry Liedtke or, recalling Brandt's photomontage, Douglas Fairbanks. Veidt's role is passionately played and the movie is given the intensity of an early horror film through Balduin's eerie double. who materializes and walks through iron gates via trick photography. Lotte Eisner gives a scene from *Der Student von Prag* as an example of atmospheric mood (*Stimmung*) in German film and its links to representations of the soul: ". . . a wavering trellis-work of hazy light is diffused through the slits of a Venetian blind on a parquet floor where the Student of Prague, in a moment of bliss, kneels at the feet of the woman he loves; the shimmer of the mullioned window is reflected in the tall mirror which, a few moments later, will betray his dark secret" (203). Here camerawork and story combine to reveal the depth of Balduin's passion for the countess. But as viewers we know that this love is doomed and made more poignant by the large mirror which, like a loaded gun bound to go off, will reveal that Balduin has no reflection.

While it is clear that Balduin is a lust object for all the women around him, it seems that the one who desires him most of all is the evil Scapinelli. In order to seduce him, Scapinelli pulls out all the stops, whipping up a supernatural storm and compelling the dogs and horses in a hunt to go where he wills them and thus to carry the countess to Balduin. While Scapinelli brings these two together, he does so because of his own desire to possess and control Balduin in reflected form. In this way, he is like

Fig. 8.5. Conrad Veidt as the pensive Balduin in Henrik Galeen's Der Student von Prag *(1926). Promotion still.*

Caligari controlling and dominating his somnambulist Cesare; significantly, the same actor, Werner Krauß, played both Scapinelli and Caligari.

Balduin has a guilty secret. But the story of his split self means that Balduin — like Cesare and Orlac — has no control over his criminal actions. Thus while others begin to fear or despise him as an agent of destruction, we must pity him, since we know that his only real crime is having been duped by Scapinelli in his desire to escape poverty. *Der Student von Prag* demonstrates Balduin's skill as a fencer, a romantic type of warrior. And the film represents his desirability and lovability even while it shows him to be unlovable and horrid through the vile acts that his double commits. We can read this combination of traits as an externalization of war guilt and a reflection on the interwar situation of veterans. Balduin lives in a society that ostensibly values his extraordinary fencing abilities, yet he is financially destitute. In this way, Veidt's character is akin to the Weimar Republic's war veterans, who had been promised rewards for their service and yet, in part because of rising inflation and food shortages, often felt treated as embarrassing burdens once they had returned home (Cohen, 62–63, 70). Further, there are questions about Balduin's mental state. While the theft of his reflection is presented as clear fact in the film's diegesis, or its narrative fictional world, other characters do not perceive any difference between the two Balduins. Thus it appears to many that he is behaving erratically and is no longer of sound mind. This too provides a point of identification for veterans who were surrounded by people who did not always understand their past experiences or their present behavior.

Lastly, the film points to the events of the First World War in its opening and closing scenes by showing a tombstone which reads, in part, "this monument is dedicated to Balduin, the best fencer in Prague. He gambled with Evil and lost." In 1926 the memory of the lost war had not yet faded; indeed, the tenth anniversary of the war's start had recently been marked with much controversy. Further, the harsh conditions of the Versailles Treaty may have made many Germans feel that they had indeed "gambled with Evil and lost." If Balduin is read as a stand-in for First World War veterans, the fact that he is ultimately only able to find happiness and a reintegration of his personality through death is a bleak conclusion to the film, but one which would have struck a chord with viewers.

Der Student von Prag combines traits amassed in Veidt's numerous previous films, including the significant surviving examples that I have analyzed here. Perhaps more than any other film, it showcases Veidt simultaneously as both a lust object and an object of sympathy or even pity. In addition, tropes of the skilled artist are here combined with the iconography of the soldier, and themes of homosexual desire are transposed into the relationship with Scapinelli.

Veidt's overwhelming popularity as a star was based in the repeating echoes of motifs through a wide array of roles in varied film genres. In performing as the sensitive gay musician, the effete but dangerous sleepwalker, the wounded and traumatized concert pianist, or the period-drama hero and lover, Veidt was also bringing to mind elements of various other masculine masquerades that spoke to essential discourses in Weimar culture: a gay man struggling with a homophobic society; a man with a criminal past; a lust object of modern men and women; and, a combination of all of these, an ex-soldier who must struggle to integrate into postwar society. Veidt's representation and exploration of these types and tropes was essential work as Weimar Germany struggled to heal from its past and imagine its future.

Notes

I wish to thank my fellow members of the 2006 German Film Institute hosted by the University of Michigan for the inspiring discussion of Veidt's work in several films, *Orlacs Hände* most prominent among them. In particular, I am grateful to Christian Rogowski, Anton Kaes, and Eric Rentschler for their insights, which helped to inspire and shape this essay.

The epigraph to this chapter is drawn from Heinz Salmon, "Charaktertyp," in *Film-Götter: Frechheiten aber Wahrheiten* (Berlin: Grübel, 1919); repr. in *Conrad Veidt: Lebensbilder: ausgewählte Fotos und Texte,* edited by Wolfgang Jacobsen (Berlin: Argon / Stiftung Deutsche Kinemathek, 1993), 15.

[1] "Ein scheinbares Mittelding zwischen Star und Charaktertyp. Die schwärmenden jungen Mädchen wollen ihn gern als Star, eine gewisse Spezie von reifen Frauen als obiges Mittelding; wir aber wollen ihn nur als Charaktertyp. Denn da ist der schlanke sehnige Asket vollkommen zu Hause. Er ist die personifizierte Vergeistigung der dritten Dimension, also vierte Dimension. Wenn er will, blicken seine Augen in das vierte Reich, sein Antlitz wird transparent, es scheint, es haben alle Leidenschaften daran genagt. Seine düstere Seele steht auf seinem Gesicht! Und dann spielt er auf dieser Seele auch noch, wie auf einer gequälten, schreienden Violine. Er ist eine unentbehrliche Bereicherung, ein Typ für sich!" Unless otherwise noted, translations are my own.

[2] "Jungfrauen von 8–80, die ein klein wenig von der Hysterie angestochen sind, haben IHM in ihrem mehr oder weniger weiten Busen einen Altar errichtet, für blaß aussehende Jünglinge ist ER überhaupt der personifizierte Lebenszweck."

[3] The 1926 version of *Der Student von Prag,* which stars Veidt, is distinct, of course, from the original 1913 version, starring Paul Wegener.

[4] Alexander Doty shows how *Caligari* lends itself to queer interpretations (23–47). For example, he reads the opening scene, where Francis meets an older man on the asylum grounds, as a cruising scenario (23–24). And when Dr. Caligari's diary is found, Doty gives a sexual spin to the doctor's recorded wish to find out "if it's true that a somnambulist can be compelled to perform acts abhorrent to him . . ." (40).

[5] Anton Kaes has spoken and written on this aspect of the film in relation to Sigmund Freud's 1919 essay, "Die Psychoanalyse der Kriegsneurose," in which Freud explores conflicts between an individual's war and peace egos (*Kriegs-Ich* and *Friedens-Ich*). While the former is compelled to kill, the latter feels a strong compulsion *not* to kill, and this conflict can cause a collapse of the psyche and mental paralysis. See Kaes, 209.

Works Cited

Andriopoulos, Stefan. *Possessed: Hypnotic Crimes, Corporate Fiction, and the Invention of Cinema*. Chicago: U of Chicago P, 2008.

Battle, Pat Wilks. "Biography." In Soister, 7–26.

Benjamin, Walter. *The Origins of German Tragic Drama*. Translated by John Osborn. New York: Verso, 1977.

Brod, Harry. "Masculinity as Masquerade." In *The Masculine Masquerade: Masculinity and Representation*, edited by Andrew Perchuk and Helaine Posner, 13–19. Cambridge, MA: MIT Press, 1995.

Cohen, Deborah. *The War Come Home: Disabled Veterans in Britain and Germany, 1914–1939*. Berkeley: U of California P, 2001.

Doty, Alexander. *Flaming Classics: Queering the Film Canon*. New York: Routledge, 2000.

Dyer, Richard. "Less and More than Women and Men: Lesbian and Gay Cinema in Weimar Germany." *New German Critique* 51 (1990): 5–60.

———. *Stars*. 1979. Reprint, London: British Film Institute, 1998.

Eisner, Lotte H. *The Haunted Screen: Expressionism in the German Cinema and the Influence of Max Reinhardt*. Translated by Roger Greaves. 1952. Reprint, Berkeley: U of California P, 1973.

Elsaesser, Thomas. "Weimar Cinema, Mobile Selves, and Anxious Males: Kracauer and Eisner Revisited." In Scheunemann, *Expressionist Film*, 33–71.

Isherwood, Christopher. "The Guardian God." In *Christopher and His Kind*. 1976. Reprinted in Jacobsen, 21–23.

Jacobsen, Wolfgang, ed. *Conrad Veidt: Lebensbilder; Ausgewählte Fotos und Texte*. Berlin: Argon / Stiftung Deutsche Kinemathek, 1993.

Janowitz, Hans. "Caligari — The Story of a Famous Story (Excerpts)." In *The Cabinet of Dr. Caligari: Texts, Contexts, Histories*, edited by Mike Budd, 221–39. New Brunswick, NJ: Rutgers UP, 1990.

Kaes, Anton. *Shell Shock Cinema: Weimar Culture and the Wounds of War*. Princeton, NJ: Princeton UP, 2009.

Kracauer, Siegfried. *From Caligari to Hitler: A Psychological History of German Film.* 1947. Reprint, Princeton, NJ: Princeton UP, 1974.

Mann, Erika, and Klaus Mann. ". . . Und diese Stimme": *Escape to Life.* 1991. Reprinted in Jacobsen, 95.

Salmon, Heinz. "Charaktertyp." *Film-Götter: Frechheiten aber Wahrheiten.* Berlin: Grübel, 1919. Reprinted in Jacobsen, 15.

Scharf, Fritz. "Crescendo und Decrescendo." *Film und Brettl* 1 (January 1922). Reprinted in Jacobsen, 43.

Scheunemann, Dietrich. "The Double, the Décor, and the Framing Device: Once More on Robert Wiene's *The Cabinet of Dr. Caligari.*" In Scheunemann, *Expressionist Film.* 125–56.

———, ed. *Expressionist Film: New Perspectives.* Rochester, NY: Camden House, 2003.

Soister, John T. *Conrad Veidt on Screen: A Comprehensive Illustrated Filmography.* Jefferson, NC: McFarland, 2002.

Steakley, James. *Anders als die Andern: Ein Film und seine Geschichte.* Hamburg: Männerschwarm Verlag, 2007.

———. "Cinema and Censorship in the Weimar Republic: The Case of *Anders als die Andern.*" *Film History* (New York) 11.2 (1999): 181–203.

Theweleit, Klaus. *Male Fantasies: Male Bodies; Psychoanalyzing the White Terror.* Vol. 2. Trans. Erica Carter. Minneapolis: U of Minnesota P, 1989.

von Hollander, Walter. "Die viel zu feinen Leute." *Uhu* (January 1930). Reprinted in *Uhu: Das Magazin der 20er Jahre,* edited by Christian Ferber, 223–26. Frankfurt am Main: Ullstein, 1979.

Walker, Julia. "'In the Grip of an Obsession': Delsarte and the Quest for Self-Possession in *The Cabinet of Dr. Caligari.*" *Theater Journal* 58 (2006): 617–31.

9: The Musical Promise of Abstract Film

Joel Westerdale

I N HIS 1916 PRESENTATION, "Die künstlerischen Möglichkeiten des Films" (The Artistic Possibilities of Film), the already renowned actor and film-maker Paul Wegener lamented that films up to that point were largely a disap-pointment. In its first twenty years, the medium had produced mostly kitsch — poor imitations of bad theater with stories reminiscent of trashy novels. This assessment notwithstanding, Wegener insists: "Das Ding ist gut!" (the thing is good). He declared that film would one day become more than sim-ply a lesser theater for the hoi polloi, and that even his own widely admired artistic achievements — starring in *Der Student von Prag* (The Student of Prague, 1913) and directing *Der Golem* (The Golem, 1914) — did not begin to approach the level of filmic artistry that was coming. One day, the medium of film would move beyond the plebeian and produce works that would deliver "an artistic experience . . . an optical vision, a great symphonic fan-tasy" (Wegener). But in 1916 the artistic possibilities of film had yet to be realized. To do so, according to Wegener, would entail liberating film from the yoke of narrative and cultivating its essence, which, as his "symphonic" vocabulary betrays, is akin not so much to stage or novel as to music.

Though Wegener himself did not take up the challenge suggested by this vision of film's future, a few short years later a handful of artists would set about making what has been termed *optische Musik* (optical or visual music). Ascribing musical qualities to film was already widespread by the early 1920s, with cinema frequently referred to as "the music of light" (King, 35), but the musical quality of these particular films was different; it was more pronounced, more distinctly "musical." Even in the heady atmosphere of experimentation that surrounded film production in early Weimar Germany, Walther Ruttmann's *Lichtspiel Opus 1* (Film Opus 1),[1] Hans Richter's *Rhythmus 21* (Rhythm 21),[2] and Viking Eggeling's *Symphonie diagonale* (Diagonal Symphony)[3] were avant-garde. Sometimes referred to as a kind of "absolute film," they refrain from narrative elements or even figurative representation. Instead, these one-act films (ranging typically from three to twelve minutes in length) offer animated geometric patterns, in many ways not entirely unlike today's screensavers. In Richter's *Rhythmus 21*, for instance, quadrilaterals traverse the screen, growing larger (appearing to advance) and shrinking (appearing to recede), exhibiting a dynamism comparable to the crescendo and decrescendo of music; additionally, the changing tempo of these developments, as well as the frequency of cuts, can create the impression of an accelerando or ritardando. Likewise, Eggeling's *Symphonie diagonale* repeatedly creates a kind of visual glissando by rapidly unmasking parallel lines of increasing length.

Certainly German film has a long association with music. One can't forget, for instance, that F. W. Murnau's *Nosferatu* (1922) is named *Eine Symphonie des Grauens* (A Symphony of Horror), as his later *Sunrise* (1927) is *A Song of Two Humans*. But as subtitles, such appellations only confirm that the principle of music is secondary to narrative content. The issue, however, is somewhat more complicated in the case of films that have no representative or narrative content and are considered "abstract." Though critics like Béla Balázs include certain documentary montage films like Ruttmann's 1927 *Berlin: Die Sinfonie der Großstadt* (Berlin: Symphony of the Big City) under the rubric *optische Musik*, in this current study I limit myself to the earliest abstract films by Ruttmann, Eggeling, and Richter. For such films enjoy a twofold association with music: first through their abstraction, and second, through their temporal development. Both of these aspects contributed to the understanding of abstract film as *optische Musik*, but whereas the first captured the imagination of critics, the second dominated discussions by the artists themselves. Each of these films, limiting itself to the play of light, shadow, color, and movement, thus seemingly responds to Wegener's challenge, producing an art form that does not subjugate itself to the demands of narrative but rather celebrates film as film. The association with music provides a means of conceptualizing these avant-garde films, playing a conspicuous role in the analyses of contemporary theorists, critics, and the artists themselves. In the end, however, this association comes to dominate the idiom of these filmmakers, contributing to the demise of the unfamiliar yet promising mode of filmmaking it initially sought to make comprehensible.

In the years before these films were made, abstract or non-figurative painting had already come to be strongly associated with music through the influence of such artists as Wassily Kandinsky and Franz Marc. In his 1911 treatise *Über das Geistige in der Kunst* (*Concerning the Spiritual in Art*), Kandinsky reciprocates composer Arnold Schönberg's concept of *Klangfarben* (sound-colors), writing of the "voices" and "harmonies" of a painting, of the "melodic" and "symphonic" extremes of technique; Marc likewise draws from the vocabulary of musical composition when he writes of the "dissonance" and "consonance" of colors (Frisch, 120). For Kandinsky, the arts had "never in recent times been closer to one another," and it was the non-figurative aspect of modern painting that enabled this confluence (Frisch, 90). Such considerations pervaded the artistic atmosphere in which those who would come to make *optische Musik* emerged.

Ruttmann, Richter, and Eggeling all began their artistic careers as painters strongly influenced by Kandinsky, and with the canvas as their point of departure, their films can be seen as non-figurative paintings put in motion. But for the early film theorist Balázs, this in no way results in optical *Musik* — he considers this description itself to be a superficial and false analogy formulated by over-hasty theorists ("Der absolute Film," 142). The forms employed in these films are abstracted from concrete manifestations, while music is no more abstract than is architecture. Balázs concedes that the rhythm of editing can have a somewhat musical quality ("Montage," 90), but abstraction itself does not lead to musicality. Kandinsky would likely take issue with this assessment, for when he writes of the contemporary proximity of the arts, he writes not simply of the relation between abstract painting and music, but of the relation between his kind of abstract painting in particular and the atonal music of Schönberg. More importantly, however, Balázs's focus on the issue of abstraction ignores the initial motivation of these filmmakers, for whom film approaches music not through the notion of abstraction but through the experience of movement.

Before they turned to film — at the animation tables of Germany's premier film production company, the Universum Film AG (Ufa) — the German Hans Richter (1888–1976) and the Swedish-born Viking Eggeling (1880–1925) were painters active with the Dada artists in Zurich. Richter had moved there in 1916, the same year the Berlin periodical *Die Aktion* devoted a special issue to his work as a painter. In 1918 Dada champion Tristan Tzara introduced him to the older Viking Eggeling, whose work responded directly to the theoretical writings of Kandinsky (Wollen, 44). Eggeling's ambition as a painter was to develop a universal graphic language, one that, like the "transnational" language of Dada poets like Tzara, Hugo Ball, Richard Huelsenbeck, and other Cabaret Voltaire regulars, overcame the linguistically defined national borders exploited in the First World War. With Richter, Eggeling would map out this idea in a pamphlet called *Universelle Sprache* (Universal Language, 1922). The painters' language itself was to be one of forms rather than words, producing a kind of musical notation for the eyes.

But associating their graphic work with music and with language forced them to confront a dilemma that had long frustrated painters and had become particularly acute in the early years of the twentieth century, namely, how to introduce the element of time into their work. Ever since G. E. Lessing published *Laokoön oder Über die Grenzen der Malerei und Poesie* (*Laocoön, An Essay on the Limits of Painting and Poetry*) in 1766, the respective structures of painting and poetry had been seen to determine what was appropriate for them to depict. Painting, which Lessing defined as the domain of "co-existent signs," was limited to depicting that which is coexistent; in order to depict a succession of events, Lessing argued, one needs a succession of signs, that is, poetry (149). This division of content between the media, relegating to painting the depiction of bodies in space and to poetry the portrayal of events through time, was widely accepted until the early twentieth century, at which point Italian Futurists, among others, began seeking ways to integrate temporal development into the painted image. In answer to this challenge, Eggeling developed a style he called "kinomorphism" (Goergen, "Kinomorphism," 249).

The influential artist and theorist László Moholy-Nagy described Eggeling as the first person who had not only recognized and pursued the problem of time in painting, but actually attempted to give it form in his works (16). Eggeling's strategy was to overcome the limitations Lessing had determined by portraying the gradual development of drawings through successive individual images drawn on rolls of paper (Goergen, "Kinomorphism," 170). His *Horizontal-Vertikal-Orchester* (Horizontal-Vertical Orchestra) consisted of thousands of constructivist drawings exhibiting minute changes that the viewer was to appreciate while walking along the painting's fifteen meters. It is not difficult to see how his and Richter's work on "Rollenbilder" (scroll paintings), as they called them, precipitated a turn to film, and indeed, the *Horizontal-Vertikal-Orchester* served as a kind of score for Eggeling's first foray into motion pictures. Unfortunately, Eggeling was unsatisfied with the results of these initial experiments and, judging from the lost film's lack of mention in German film censorship records, it was never screened publicly (O'Konor, 252 n. 32).

Certainly the constructivist images Eggeling and Richter painted were abstract, but it is not the moment of abstraction or an expressed desire to create a visual form of music that spurs the artists' real innovation, but rather the interest in adding movement and, thus, temporal development to already abstract works. As Richter put it: the "scrolls implied movement . . . and movement implied film" ("Avant-Garde," 221). For him, rhythm is "the essence of filmmaking, because it's . . . the conscious articulation of time, and if anything is at the bottom of filmmaking," Richter says, "it is the articulation of time, of movement" (interview in Starr). By withholding narrative and figurative representation, the two time-dependent elements of movement and rhythm become the stars of the film. In reducing film to these essential elements, Richter was convinced that he and Eggeling had entered into uncharted waters where music simply provided the only suitable point of orientation (Richter, "Viking Eggeling," 46).

Music thus serves not as the expressed ambition but as an explanation by analogy. And this is evident in an article published in 1921 in the revolutionary Dutch art journal *De Stijl*, in which Richter describes the transition from scrolls to film. He writes:

> The reproduced drawings represent major moments in processes that are intended to be in motion. The works will be realized in film. The process itself: evolutions and revolutions forming in the sphere of the purely artistic (abstract shapes), analogous somewhat to the events of music to which our ear is accustomed.[4]

In this passage, music serves an important explanatory function, but its relation to the artistic enterprise described is not defining. Rather, the project is simply analogous (*analog*) to music, and that only somewhat (*etwa*). This is also how Eggeling had described the relationship between the two arts in the Hungarian journal *MA* earlier that same year (105). The articles by the two artists are in fact so univocal in their use of music as an explanation rather than ambition that one scholar claims Richter lifted his article directly from Eggeling's (O'Konor, 70). In each case music serves to clarify and not to direct their objectives.

While Richter and Eggeling were putting their plans into motion, Walther Ruttmann (1887–1941) was completing *Lichtspiel Opus 1*, which had its Berlin premiere — and with it, the public premiere of *optische Musik* — at the Marmorhaus cinema on 27 April 1921. Ruttmann is perhaps best known for his 1927 *Berlin* film and for the animated sequence of Kriemhild's dream in Fritz Lang's *Die Nibelungen* (The Nibelungs, 1924). Like Richter and Eggeling, Ruttmann too began his artistic career as a painter, and this likewise helped to shape his portrayal of film's purpose and potential. In an essay written some time between 1913 and 1917, he classifies film (*Kinematographie*) as one of the "bildenden Künste" (visual arts), likening it to painting and dance rather than to music directly ("Kunst und Kino," 73). For Ruttmann, cinema's most important means of expression is "die Bewegung . . . optische[r] Phänomene, die zeitliche Entwicklung einer Form aus der andern" (the movement . . . of optical phenomena, the temporal development of one form out of another), and this is evident in his *Opus 1*, as well as in his similar early works, *Opus 2* (1921), *Opus 3* (1925), and *Opus 4* (1925).[5] In keeping with his statement, his films display a degree of dynamism alien to those of Richter and Eggeling. Richter's *Rhythmus 21* is limited primarily to quadrilaterals which, though mobile, do not actually change in shape (fig. 9.1), and even the larger repertoire of figures that make up Eggeling's *Symphonie diagonale* (fig. 9.2) do not transform or evolve; rather they expand as new fields are revealed, and disappear as portions are masked. The figures in Ruttmann's *Opera* (fig. 9.3), on the other hand, are themselves malleable, altering their form like amoebae. As Alfred Kerr put it in his review for the *Berliner Tageblatt*:

> One thinks of the images of the Expressionists. But they are immobile. Chagall's luminous paradises remain fixed. The glittering futurisms of the latest Parisians petrify motionlessly — in the frame. Here, however, things dart, they paddle, burn, climb, bump, billow, glide, stride, wilt, flow, swell, grow light or dark; unfold, arch, spread, diminish, roll up, narrow, sharpen, divide, bend, raise, fill, empty, distend themselves, cower; flirt, and slip away. In short: Expressionism in motion.[6]

Fig. 9.1. Quadrilaterals appear to approach and recede in Hans Richter's
Rhythmus 21 *(1923). Screenshot.*

Though the works of Richter and Eggeling have their distinctive style
and charm, the kind of dynamism that elicits such journalistic bombast is
lacking.

Despite these differences, Ruttmann's account of his films shares with
those of Richter and Eggeling an emphasis on movement and development rather than music. Though called *Opera*, these films were efforts in
what Ruttmann, in an undated essay written around 1919 or 1920, called
"Malerei mit Zeit" (painting with time). This project sought to create

> an art for the eye that differs from painting, in that it proceeds tempo-
> rally (like music), and that the main artistic focus is not (as in a picture)
> in the reduction of a (real or formal) process to a single moment, but
> rather precisely in the temporal development of the formal.[7]

The introduction of the temporal element into painting, Ruttmann
recognizes, demands a reconsideration of the painter's enterprise. According
to Lessing, painting could imitate action only by choosing the most preg-
nant moment that would indicate rather than represent the action (150).
By "painting with time," Ruttmann need not reduce his image to that
single moment.

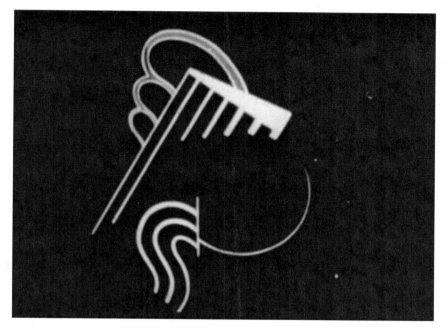

Fig. 9.2. A more complex yet less mobile image from Viking Eggeling's
Diagonalsymphonie *(1924). Screenshot.*

As Theodor W. Adorno points out in the spirit of Lessing, painting is still a *Raumkunst* (a spatial art), whereas music, unfolding in time, is a *Zeitkunst* (a temporal art). Though closely aligned with painting, film, with its rhythm, development and movement, shares a temporal aspect with music that distinguishes it from painting (Adorno). And for Ruttmann, as for Richter and Eggeling, it is from film's capacity to do what painting precisely *cannot* do that it derives its musicality.

The abstract form of these films contributes to their musicality largely by suppressing the narrative impulse. Lessing had positioned poetry, that is, epic poetry, as that which develops along the temporal axis — a narrative presentation that unfolds in time is suitable for portraying actions that also unfold in time. Through the use of abstract forms in film, the narrative impulse is stifled, leaving music as the appropriate remaining artistic analogy. The result is an art form that, as both a *Raumkunst* and a *Zeitkunst*, openly challenges Lessing's partition of the arts. Devoid of figurative representation, these films cannot be mistaken for filmed plays or dramatized novels; they challenge both filmic convention and Lessing's typology in becoming paintings in motion.

Fig. 9.3. Walther Ruttmann's dancing "amoebae" in his pioneering Lichtspiel Opus 1 *(1921). Screenshot.*

It is easy to forget that it is precisely in terms of the juxtaposition of the still image with the image in motion that film was first experienced: doing what a picture cannot do was the essence of the film spectacle in cinema's early years. Though we have naturalized the oxymoron "motion picture," the cinema of attractions at the turn of the century centered on the transition from still to moving image. The primary astonishment elicited by early film lay not in the verisimilitude of the image but rather in the image's ability to transgress its generic limitations (Gunning, 822–23). The story of panic in the aisles, of spectators fleeing what they take to be an actual oncoming train, is likely a myth. Spectators were not so naive as to mistake a colorless, silent world for reality; they had no experience, however, seeing a still image come to life. This transition was in fact the *raison d'être* of the early filmic performance, and the presenters would emphasize this impossible transformation by first projecting the static image for a few seconds, and only after initially withholding the illusion of movement would they then set the apparatus — and thereby the image — in motion.

The accounts of Richter, Eggeling, and Ruttmann return to this fascination with motion, emphasizing less what is depicted than the image's movement itself. Balázs's critique of *optische Musik* takes issue with the abstract nature of these works, but abstraction itself has little bearing on the musical characterization of these films, which the artists ascribe rather to the films' temporal unfolding. In defying Lessing's distinction between painting and poetry, these artworks enter into a generic no-man's-land, leaving the artists with music as the only suitable analogy to understand and explain their enterprise. But this comparison comes with pitfalls that neither the artists nor subsequent critics seem to have realized.

The association with music helps the relatively young and still largely plebeian art of film to establish its cultural pedigree by confirming its close relation to not just any recognized art form, but to the art form that, through the advocacy of the likes of philosophers Arthur Schopenhauer and Friedrich Nietzsche, was arguably the one most privileged in Germany in the nineteenth and early twentieth centuries. Precisely by severing its ties with the representational, story-telling forms of the novel and the drama, and reinforcing its intrinsic musicality, film would prove its aesthetic autonomy. Through its association with music, it could establish its legitimacy among the arts.

This association, however, is not without its danger. Though the interest in motion precedes the analogy of music in the projects of these filmmakers, the gravitational pull of the older sister-art is strong and alters their trajectory. Richter would come to dismiss the rhythm of Ruttmann's *Opus*-films as "accidental" ("Avant-Garde," 222); he would criticize their lack of melodic units, musical structure, or developed form (LeGrice, 27). Richter never had much love for Ruttmann, but the implied criteria of his criticism are telling. While the analogy of music may help to explain and legitimize their films, it takes an extra step to criticize these works according to standards developed for the older medium. Ruttmann, indeed, opens himself up to such criticism. Even if early on he associates film with painting and dance in his writings, the will to music takes over, as becomes clear in 1927, when Ruttmann lays out his intentions for *Berlin: Die Sinfonie der Großstadt* in an article for the daily *Film-Kurier*. His first intention, he explains, is to exploit what he considers film's uncompromising objectivity to record the behavior of people who don't realize they are being filmed. His second is to take this material and submit it to the "straffste Organisation des Zeitlichen nach streng musikalischen Prinzipien" (strictest organization of the temporal according to rigorous musical principles; "Der neue Film," 80). This agenda signals a subtle yet fundamental shift in his artistic objectives.

Now Richter would also produce a shorter visual "symphony," his *Rennsymphonie* (Race Symphony, 1928), which in many ways resembles Ruttmann's Berlin film. Like Ruttmann's film, it comprises unnarrated documentary footage presented in apparently chronological order, here tracing a trip to the racetrack Hoppegarten outside Berlin, including an opening approach via train and automobile. Images of traffic and police-men, as well as close-ups of hands, legs, and money, reinforce the similarity between the films, as do the editing techniques, which invite comparison between humans and animals, all the while increasing in tempo, building in an ecstatic crescendo. Despite these many similarities, Richter does not suggest that the musical title reveals an organizational principle that guides the making of the film. Rather, it seems to perform the kind of explanatory function that aligns it with his earlier *Rhythmus 21*. The title tells us not to expect a standard narrative short, but that we should focus on other qualities, like composition and rhythm.

In his piece for the *Film-Kurier*, however, Ruttmann claims to deliber-ately adopt musical conventions as guiding principles, which scholars have subsequently sought to distinguish in the film (see Hake). And this agenda reveals what political analysts sometimes call "mission creep": what begins as a means of explaining and legitimizing something comes to define the standards against which something is being judged. Richter's critique of Ruttmann shows just such a slippage from auxiliary concept to normative standard. By organizing his film according to musical rather than filmic principles, Ruttmann invites such criticism, and such criticism privileges the analogy of music, with its accompanying musical criteria, over the immediate filmic artwork.

In turning to music, film turns away from itself, and the constant refer-ence to music in the titles of these films and in the writings of these film-makers actually sabotages the "musicality" of these works by subjugating the newer medium to the older. While the light, shadow, and color of film can provide abstract shapes that stand in analogical relation to music like Kandinsky's painterly "Kompositionen" (compositions), the movement of these forms, enabled by film's temporal aspect, does not stand in some kind of analogical relation to music. Rather, the temporal aspect is a genuine commonality between the two media — it is just as essential to film as it is to music. The association of the former with the latter through the use of musical terminology may have augmented the cultural legitimacy of the newer form, but only at the cost of the autonomy it sought to establish.

On 3 May 1925 a group of radical artists and architects called the *Novembergruppe* (see "Richtlinien"), in conjunction with Ufa, presented a matinee called "Der absolute Film" (Absolute Film) at the small Ufa-Theater on the Kurfürstendamm in Berlin. The program included the public premiere of Eggeling's *Symphonie diagonale*, and Ruttmann's *Opus 2, 3*, and *4*, *Images mobiles* from Fernand Léger and Dudley Murphy, Francis Picabia and René Clair's *Entr'acte*, and a performance of Ludwig Hirschfeld-Mack's "color organ." The following week it included Richter's *Film ist Rhythmus* (Film Is Rhythm; a mixture of footage from his *Rhythmus 21* and *Rhythmus 23*), which, despite its inclusion on the pro-gram, had not been available the week before. Judging from the account of the young Rudolf Arnheim, Ruttmann's *Opera* were the most successful of the abstract films, but not exactly for their musical quality. Whereas he describes Eggeling's film as little more than "a melee of lines, creating variation rather than ingenuity," he notes that Ruttmann's films were far more evocative:

> The absolute forms behaved themselves in a very human way and thus greatly exceeded the intentions of their creator. At the same time, however, they produced a cheery mood. Two spongy forms are cute and cozy flirters, and a gaunt rectangle runs restlessly here and there like a man whose wife is taking too much time to dress. A domestic scene in the realm of mathematical embarrassment showing how easy it is to imitate our most basic traits. (Schobert, 241)

It is not the musical qualities of Ruttmann's films that draw Arnheim's praise, but rather their potential anthropomorphic aspects. Not symphonic rapture, but cuteness, domesticity, embarrassment reduced to their most basic visual manifestation. Representation, it would seem, trumps musicality.

The program, billed as a one-time event, was popular enough to warrant repeating the following Sunday. But even as it marked the pinnacle, it also marked the passing of *optische Musik* in its earliest abstract form. A few weeks later, Eggeling would die in a Berlin hospital. And perhaps inspired by the other films on the program, Richter and Ruttmann would turn away from animated abstraction and continue their formal experimentation with documentary and staged footage (Schobert, 242). Richter went on to make such surrealist-influenced montage films as *Inflation* (1927) and *Vormittagsspuk* (Ghosts before Breakfast, 1928). Leaving Germany in 1933, he emigrated to the United States in 1940, where he became an important representative of the European avant-garde. Ruttmann stayed in Germany, where he died in 1941. Beyond his *Opera* and *Berlin*, he went on to make many more documentary and industrial films, while experimenting with sound, creating such innovative films as *Melodie der Welt* (World Melody, 1929) and the sound-montage film without images, *Weekend* (1930).

Even the initial advocates of abstract *optische Musik* did not see the need to continue in this vein. It would not be the seed of a filmic revolution, but merely a hiccup in film's development toward an almost exclusively narrative repertoire. Their initial efforts to create paintings that move might have proved a challenge to Lessing's division of the arts, but in the end, the demise of these early productions suggests a corollary to his assessment: not only are poetry and narrative appropriate for depicting events in time, but even the most remotely representational images unfolding in time, as in film, have a tendency toward narrative, even if, on occasion, we might consider them musical.

Notes

[1] *Lichtspiel Opus 1*, produced, directed, animated, and edited by Walther Ruttmann for Ruttmann-Film GmbH; original music by Max Butting; original length: 243m; original format: 35mm, 1:1.33, hand-colored; censorship number: M.00789, 29 October 1921; previewed 1 April 1921 in Frankfurt, U.T. im Schwan; premiere: 27 April 1921, Berlin Marmorhaus; available on DVD, *Berlin: Symphony of a Great City* (Image Entertainment, 1999).

[2] *Rhythmus 21*, directed and produced by Hans Richter, director of photography: Svend Noldan, Otto Schmalhausen from Ufa's animation department; commissioned by Ufa; original format: 35mm, 1:1.33, b/w (partially negative); premiere: Théâtre Michel, Paris, 6 July 1923; available on DVD: *Avant-Garde — Experimental Cinema of the 1920s & 1930s* (Kino Video, 2005).

[3] *Symphonie diagonale* (also known as *Diagonalsinfonie* or *Diagonalsymphonie*), directed and edited by Viking Eggeling and Erna Niemeyer; produced by Viking Eggeling; shot in Eggeling's apartment, in Berlin, 1923–1924; original length: 149m; original format: 35mm; b/w; premiere: 3 May 1925, U.T. Kurfürstendamm, as part of matinee "Der absolute Film"; available on DVD: *Avant-Garde — Experimental Cinema of the 1920s & 1930s* (Kino Video, 2005).

[4] "Die abgebildeten Zeichnungen stellen Hauptmomente von Vorgängen dar, die in Bewegung gedacht sind. Die Arbeiten werden im Film ihre Verwirklichung finden. Der Vorgang selbst: gestaltende Evolutionen und Revolutionen in der Sphäre des rein künstlerischen (abstrakte Formen) analog etwa den unserem Ohr geläufigen Geschehnissen der Musik" (Richter, "Prinzipielles," 81; my translation).

[5] *Lichtspiel Opus 2*, produced, directed, animated, and edited by Walther Ruttmann for Ruttmann-Film GmbH; original length: 78m; original format: 35mm, 1.33:1; b/w (tinted); censorship number: M.00889, 15 February 1922; preview: January 1922; *Lichtspiel Opus 3*, produced, directed, animated, and edited by Walther Ruttmann for the production firm Kunstmaler W. Ruttmann; assistant director: Lore Leudesdorff; original length: 66m; original format: 35mm; 1.33:1; b/w (colored); censorship number: B10332, 21 April 1925; *Lichtspiel Opus 4*, produced, directed, animated, and edited by Walther Ruttmann for the production firm Kunstmaler W. Ruttmann; assistant director: Lore Leudesdorff; original length: 70m; original format: 35mm; 1.33:1; b/w (partly colored); censorship number: B.10333, 21 April 1925. All three films were premiered on 3 May 1925, U.T. Kurfürstendamm, as part of the matinee "Der absolute Film."

[6] "Man denkt an Expressionistenbilder. Die sind aber unbewegsam. Chagalls Leuchtparadiese bleiben doch starr. Die Funkelfuturismen der neuesten Pariser versteinern reglos — im Rahmen. Hier aber flitzen Dinge, rudern, brennen, steigen, stoßen, quellen, gleiten, schreiten, welken, fließen, schwellen, dämmern; entfalten sich, wölben sich, breiten sich, verringern sich, kugeln sich, engen sich, schärfen sich, teilen sich, krümmen sich, heben sich, füllen sich, leeren sich, blähen sich, ducken sich; blümeln und verkrümeln sich. Kurz: Expressionismus in Bewegtheit" (Kerr, 99; my translation).

7 "Eine Kunst für das Auge, die sich von der Malerei dadurch unterscheidet, daß sie sich zeitlich abspielt (wie Musik), und daß der Schwerpunkt des Künstlerischen nicht (wie im Bild) in der Reduktion eines (realen oder formalen) Vorgangs auf einen Moment liegt, sondern gerade in der zeitlichen Entwicklung des Formalen" (Ruttmann, "Malerei mit Zeit," 64; my translation).

Works Cited

Adorno, Theodor W. "On Some Relationships between Music and Painting." Translated by Susan Gillespie. *The Musical Quarterly* 79.1 (Spring 1995): 66–79.

Balázs, Béla. "Der absolute Film." In Diederichs, Gersch, and Nagy, 2:124–44. Originally appeared in *Der Geist des Films*, 1930.

———. "Montage." In Diederichs, Gersch, and Nagy, 2:82–93. Originally appeared in *Der Geist des Films,* 1930.

Diederichs, Helmut H., Wolfgang Gersch, and Magda Nagy, eds. *Schriften zum Film.* 2 vols. Munich: Hanser, 1982.

Eggeling, Viking. "Elvi fejtegetések a mozgómüvészetröl." *MA* 6.8 (1921): 105–6.

Eggeling, Viking, and Hans Richter. *Universelle Sprache.* Germany, 1919.

Frisch, Walter. *German Modernism: Music and the Arts.* Berkeley: U of California P, 2005.

Goergen, Jeanpaul, ed. "Viking Eggeling's Kinomorphism: Zurich Dada and the Film." In *Dada Zurich, a Clown's Game from Nothing*, edited by Brigitte Pichon and Karl Riha, 153–75. New York: G. K. Hall, 1996.

———, ed. *Walter Ruttmann: Eine Dokumentation.* Berlin: Freunde der Deutschen Kinemathek, 1989.

Gunning, Tom. "An Aesthetics of Astonishment: Early Film and the (In)Credulous Spectator." In *Film Theory and Criticism: Introductory Readings*, 5th ed., edited by Leo Braudy and Marshall Cohen, 818–32. New York and Oxford: Oxford UP, 1999.

Hake, Sabine. "Urban Spectacle in Walter Ruttmann's *Berlin, Symphony of the Big City.*" In *Dancing on the Volcano: Essays on the Culture of the Weimar Republic*, edited by Thomas W. Kniesche and Stephen Brockmann, 127–42. Columbia, SC: Camden House, 1994.

Kerr, Alfred. "Der Vorstoß im Film." *Berliner Tageblatt,* 16 June 1921. Reprinted in Goergen, *Walter Ruttmann,* 99.

King, Norman. "The Sounds of Silents." In *Silent Film*, edited by Richard Abel, 31–44. New Brunswick, NJ: Rutgers UP, 1996.

LeGrice, Malcolm. *Abstract Film and Beyond.* Cambridge, MA: MIT Press, 1977.

Lessing, G. E. *Laocoön, An Essay on the Limits of Painting and Poetry.* Translated by Robert Phillimore. London: MacMillan, 1874.

Moholy-Nagy, László. *Malerei, Photographie, Film.* Munich: Albert Langen, 1925.

O'Konor, Louise. *Viking Eggeling, 1880–1925, Artist and Filmmaker, Life and Work.* Stockholm: Almqvist & Wiksell, 1971.

Richter, Hans. "Avant-Garde Film in Germany." In *Experiment in Film*, edited by Roger Manvell, 219–33. New York: Arno, 1970.

———. "Prinzipielles zur Bewegungskunst." *De Stijl* 4.7 (1921): 81–82. Reprinted in *De Stijl, 1921–1932*, 2:81–82; 3 vols. Amsterdam: Athenaeum, Bert Bakker, Polak & Van Gennep, 1968.

———. "Viking Eggeling." In *Experimental Animation: An Illustrated Anthology*, edited by Robert Russett and Cecile Starr, 45–46. New York: Van Nostrand Reinhold, 1976.

"Richtlinien der 'Novembergruppe.'" Berlin: Novembergruppe, January 1919. Reprinted in *Manifeste Manifeste, 1905–1933*, edited by Diether Schmidt, 159. Dresden: Verlag der Kunst, 1965.

Ruttmann, Walther. "Kunst und Kino." In Goergen, *Walter Ruttmann*, 73.

———. "Malerei mit Zeit." In *Film als Film, 1910 bis heute*, edited by Birgit Hein and Wulf Herzogenrath, 64. Cologne: Kölnischer Kunstverein, 1977.

———. "Der neue Film." In Goergen, *Walter Ruttmann*, 78–80.

Schobert, Walter. "'Painting in Time' and 'Visual Music': On German Avant-Garde Films in the 1920s." In *Expressionist Film: New Perspectives*, edited by Dietrich Scheuneman, 237–49. Rochester, NY: Camden House, 2003.

Starr, Cecile. "Richter on Film." 1972 film interview. In *Hans Richter: Early Avant-Garde Films.* New York: Arthouse, 1996.

Wegener, Paul. "Paul Wegener: Die künstlerischen Möglichkeiten des Films." In *Paul Wegener: Der Regisseur und Schauspieler*, edited by Rudolph S. Joseph, pages unnumbered. Munich: Münchner Stadtmuseum, Photo- und Filmmuseum, 1967.

Wollen, Peter, "Viking Eggeling." In *Paris Hollywood: Writings on Film*, 39–54. London and New York: Verso, 2002.

10: The International Project of National(ist) Film: Franz Osten in India

Veronika Fuechtner

T HE POPULAR IMAGINATION frequently associates German silent film with an aesthetic of shadows and excessive décor and identifies it as a distinctive high-art national cinema. However, Weimar Republic Cinema was also a popular cinema with international production and distribution mechanisms firmly in place. The crucial role that the Bavarian film director Franz Osten played in the beginnings of Bombay's film industry subverts the notion of a monolithic German national film history. In the following, I will provide historical background on Osten, his collaborators in Bombay, and the context of the Indian film industry, before focusing on his first silent German-Indian coproduction, *Prem Sanyas / Die Leuchte Asiens / The Light of Asia* (1925). This will highlight some of the often strange and surprising connections between Weimar German Cinema and early Hindi cinema, which preceded, but not necessarily produced, what is now known as "Bollywood." While Franz Osten's films and the stars they created, especially Devika Rani and Ashok Kumar, hold a firm place in the historiography of Hindi cinema, they have only recently been reclaimed to the European cinematic canon.

Heimat in Many Places: Franz Osten's Life Between Bavaria, Berlin, and Bombay

Osten's biography presents an example of the close interplay of silent cinema with photography, the documentary film genre, and the world of theater. Franz Osten was born Franz Ostermayr in Munich in 1876. His father was a photographer, and Osten took over the studio with his brother, Peter. Soon the Ostermayrs started their own new business, screening short silent films by the French film companies Gaumont and Pathé, for which Franz Osten subsequently worked as a cameraman. In 1909 Osten and his brother founded the *Münchner Kunstfilm Kompanie*. Both brothers also started working with director Max Reinhardt on the summer productions of the *Künstlertheater*, and in 1910 Osten began directing his first feature films. During the First World War Osten first worked as a war correspondent and then fought in the war in Tyrol, Galicia, France, and Italy. After the war he rejoined Peter Ostermayr at the film production company Emelka (representing MLK — *Münchner Lichtspielkunst*), and became its chief director in 1920. In the following years, Osten distinguished himself as a director of *Heimat* films such as *Der Ochsenkrieg* (The Oxen War, 1920). based on a novel by Ludwig Ganghofer, or lighter popular fare, such as the comedy *Die raffinierteste Frau Berlins* (Berlin's Most Cunning Woman, 1927).[1] Later, in the 1920s, Osten directed three silent German-Indian coproductions on location in India: *Prem Sanyas* (1925), *Shiraz* (1928), and *Prapansha Pash* — *Throw of Dice* (1929).

When he was not in India, Osten commuted between Berlin and Munich, where he produced the first feature-length film with Bavarian comedian Karl Valentin, *Der Sonderling* (The Odd Man, 1929). In 1935, a few years after directing his first German sound film, *Im Banne der Berge* (Under the Spell of the Mountains, 1931), Osten returned to India. There he joined the coproducer and star of his three silent German-Indian films, Himansu Rai and his wife Devika Rani, who had just founded their own studio, the influential and successful Bombay Talkies. All in all, Osten directed sixteen Hindi sound and music films for Bombay Talkies. At the onset of the Second World War, Osten, who was a member of the Nazi party (NSDAP), was arrested by the British colonial authorities and interned for eight months. Shortly after his release, Himansu Rai died prematurely, and there was no space for Osten at Bombay Talkies any more. Osten left for Germany in poor health and once again found employment back at his brother's company in Munich, now named Bavaria films. Until the end of the Second World War he headed the artistic staff department and film archive. In 1946 Osten became the director of a spa in Bad Aibling, where he died in relative obscurity in 1956.

The Story of *Prem Sanyas*

As the film critic Amrit Gangar writes, the story of *Prem Sanyas*, Osten's first silent film shot in India from 1925, begins with Himansu Rai (1892–1940), the film's star and coproducer. Rai was born in Bombay and studied law in Calcutta and London, where he decided to devote himself full-time to acting on stage and consulting on film productions with exotic themes. In London, Rai also met Devika Rani (1908–94), the daughter of the first Indian surgeon-general of Madras and the grandniece of the Bengali poet Rabindranath Tagore. Rani had attended boarding school in England since she was nine, had studied at London's Royal Academy of Dramatic Arts, and was designing art, textiles, and sets for the English film producer Bruce

Wolfe. Rani worked as a set-design assistant for Osten's third silent film, *Prapansha Pash* (1929), and married Himansu Rai shortly thereafter. Like many early Indian film pioneers before them, the young couple went to Berlin. As Devika Rani describes in her memoirs, Himansu Rai was "the only Asian to have the position of producer in a Western studio, and to be treated at par" (Gangar, *Osten*, 2). As Erik Barnouw and S. Krishnaswamy report (97), Devika Rani became a trainee at the Ufa film company with Erich Pommer, attended film-acting seminars with G. W. Pabst, met Fritz Lang, Emil Jannings, Josef von Sternberg, and Max Reinhardt, and watched Marlene Dietrich during the shooting of *Der blaue Engel* (The Blue Angel, 1930). Rani would later evoke Dietrich's appearance and performance style in her starring role in the crime thriller *Jawani Ki Hawa* (1935), the first sound film that Osten directed for Bombay Talkies. On the wave of their success with their first Indian English-language sound film, *Karma* (1933), Rai and Rani founded their own production company and film studio, Bombay Talkies, a huge complex in Malad, a suburb of Bombay. The site included a sound stage, a recording room, a laboratory, a library, and a preview theater; furthermore, publicity, camera, and engineering departments, and even a small school for child performers (Ramachandran, *70 Years*, 91). After Rai's death in 1940, Rani took over the direction of Bombay Talkies and went on to produce and star in many more films. Ashok Kumar was the other leading star of Bombay Talkies, until he founded his own production company, Filmistan, with Sashadhar Mukherjee in 1943. When Rani retired in 1945 after marrying the Russian painter Svetoslav Roerich, Kumar and Mukherjee retook control of Bombay Talkies. However, after initial successes the company folded in 1954. Devika Rani was to be honored and remembered as the "first lady of the Indian screen" beyond her death in 1994.

The story of *Prem Sanyas* and the beginning of Osten's long-term involvement with Indian cinema is also the story of how various theater traditions, popular or art film registers, and differing artistic and political agendas came together: Bavarian theater and Bengali theater, Christian passion plays and Hindu mythology, and German *Heimatfilm* and Indian nation-building film. In 1922, during his time in London, Himansu Rai had acted in a play titled *The Goddess* by the London-based author Niranjan Pal (1889–1959). Rai became close to Pal, with whom he shared a Bengali background. Pal was to write all the scripts for Osten's silent movies as well as to produce, direct, or write many other films, especially for Bombay Talkies. Pal wrote an adaptation of the 1879 epic poem *Light of Asia* by Sir Edwin Arnold (1832–1904) about the life of Buddha. Arnold, a British journalist and educator, spent several years in India as a colonial officer and published several translations and adaptations of Hindu scriptures, such as the *Bhagavad Gita*. Arnold's *Light of Asia* frames much of Buddha's life with Christian and Graeco-Roman iconography; that is, Buddha's birth is celebrated by four angels representing

the cardinal points of the compass, or ethereal devas sing to Buddha like
sirens. Connecting Buddhism with what he describes as Brahminical noblesse,
Arnold directs his poem against the spirit of abstraction and nothingness that
seemed to have overtaken the West. Despite the poem's championing of a
nobility inflected by caste, religion, and race, Mahatma Gandhi later declared
that Arnold's piece had impacted him profoundly in its depiction of worldly
renunciation. Pal's adaptation, as evidenced in Osten's film, was indebted to
a more realist aesthetic and toned down some of the supernatural elements
of Arnold's poem. But it retained Arnold's vision of nobility and his representation of Buddha as a Jesus-like figure.

Himansu Rai had been keen to create a film series on world religions,
starting with one film based on the Oberammergau Passion Play and another
on the life of Buddha, so it is likely that Pal's script of *Prem Sanyas* was
impacted by Rai's plan.[2] Even before Rai, several other Indian film pioneers
had been attracted to the idea of creating filmic monuments to Hindu or
Buddhist mythology. Dadasaheb Phalke (1870–1944), for example, decided
to become a filmmaker after seeing the 1906 Pathé film *Life of Christ* and
had been directing silent feature films based on religious mythologies since
1913, among others *Buddha Dev* (Life of Lord Buddha, 1923). After having
sold his script of *Light of Asia* to the Great Eastern Film Corporation in
Delhi, Niranjan Pal traveled to Munich with Himansu Rai in early 1924 to
negotiate a coproduction with the Emelka Film Company.

Prem Sanyas was by no means the first international coproduction
involving India — Phalke had worked with the French company Pathé; the
Italian director Eugenio de Liguoro and the French director Camille Le
Grand shot films for the production company of the Madan family in
Bombay; and in 1924 the Madans shot the film *Savitri,* based on Hindu
mythology, in Rome with an Italian cast (the film was later remade by
Osten in Bombay in 1937).[3] Ironically, *Prem Sanyas,* with its strong claim
of Indian authenticity, only survived because it was an international coproduction (Garga, 60). Most of the 1,300 Indian films made during the
silent era were destroyed by neglect or fire, which unfortunately limits the
possibility of creating a visual context for Osten's work — at least where
films shot in India are concerned.

From the perspective of the German production company Emelka, the
proposed project of *Prem Sanyas* must have been promising. As historian
Thomas J. Saunders has noted, the main question confronting the German
film industry in the immediate postwar period was "whether to pursue a
national or international motion picture identity" (Saunders, 89). Emelka
had already undertaken coproductions with British and Hungarian companies and was seeking to raise its international profile. Furthermore,
Germany's longstanding fascination with India had gained momentum
with the 1921 Germany visit by Bengali poet and Nobel laureate
Rabindranath Tagore, and Emelka was trying to capitalize on the wave of

successful books and films with Indian themes, such as Count Hermann Keyserling's *Travel Diary of a Philosopher* (1919) or the films *The Yogi* (Paul Wegener, 1916) and *The Indian Tomb* (Joe May, 1921). May's *The Indian Tomb* was based on a 1918 novel by Thea von Harbou, and it experienced several film adaptations: remakes were shot on location in India by Richard Eichberg in 1938 and by Fritz Lang in 1959 (Rogowski, 64–66). Much earlier, in 1928, Franz Osten also remade *The Indian Tomb* under the title *Shiraz*, his second silent film shot in India. Osten's version was based on a stage play by Niranjan Pal, and much of Eichberg's 1938 remake follows Osten's dramaturgy and use of locations.[4]

Not only did the proposed project of *Prem Sanyas* involve the fashionable topic of India, but it could also tie into the recent German neo-Buddhist revival. In 1924, for instance, the physician Paul Dahlke had opened an influential Buddhist center in Berlin (Zotz, 161; Payer). The institutionalization of Buddhism in Germany was preceded by the publication of Hermann Hesse's novel of a spiritual journey, *Siddhartha*, in 1922 and Alfred Döblin's essay "Buddho und die Natur" (Buddha and Nature) in 1921, in which Döblin merged his psychoanalytically inflected vision of the soul with a Buddhist vision of oneness, declaring it his form of "patriotism" (Döblin, 1200).

Given this background, *Prem Sanyas* was poised to find a German audience. While the Great Eastern Film Company retained the rights for the Indian market and received enough money to cover shooting costs, Emelka was to get the European rights in return for processing and editing the film in Munich and for sending equipment and a film team to India (Barnouw/Krishnaswamy, 95). At this point Franz Osten became involved in the project as the film's director. In February 1925, three months after Pal and Rai had started pre-production in Bombay, Osten embarked on his first of many trips to India as an ambassador of "German cinematic art," with the declared project to make an "authentic Indian film" or — ignoring the rich history of Indian cinema up to that point — "the first specifically Indian film" (Koch, 29). With him traveled three fellow Bavarians, the cameraman Willi Kiermeier, the comedian Bertl Schultes, who served as interpreter, and finally Josef Wirsching, the principal cameraman for *Prem Sanyas*, who was to return to Bombay in the mid-1930s to shoot many films for Bombay Talkies and other studios until 1971.[5] *Prem Sanyas* was shot within five months in many different locations all over India, including Calcutta, Jaipur, Udaipur, Agra, and Benares.

Prem Sanyas found a wider audience than its predecessor, Phalke's *Buddha Dev*. The film opened in Munich on 22 October 1925 and had a successful run in several other European countries. After initial difficulties finding a distributor in Great Britain, *Prem Sanyas* was released with a special screening for the royal family at Windsor Castle on 27 April 1926 and ran in London for one year straight. In Bombay itself the film ran for just two weeks to critical acclaim, but to a disappointing box office (Barnouw/ Krishnaswamy, 96). Reviews in Germany hailed *Prem Sanyas* as "a new achievement of the German film industry," "a glory of German cinematic art" that could conquer new foreign markets for other German films, or — from a proudly Bavarian perspective — simply as the "most beautiful German film ever" (Koch, 22–25). The writer Alfons Paquet remarked that Indians had finally overcome their "shyness of cinematographic technique" and probably were acting in this film not for the sake of money but for "pride in their race" (Koch, 26). In contrast, in the Indian marketing material Franz Osten is barely mentioned, and if at all, he is thanked for his technical support. In that context, the film was clearly presented as an all-Indian enterprise with Niranjan Pal as its visionary author and Himansu Rai as its enterprising producer and star. The *Indian Daily Mail*, for example, saw *Prem Sanyas* as an example of Indian cinema, notwithstanding its international production history: "Western producers begin to realize that Indian folk are just as eager to see the 'real' life of Occidental races depicted on screen" (Great Eastern). The two differing perspectives also have impacted the available secondary literature on *Prem Sanyas*: the film is often labeled either as an Osten film or as a Rai/Pal film. Nevertheless, contemporary reviews in Germany as well as in India agreed in their critique of what they perceived as the film's slow pace and lack of dramatic movement.

Simply Authentic — Excessively Exotic

Prem Sanyas presents the story of Buddha's life: his birth and upbringing as the noble prince Gautama, shielded from all sadness, his opulent marriage with Gopa, his discovery of suffering, his final renunciation of his wealth and his family, and his liberation from all attachments. *Prem Sanyas* opens with a strong claim of Indian authenticity. The viewer reads:

> The Indian Players present / The Light of Asia / By Niranjan Pal with specially selected titles from Sir Edwin Arnold's Masterpiece / As shown by Royal Command at Windsor Castle on April 27th, 1926 / This unique film was produced entirely in India without the aid of studio sets, artificial lights, faked-up properties or make-ups. / His Highness, the Maharajah of Jaipur placed the whole of the resources of his State for the making of the picture. / All the principal characters in the film are portrayed by members of the Indian Players Company, each of whom gave up his or her career as Doctor, Lawyer, Engineer and Professor to bring about a renaissance of the Dramatic Art of India.[6]

At first glance this manifesto reads like a predecessor of the manifestos of the 1990s Danish film movement *Dogma*: no artificial lights, lots of lay actors, and an indigenous independent production. However, the initial

Fig. 10.1. Exotic excess in the marriage ceremony of Gautama and Gopa, Die Leuchte Asiens / Prem Sanyas *(1925). Publicity still. The National Film Archive of India, Pune.*

gesturing at a "less is more" aesthetic is already paired with the anticipation of the pleasures of exotic excess mobilized by the announcement that the film benefited from all that the Maharajah of Jaipur had to offer. The interplay between claims of authenticity and promises of pleasures of excess is programmatic for the entire film: on the one hand it is clearly schooled in the naturalist theater tradition, with its social critique and its attention to milieu detail, and on the other hand it is indebted to the expressionist film tradition in its play with symmetries, its framing of the action through windows and palace arcs, and its reveling in Indian décor, dress, and jewelry. For example, in the wedding of Gautama and Gopa, the attempt at ethnographic realism in the depiction of the religious ceremony and its attention to ritual detail is followed by a carefully framed exit from the temple and luscious shots of the couple riding bejeweled elephants in an opulent wedding procession (fig. 10.1). In general, *Prem Sanyas* pays great attention to animal behavior. At times the story line justifies the emphasis given to these sequences, for example, when Gautama realizes that animal hunting and slaughter is no less evil than human suffering. In other instances the animals seem to become part of an ethnographic gaze that encompasses animals and Indians alike as forms of "wild life."

The film's opening claim of authenticity and the ethnographic gaze that follows are a careful construction, not only in regard to their conflicting aesthetic signals, simplicity and excess, but also in regard to the question of how the film defines Indianness and, of course, Indians. Who are these Indian players who are purportedly presenting this story? To begin with, they are not all just Indian. The female star of *Prem Sanyas*, who played the role of Buddha's wife Gopa, is credited as Seeta (Sita) Devi. Seeta Devi was the screen name created for this film for the thirteen-year-old Anglo-Indian Renée Smith, who also starred in Franz Osten's two subsequent silent films, *Shiraz* (1928) and *Prapansha Pash* (1929). She continued her success in productions of the influential Madan family. However, since Devi did not speak Hindi, she was unable to continue her career in Hindi sound film (Bose, 109). Like Devi, many of the early Indian female leads were Anglo-Indian (for example, Patience Cooper, another Madan star) or had been educated entirely in England (like Devika Rani) — the secondary literature outlines that there was less prejudice in Anglo-Indian circles against acting as a profession for women. In addition, Anglo-Indians represented what was described as the "upper crust" of colonial Indian society. For *Prem Sanyas*, the purity of the artistic enterprise as well as the purity of the spiritual tale should be reflected in the class, caste, and educational background of the actors: therefore the naming of the professions, doctor, lawyer, engineer, and professor, is crucial at that point. Yet the actor and producer Himansu Rai had ceased practicing as a lawyer long before he played the lead in *Prem Sanyas*, and the evocation of the professional sacrifice together with the emphasis on the lay character of the production was to simultaneously cast the production in terms of an Indian national cinema and of an exotic innocence unspoiled by Western acting technique. Moreover, Indian acting here becomes part of the story of the film: it is a story of renunciation and spirituality.

I would go further and argue that besides erasing any international connection that the actors might have had and invoking a notion of spiritual sacrifice, *Prem Sanyas* presented a specifically North Indian vision of India to a European audience. This North Indian vision included the ideological investment in the idea of Aryanism, which — as the historian Thomas R. Trautmann has demonstrated — also played a role in British colonial rule and fantasy: namely the historically untenable theory that the light-skinned Aryans invaded Northern India in ancient times, forced the dark-skinned Dravidians to the south, and established a superior, sophisticated Hindu culture. In the Third Reich, Indians would be described as a type of racial predecessor of the "master race," as Vedic Aryans. Together with the sense of a common enemy, Great Britain, the idea of Aryanism led to ideological affinities between India and the Third Reich, of which Franz Osten's 1936 film *Achhut Kanya* provides an example that cannot easily be categorized.

Fig. 10.2. The dark-skinned baby Buddha in Die Leuchte Asiens / Prem Sanyas *(1925). Publicity still. The National Film Archive of India, Pune.*

What one could call "Aryan fantasies" can also be found before the Third Reich, in Germany's India enthusiasm and the neo-Buddhist wave of the 1920s. In his 1919 *Travel Diary of a Philosopher*, Count Hermann Keyserling, for example, critiqued the idea of heredity in the Indian caste system as at least in part imaginary, but gushed about the perfect specimens of Indian breeding and aristocracy and their inherited spiritual depth, which he encountered in Jaipur, which was where much of *Prem Sanyas* was filmed (Keyserling, 219). Thus it is not surprising that the German press did not shy away from describing the film's star and coproducer, Himansu Rai, as a "pure-blooded Indian" (Koch, 25), which projected a homogenizing racial discourse onto India that made even less sense in regard to the ethnically, linguistically, and culturally heterogeneous Indian subcontinent.

It would be too easy, though, to assume that these notions only worked as communal fantasies in the shooting of the film. Niranjan Pal, who wrote the script of *Prem Sanyas*, relates that he had very serious differences with Osten around the casting of baby Buddha. The boy Pal had chosen was deemed too light-skinned by Osten, who insisted that little Buddha had to be dark, so as not to be mistaken for a German child (Garga, 62) (fig. 10.2). In the same vein, the German film-trade magazine

LichtBildBühne reported that Osten was intent on casting lay extras who would truly be what they were supposed to represent: priests, beggars, or fortunetellers (Koch, 35). Again, in this instance Osten's sense of cinematic realism and Indian authenticity clashed with Pal's vision of artistic purity and exemplary stagecraft. The construction of the "Indian players" presented in the opening titles points to this theatrical vision, which is specifically Bengali. Himansu Rai's family owned a theater, and Rai was indebted to the longstanding and vibrant Bengali theater tradition in Calcutta. The film's reference to the "renaissance of the Dramatic Art of India," as well as the setup of the film as a narration within a narration with the audience reaction built in, supports the impression that for this sacred story of Buddha's life the film was recreating the Bengali stage in the spirit of poets Rabindranath Tagore or Girish Ghosh.[7]

The stage, rather the national stage, is set in the opening sequences of the film as follows:

> Every winter large numbers of European tourists are attracted to romantic India, The land of many wonders and contrasts, / Where the relic of an age-old civilization still holds magic sway over its teeming population, / And the fastest of motor cars vie for popularity with the slow pacing oxen carts.

Images of elephants and camels are contrasted with city traffic, denoting India as a land of contrasts between modernization and primitiveness, modernity and myth. The holy places of Hinduism and Islam in India are presented in this mix of travelogue and ethnography, emphasizing its religious diversity. In Gaya, where the temple of Buddha stands, the perspective shifts from the national stage to the stage for this passion play, and slowly, a group of tourists — three women, three men — comes into view, walking down the street toward the audience, viewing the merchandise in the stalls and negotiating with a street vendor. Their guide shows them the local fruit and leads them to a snake charmer and a dancing bear, and the tourists watch with amusement. The common silent film trope of depicting the fascination with a circus act prefaces their encounter with an expressively gesticulating old sage at Buddha's temple, therefore functioning not only as a meta-media moment but also as a setup for a colonial gaze. The sage narrates the story of Buddha, the story of the film (fig. 10.3). At the end, the film returns to the frame narration of the sage and the tourists, and the camera slowly zooms out until a palm leaf, an exotic stand-in for the familiar stage curtain, obscures the image.

In *Cinema at the End of Empire*, Priya Jaikumar recently described *Prem Sanyas* as part of Himansu Rai's efforts "to aim for an international audience with a self-consciously elite creative group" that ultimately produced "orientalist depictions of India" (Jaikumar, 96). While the presentation of the narrative frame obviously supports this claim, it seems that this

Fig. 10.3. The Indian sage explains his culture to the European tourists in Die Leuchte Asiens / Prem Sanyas *(1925). Publicity still. The National Film Archive of India, Pune.*

framing still simultaneously allows for different and conflicting identifications. On the one hand the audience could attach to the gaze of the tourists, on the other the tourists could also be viewed as the spectacle. Their white tropical suits and silly helmets stick out in the crowd, everything quotidian has to be explained to them by the guide, and their movements are no less fumbling than those of the dancing bear right next to them. The ambiguity of this scene also plays out on a larger scale: on the one hand, telling the life of Buddha could be and was viewed by some as part of an effort to create an Indian national cinema with its own stories; on the other hand, the images cite Christian iconography or European myth-making productions such as Fritz Lang's two-part *Die Nibelungen* (The Nibelungs, 1924), which was released in the year before *Prem Sanyas* was shot.

The divergent agendas in the production of *Prem Sanyas* led to visual ambiguities that go beyond a simple dichotomy of foreign vs. familiar. While the film was pitched to a German audience as an exotic pleasure ride, and to an Indian audience as a "record of the real life of Indian peo-

ple" (*Indian Daily Mail*), it still could easily be hailed by reviewers in
Germany as representative of German cinema, or it still could be rejected
by audiences in India as factually flawed and, ultimately, too exoticizing.[8]
Ironically, Osten's subsequent two silent collaborations with Himansu
Rai, *Shiraz* and *Prapansha Pash*, which were coproduced with the Ufa
film studio and took a turn toward a less subtle orientalism and more
opulent melodrama, were successful in India, while *Prem Sanyas* was
not.

Beyond the Weimar Republic: Melodrama, Caste and Race

When their time at Ufa in Berlin ended in 1933, Himansu Rai and Devika
Rani founded Bombay Talkies, in order to produce nation-building films
for Indian audiences. Rai's vision of film as international art that could
only be improved with foreign collaboration was increasingly in conflict
with the cultural agenda of the national independence movement. This
becomes especially apparent in the 1936 Rai-Osten collaboration of
Achhut Kanya, a tragic inter-caste love story starring Rani and Kumar. This
landmark film of Hindi cinema was an attack on colonial rule and untouchability, which Gandhi had decried as an archaic plague. However, as film
scholar Vijay Mishra has noted, the depiction of the untouchable by the
movie star Devika Rani "removes the politics of the subaltern untouchable
completely from the text" (Mishra, 19). To Mishra, the logic of melodrama and its evocation of fate completely exclude the possibility of a
politically relevant social critique of caste at the time. Himansu Rai tried in
vain to persuade Gandhi to see *Achhut Kanya*. Franz Osten was more successful in connecting to political circles back in Berlin, arranging a special
screening for Joseph Goebbels, who purportedly enjoyed the film. The
critique of caste, which at this specific historic moment of Indian nationalism was described as an oppressive, feudal system, could align with the
National Socialist vision of a racially unified *Volk* liberating itself from hierarchies imposed by a small elite. While it is certainly true that in *Achhut
Kanya* untouchability is at times reduced to a fairy tale of poverty (and the
pleasure of seeing a star suffer), the film gains political urgency in its powerful depiction of mob violence. The social control of friendly neighbors
in a village can easily and accidentally turn into mass hysteria, which is
visually associated with an uncontrollable murderous fire. Moreover,
Achhut Kanya deals with the social taboo of inter-caste marriage (it was
released a year after the Nuremberg Laws were passed, which rendered
marriage between Jews and non-Jews illegal in Nazi Germany). The film
remains ambiguous enough to make it possible to read it either way — as
a melodrama in which the final sacrifice ultimately reasserts the order of

things or as a melodrama in which the excess allows for subversive viewings.

It is telling that some accounts of Franz Osten's three silent films shot in India and his Bombay Talkies films downplay his role to that of a "technician." In turn, other accounts credit Himansu Rai simply as an actor and not as the enterprising producer and cinematic visionary that he was. It seems crucial for further readings of Osten's work in India to see these films in the context of European as well as Indian silent cinema as dynamic, transnational collaborations of different theater and film traditions and political interests, which do not neatly align with national cinema or national politics.

Notes

I wish to thank the following persons and institutions for their generous support of this research: The National Film Archive of India in Pune and its now retired director K. S. Sashidharan, Shekhar Krishnan, Amrit Gangar, Kaushik Bhaumik, Shridhar Raghavan, and Raju Bharathan. This article also benefited from the intensive discussions in the second *Unknown Weimar* workshop directed by Anton Kaes and Eric Rentschler in the summer of 2006. Other works I consulted beyond those referenced in the text are: Lahoti, Rangoonwalla, Schoenfeld, and Roerich.

[1] Franz Osten's brother, Peter Ostermayr, had secured the rights for Ludwig Ganghofer's novels and oversaw the production and in most cases the direction of the Ganghofer film series. Ostermayr's particular branding of the Alps as what film scholar Johannes von Moltke has termed "therapeutic topography" led him to be remembered as the "father of Heimatfilm" (36).

[2] According to Pal's son, Colin Pal, Rai and Pal worked on scripts together (Gangar, *Osten,* 12).

[3] There were many instances where Indian filmmakers sought technical support in Germany, especially with the advent of sound and color film; for example, V. Shanataram had the color prints for his 1933 film *Sairandhiri* processed in Germany (Ramachandran, *50 Years*).

[4] For example, the dramatic execution scene with the elephant and the subsequent death of the maid are almost identical in shot sequence.

[5] Excerpts of Schultes's memoirs regarding the shooting of *Prem Sanyas* are reprinted in Koch's catalogue. Other Germans actively involved in the early Bombay film scene were Karl von Spreti, a set designer for many Bombay Talkies movies, Willie Zolle, the head of the Bombay Talkies laboratory, the author Willy Haas, who was exiled to Bombay for a few years and wrote the script for *Prem Nagar — City of Love* (1940), and Paul Zils, who became a crucial figure in the Indian documentary film movement in the late 1940s and 1950s. (See Gangar, *Osten*; Gangar, *Zils*; and von Ungern-Sternberg.)

6 My discussion of the film is based on the version in The National Film Archive of India in Pune.

7 Brandlmeier points out the various anachronisms and inconsistencies in the film; for example, the film's wedding costumes and rituals were in accordance with Bengali tradition (91).

8 Bollywood scholar Rachel Dwyer has pointed out the blatant anachronisms of this film, for example, the depiction of Muslim architecture as classical heritage or the fact that Jaipur, established in the eighteenth century, "passes for ancient India" (Dwyer, 21).

Works Cited

Barnouw, Erik, and S. Krishnaswamy. *Indian Film.* New York, Oxford, and New Delhi: Oxford UP, 1980.

Bose, Mihir. *Bollywood: A History.* New Delhi: Roli Books, 2006.

Brandlmeier, Thomas. "Franz Osten (Ostermayr): A Bavarian in Bombay." *Griffithiana* 53 (1995): 76–93.

Döblin, Alfred. "Buddho und die Natur." *Die Neue Rundschau* 32.2 (1921): 1192–1200.

Dwyer, Rachel. *Filming the Gods: Religion and Indian Cinema.* London and New York: Routledge, 2006.

Gangar, Amrit. *Franz Osten and the Bombay Talkies: A Journey from Munich to Malad.* Mumbai: Max Mueller Bhavan (Goethe-Institut Mumbai), 2001.

———. *Paul Zils and the Indian Documentary.* Mumbai: Max Mueller Bhavan (Goethe-Institut Mumbai), 2003.

Garga, B. D. *So Many Cinemas: The Motion Picture in India.* Mumbai: Eminence Designs, 1996.

The Great Eastern Corporation Ld. *The Light of Asia.* Promotional booklet. New Delhi: G. E. C. Ld., 1926.

Jaikumar, Priya. *Cinema at the End of Empire.* Durham, NC, and London: Duke UP, 2006.

Koch, Gerhard. *Franz Osten's Indian Silent Films.* New Delhi: Max Mueller Bhavan, 1983.

Lahoti, Devendra Pratap. "Pioneering Works of Himansu Rai" and "India's Dream Girl No.1 — Devika Rani." In *70 Years of Indian Cinema (1913–1983),* edited by T. M. Ramachandran, 85–99. Bombay: Cinema-India International, 1985.

Mishra, Vijay. *Bollywood Cinema: Temples of Desire.* London and New York: Routledge, 2002.

Payer, Alois. "Materialien zum Neobuddhismus: Lehrveranstaltung Neobuddhismus, Univ. Tübingen." http://www.payer.de/neobuddhismus/neobud0305.htm (accessed 15 January 2008).

Ramachandran, T. M., ed. *50 Years of Indian Talkies (1931–1981)*. Bombay: Indian Academy of Motion Picture Arts & Sciences, 1981.

———, ed. *70 Years of Indian Cinema (1913–1983)*. Bombay: Cinema India-International, 1985.

Rangoonwalla, Firoze. *A Retrospective of Bombay Talkies Films*. Bombay: Film Forum, n.d.

Rogowski, Christian. "Movies, Money, and Mystique: Joe May's Early Weimar Blockbuster, *The Indian Tomb* (1921)." In *Weimar Cinema: An Essential Guide to Classic Films of the Era*, edited by Noah Isenberg, 55–77. New York: Columbia UP, 2009.

Saunders, Thomas J. *Hollywood in Berlin: American Cinema and Weimar Germany*. Berkeley: U of California P, 1994.

Schoenfeld, Carl-Erdmann. "Franz Osten's 'the Light of Asia': A German-Indian Film of Prince Buddha — 1926." *Historical Journal of Film, Radio and Television* 15/4 (1995): 555–61.

The Light of Asia: Struggle of Gautama Buddha through Love and Renunciation (Film Booklet). New Delhi: The Great Eastern Corporation Ld., 1926.

The Roerich and Devika Rani Roerich Estate Board. "Devika Rani Roerich." http://www.roerich.kar.nic.in/devikarani.htm (accessed 11 January 2008).

Trautmann, Thomas R. *Aryans and British India*. Berkeley, Los Angeles, and London: U of California P, 1997.

von Moltke, Johannes. *No Place Like Home: Locations of Heimat in German Cinema*. Berkeley: U of California P, 2005.

von Ungern-Sternberg, Christoph. "Willy Haas: A German Jewish Scriptwriter Exiled in India." *Cinemaya* 65 (2005): 43–54.

Zotz, Volker. *Auf den glückseligen Inseln: Buddhismus in der deutschen Kultur*. Berlin: Theseus, 2000.

11: The Body in Time: Wilhelm Prager's *Wege zu Kraft und Schönheit* (1925)

Theodore F. Rippey

> *Exposed and naked is our thinking. Now we comprehend the body, uncaged and without veiling insinuations. Radiant bronze skin mirrors the light of the Olympian sun with the same pure sobriety as the sparkling pistons of clearly formed machines.*
>
> — Wolfgang Graeser, 1927

> *Outside: harmony and softness; inside: function and anatomy — that is becoming the formula. But now we see even more: consciousness instead of gesture. Instead of the limbs as a system of signals, instead of the modified semaphore-culture spawned by war, a corporal will. A body-culture.*
>
> — Fritz Giese, 1925

CHAMPIONS OF WEIMAR REPUBLICANISM draped the postwar democracy in the mantle of poets and thinkers, harking back to the classic achievements of a nation of culture. But even as they did so, the citizens of the republic were going mad for prizefighters, revue girls, and record-setting sprinters. Observers of the times framed the rising currency of and fascination with performing bodies as both symptom and catalyst of important shifts in interwar German life — and modernity generally. *Wege zu Kraft und Schönheit* (Paths to Strength and Beauty), which premiered on 16 March 1925 at Berlin's opulent Ufa-Palast am Zoo cinema, occupies an interstice between the dizzying expanse of *Körperkultur* (body culture) and those who sought to define it.[1]

Paths to Strength and Beauty strikes today's eye as an unintentionally comic melange. One grins at the documentary images of the modern body beautiful, chuckles at the contrived sequences that admonish viewers to kick-start fitness regimens, and nearly guffaws at the hackneyed reenactments of grand physical achievements of ages past (classical Greece in particular). Weimar-era critics, however, took this film as an impressive and important part of an emerging body culture, the seriousness of which is reflected in the attempts of the authors quoted above to bring gravity to the discourse of the physical and rescue the body from its equation with superficies. "Unfortunately, body-culture is still too neglected in Germany, unlike in other nations," wrote one reviewer in the *Reichsfilmblatt*. "This film will open the eyes of many people and show them the debt they have incurred to themselves."[2]

In its demonstration of how to settle that debt, the film unleashes what Siegfried Kracauer called a "frenetic gush" of body images (146). I do not pretend to offer an exhaustive analysis of this unwieldy flow here. In exploring how the film sets bodies in time, however, I will characterize the problems of corporality, modernity, and identity that underlie the film and assess the political implications of how the film tackles these issues. The film's depictions of bodies in history and decelerated movement are the focal points of my analysis, and two initial overviews provide context for my close readings: first, of the broad public discourse on physical culture and more specialized scientific study of perceived links between physical and psychological constitution; second, of the film's content and production circumstances. I argue that the filmic rendering of an ideal morphology, which could stand outside time, is fueled by the desire to resolve the contradiction between the modern concept of the sovereign subject and the modern social, economic, and cultural systems that thwart such sovereignty.

Body Culture and Constitution Research

Weimar Germany saw an explosion of physical culture that included reinvigoration of amateur gymnastics, track, boxing, and team-sport clubs across all regions, classes, and political factions; the emergence of professional sports competitions (prize fights in particular) as mass spectacles; a revue and film culture in which elaborate choreography of performing bodies became a prominent aesthetic component (from the chorus girls at Berlin's *Admiralspalast* to the throngs of Ernst Lubitsch's historical epics or Fritz Lang's *Metropolis*); and a range of print media that saturated the interwar cultural landscape with images of the body (Cowan, *Cult*). Outright hostility to the development of physical culture as body-conditioning was rare. Who, after all, could argue with the notion that a defeated and depleted nation would be well served by a reinvigoration of the body? Quite common, however, were critical voices troubled by the prospect of an excess of the physical, be it in the form of a threatening mass or in the obsession with toning muscles at the expense of tuning the mind. For every Paul Samson Körner, the German boxing star of the early and mid-1920s who wrote and spoke publicly about the need for German youth to develop their strength and advance the discipline of their "outer and inner selves" through sport (Samson Körner), there was a Gustav Stresemann, the German foreign minister who saw the displacement of the "aristocracy of mind and spirit" by an "aristocracy of the biceps" as a net loss for his country.[3]

Accompanying the adversarial public debates, there was a critical discourse that sought to characterize the deeper significance of postwar

German society's embrace of the physical. The quotations that head this essay exemplify this discourse, and the text from which the second is taken, Fritz Giese's *Girlkultur* (Girl Culture), typifies the Weimar-era effort to isolate what were viewed as the American qualities of physical culture (and culture generally) and strategize about the most productive appropriation of those qualities. Giese, a Social-Democratic labor psychologist and cultural critic, published broadly on the scientific organization of the workplace as well as on physical culture. *Girlkultur* was preceded by an influential book on conditioning the female body, a collaboration with Hedwig Hagemann (whose school is featured in *Paths to Strength and Beauty*) and other proponents of systems of nude exercise for women as developed by American fitness pioneer Dr. Bess Mensendieck. As Karl Toepfer notes, Giese saw in this system a means of fostering a "highly unique identity, which can adapt well to the complexities and instabilities of a modern life driven above all by 'technology'" (74). Giese was a "rationalist" in his approach to nudity, because he grounded his "nudist discourse in the rhetorics of science, history, and aesthetic theory, rather than in the rhetorics of myths, nature, and national will" (74). Giese's general approach to body culture overlaps significantly with that of *Paths to Strength and Beauty*. For Giese, the phenomenon of the *Girl*, embodied most perfectly by the dancers of the internationally famous Tiller Girls revue troupe, came into being at the convergence of visual mass media (film in particular), multi-racial American society, and a specifically modern aesthetic sensibility that values rhythmic, dynamic form, and sensually (as opposed to intellectually) graspable performance. "The American human being manifests itself in the girl," this "mini-machine" (17) whose performance is itself a substance that transports the *Girl* beyond mere show.

Giese seeks not the destruction of the rational subject (the absolute triumph of the body over the mind) but the re-setting of thought in the body's register. The body is the concrete, sensual matrix of our interaction with the world, and Giese surveys a whole history of German intellectual abstraction that has, in its progress, literally separated the nation from reality. "How does Kant's theory help us?" he asks. "Schelling's theory of nature? And what are we supposed to do with Hegel's abstraction? What practical value does one find in Spengler's conclusions? The people who committed suicide after reading *The Decline of the West* did the rest of us a service: we cannot really use them, just as we cannot put Spengler's conclusions to use" (131). In Giese's eyes, postwar Germany needs less inhibition, less rumination, more pragmatism, more optimism, more *action*. And here the older culture can learn from the younger the virtues of a special naiveté that can place relishing the physical in a symbiotic relationship with economic productivity and social harmony.

Giese's notion of corporal will (*Wollen des Körperlichen*) is awkward when translated literally: *wanting of the bodily*. The German genitive (even more so than the English) undermines a clear sense of whether the bodily is the subject or object of desire. One suspects a design behind the imprecision, for Giese posits the corporal as a desiring entity unto itself while at the same time pushing a model of intellect that forges objectives in a more corporally conscious way. In Giese's descriptive model, a body consciousness heightened from both sides of the traditional body/mind divide forms a powerful elective affinity with the pragmatic intelligence that has so empowered America. This symbiosis differs greatly from the German reduction of the body to a semaphore instrument by a martial intelligence that had become too abstracted from the corporal realm. In the proliferation of body culture Giese sees an opportunity for Germany to gain something crucial that it has thus far lacked.

Surveying the postwar world through a more narrowly focused, scientific lens, proponents of constitution research saw another lack that they also considered an impediment to social progress: a set of blank areas in the typological map of the human character. Filling these in was the objective of *Körperbau und Charakter* (Physique and Character), the internationally influential work by the field's best-known representative, Ernst Kretschmer. Kretschmer was a professor of psychiatry at Marburg, and his 1921 text saw eight editions by 1930. The core elements of his diagnostic system were three physiological and two psychological types, which in myriad subdivisions and combinations could account for the vast range of human personalities. This typology began with seeing the body anew:

> We must tread the laborious path of systematic written descriptive sketching of the body from head to toe, with caliper-compass and measuring tape whenever possible, simultaneously photographing and drawing what we see. [. . .] We must make series of hundreds of observations of every single patient we can reach, always following the same rigorous scheme. Above all, however, *we must learn again to make use of our eyes, simply to see and observe*, without aid of microscope and laboratory. (2; my emphasis)

The description of medical method sets an objective for visual perception training that reaches beyond the borders of psychiatric practice. To view intently and efficiently, recognizing defining features quickly, is to bring order to the potential chaos of any newly encountered corporal material. This is an impulse central to the agenda of *Paths to Strength and Beauty*, and evidence of its broad expression in Weimar pop culture abounds.

Kretschmer's ideas were disseminated by a plethora of journalists, who peppered the daily and weekly press with features on physiology and character research in the 1920s and early 1930s. As Lynne Frame demonstrates in a compelling analysis of journalistic and popular-novel portrayals of women's physiques and personalities, the efforts of constitution research to "give contours to a society in disarray" (13) are as traceable in a tabloid feature on the characterological implications of women's sitting leg position as they are in clinical literature. In both forums, one detects the urgent effort to make the body readable as a means of mapping the mind.

Such a process of physiological and psychological characterization offered the prospect of scoring a dual victory in the struggle to overcome the epistemological instability that plagued what Helmut Lethen aptly calls the "improvised" republic (7) as it sought to establish its own formal and informal structures amid Wilhelmine ruins. In his seminal study *Verhaltenslehren der Kälte* (translated as *Cool Conduct*),[4] Lethen elaborates the compelling thesis that moments of "social disorganization" intensify the need for behavioral paradigms that enable distinction of the known from the foreign, the inner from the outer — the distinctions without which identity is not possible. These are the imperatives that fueled the work of Giese and Kretschmer just as they fueled *Paths to Strength and Beauty*.

Ufa, the *Kulturfilm*, and *Paths to Strength and Beauty*

Dominating the domestic film market by 1920, *Universum Film Aktiengesellschaft* (Ufa) embarked on an ambitious program to increase its economic strength and cultural prestige on an international scale.[5] As part of the latter effort, the conglomerate established a special production arm for "cultural films" (*Kulturfilme*).[6] Designed to have a didactic or edifying function, their content ranged from sexual hygiene (often controversial for their frankness) to geographical/anthropological subjects (often rife with colonialist imagery) to more technical and pop-cultural topics of current interest (sport, factories, expeditions, and so on). The cultural films generally maintained documentary and/or didactic conventions (audience address, reporting, analysis, "lessons"), but staged scenes were frequently combined with documentary footage to flesh out filmmakers' designs. Ufa's *Kulturfilm* division was anything but an afterthought: it produced over one hundred and thirty films from 1919 to 1944, reaching a high point in 1930 with fifteen films, many of which had a length of over 2,000 meters.

The most important single figure over the history of the *Kulturfilm* division was arguably Nicholas Kaufmann, a Swiss citizen and physician who worked at Berlin's prestigious Charité clinic before coming to Ufa in 1919 to work on the first cultural film, *Die Geschlechtskrankheiten und ihre Folgen* (Sexually Transmitted Diseases and their Consequences). The relationship thus begun proved durable: Kaufmann stayed with Ufa throughout the Weimar years and beyond, emigrating back to Switzerland in 1944.[7]

In the early 1920s the *Kulturfilm* frequently thematized hygiene and fitness; technology and its impact on modern life; historical and regional foundations of German identity; and race; much of which dovetailed with Kaufmann's interest in medically and scientifically themed films. All these concerns are present in *Paths to Strength and Beauty*, which uses the overarching subject of "modern physical culture" as a vehicle for communicating a diverse set of messages pertaining to national health at this juncture in German history. The film, in production during 1923 and 1924, was scripted and overseen by Kaufmann (by then the head of *Kulturfilm* production), and he shared directing credit with Wilhelm Prager, an important *Kulturfilm* director in his own right. At a final cut length of 2,567 meters it was the longest cultural film to date, and its length was surpassed only on rare occasions in the two decades following.

The film itself consists of six parts, covering the Ancient Greeks and the Weimar present; gymnastics for fitness; rhythmic gymnastics; dance; sport; and the open-air, active lifestyle. It surveys the state of interwar German corporal affairs and efforts to improve physical conditioning, and it also establishes a historical narrative that begins with the ancient synthesis of physical and mental health. The film assumes that this synthesis was destroyed as a consequence of the industrialization and mechanization of modern life, and it bemoans the atrophying of the body among professionals and white-collar workers, whose labor no longer requires physical exertion. As the body deteriorates, so does the collective national condition, and while the film does not fixate on the national, it clearly frames the effort to reclaim the Greek ideal as both empowering for the citizen and crucial for the nation-state.

Bodies in History

The film opens with three quick images of ancient Greece (a temple and two statues), and the initial titles and images establish the chasm separating the classical harmony of body-and-mind cultivation from a postwar Europe that breeds inadequately exercised, stressed, nervous bodies. After a comic illustration of a bourgeois apartment filled with irritable types (portly father, nagging/hovering wife, high-strung daughter), a title announces the ancient *Gymnasium* as the place where actual gymnastics was a core component of the educational process. The image that follows graphically matches the front view of the temple roof from the film's opening shot. The pigeons perched atop it immediately give away its dimensions, though, and the following shot reveals that this is the entrance to a contemporary prep school. This place is still called *Gymnasium*, despite the fact that grammar has displaced physical training at the curricular core. Thus the graphic match is ironic, the visual resonance serving only to underscore how far removed modern educational institutions and the cities that they serve have become from the mind-body harmony of ancient Athens.

The culprits? Books and machines. The mechanization of modern life is represented here by a montage sequence that anticipates Walther Ruttmann's *Berlin: Symphony of a Great City*, and shots of frail, bookish types and harried office workers illustrate the increasing specialization of the knowledge economy. Those seeking release from the workday grind only sap their strength further by gallivanting about in nightclubs and filling themselves with alcohol. A title explicitly designates such behavior as sinful, admonishing viewers that such transgressions will be exposed and punished.

Moments later we receive our second visual dose of reconstructed Greece, this one a richer and more dynamic seven-shot sequence lasting approximately one minute and five seconds. These shots provide a quick rundown of classical-age sprinting, discus, wrestling, and boxing. The medium and medium-long shots of the competitors are bookended by an establishing shot, which shows athletes entering the stadium and allows us to survey the arena, and a closing shot, in which setting and camera position mirror the first. This sequence is followed by a scene in which a cross-section of the Weimar physically unfit (stout burghers, sunken-eyed intellectuals, decadent socialites) is paraded in front of a classical female nude. The lookers have only indignation, blank stares, or disinterest to offer — none can engage meaningfully with the statue, which, as suddenly becomes clear, is actually a young woman in a tableau vivant-style frozen pose. Together with the Greek sports sequence, the living statue reinforces the distance — not only in time, but also in attitude — that separates the invigorating Greek celebration of the body and the current day.

The next historical sequence focuses on the corset. A title announces that fashion has forced women into corsets for centuries and complains that contemporary fashion still inhibits female fitness: we view a close-up of a woman's back, which then turns to an animated image that shows a corset being put on and tightened. An animated X-ray effect shows the ribs and organs being squeezed beneath. A title proclaims, "A truly beautiful woman needs no corset," and the next image is a medium shot of a Greek female torso statue. In neither case do we see a face, and the sequence advances its argument about beauty as harmonic muscular development. The next image is a long shot of two nude women from behind, posing on a beach, whose bodies echo the proportions of the statue. A title, "The harmonic proportionality of the body was the ideal of the ancient Greeks," forms the transition to the next Greek reenactment scene (the myth of the "Judgment of Paris"), in which three women disrobe and strike classical poses for their male admirers (fig. 11.1). We see them from head to toe, and the gaze we are allowed upon the full and fully proportioned body in both the contemporary and the classical shot becomes a means of overcoming the distance established in the earlier ancient Greek juxtapositions. A connection, this part of the film visually suggests, can indeed be made between Germany in the 1920s and the Greek Golden Age.

Fig. 11.1. *"Greek goddesses" disrobe in a reenactment of the "Judgment of Paris" in* Wege zu Kraft und Schönheit. *Promotion still.*

The evidence for such a connection then mounts steadily. Moments later a title and establishing shot introduce us to Hellerau, Émile Jaques-Dalcroze's academy for rhythmic gymnastics near Dresden, the cradle of the eurhythmics movement. The Hellerau façade recalls the ancient temple from the outset of the film, and the Hellerau students that we see demonstrate repeatedly those movements that the film designates as evidence of muscular harmony, thus beauty. At this juncture we begin to see multibody groupings and coordinated programs of movement. Lines or small formations of bodies in synchronized motion hint in the direction of conditioning as a collective endeavor. The film now also begins to couple its discourse on harmony as the root of beauty of form with rhythm as the root of beauty in movement.

Here the film underscores that the body in motion must be cultivated, just like the body at rest, and that the objective is nothing short of complete physical control. The Hellerau students demonstrate synchronized movement as well as poses, modeling for viewers the proper ways to contract and relax their muscles. The images posit a state of harmonic proportionality in which the body becomes its own natural corset, its exercise reflecting a full consciousness of limits and a full realization of potential. The Mensendieck student sequences that follow elaborate this ideal oscillation between movement and stillness under the sign of control, reinforcing the film's case for a vibrant interactivity between the body cultures of ancient Greece and Weimar Germany. At the end of part 3 the antithesis of the two, established in the film's opening sequences, achieves its synthesis.

That synthesis is the grounds for a visual equation offered near the conclusion of the film, in which editing and mise-en-scène work in concert to match the classical model with the modern situation. Essentially summarizing the film, a title announces, "And that is the way that the classical ideals of body culture again receive what they are due." To underscore the synopsis visually, Prager and Kaufmann use the exact same opening shot from the Greek athletics survey discussed above, which shows three loincloth-clad youths entering a re-created Greek stadium. This is followed by a shot (same camera height, angle, and distance) of a 1920s stadium, with a steam of bare-backed youths entering the frame from our right.

The film is quite preachy on matters of health and strength, but it tends to avoid sermonizing about national rejuvenation. Reviews suggest, however, that the point was clear enough. "This film," wrote one critic in *LichtBildBühne*, "shows the place where the building-up of the German people must begin anew" ("Wege zu Kraft und Schönheit"). But if these sequences labor openly to restore the physical to its rightful place and implicitly to demarcate a point of departure for national rebuilding, then the series of images I will now treat open the door to the body's virtual apotheosis — a process with the potential to both reinforce and undermine the Hellenistic narrative.

Stretching Seconds

At just short of four-and-a-half minutes, the Mensendieck images are unusually long for a sequence devoted to a single body-culture proponent. The sequence uses no slow motion at all: deceleration in this case comes from the performing bodies themselves, as the women, nude or in form-fitting, gauzy singlets, demonstrate their deliberate yet fluid movement-forms — reminiscent of yoga poses rather than hard workouts — individually or in small groups. In one shot, a single woman in profile executes a knee-bend that lasts fourteen seconds from initial standing position, through the half-squat to the return to upright position. In a long take eight shots later, two women face each other in profile, approach one another with one mirrored step, then kneel and perform a deep bow that takes their chests to their thighs and their heads near the ground. Those movements total thirty-six seconds. The final shot of the sequence is another "mirror" exercise, in which two women, facing each other in quarter-profile with their backs to the camera, go from a standing position to balancing on one foot as they lean toward each other. They then clasp one hand and raise the other and, drawing their faces very close to one another, rise to a tip-toe stance. The last movement takes five seconds; the entire exercise takes fifty.

The sequence compels the viewer (just as the exercise method compels the women) to train in on the bodies in motion, focusing both on distinct performing parts (an arm, a foot, a knee) and organic performing wholes. Mise-en-scène establishes the classical aesthetic evoked at the film's outset: when shot straight-on, the women exercise against simple natural backgrounds (lakes, meadows, trees); when shot from below, they are silhouetted against the sky. Most of the shots are framed at the threshold between medium and long, enabling the photographed bodies to fill the frame in a way that violates the conventions of narrative cinema but performs the documentary function desired here perfectly.

In moments when the deliberate slowness grinds down to virtual stillness, we reach the kinetic opposite of the scenario sketched humorously at the outset of the film, in which the harried and portly bourgeois is jostled and propelled by impatient taxi driver, screaming baby, pestering wife, and pressing appointments — none of which he can control — and literally choked by a recalcitrant starched collar. The Mensendieck sequences elide all that is hectic, removing the clutter (including clothes) of frenetic urban civilization, and visually argue that a program of concentrated exercise can literally undo the damage that civilization inflicts. The objective is the removal of all impediments to the perfection (*Vollendung*) to which, according to the film, the body naturally aspires and the recovery of an organic rhythm long obliterated by the "machinic *Takt*" of modernity (Cowan, "The Heart Machine"). Here is the stability that the citizens of Lethen's improvised republic so desperately sought.

Corporal control and high performance converge in the sequence on Russian ballerina Tamara Karsavina in the film's fourth part. There are three sub-sequences here: the first shows Karsavina doing balance and flexibility exercises, the second shows her performing with a partner, and the third (a single shot) shows a brief solo sequence of jumps, turns, and *battements* in slow motion. The third shot, set up by the title "Only the slow-motion camera can demonstrate the full beauty and power of Karsavina's art," is of principal interest here as a compelling illustration of the film's objectives in physical and visual training. Here the viewer can actually trace alternating muscular tension and relaxation on the contours of Karsavina's arms and legs, and the deceleration of the moving image allows us to consume visually that effort in Karsavina's elegance and fluidity which, at normal speed, we would note but not be able to process. The camera performs what Walter Benjamin characterizes as a surgical function, discovering things heretofore unknown to the naked eye (499–500). In so doing, though, it alters the very process of visual apprehension, giving the eye a new level of focus to aspire to.

Seeing the body defy gravity is exciting, and that excitement in the Karsavina sequence facilitates the film's rhetorical objective of rendering a *transcendent* body that breaks the bounds to which we assume bodies to be subject. This effect intensifies in a sequence in part 5, featuring German champion gymnast Rudolf Kobs on the horizontal bar. Watching the one-minute-and-fifty-seconds' worth of slow-motion footage of Kobs's routine, today's viewer acquires a deep sense of the cultural logic of Graeser's effusive proclamations about naked thinking, bronze skin, and clearly formed machines. With camera and sun angle working to produce a natural-light chiaroscuro effect on Kobs's body, and with the gymnast clad only in a brief singlet, the spectator takes in an image-stream of rippling, flexing, and undulating muscles as Kobs flies, flips, and turns. The light-and-shadow contrast enhances our perception of tension and relaxation, and unlike the Karsavina sequence, Kobs's muscles bulge — creating ridges and plateaus on the skin that impress without becoming grotesque. Again, gravity is defied, and the eye lingers over the biceps, triceps, quadriceps, abdominals, glutei, and the smaller muscles that encase the skeletal torso. Again, the ideal is forged: a body stripped bare of cultural and historical marking, achieving a new level of perfection and empowerment in its performance, cinematographically captured in a way that enables it to float outside time (fig. 11.2).

Not much is made (explicitly at least) of gender difference in these sequences. Nonetheless, Kobs's musculature forms a set of concrete, gendered contours, emphasizing the *strength* in *Strength and Beauty* and distinguishing a masculine ideal of corporal performance from the feminine ideal embodied by Karsavina. Gender differences established implicitly or explicitly in the film are backed by the traditional distinction of stronger/fairer and/or the force of modern science. Dr. Mensendieck, it is explained, has developed a conditioning system perfect for the *female* body, and it is always men who are featured in activities like discus, hammer-throw, and boxing. Thus the film allows a traditional separation to persist without becoming anxiously invested in denying women access: the rhetoric of its images make the case that both women and men must pursue those activities best suited to *their own* gendered and individuated ideal physical development.

This by no means bars women from competitive sport, a fact the film illustrates with its footage of American tennis star Helen Wills. This brief sequence opens with a close-up of a woman's hand catching three balls, run first at normal speed, then in slow motion. Here again, the camera catches what the eye would miss: the concrete visual details of the dexterity, speed, and elegance with which the fingers and palm pluck the objects from their line of flight. We then see a brief close-up of Wills (shot from a medium-high angle), followed by a forty-five-second slow-motion sequence of one tennis point. This single take is a long, high-angle shot that allows us to concentrate on Wills in the foreground while monitoring her opponent in the background. As the player's signature sailor suit flows and flaps

Fig. 11.2. German gymnast Rudolf Kobs on the high bar. The sequence makes extensive use of slow-motion cinematography. Screenshot.

in response to her deft movements, the Wills-figure floating across the screen bears a noticeable resemblance to the Karsavina-figure that glided through our field of vision in part 4. The bodies are oriented differently vis-à-vis the plane on which they perform, of course, and the game does not permit Wills the premeditation of sequenced moves that dance permits Karsavina. But the brief, bouncing movements and rapid, purposeful strides visually evoke the dancer's steps, and each demonstrates a remarkable ability to lift off. Both sequences captivate in their display of elasticity, lightness, and grace, all of which rests in strength but has nothing to do with brute force. Thus both reinforce the gendered paradigms of optimal corporal performance that the film generally maintains, even as the Wills sequence specifically endorses the appropriateness of women's claim on select fields of competitive struggle.

To what effect does the film objectify female bodies? There is ample erotic charge in many of the slow-motion sequences of the bodies on display. But erotic in this case is neither reducible to titillating nor accurately characterized with a vocabulary of genitally focused sexual lack, possession, and gratification. The clinical contrivance of the film, its openly demonstrative approach, further distances it from the Oedipal scene: its pleasures are more morphological than libidinal; the desire it stokes has corporal optimization, not sexual release, as its object.

Master Narratives, Contending Narratives

What did the filmmakers overlook in their construction of ideal corporal morphology along classical lines? What threats to their project did those oversights generate? Pursuing these questions, one achieves deeper insight into the film and a more refined sense of how Weimar body culture was implicated in the encompassing problem of modern subjectivity.

Simply stated, the two biggest things that the filmmakers overlooked in their document of modern body culture and its historical antecedents were culture and history. *Paths to Strength and Beauty* indulges liberally in reenactment to shore up its arguments about restoring the balance of body and mind, but it is essentially — and here deceleration is crucial — about positing an ideal morphology that transcends the bounds of temporal and cultural setting. Watching the film, the audience could actually contemplate the *meaning* of a rippling thigh, an especially taut buttock or an elegant hand, often as semantic surfaces apparently bare of any ideological or sociohistorical referentiality. The reconstructed Greek world is offered as the context in which this ideal was discovered, and the surveyed 1920s are offered as the context in which the ideal can and must be recovered. In no case is the supposed self-evidence of that ideal quality questioned; at no point does the film hint that the timeless model is itself rife with ideological and sociohistorical contingency.

But I suspect that the filmmakers knew all this, for even as the sheer quantity and diversity of its images strain the film's Hellenistic master narrative (it is hard, after all, to make an image of David Lloyd George playing golf evoke the Greek Golden Age), the selection seems too canny to support the charge of naive body-aestheticism. If the Greek story is not compelling, then perhaps the rationalist-Americanist story (à la Giese) is. If neither of those work, then the more mythically intoned story of German national renewal stands duty-ready — an image of Turnvater Jahn, the gymnastics pioneer and champion of German liberation in the Napoleonic era, is superimposed on a regiment engaged in calisthenics at the end of the film. The filmmakers may well have recognized the contradiction in their effort to thrust a culturally and historically bound vision of optimal corporality beyond all cultural and historical limits, but they pursued that objective with great purpose nonetheless.

This pursuit follows a path of flight from modernity, along which the body could be conceptualized as a means of mastering modern problems without ever actually tackling them. For regardless of the narrative summoned to buttress the argument, the core assertion of the film involves identifying the body as the prime recipient of the damage of economy and society and corporal optimization as the prime means of undoing that damage. If social, economic, and cultural codes, rules, structures, and institutions have traditionally denigrated, debilitated, and destroyed the body; and if such damage has become the most compelling, concrete expression of the myriad ways that life in the world thwarts the vision of individual sovereignty bequeathed by the Enlightenment; then body culture magically becomes a *modern* solution to both problems. In undoing the damage, one gains autonomy. The only catch, of course, is that the traditional conditions of corporal damage and individual disempowerment tend only to have intensified with modernization, and perfecting a Mensendieck exercise sequence or working the horizontal bar like Rudolf Kobs does little to alter those conditions.

This line of flight thus traces obliquely a shift in the very concept of self-actualization, away from the paradigm of individual sovereignty (which modern philosophy may promise but modern reality will never allow) and toward a radical notion of liberation that involves *release from*, not mastery over, debilitating and disempowering contingencies. The bareness of the bodies in *Paths to Strength and Beauty* signifies the dream of that deliverance, but the film as a whole overdetermines that bareness. The spectator is left wondering about a more anarchic corporal imaginary that could actually have transformative consequences for the conditions that the film simultaneously acknowledges and elides. Then again, those slow-motion sequences may remain mesmerizing diversions too strong and beautiful to penetrate analytically in the name of social transformation. *Vollendung*, after all, is a state of being that renders the very idea of change insignificant; and visually captured movement, once decelerated, gains a seductive sheen of immunity to time's passage and history's states of flux.

Notes

The first epigraph to this chapter is drawn from Graeser, *Körpersinn* (Body-Sense), quoted in Toepfer, 66. Translation by Toepfer. Graeser, a Bach scholar, came under the influence of Oswald Spengler (author of *The Decline of the West*), and dedicated *Body-Sense* to him. The second epigraph is drawn from Giese, *Girlkultur* (Girl-Culture), 1011.

[1] *Wege zu Kraft und Schönheit*, Universum Film Aktiengesellschaft (Ufa), 1925, directed by Wilhelm Prager, written by Nicholas Kaufmann; cinematography by Friedrich Weinmann, Eugen Hrich, Kurt Neubert, and Friedrich Paulmann (slow-

motion sequences by Jakob Schatzow and Erich Stöcker). English titles: *Paths to Strength and Beauty* or *Ways to Strength and Beauty*.

[2] "Körperkultur." This review and seven others are accessible via the Deutsches Filminstitut website under http://www.deutsches-filminstitut.de/zengut/df2tb542k.pdf (accessed 4 Nov. 2007).

[3] "Für den Sport, gegen die Sportauswüchse." For more on sports and body culture in Weimar Germany, see Bathrick; Eggers; Jensen; Rippey; von Saldern; and Wesp.

[4] I use the German version because the English version has its own, somewhat different, introduction.

[5] For more on the evolution of Ufa, see Elsaesser; Hake; and Kreimeier.

[6] See Kreimeier/Ehmann/Goergen, sections 3 (151–228) and 4 (229–300).

[7] The Deutsches Filminstitut maintains pages on *Paths to Strength and Beauty* http://www.deutsches-filminstitut.de/filme/f018491.htm and the *Kulturfilm* http://www.deutsches-filminstitut.de/thema/dt2t001.htm, as well as a concise biography of Nicholas Kaufmann http://www.deutsches-filminstitut.de/dt2tp0142.htm (all accessed 4 Nov. 2007).

Works Cited

Bathrick, David. "Max Schmeling on the Canvas: Boxing as an Icon of Weimar Culture." *New German Critique* 51 (1990): 113–36.

Benjamin, Walter. "Das Kunstwerk im Zeitalter seiner technischen Reproduzierbarkeit." 1936. Reprinted in *Gesammelte Schriften*, edited by Rolf Tiedemann, 1:471–508. Frankfurt am Main: Suhrkamp, 1991.

Cowan, Michael. *The Cult of the Will: Nervousness and German Modernity.* University Park: Pennsylvania UP, 2008.

———. "The Heart Machine: 'Rhythm' and Body in Weimar Film and Fritz Lang's *Metropolis*." *Modernism/Modernity* 14:2 (2007): 225–48.

Eggers, Erik. *Fußball in der Weimarer Republik.* Kassel: Agon, 2001.

Elsaesser, Thomas. *Weimar Cinema and After: Germany's Historical Imaginary.* New York: Routledge, 2000.

Frame, Lynne. "Gretchen, Girl, Garçonne? Weimar Science and Popular Culture in Search of the Ideal New Woman." In *Women in the Metropolis: Gender and Modernity in Weimar Culture*, edited by Katharina von Ankum, 12–40. Berkeley: U of California P, 1997.

Giese, Fritz. *Girlkultur: Vergleiche zwischen amerikanischem und europäischem Rhythmus und Lebensgefühl.* Munich: Delphin-Verlag, 1925.

Graeser, Wolfgang. *Körpersinn.* Munich: C. H. Beck, 1927.

Hake, Sabine. *German National Cinema.* New York: Routledge, 2002.

Jensen, Erik "Crowd Control: Boxing Spectatorship and Social Order in Weimar Germany." In *Histories of Leisure,* edited by Rudy Koshar, 79–104. New York: Berg, 2002.

"Körperkultur." *Reichsfilmblatt,* 14 April 1925.

Kracauer, Siegfried. "Wege zu Kraft und Schönheit." 1925. Reprinted in *Kleine Schriften zum Film, 1921–1927,* ed. Inka Mülder-Bach, 143–46. Frankfurt am Main: Suhrkamp, 2004.

Kreimeier, Klaus. *The Ufa Story: A History of Germany's Greatest Film Company, 1918–1945.* Translated by Robert Kimber. Berkeley: U of California P, 1999.

Kreimeier, Klaus, Antje Ehmann, and Jeanpaul Goergen, eds. *Geschichte des dokumentarischen Films in Deutschland.* Vol. 2: *Weimarer Republik, 1918–1933.* Stuttgart: Reclam 2005.

Kretschmer, Ernst. *Körperbau und Charakter: Untersuchungen zum Konstitutionsproblem und zur Lehre von den Temperamenten.* 12th ed. Berlin: Springer, 1936.

Lethen, Helmut. *Verhaltenslehren der Kälte: Lebensversuche zwischen den Kriegen.* Frankfurt am Main: Suhrkamp, 1994.

Rippey, Theodore F. "Athletics, Aesthetics, and Politics in the Weimar Press." *German Studies Review* 28:1 (2005): 85–106.

Samson Körner, Paul. "Jugend und Sport." *Berliner Börsen-Courier,* 12 April 1925, 4.

Stresemann, Gustav. "Für den Sport, gegen die Sportauswüchse." *Berliner Tageblatt,* 28 January 1927, Sportblatt.

Toepfer, Karl. "Nudity and Modernity in German Dance, 1910–1930." *Journal of the History of Sexuality* 3.1 (1992): 58–108.

von Saldern, Adelheid. "Sports and Public Culture: The Opening Ceremonies of the Hanover Stadium in 1922." In *The Challenge of Modernity: German Social and Cultural Studies,* translated by Bruce Little, 215–47. Ann Arbor: U of Michigan P, 2002.

"Wege zu Kraft und Schönheit." *LichtBildBühne,* 17 March 1923.

Wesp, Gabriele. *Frisch, fromm, fröhlich, Frau: Frauen und Sport zur Zeit der Weimarer Republik.* Königstein: Helmer, 1998.

12: Henrik Galeen's *Alraune* (1927): The Vamp and the Root of Horror

Valerie Weinstein

HENRIK GALEEN'S *ALRAUNE* (Mandrake, 1927)[1] is the tale of a dangerous vamp: inspired by a medieval myth in which the mandrake root at the base of the gallows becomes a living being after being fertilized by a hanged man and harvested at midnight, Professor ten Brinken creates a woman, artificially inseminating a prostitute with the semen from a hanged murderer. The product, Alraune, ruins every man who loves her and takes revenge on her maker, seducing and destroying him.

In his discussion of the vamp figure, conservative film critic Oskar Kalbus cites Brigitte Helm's Alraune as the prime example.[2] To Kalbus, writing in 1935, the vamp is a "contemporary" phenomenon that unites pleasure and horror and hides traces of her difference from normal women. He compares the vamp to a vampire, an Indian dancer, and a gypsy — with "glowing eyes" and "snakelike movements" (129) — construing her as monstrous and racially other. In contrast to a healthy woman, the vamp does not love, but rather cruelly uses her strengths to reach her goals; her difference from others, however, is hard to see, for the vamp can be blonde and blue-eyed (Kalbus, 129) — accepted signs of Northern European racial identity at the time.

Kalbus's account inspires many of the questions central to this inquiry: How and why does *Alraune* make the vamp an object of horror? What is the relationship between *Alraune* and contemporary discourses of sex, race, and health? And what is the significance of the problem that the vamp cannot be distinguished visually from the healthy woman? By combining a close reading with attention to discussions of race, heredity, and the New Woman in the Weimar era, theories of the horror film, and Sigmund Freud's "Uncanny," I will show how *Alraune* preys on fears of racial pollution and anxieties about the New Woman and debunks science as an effective source of knowledge.

The first scene of *Alraune* prepares spectators for a horror film. Titles narrating the Alraune legend alternate with abstract, distorted images of a gallows and cemetery, obscured by fog and high-contrast lighting. By contrast, the film's second scene makes marked realist claims. It takes place in the home of Professor ten Brinken, "a world-famous authority on genetic crossbreeding." The mise-en-scène is consistent with what one might expect of the home of an eminent scientist in the early twentieth century. Three-point lighting erases any unruly shadows, and Brinken and his audience wear neat formal dress and move naturally, quite unlike the shapeless form that lurches its way across the cemetery in the first scene.

The second scene does not necessarily disavow the expectation that we are in for a horror film. As S. S. Prawer points out, "the monster-maker," whose ambition leads to his downfall, is a stock figure in horror films (38). Nevertheless, a stylistic break between the first and second scenes of *Alraune* marks the intrusion of science into the film. Science and the horrific narrative merge thematically and stylistically as the film progresses, and the imbrication of horror and realist claims, superstition and science, is accompanied throughout the film by the use of techniques associated with Expressionism and the New Objectivity.[3] This mixture of styles in *Alraune* highlights the event the film locates at the intersection of superstition and science: genetic crossbreeding. Alraune is a product of this genetic crossbreeding, the offspring of a criminal and prostitute, and she is visually associated with a real social phenomenon of Weimar Germany, the "New Woman." Styles and structures typical of the horror film render her monstrous, as strategies with realist claims locate her in the spectators' real world. Thus Galeen's *Alraune* carves out a position within socially significant debates on behavior, environment, and genetics, and within cultural explorations of the ideal New Woman.

In the scene discussed above, Brinken announces the plans for his next experiment:

> I am going to conduct scientific research into this old superstition [the Alraune legend]. [. . .] We need to establish whether the parents' genetic make-up has a purely random effect on the offspring. I always tell my students we must continue in the direction indicated by Doctor Voronoff with his genetic experiments. Above all, we must monitor the results. They could bring new possibilities into the study of humanity.

This title positions Brinken, the audience, and the film in relation to genetic research. The use of Voronoff's well-known name[4] situates Brinken within an extra-textual and non-fictional scientific genealogy. The use of "we" implicates the audience in Brinken's experiment: by observing Alraune, we should be able to make some determination about the impact of heredity on her. This frames the rest of the film as a quasi-scientific exploration.

The question on the effect of the parents' "genetic make-up" on the offspring that Brinken's experiment proposes to answer, and its ramifications, would have been familiar to Weimar audiences: in the early 1900s, German biologists "rediscovered" Mendel's laws of inheritance and extended them to human beings (Weindling, 232–37). By contrast, Lamarckian scientists believed that organisms were shaped by their environments and that acquired characteristics could be inherited,[5] a position that offered earnest alternatives to Mendelian understandings of genetics well through the 1920s (Weindling, 328–31, 376). The question of human genetic inheritance had profound implications for social thought and policy in the 1920s.[6] At that time human reproductive science was the focus of a variety of movements and disciplines, among them genetics, eugenics, sexology, social biology, anthropology, hygiene, sexual reform, homosexual emancipation, feminism, and endocrinology. Politicians from the far Left to the far Right supported different policies meant to improve the population in both qualitative and quantitative ways, for the German population was seen as decreasing in health and size. These decreases, including a range of health problems and social ills, were attributed to degeneration — the proliferation of poor genetic stock among the German population, which reversed evolutionary development and progress. Conflicting understandings of heredity, constitutional predisposition, and environment complicated these discourses, which were in any case not internally coherent, and much was grouped under the rubric of heredity and degeneration that many today would view as social or environmental.

Health and reproductive concerns were central to the expansion and shape of the welfare state in the Weimar Republic. Scientific research influenced a range of debates and legislation on birth control, abortion, sexually transmitted diseases, marriage counseling and certificates, health care, health insurance, labor law, housing, sterilization, euthanasia, and more, with a variety of groups tapping into a voracious demand for health and eugenic propaganda (Weindling, 405). A Lamarckian emphasis suggested that through an extension of education, legislation, and welfare the working classes and the national population at large could regenerate. A Mendelian approach to genes and heredity could at times impede welfare. For example, Otmar von Verschuer's research suggested that genetics was responsible for industrial lung diseases (Weindling, 403). Ideally, counseling and education would dissuade unfit individuals from reproducing, so long as compulsory sterilization remained unpopular (Adams, 218–19).

Alraune appeared at a time of growing popular awareness of genetics, eugenics, and hygiene. Many people visited traveling exhibits, like the seven and a half million visitors who took in the eugenic *Gesolei* (*Gesundheit, soziale Fürsorge und Leibesübungen* = Health, welfare, and exercise) exhibit held in Düsseldorf from May through October 1926 (Weindling, 414). As part of a spate of health-education films Ufa, Germany's largest production company, produced *Nature and Love* on the history of evolution in 1927 and in 1928, *The Curse of Heredity: Those Who Should Not Be Mothers, or, a Film of Love and Duty*.[7] *Gesolei* and the *Reichsgesundheitswoche* (Reich Health Week) in April 1926 helped spread genetic and eugenic messages and used attractive modern media such as radio, film, cartoons, and popular literature (Weindling, 410).

To examine the question of heredity, Brinken crosses a criminal and a prostitute (two major figures in degeneracy discourse dating back to the work of Cesare Lombroso in the mid-nineteenth century) and has the child raised in a convent. Despite her biological origins, Alraune does not show any obvious symptoms of physical or mental illness. Instead, several scenes feature her athleticism and her delicate, symmetrical physiognomy and blonde hair, which would have appealed to the promoters of Germanic racial health.

If Alraune displays any hereditary imperfection, it is emotional and behavioral. Not traditionally feminine, she is cruel and fearless. She convinces a boy named Wölfchen ("little wolf") to help her run away, and they take a train, where she meets her next lover, a magician with the circus. The magician produces a white mouse that crawls up Alraune's leg and under her skirt. A look of childish pleasure crosses her face, as the magician's is stricken with horror, followed by admiration. Later, working at the circus as his assistant, Alraune causes a scene of panic and chaos by letting herself in with the lions and terrifying them, rather than the reverse.

Alraune's fearlessness and lack of empathy extend to her relationships with men. Alraune seduces each man to help her escape from and destroy the last. Because Alraune manipulates Wölfchen into stealing money from his father, he can never return home, even after she abandons him. Multiple shots of Wölfchen wandering in a trance-like state to do her bidding, unblinking and wide-eyed, under harsh frontal lighting, show how thoroughly she has devastated him. She leaves the magician and the lion tamer in rapid succession. Brinken takes her from the circus, but she turns on him when he refuses to let her marry the viscount who has asked for her hand and she finds out that he created her as "the whim of a cynical scientist." She ruins her creator emotionally and financially and then elopes with the viscount, leaving Brinken to suffer "the hell of loneliness and insanity."

The film's repeated references to Alraune's inhumanity and sexual libertinage would help a Weimar German audience associate the screen vamp with familiar debates about women in modern society. In her essay, "Gretchen, Girl, Garçonne?" Lynne Frame describes typologies of the New Woman created by biomedical and popular discourses in the Weimar Republic. One type, the *Girl*, is defined in an article from the *8-Uhr-Abendblatt* thus: "The *Girl*, originating in America as the child of pioneers and immigrants, is . . . a daring athlete, sexy but without sizzle — rather coolly calculating — she succeeds whenever she encounters the sexually bourgeois man of the old school" (Frame, 12). The Berlin daily attributes a genetic component to the *Girl* — a heritage of American pioneers and immigrants — which ties her to the neurasthenia and degeneracy associated with American modernity.[8] Alraune, like the *Girl*, is an athlete, and they both take a "coolly calculating" approach to men, an approach shared by the vamp.

The *8-Uhr-Abendblatt*'s description of the cool, degenerate, athletic *Girl* also resonates with contemporary biomedical paradigms that link the *Girl* with scientific discussions of female "intersexuality," a form of degenerate "masculinization" of modern women leading to the qualitative and quantitative decline of the German population (Frame, 18–20). "Intersexual" women were allegedly more intelligent, athletic, and ambitious, and had more masculine bodies — all features of the New Woman, making the true "intersexual" harder to recognize (Frame, 20). From a eugenic standpoint "intersexual" women posed a problem, since they were purportedly less fertile, according to P. Mathes, on account of crossbreeding arising from the racial diversity in the modern metropolis (Frame, 19).[9] Galeen's *Alraune* invites the viewers to observe an experiment with crossbreeding, construing the results as monstrous.

Noël Carroll argues that the monster, the definitive figure for the horror genre (84), disrupts an otherwise realistic setting; it is "an extraordinary character in our ordinary world . . ." (16). Galeen's film presents Alraune in this way, as unnatural and monstrous, by using realistic representational techniques and settings. Building on the work of anthropologist Mary Douglas, Carroll argues that monsters are categorically "threatening *and* impure," evoking disgust and horror because they violate cultural categories (28–32). Alraune's threat is that of the vamp or the *Girl* who ruins the respectable men she seduces. Her impurity is derived from her "fantastic biolog[y]."[10] Alraune is a "fusion figure," the perverse product of modern reproductive technologies and genetic experimentation (Carroll, 44). "K. r.," the reviewer for *LichtBildBühne*, praised such disjuncture and fusion in Helm's performance, first volcanic, then icy, which brings out Alraune's "special, half-gothic, half-Asiatic demonry" ("sonderbare, halb gotische, halb asiatische Dämonie," 72). Alraune's conflicted, racially blended, and demonic character stem from her origin as test-tube spawn of murderer, prostitute, and mandrake root.

Alraune's origin as the product of artificial insemination alone would not render her monstrous in Carroll's sense. Instead she would merely represent a new and unfamiliar reproductive technology. Although rather obscure, experiments in human artificial insemination existed as early as 1907 within "the liberal wing of the eugenics movement" (Weindling, 376). As late as 1934, however, Hermann Rohleder, a pioneer in artificial insemination, admitted that the German public knew little about this technology (162) and cited *Alraune* as an example of the public's ignorance (156). Rather than instructing the public about artificial insemination, the film obscures it so thoroughly that it is unclear what happens to Alraune's mother after Brinken drags her into his lab. Moreover, the film emphasizes

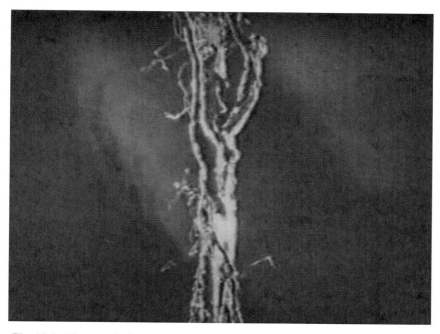

Fig. 12.1. The mandrake root morphs into Alraune, the woman and vamp (Brigitte Helm). Screenshot.

the roles of the mandrake root and scientist Brinken in Alraune's parentage. It is the shift from biological to technological and fantastic parentage that leads us to read Alraune's origins as monstrous: her "fantastic biology" blends these normally distinct identities.

The film repeatedly suggests that Alraune is the embodiment of the mandrake root. Her name and her facile destruction of every man who tries to possess her recall the medieval myth as told at the start of the film. Brinken's repeated musings reinforce this narrative thread. It is also affirmed visually, both when he regularly fondles his treasured mandrake root, which has a noticeably feminine, humanlike shape, and, during his decline, when the root appears in a vision. In this vision, the mandrake root spins against an abstract, hazy background, and as the root spins, it dissolves into the spinning Alraune. The dissolve in this sequence blurs the boundaries between the magic object and the vamp (fig. 12.1).[11] The film explicitly codes the mixings that created Alraune as impure. Frank Braun tells his uncle Brinken, "You have blasphemed against God!" The nephew's sentiment is echoed by intertitles at the close of the film that accuse Brinken of "violating nature."

Yet, more than fantastic biology and violation of God and nature render Alraune horrible and impure. Alraune is pointedly not sexually pure; her interactions with her creator Brinken even evoke incest. The first half of the film and the ambiguous coding of Alraune's origins establish a father-daughter relationship between the two. This relationship becomes sexually charged after Brinken removes Alraune from the circus. Brinken keeps Alraune apart from others, gives her expensive presents, and becomes very jealous about her interactions with other men — to the point that he threatens to kill her if she leaves him.

Our very first glimpse of Alraune is preceded by a close-up of a fly crawling in a bowl of gelatin, a fly that she squashes with her bare finger. She uses her bare hands to lift an extraordinarily large, nasty insect from a matchbox she carries, in order to drop it down the Mother Superior's back. She glows with pleasure when the magician's mouse crawls up her leg and under her skirt. Alraune is in direct physical contact with disgusting vermin, yet she is akin enough to them that they do not disgust her. Alraune is thus depicted as impure by a filmic technique that Carroll calls "horrific metonymy," where the horrific being appears so due to its association with "objects of disgust and/or phobia" (51).

Another form of horrific metonymy in the film is less straightforward. We first see the gnarled and disturbingly humanoid mandrake root when Brinken takes it out of a display cabinet. It is just one of many unusual objects in a collection of bizarre artifacts, among them monstrous, semi-anthropomorphic masks that decorate the background of most shots in Brinken's home. The narrative and visual analogies that suggest Alraune is the incarnation of the mandrake root also imply she is one of his collectibles with exotic or primitive and half-human attributes.

On the eve of Alraune's conception, the objects in Brinken's collection and the reaction of Alraune's biological mother to them accentuate the horror of Alraune's origins among the primitive and half-human. Frank Braun has brought the prostitute into his uncle's sitting room. As she nervously waits, she glances around. We see a close-up of a grimacing mask on the wall with broad features exaggerated by carved lines and topped with a shock of hair. The reaction shot shows the back of the woman's head, her gaze fixed in the direction of the mask, from which she slowly turns away. She looks around more until the camera takes a close up of a pointy devilish mask with long hair, horns, nose, and teeth. Another reaction shot shows her widen her eyes and begin to hyperventilate. She crosses over to Frank Braun, grabs his lapel and pleads with him. He exits to another room. She turns to look at the mural of a giant serpent with a human head, which dominates the parlor wall, and the camera cuts in to a close-up of its grinning, fat-cheeked face. In the other room, Braun tries to convince Brinken to renounce his "terrible plan." A secret door opens up in the belly of the serpent mural, and Brinken emerges, rolling up his sleeves. The camera cuts to the woman's shocked face before it cuts to the intertitles introducing Alraune's life in the convent school. The prostitute's reaction shots give the audience an interpretive framework, suggesting that these half-human monsters are horrible, as is the possibility of unexpected life emerging from them. The scene also stages a visual metaphor that emphasizes the monstrosity of Alraune's birth: Alraune's conception and gestation will take place inside the lab through the secret door — visually and spatially in the belly of the giant human-headed serpent.

The depiction of Alraune as monstrous, half-human, and primitive resonates with other Weimar discourses,[12] including Sigmund Freud's "Das Unheimliche" (The Uncanny, 1919), which can help us interpret the film. Freud argues that the uncanny is the return of something once trusted or *heimlich* that has since become alienated from the individual through repression (263–64). The uncanny can originate in the individual's repressed childhood fantasies, wishes, fears, and complexes (Freud, 256–57), or it can derive from suppressed beliefs from earlier phases of human development. According to Freud, civilized peoples have abandoned primitive animism, the belief in the all-powerful magic of people, thoughts, and things (263). Yet the primitive returns as the uncanny (265) when coincidences make thoughts or objects seem all-powerful and affirm our primitive convictions (271).

Some of *Alraune*'s uncanny quality stems from what Freud would describe as the reaffirmation of primitive animism. A casino scene late in the film emphasizes Alraune's status as the all-powerful animistic fetish and as the embodiment of the mythic root described in the first scene, which can bring luck but will bring torment to anyone who tries to own it. Alraune has enticed Brinken to spend money lavishly on her, and inexplicably his investments collapse. The film casts this as horrific or uncanny through the language of Brinken's telegram, which reads "Dear Professor, it's as if you were pursued by a *ghost*, as if one *devil* were wishing ill on another. All your speculative ventures have failed. You are ruined" (emphasis mine). Brinken decides to try his last chances at the casino. Alraune, standing at his side, tells him to bet red, "the color of luck." The roulette ball lands on red ten times. The professor's chips pile up in front of him, and as he bets all on the eleventh round, Alraune slips out of the room. Panic spreads across the professor's face as his eyes dart about, looking for his missing creation, and the ball lands on black, seemingly as a function of Alraune's animistic power.

Yet Freud reminds us that not everything that evokes repressed wishes or drives or reinforces primitive beliefs and superstitions is experienced as uncanny (268). What further differentiates the uncanny is primarily an aesthetic question (269). On the one hand, a certain level of realism in fiction — such as we see in *Alraune* — facilitates perception of the uncanny, in order for the affirmation of superstition to be perceived as real (271–73). On the other hand, the manipulation of *Stimmung* (atmosphere) also can

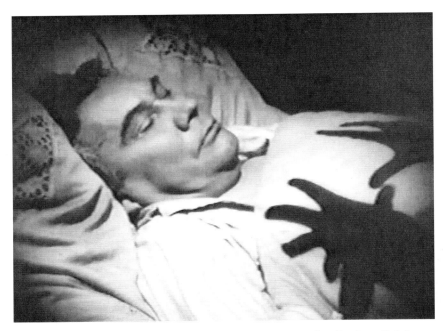

Fig. 12.2. Alraune's hands ominously threatening her maker, Prof. ten Brinken (Paul Wegener). Screenshot.

affect whether or not an audience experiences something as uncanny (273). Expressionist techniques throughout the film create an uncanny *Stimmung*. The opening scene is the best example, but outdoor scenes throughout the film perpetuate the uncanny mood, from ominous landscapes crossed by a speeding train to winding city alleyways and shaded archways. The indoor shots take a tone that has grown to signify realism in narrative film, but the lighting is still higher contrast than in classics of the New Objectivity. Clouds of cigarette, pipe, and cigar smoke shroud the characters in mystery and drama. Strong single light sources cast foreboding shadows, as when Alraune signals to a lover from her window. The night Alraune finds out about her dubious origins and vows to take revenge on her maker, her shadow creeps along the wall and the shadows of her hands threaten to encircle his neck, similar to shots familiar from such Expressionist classics as *The Cabinet of Dr. Caligari* and *Nosferatu* (fig. 12.2). Thus both the realism and the *Stimmung* of the blended style of *Alraune* exaggerate the film's uncanny structure.

According to Freud, one of the most common uncanny structures is repetition, which makes the otherwise harmless seem uncanny, fated, and unavoidable (Freud, 259–60). Freud suggests that this uncanny return of the same also stems from infantile psychic life; it is a repetition compulsion arising from deep drives that reach out from beyond the pleasure principle and lend part of psychic life its "demonic" character. Anything that reminds one of this repetition compulsion can be experienced as uncanny (261).

Alraune's repetition of already unoriginal motifs and stories — even if driven by market concerns — contributes to the film's uncanny effects. Galeen's is one of several films based on Hanns Heinz Ewers's 1911 best-selling novel.[13] The title character is a repetition of already hackneyed fictional tropes: the vamp, the monster that appears human, the inanimate being brought to life. Repetition also occurs within the film: the recurrent motif of smoke or fog, repeated analogies between woman and root, phrases reiterated in the titles, multiple scenes of fearlessness, and the cycles of seduction and destruction. While the use of leitmotifs and thematic and visual repetition are not always uncanny, they can be read as such in the context of *Alraune*'s other uncanny features.

The uncanny is everything that should have stayed hidden and secret but instead has come to the fore (Freud, 249), manifesting itself in structures that reveal a frightening return of the repressed (263–64). *Alraune*'s repetition compulsion suggests that the film discloses some secret, has rendered something *heimlich unheimlich*; but what? The answer lies in what the film codes as monstrous, namely, Alraune herself, and it is her secret alterity that is so disturbing. A product of "fantastic biology," Alraune dissolves multiple boundaries, between woman and root, primitive and modern, science and superstition — a mixture associated by the film and the contemporary discourses with sexual temptation and racial admixture. Her monstrosity erupts in fits and spurts, in scenes of blending, superstition, repetition, and uncanny *Stimmung*. The threat of this monstrosity is amplified, because we see it only in its occasional uncanny eruptions. Through much of the film, Alraune too easily is confused with Kalbus's healthy-looking blonde and blue-eyed woman (Kalbus, 129). Because Alraune's difference emerges only momentarily, we can never know for sure whether this New Woman is monstrous or degenerate at all.

In the end, *Alraune* takes an ambivalent position toward modern female sexuality. The title figure has refused objectification and instead has taken her pleasure at the expense of her male admirers, non-reproductive behavior inconsistent with policies targeted at improving the German birthrate. This form of female sexuality not only appears monstrous and uncanny but also is a source of pleasure for both Alraune and her audience. The final scene, in which Alraune elopes with the viscount, whom she claims to love, promises to domesticate Alraune, to recover her into normative reproductive heterosexuality. Yet the narrative leaves open whether she actually will stay with her lover, and it is unlikely that this domestic future could be more pleasurable than Helm's previous performance. Unharnessed female sexuality retains some of its appeal, even as the film lays out its genetic implications.

Alraune stages an experiment intended, as Brinken tells us, to answer the question of "whether the parents' genetic make-up has a purely random effect on the offspring," a question that had significant social and political ramifications during the Weimar Republic. Brinken's experiment, however, fails to answer this fundamental question: Alraune is neither a murderer nor a prostitute but rather some variation on the New Woman — a *Girl*, or, at worst, a vamp — who may, perhaps, kill men with sex. She looks like any other woman and, at the end of the film, claims plans to adopt a more normative lifestyle. By leaving the narrative open and Alraune difficult to pin down, the film suggests that Brinken's question cannot be answered definitively through observation. *Alraune* challenges science's ability to know and — indirectly — the prudence of basing policy on scientific knowledge.

Instead, *Alraune* illustrates that Brinken's question, which cannot be answered empirically, is best answered affectively. It is Alraune's monstrosity — created by the weaving of the Alraune legend into the scientific narrative — that appears to answer the question that has not been answered: the test-tube baby who becomes a New Woman is not merely degenerate but monstrous. Because the film makes stylistic and narrative efforts to situate itself in the world of the spectator, it appears to claim that, in the real world, the question of genetic inheritance produces not a rational answer but instead the pleasure and horror, the temptation and destruction, that surround Alraune. This sleight of hand suggests that the product of genetic experimentation is a monster that masquerades as human, but also that the ideological edifices of degeneracy and eugenics and the politics with which they are intertwined are built on conjecture and affective responses — on the fantasy of the monster vamp that results from degenerate heredity. On the one hand, *Alraune* warns against genetic mixing and aggressive female sexuality and, on the other, questions the efficacy of science to set its own projects and goals, to predict degeneracy, and to control sexuality — tasks at which Brinken fails miserably.

Notes

[1] Galeen was a successful scriptwriter, director, and occasional actor. His best-known scripts include *Nosferatu* (F. W. Murnau, 1921), *The Golem* (Paul Wegener, 1920), and *Waxworks* (Paul Leni and Leo Birinski, 1923/24). He directed a number of films, including *The Golem* (1914) and *The Student of Prague* (1926). Galeen's *Alraune* was so popular that its run in the Capitol Theater in Berlin had to be extended, postponing the opening of Charlie Chaplin's *Circus* and leading to contractual problems ("'Alraune' um eine Woche im Capitol verlängert," 3; "Alraune contra Chaplin," 2).

[2] Helm played Alraune in both the Galeen film and the 1930 version directed by Richard Oswald.

[3] Expressionist German film focuses on the essence of emotions and objects, psychology, and the supernatural, and employs techniques such as *chiaroscuro* lighting, distorted or non-naturalistic mise-en-scène, and highly stylized acting. The New Objectivity refers to a range of material that is matter-of-fact, makes realist claims, embraces modernity, technology, and mass culture, and focuses on surface appearance and social realities.

[4] Sergei Voronoff was internationally renowned for his experiments implanting monkey testicles into humans as a form of rejuvenation, a technique not discredited until the 1930s (Weindling, 377 and Clarke, 244).

[5] For a concise summary of Lamarck's ideas as relevant to eugenic debates, see Richardson, 10–11.

[6] See Schwartz; Weindling; Weiss.

[7] *Natur und Liebe* (Nature and Love; directed by Wolfram Junghans, Willy Achsel, and Ulrich K. T. Schulz, 1926–27) and *Der Fluch der Vererbung* (The Curse of Heredity; directed by Adolf Trotz, 1927) were feature films shown in popular movie houses. Several shorts were also produced and screened before other features (Weindling, 412–13).

[8] See Gilman, 156.

[9] One of the scenes removed from *Alraune* on 20 January 1928 (Censorship no. O. 00067) included a "negro" approaching a prostitute climbing out of the window of the brothel where Alraune's mother was found.

[10] Carroll uses the term "Fantastic Biologies" to head his discussion of the "fission" and "fusion" composition of monsters (42).

[11] The casting of Brigitte Helm, well known for her role as the robot-woman in Fritz Lang's *Metropolis*, also urges the viewer to conflate object and vamp. Richard McCormick has connected the vamp, the New Woman, and the monster via Helm in that film: "Outwardly, the false, robot Maria is a vamp, a monstrous version of the New Woman" (29; see also 30, 114). On Helm's discomfort with being typecast in this manner, see Semler, 82–88.

[12] For example, the "primitive" appears in discussions of the *Girl* (Frame, 12, 34).

[13] *Alraune, die Henkerstochter, genannt die rote Hanne* (Alraune, the Hangman's Daughter, Called the Red Hanne; Eugen Illés, 1918); *Alraune* (Mihaly Kertész [=Michael Curtiz], 1918); *Alraune und der Golem* (Alraune and the Golem; Nils Chrisander, 1919); *Alraune* (Henrik Galeen, 1927); *Alraune* (Richard Oswald, 1930); *Alraune* (Arthur-Maria Rabenalt, 1952).

Works Cited

Adams, Mark B. "Towards a Comparative History of Eugenics." In *The Wellborn Science: Eugenics in Germany, France, Brazil, and Russia*, edited by Mark B. Adam, 217–32. New York: Oxford UP, 1990.

"'Alraune' um eine Woche im Capitol verlängert." *Film Kurier*, 1 February 1928, 3.

"Alraune contra Chaplin." *Film Kurier*, 6 February 1928, 2.

Carroll, Noël. *The Philosophy of Horror or Paradoxes of the Heart*. New York: Routledge, 1990.

Clarke, Adele. *Disciplining Reproduction: Modernity, American Life Sciences, and the Problems of Sex*. Berkeley: U of California P, 1998.

Frame, Lynne. "Gretchen, Girl, Garçonne? Weimar Science and Popular Culture in Search of the Ideal New Woman." In *Women in the Metropolis*, edited by Katharina von Ankum, 12–40. Berkeley: U of California P, 1997.

Freud, Sigmund. "Das Unheimliche." In *Gesammelte Werke: Werke aus den Jahren 1917–1920*, 12:242–74. Frankfurt am Main: Fischer, 1978.

Gilman, Sander. *Difference and Pathology: Stereotypes of Sexuality, Race, and Madness*. Ithaca, NY: Cornell UP, 1985.

K. r. [pseud.]. Review of *Alraune*. *LichtBildBühne*, 26 January 1928, 2.

Kalbus, Oskar. *Vom Werden Deutscher Filmkunst: Der stumme Film*. Altona-Bahrenfeld: Cigaretten Bilderdienst, 1935.

McCormick, Richard W. *Gender and Sexuality in Weimar Modernity: Film, Literature, and "New Objectivity."* New York: Palgrave, 2001.

Prawer, S. S. *Caligari's Children: The Film as Tale of Terror*. New York: Da Capo, 1980.

Richardson, Angelique. *Love and Eugenics in the Late Nineteenth Century: Rational Reproduction and the New Woman*. Oxford: Oxford UP, 2003.

Rohleder, Hermann. *Test Tube Babies: A History of the Artificial Impregnation of Human Beings, Including a Detailed Account of its Technique, Together with Personal Experiences, Clinical Cases, a Review of Its Literature, and the Medical and Legal Aspects Involved*. New York: Panurge, 1934.

Schwartz, Michael. *Sozialistische Eugenik: Eugenische Sozialtechnologien in Debatten und Politik der deutschen Sozialdemokratie, 1890–1933*. Bonn: Dietz, 1995.

Semler, Daniel. *Brigitte Helm: Der Vamp des deutschen Films*. Munich: Belleville, 2008.

Weindling, Paul. *Health, Race and German Politics between National Unification and Nazism, 1870–1945*. Cambridge: Cambridge UP, 1989.

Weiss, Sheila Faith. "The Race Hygiene Movement in Germany, 1904–1945." In Adams, 8–68.

13: The Dialectic of (Sexual) Enlightenment: Wilhelm Dieterle's *Geschlecht in Fesseln* (1928)

Christian Rogowski

"Strictly Confidential"

IN LATE NOVEMBER 1928, Berlin newspapers reported strange goings-on in some of the city's grimiest neighborhoods: in the working-class districts in the north people were surprised to find letters in their mailboxes marked, "*Streng vertraulich*" (Strictly Confidential). Likewise, passers-by on Müllerstraße in the district of Wedding were handed sealed envelopes with the imprint, "*Nur öffnen, wenn Sie allein sind*" (To be opened only when you are alone). What was the secret that ostensibly needed to be carefully guarded, yet shared with "almost everybody whose name appears in the address book?"[1] Those adventurous enough to open these envelopes found that they contained an ad for a film with the titillating title, *Geschlecht in Fesseln* (Fettered Sexuality, or Sex in Chains) that was to be shown in a local movie theater. The title and the aura of secrecy surrounding the film may very well have created the impression that what was advertised was a pornographic film catering to the more unusual sexual tastes. The whole thing, it turned out, was a clever publicity stunt devised by the owner of a local cinema, eager to exploit people's penchant for secrecy and to capitalize on the title of a film that seemed to cater to prurient desires.

Such lowbrow advertising tactics were a far cry from the official publicity surrounding Wilhelm Dieterle's film a month earlier when it opened, on 24 October 1928, at the prestigious Tauentzienpalast in Berlin's affluent West End. The official program brochure oozes high-minded seriousness: the plot summary of the film is preceded by a quote from the beginning of the Third Canto of Dante's *Inferno*, when Dante and his guide Virgil pass through the gates of hell: "Through me the way into the suffering city / Through me the way to the eternal pain / Through me the way that runs among the lost." The quote is followed by the somewhat pompous admonition that "Dante's words ought to shine ("glühen") on the main portal of every prison."[2] On a more somber note, the film's subtitle, *Die Sexualnot der Gefangenen* (The Sexual Distress of Prisoners) highlights an explicit political agenda: *Geschlecht in Fesseln* presents itself as an intervention in debates concerning prison reform, based on the notion that sexuality constitutes a basic human right. The official publicity surrounding Dieterle's film mobilized one of Western civilization's most auspicious classics, Dante's *Inferno*, to bolster its respectability (and to enhance its emotional appeal), presenting the sexual predicament of prisoners in terms at once culturally palatable and urgent.

We are fortunate that Wilhelm Dieterle's remarkable silent film of 1928 is now available again in a beautifully restored print issued on DVD by Kino International, in cooperation with Filmmuseum Munich. The disc allows us to reconstruct the unique aesthetic qualities and the emotional appeal the film must have had on Weimar German audiences and to assess its distinctive position within Weimar Cinema. Oddly enough, the film is mentioned only briefly in Siegfried Kracauer's seminal account of Weimar Cinema, *From Caligari to Hitler* (1947).[3] Kracauer places *Geschlecht in Fesseln* among a number of socially critical films of the mid-1920s that, he argues, lacked any real political impetus. Rather than focusing on the main political questions of the day, Kracauer claims, such films "tried to neutralize pent-up indignation by directing it against evils of small importance." The main function of such films, in Kracauer's view, is to act as "safety valves" that distract audiences from the real political problems (Kracauer, 145). The question of reproductive rights (including access to birth control and the problem of abortion) concerned all women in Weimar Germany and, of course, their male partners as well (Usborne, 203). The question of sexual rights and prison reform affected a smaller sector of the German population, the roughly 450,000 inmates in prisons, among them an estimated 20,000 left-wing political prisoners, whose activities on behalf of the causes they believed in had presumably been important enough to bring them into conflict with the law (Plättner, 11). Kracauer's roundabout dismissal of such political activities (and the films that took up these causes) as of "small importance" appears callous today.

As Kracauer's gingerly handling of the film suggests, its title, *Geschlecht in Fesseln*, to a certain extent invited misunderstandings even among contemporary audiences when the film was first released. Today the title of its American release, *Sex in Chains*, may be more fitting for a quasi-pornographic film rather than a finely crafted melodrama that puts itself in the service of social reform. Curiously, the American distributor employs advertising stratagems not unlike those of the clever cinema owner of 1928 mentioned above: the cover of the DVD release sports a screen shot of a moment when one of the prisoners reaches out from his bed to a fellow inmate, and a caption places the film among "Gay-Themed Films of the German Silent Era." This is very different from the film's original advertising: the cover of the *Illustrierte Film-Kurier*, the illustrated program booklet that accompanied the 1928 release of the film, features a montage of two images: a big picture of Franz Sommer (Wilhelm Dieterle), standing in front of a barred window, pensively holding a small bird in the palm of his hand, provides the background for a round cameo portrait of his wife Helene (Mary Johnson), inserted in the lower right (fig. 13.1). Helene is shown looking into the distance, her eyes cast downward. The combined images highlight both the separation of the two spouses and the bond between them: their eyelines are mismatched, yet the affection that Sommer displays for the bird, in combination with Helene's wistful look, signals their longing for reunion. Visually, the official advertising of the film at its original release offers no suggestion of homosexuality as one of its themes. While the film indeed addresses questions of sexual desire in a same-sex environment (the prison), it is misleading to reduce the film to the label "gay-themed."[4] In fact, as I will show, the film to a certain extent calls into question what constitutes homosexuality. Moreover, there is a peculiar contradiction between the film's overt agenda of propagating universal sexual rights and the manner in which the question of whether such general rights extend to gays is to a certain extent obfuscated in the narrative.

In what follows, I wish to explore the distinctive strategies with which Dieterle's film negotiates the delicate balance between social advocacy and emotional impact, between artistic seriousness and popular appeal, as it addresses the sexual dimension of contemporary social and political problems. I will place the film in a variety of historical, cultural, and social contexts surrounding its production and release. In my analysis, I will focus on three key moments in the film: first, the exposition, which places the issue of prisoners' sexual needs and rights in a broad humanitarian frame; second, what could be called the "seduction scene," which raises the specter of "inappropriate" — specifically, homosexual — sexual activity; and third, the film's ending, which demonstrates the extremely narrow discursive confines within which homosexuality could be addressed publicly during the Weimar Republic. As we will see, the film's narrative trajectory and its visual organization are, to a certain extent, at odds with one another. A close reading of the film reveals a largely unresolved tension between the progressivist rationalistic impulse behind the film and the melodramatic format chosen to convey its reformist agenda. While the film advocates an enlightened acceptance of sexual desire as a natural tendency of all human beings, including those incarcerated, the melodramatic mode of narration seems to reinforce a normative notion of only one "natural" form in which this tendency is allowed to manifest itself — firmly within the confines of bourgeois, heterosexual, monogamous marriage. Paradoxically, it seems, the effort to call into question oppressive social practices is articulated in a form that ultimately appears to affirm the very social model that produces oppressive effects. Yet at the same time the emotional power of the film, based on its visual construction, retains the potential to undercut the very stability concerning sexual norms that its narrative seems to reinforce.

Fig. 13.1. Cover of Illustrierter Film-Kurier *255 (28 October 1928). Courtesy of Deutsches Filminstitut, Frankfurt am Main and Verlag für Filmschriften, Christian Unucka, 85241 Hebertshausen.*

Delicate Subjects

When Wilhelm Dieterle's *Geschlecht in Fesseln* premiered in the fall of 1928, the critical and audience response was generally very favorable. Fritz Olimsky, of the *Berliner Börsen-Zeitung*, for instance, notes that the audience appreciated "that the scriptwriters and the sensitive director Wilhelm Dieterle approach the subject matter with utmost delicacy without diminishing any of its impact."[5] The reviewer of the *Reichsfilmblatt* likewise expresses his admiration for the manner in which the film combines advocacy for a cause with artistic integrity:

> A passionate tendential film (*Tendenzfilm*) — but with a tendency on which we all can agree: this is a film that fights for liberality and human dignity, against insensitivity and intolerance. What's more, [it is] a film that raises a delicate subject with seriousness.[6]

In the parlance of the day, political "tendentiousness" and artistic quality were generally assumed to be mutually exclusive (Murray). Most positive reviews of the Berlin premiere thus take great pains to downplay the film's political dimension (much, we shall see, as the film itself does) and instead emphasize its artistic qualities: to these reviewers the film is a masterwork because it manages, despite its potentially controversial subject matter, to speak to the viewers' emotions.

The concepts employed in the mainstream press, even those that reviewed the film positively, highlight the discursive force fields within which the film had to operate: as a film addressing social and political concerns, it had to distance itself from the suspicion of party-political, especially left-wing, advocacy (*Tendenz*); as a film addressing sexual questions, it had to associate itself with "art" in order to distinguish itself from the negative reputation of the so-called *Aufklärungsfilme*, the wave of "sexploitation films" of the immediate postwar period (see the essay by Jill Smith in this volume). To intervene in public debates on the necessity for a humane reform of the German penal system, the film had to appeal to the general electorate, primarily middle-class voters who could exert pressure upon political power brokers; and it had to conform to the bourgeois values of the educated social and political elites, such as mainstream journalists, elected officials, parliamentary representatives, and judicial authorities. In early 1929, with clear reference to *Geschlecht in Fesseln*, Dieterle joined the public debate about the tension between politics and art with an essay entitled "Tendenz im Film" (Tendentiousness in Film). There he passionately contended that the two terms were not mutually exclusive but compatible, indeed complementary, arguing for "Tendentiousness as art! Tendentious toward making the subject matter come alive, not to bore, but to go ahead and entertain, to stimulate thinking. Depicting conditions, offering a warning, and making things better."[7] Given the politically volatile climate of the Weimar Republic even during the "stabilization period" of 1924–29, any direct association with left-wing party politics or sexual prurience had to be avoided to appease censors and audiences alike. Instead, the focus had to be placed upon the transformation of authentic, that is, verifiably relevant, subject matter into art. This strategy, it seems, was largely successful: after its initial release the film earned the predicate "of artistic value" ("künstlerisch wertvoll") and was exempted from entertainment tax normally levied upon feature films.[8]

Even so, Dieterle's interventionist film quickly became the object of politically motivated attacks. Within days of the film's release, in the fall of 1928, a representative of the right-wing *Deutsch-Nationale Volkspartei* (German National People's Party) launched an inquiry in the Prussian Parliament on the basis of the use of footage of state-owned facilities, such as prisons. How, the representative argued, could public authorities permit the use of such images in the production of politically suspect "tendential films" (*Tendenzfilme*) that in his view "offended very large circles of the population?" The Prussian Ministry of Justice responded coolly, along purely formal lines: no government officials were involved in the making of the film, and the filming of the facades of public buildings could not be prevented, nor did it require permission. Over a year later, on 9 December 1929, the Bavarian government appealed to the Upper Chamber (*Oberprüfstelle*) of the Berlin Censorship Board to ban the film. The film, the argument ran, undermined the public's trust in official authorities by depicting the judicial and penal system as inhumane. The board denied the appeal for a total ban, noting that it displayed "a certain tactfulness in the treatment of the most daring subject matter" and that the film did not lack "a certain delicacy."[9] All the same, the Censorship Board agreed that some moments in the film overstepped the limit, ordering that seven cuts be made (totaling about fifty-eight meters), as well as several changes in the wording of the intertitles.

The Film and Its Background

Geschlecht in Fesseln opens with the credits and the title screen, followed by two intertitles that position the film within two interconnected contexts: the first screen assures the viewer that the story is based on real incidents, as collected by Karl Plättner (1893–1945), a well-known left-wing radical and political prisoner, who documented the sexual dimension of incarceration in his book, *Eros im Zuchthaus* (Eros in Prison, 1929), with the help of Magnus Hirschfeld's Berlin *Institut für Sexualforschung* (Institute for Sexual Research). The second intertitle informs us that the film was endorsed after its Berlin premiere by the German branch of the League for Human Rights (*Liga für Menschenrechte*). The *Liga* was an organization based on liberal humanist principles that included among its members such prominent figures as Albert Einstein and women's rights pioneer Helene Stöcker.[10] The two intertitles highlight the film's aspirations to quasi-scientific stature of empirical verifiability and the political importance of the issues it addresses. The first intertitle, however, also aligns Dieterle's film with two potentially problematic traditions: the sphere of left-wing political activism and that of *Sexualwissenschaft* (Sexual Science), often denounced by its opponents as a "Jewish science" (Haeberle, 306). The film thus faced the challenge of advancing its interventionist agenda in a manner that would not alienate large segments of the audience, who might have objected to the nexus of politics and sexuality.

The question of the sexual rights of prisoners had attracted widespread attention in the wake of a lecture given by the German-Jewish intellectual and writer Erich Mühsam (1878–1934) at Hirschfeld's Berlin *Institut* in the fall of 1926 (Plättner, 10). As an anarchist and radical pacifist, Mühsam had been imprisoned from April to November 1918 for his opposition to the war and in 1919 had been sentenced to fifteen years in jail for his participation in the short-lived Munich Soviet Republic (*Räterepublik*). In 1924, he was released as part of a general amnesty for political prisoners. Hirschfeld and the Berlin *Institut* operated within a tradition of bourgeois liberalism that sought political reform on the basis of enlightened humanistic rationality. All the same, as Veronika Fuechter notes (158–61), the *Institut* maintained close contacts with left-wing activist individuals and groups, among them the *Verein sozialistischer Ärzte* (VSA; Association of Socialist Doctors). Some members of the VSA and of Hirschfeld's *Institut* worked in Berlin's poorest neighborhoods and were on occasion willing to use their authority as licensed physicians to provide to their indigent clients services that overstepped the limits of legality, such as referrals for abortions (prohibited under §218 of the German penal code). Moreover, many of the routine activities at the *Institut*, such as sex education, consultations about contraceptives and methods of birth control, and advocacy for the rights of sexual minorities (homosexuals, lesbians, and transsexuals) were politically controversial. In this context it is perhaps surprising that Hirschfeld and Felix Abraham of the *Institut* took a notorious political radical like Karl Plättner under their wing as he embarked on his book documenting the sexual plight of prisoners.

Karl Plättner was, by all accounts, a colorful character who had come into conflict with the law on many occasions on account of his left-wing political activism. In the early 1920s Plättner led a gang of thugs that terrorized parts of central Germany in spontaneous acts of "expropriation" and "redistribution of property" from banks, businesses, and post offices, achieving a kind of folk-hero status before his arrest in 1922.[11] He was released in 1928 after serving six years of a ten-year sentence. Plättner used the time in prison to conduct research on the sexual predicament of prisoners, interviewing his fellow inmates and reading whatever literature on the subject he could lay hands on. The result was the book *Eros im Zuchthaus*, which was published in 1929 with a foreword by Magnus Hirschfeld and Felix Abraham.

The exact nature of Dieterle's involvement with Plättner and with Hirschfeld's Institute for Sexual Research is not known. It would appear that Dieterle had access to a manuscript version of Plättner's book (which only came out after the film was released), probably via Franz Höllering, the prominent leftist journalist whose name appears in the opening credits.[12] It is not known how Dieterle found out about Plättner's project of detailing the sexual situation of prisoners and whether there was any direct contact between Dieterle and Plättner. It is likely that Dieterle asked Höllering, who may have had connections with Plättner and/or the *Institut*, to create an exposé for the film from Plättner's manuscript.[13]

Dieterle's film features many episodes that find a correlative in Plättner's book: there is a scene showing the prisoners sculpting female bodies out of bread, something Plättner had listed among many compensatory activities as symptoms of repressed sexuality. Sommer's handling of his wife's kerchief recalls the fetishistic practices surrounding objects associated with women in general, and love partners in particular, detailed by Plättner. Most notably, Plättner recounts acts of self-mutilation, self-castration, and suicide as results of sexual deprivation that appear in the film in two scenes: at one point, a desperate prisoner picks up a piece of broken glass in order to do harm to himself; later, he steals a gun from a prison guard in order to commit suicide. Dieterle's film also echoes Plättner's book in the remarkable attention both give to the plight of the spouses of the incarcerated: Plättner provides extensive accounts of the emotional and psychological distress imposed upon the innocent through enforced separation. Dieterle condenses such ideas in the scene where Sommer's wife Helene nearly goes insane with longing and bangs on the doors of the prison where her husband is held.

Plättner's book culminates in a series of practical demands for prison reform, including regulations about leave policies, visitation rights, and so on. Its activist agenda is enhanced by an appendix, which includes three form letters that can be torn out and filled in.[14] Such direct activism is transformed in the film into a scene in which one of the main characters visits a member of parliament: after his release, industrialist Steinau (Gunnar Tölness), who had been imprisoned as the result of an anonymous denunciation, seeks to persuade a political dignitary of the sexual rights of prisoners. Yet the unnamed parliamentarian, self-satisfied and coolly smoking his cigar, remains unmoved and espouses many of the clichés that Plättner in his book attributes to opponents of penal reform, while Steinau articulates many of Plättner's key points.

Unlike the film, which mostly operates with subtle suggestion and understated hints, Plättner's book goes into graphic detail about the sexual

Fig. 13.2. Opening shot: Helene Sommer's hand wiping the name plate. Screenshot.

practices to which the prisoners resort in their despair. Dieterle's film condenses and visualizes some of the key elements of Plättner's book by creating a sequence of dramatic vignettes replete with visual symbolism. Whereas Plättner collates a large number of reports and accounts from dozens of sources, Dieterle's film centers on the story of two individuals placed into a carefully crafted multi-layered scenario.

Setting the Terms

The film proper begins with a close-up of a female hand wiping clean the name plate above a doorbell, "Franz Sommer, Ingenieur (engineer)" (fig. 13.2). The hand, we soon find out, belongs to Helene, Sommer's wife, who has to do her own household work, because the couple can no longer afford to keep a maid, as Sommer has lost his job. Helene tries to hide both these facts from her visiting father by pretending that the maid has her night off and by feigning a phone call to Sommer's old office. After this introductory scene, the film cuts to a close-up of a newspaper being held by the hands of an impeccably dressed male, who is perusing the "help wanted" ads. The man is initially presented as an anonymous member of the unemployed masses, as we see him reduced to sitting on a bench in a park and trying to make a living by doing frustrating occasional work: he has teamed up with a partner who is filming passers-by in hopes of making them pay for the random filmic snapshots. It is quickly made clear that this is not a reliable or bountiful source of income when a young woman rejects the request to pay for the film footage. Viewers may at that point already have recognized Wilhelm Dieterle, who plays Sommer, but it is not until a few moments later that we are actually introduced to the character's name and distinct identity: one of the passers-by recognizes him as a former colleague and offers help by providing a lead to a more respectable job, as a sales representative of a vacuum-cleaner company.

The opening sequence, then, firmly establishes the social, psychological, and economic parameters within which the audience is supposed to place Sommer's story: he is a well-educated, skilled professional; he is a respectable middle-class man, living in a happy marriage with an emotionally supportive spouse; and he has fallen upon hard times in a climate of increasing unemployment that puts his marriage under severe economic pressure. It has to be remembered that at the time the film was shot and released (in the summer and fall of 1928), there were already nearly 1.5 million unemployed in Germany, even before the onset of the Great Depression in October 1929. Dieterle's film thus speaks to widespread economic worries and status anxieties in the German educated middle class, the white-collar employees, which Siegfried Kracauer would famously document in his sociological vignettes, *Die Angestellten* (The Salaried Masses, 1929/30). Dieterle's film endows Sommer with a kind of "everyman" quality that allows large segments of the general audience to identify with him. The opening shot subtly introduces a key theme of the film: the effort to keep one's name and reputation clean in times of severe economic pressure.

Another important aspect of the opening sequence is the image of marriage it presents. There is a palpable sexual chemistry between Sommer and his wife. When Sommer, delighted at seemingly having landed a promising job, returns home, he is shown playing a light-hearted game with Helene: he places the case that contains the sample vacuum in front of the door, rings the doorbell, and hides behind the banister of the staircase leading up to his apartment, taking childlike delight at her disorientation and surprise when she comes to the door. The enthusiastic presentation of the accoutrements of his new job continues with excited banter that culminates in a passionate kiss: a medium close-up shot focuses on Sommer's hand as he embraces Helene with his right arm around her shoulder, prominently displaying his wedding ring (which Sommer wears, European-style, on his right hand). The camera then discretely withdraws as Helene leans back and Sommer picks her up to carry her away and the screen fades to black. It is clear that Franz and Helene Sommer are a happy couple in a loving and mutually supportive relationship, with an active — "normal" — sex life. The norm established here is that of monogamous heterosexuality, within the officially sanctioned form of marriage.

The film's narrative structure continues to maintain a dual trajectory, initially in a realistic mode of representation. Much of the outdoor footage was clearly shot on real locations: Sommer is shown doing his "film work" in a public park, and during his job interview at the vacuum-cleaner shop we can see the hustle and bustle of Berlin's Kurfürstendamm through the window in the background. By contrast, most of the interior scenes were clearly shot in a studio, with carefully calibrated (rather than natural) lighting. At dramatically significant moments the largely conventional visual approach is punctured by artistically ambitious "experimental" flourishes. For instance, the repetitiveness and tedium of Sommer's "job" going from door to door trying to sell vacuum cleaners is represented by a short sequence in which his image is multiplied and refracted as it begins to rotate on the screen in the manner of a kaleidoscope. The visual "shorthand" of this narrative ellipsis highlights the futility of Sommer's efforts to make a decent living in this way. It also creates empathy for the protagonist and his increasing emotional distress.

Through constant crosscutting the film carefully interweaves and balances the story of Franz Sommer with that of his wife Helene. As Sommer struggles to recover from the loss of status and financial security, Helene increasingly takes over the role of breadwinner: she takes up employment selling cigarettes in a restaurant to make up for the shortfall in income. The two protagonists become objects of identification for a general audience, regardless of gender and social class, in that both characters are associated with the struggle to support themselves and maintain their marriage in difficult economic times. And it is Sommer's love for his wife that leads to his downfall: emotionally worn out by his futile efforts to secure a living for himself and his wife, Sommer tries to help Helene ward off the lecherous advances of a restaurant guest. An altercation ensues that leads to the man's fall and to Sommer's imprisonment, first on charges of physical assault, and later — after the man dies of his injuries — on charges of manslaughter.

Sexual Economies

The exposition and the dual storyline suggest that the institution of marriage is threatened by economic and psychological pressures as the economic basis of existence collapses for the Sommers. The film strips their predicament of any explicitly political implications. The reasons for Franz's unemployment are left unexplored and, like the unfortunate incident with the stranger, the loss of his job is presented as an act of fate. While aligning itself with left-wing Weimar politics through its advocacy of prisoners' rights, the film carefully de-politicizes the issue and frames it primarily in moral and psychological terms.

In its portrayal of sexuality as a basic human need, Dieterle's film is indebted to contemporary progressive notions of human sexuality: sexual reformers like Magnus Hirschfeld and Iwan Bloch, following Sigmund Freud, employed a pressure/release model of sexual drives (Gallwitz). All humans, it was argued, are biologically dominated by sexual urges that seek an outlet. If this outlet cannot be found in a "regular" or "normal" way, it will seek other, "deviant" or "perverse" forms. From this assumption it follows logically that in situations in which partners of the opposite sex are not available, the sexual needs will inevitably seek to find release in same-sex activity. In the context of prison reform, the pressure/release model of sexuality made it possible to posit sexual activity as a basic human right that should not be denied to anyone. The argument was that prisoners, regardless of the offense that led to their incarceration, do not forfeit their basic human rights: authorities have an obligation to see to it that the prisoners' sexual needs are met along with their other basic needs, such as sustenance, shelter, and protection from violence.

Interestingly enough, the sexual reformers cast the issue of prisoners' sexual needs not only in terms of human rights but also in terms of social expediency: they argued that if society did not want to corrupt male prisoners morally (for instance by indirectly forcing them to adopt homosexual behavior), it needed to ensure that prisoners were provided with acceptable sexual outlets (that is, regular contact with members of the opposite sex). The prison reform debate thus revolved almost exclusively around visitation rights, in the shape of unsupervised conjugal visits, thus bracketing the rights and needs of those prisoners who were not married or — for one reason or another — not otherwise involved in a stable heterosexual relationship.[15]

The ostensible prudishness of the discourse of sexual reform may seem surprising, given the well-known sexual cynicism of the Weimar Republic, where any imaginable form of gratification was available for purchase on the streets of big cities like Berlin, and all sorts of sexual subcultures seemed to flourish, calling into question the idea that all humans naturally aspired to monogamous unions or restricted their sexual activities to heterosexual genital intercourse. Yet it is clear that the advocates of sexual reform had little choice but to employ a normative, bourgeois rhetoric, as they were aiming to influence the decisions of the power brokers, legislators, civil servants, and public leaders, who — at least publically — firmly subscribed to staunchly bourgeois ideas of morality.

Opponents of penal reform routinely employed a set of interrelated arguments: sexual aberrations, they insisted, concerned only those prisoners whose sexuality had already been abnormal outside of prison. For instance, Hugo Dingeldey tells us (24) that this was the much publicized stance of Erich Wulffen (1862–1936), one of the top officials in the Ministry of Justice of Saxony and the author of the leading handbook on criminal psychology in the Weimar Republic, *Kriminalpsychologie: Psychologie des Täters* (Criminal Psychology: Psychology of the Perpetrator, 1926; republished 1931). Wulffen, who delighted in his reputation as a mild-mannered advocate of justice, went on record as claiming that "only those who already had trouble relating to females outside of prison had sexual problems inside."[16] The general consensus was that the *Sexualnot* (sexual distress) experienced by prisoners was a perhaps unfortunate but often valuable byproduct of imprisonment: those who had committed a crime were depraved and degenerate individuals who deserved no better. If the loss of freedom involved a component of psychic suffering through sexual deprivation, punishment would be enhanced by driving home a moral lesson through suffering. Complaints from prisoners concerning their sexual needs were routinely dismissed as the rantings of troublemakers.

Yet the war had created a fundamentally new constellation: innumerable German men had violated the sanctity of bourgeois marriage by frequenting the official brothels that military authorities had established all along the various front lines to provide German soldiers with the kind of sexual release the reformers were advocating for peacetime prisoners; and hundreds of thousands of German men had also been subjected to the experience of sexual deprivation in the same-sex environment of the POW camps. In his comprehensive *Sittengeschichte des Weltkriegs* (The Sexual History of the World War, 1930), Magnus Hirschfeld notes that same-sex activities constituted a "very common form of substitute satisfaction" in POW camps (Hirschfeld, 236). The survivors of the POW camps, Hirschfeld argues, returned home as "psychic invalids," displaying a pathological sexuality, because they had succumbed to harmful "vices," namely autoerotic and same-sex activities (whose moral and psychological implications Hirschfeld oddly equates).

For Dieterle's film it is important that the issue of *Sexualnot* inflicted by imprisonment had been experienced by regular German men, like Dieterle's protagonist, against whom the depravity/degeneracy argument and the "just deserts" argument could not be advanced, and by German women who had been separated from their male partners. The framing provided by the film's narrative structure is of prime importance: the film focuses for a surprisingly long time on the sexual predicament of Sommer's wife, Helene. After suffering sexual deprivation through the separation from her husband for over two years, Helene is shown in a pivotal scene frantically banging her fists against the prison doors (fig. 13.3). Her shouts turn from "Mein Mann!" to ". . . Mann!" indicating the moment at which her desire for sexual congress with her husband turns into an undifferentiated desperate longing for any sort of sexual contact.[17] Helene's yearnings

Fig. 13.3. Helene (Mary Johnson) banging on the prison doors. Screenshot.

lead her to seek refuge with her benefactor, Steinau, who has secretly loved Helene all along and who now provides the male attention Helene has been screaming for.

The scene in which Helene suffers a kind of moral and mental break-down signals the film's slide into a totally melodramatic mode of narration. The hand-held camera, moving backward and forward perpendicular to the image plane, mimics Helene's extreme agitation and, with its thrusting motion, aligns the viewer with her subjective predicament as she storms the prison gate. Melodrama, critics like Peter Brooks, Christine Glenhill, and Linda Williams have argued, is predicated on the essential goodness and innocence of the protagonists caught up in undeserved suffering (Mercer/Shingler, 95). The film's exposition establishes Franz and Helene as fundamentally decent people subjected to unfair circumstances, setting up a clear-cut Manichean opposition between "good and evil as opposites not subject to compromise" (Brooks, 36). Unlike regular melodrama, Dieterle's film does not represent "evil" in the shape of a particular char-acter (although various individuals, such as a brutal prison guard or the callous politician, come close) but as a disembodied entity — a legal system unresponsive to basic human needs. Structurally the juxtaposition of the two storylines of Franz and Helene creates a melodramatic constellation: the viewers are made to be intensely involved with the characters emotionally and they are given more knowledge about the situation than the characters themselves. Now the visual excess of the camera work in the scene with Helene banging on the prison gates revs up the emotions to fever pitch, another characteristic of the "melodramatic imagination," as described by Peter Brooks, as a "mode of high emotionalism and stark ethical conflict" (Brooks, 12).

Significantly, Helene's resolve to remain faithful to her spouse is shown to fail *before* Sommer in turn succumbs to the sexual temptations present in the same-sex environment of the prison. Moreover, the film takes great pains to make it clear that Sommer never actively seeks a sexual engagement with his fellow prisoners. Whereas the film associates Helene's transgression with a discourse of physical desire (along the lines of the pressure/release model), it links Sommer's transgression with a discourse of love (a more elevated expression of sexual desire): we witness the gradual evolution of an emotional bond that develops between Sommer and the new young prisoner, Alfred. One evening we see a medium shot of the corner of the cell where the two men's beds are placed. If Helene's lapse, with its shaky camerawork and hysterical body language, is associated with emotional hyperbole, Sommer's transgression is characterized by allusion, restraint, and understated tension: young Alfred is shown lying in his bed, which is parallel to the visual plane, while Sommer's bed is at a right angle at the foot of Alfred's bed. Slowly, the camera repeatedly pans from side to side in this scene, every now and then revealing Sommer's head in the extreme left of the frame. The movement of the camera creates a strange tension in repeatedly scanning, as it were, Alfred's entire body while largely keeping Sommer outside the frame altogether. The camera thus partly aligns the viewer with Sommer's position, seemingly affirming the attractiveness of the young man as an object of desire, with the sideways camera movement at the same time subliminally mimicking a shaking of the head in negation, as if to ward off that desire. The visual tension is intensified by the dialog that centers on Alfred's apprehensiveness as he cautiously launches his declaration of love for Sommer. The actual confession, however, is left out of the intertitles; viewers have to figure out what Alfred says by inference or by reading his lips — presumably he is confessing his love.[18] Alfred's fear of rejection and ridicule is palpable as he seeks assurance from Sommer, who has remained silent. It is only after Sommer gives this verbal reassurance ("I will never despise you.") that Alfred stretches out his left hand towards Sommer. As the camera pans left, Sommer's right hand enters the frame from above to meet Alfred's, and we see Alfred clutch Sommer's hand, which — ironically — offers us a brief glimpse of Sommer's wedding ring (fig. 13.4). The screen discretely fades to black, leaving viewers to infer what the exchange may have signified. In not providing the intertitles for what Alfred says, and in allowing for only the subtlest hint of physical contact between the two men, Dieterle's film clearly frames homo-

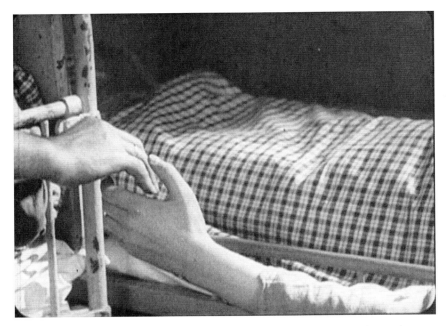

Fig. 13.4. Sommer's hand meets Alfred's in the "seduction" scene. Screenshot.

sexuality as a social taboo, something that cannot be acknowledged directly, but that needs to remain unsaid. Here, literally, "melodrama speaks the unspeakable and represents the unrepresentable" (Mercer/Shingler, 97).

Dieterle's film sanitizes the issue of homosexuality by obscuring any aspects that his audiences most likely would have found unsavory and disturbing. Karl Plättner's book, to which the film alluded at the beginning, gives graphic accounts of the sexual practices prevalent in prison settings, including male-on-male rape, prostitution, and group orgies. Plättner makes it clear that sexual contacts in prisons were usually initiated by older prisoners, who often enough forced themselves upon younger inmates, not only to seek sexual gratification but also to establish and maintain hierarchies of power. Dieterle's film not only reverses the situation (with young Alfred making, however cautious, overtures and Sommer responding by letting go of his defenses) but it also humanizes the potentially objectionable same-sex relationship in terms of emotional bonding and love. The film at this point presents homosexuality as one variant among other expressions of human sexuality — a "normal" choice given the exceptional circumstances — eschewing the discourses of pathology, moral depravity, or sin with which same-sex relationships were usually associated.

Embedded in a multiple set of contexts, the "seduction scene" is perhaps director Dieterle's most remarkable artistic achievement. Through its complex layering of situational and psychological factors, the film manages to overcome potential moral objections on the part of diverse audiences, first to the issue of marital infidelity and then to the issue of same-sex activity; the carefully calibrated mise-en-scène leads audiences to a point at which viewers can put themselves in the shoes of the characters. Sommer's same-sex encounter, like Helene's sexual lapse before, is presented as something that, given the circumstances, can happen to anyone. All "normal" categories have been reversed: in her "active" pursuit of a random sexual partner, after she has been denied access to her husband, Helene Sommer exhibits male characteristics; conversely, the "passive" response to the emotional solicitation of a loving individual completes the emasculation and feminization of Franz Sommer.

The melodramatic mode of representation encourages viewers, regardless of their moral convictions, to empathize with Sommer's and Helene's predicament. Judging from the mostly positive and thoughtful response the film elicited at its premiere, it would appear that the film managed to persuade its audiences of the necessity to reform the German penal system so that the sexual and emotional needs of prisoners be addressed in terms of a fundamental human right. Most critics professed to be deeply moved by the humanist vision of the film, and the film was very successful at the box office, despite its potentially controversial subject matter. Yet even then, some critics found fault with the supposed inevitability of the film's tragic conclusion.

Inevitabilities?

After Franz Sommer is released from prison, it appears that neither he nor his wife can forgive themselves for their own moral lapses, which violated their bond in marriage and which, as noted above, reversed their respective gender roles. When they realize the extent of their transgressions, they decide to die together. Paradoxically, they are unable to overcome their estrangement and their feelings of guilt while at the same time feeling compelled to affirm their marital bond by committing double suicide: as Helene emphasizes, "We belong together. In love and in guilt." The film had presented their predicament as contingent upon circumstance, as the inevitable and logical consequence of an inhumane and untenable situation. Millions of German returnees from the war and the prison camps had been forced to renegotiate their marriages and their other relationships in the face of similar circumstances. Most of them had found a way to continue living, with all the tensions and contradictions the new situation entailed.

Fig. 13.5. Alfred (Hans Heinrich von Twardowski) as the intruder between Sommer (Wilhelm Dieterle) and Helene (Mary Johnson). Screenshot.

Alfred's role in the destruction of Franz and Helene Sommer remains altogether ambivalent. Upon his release from prison he is shown in a low-class urban neighborhood with a male friend, who suggests to him that Franz Sommer would be a good object for blackmail, a reference to § 175 of the German penal code, which made homosexual acts between men a crime. Richard Oswald's pioneering gay-rights film, *Anders als die Andern* (Different from the Others, 1919; see Jill Smith's essay in this volume) had highlighted the role of blackmail in the suicide of homosexual violin virtuoso Paul Körner (played by Conrad Veidt).[19] On the one hand, Dieterle's film thus makes a point many advocates of penal reform had made: enforced isolation in same-sex environments exposed men who may have entered jail for minor offenses to a situation in which they committed more serious "crimes," starting a vicious cycle, a self-reinforcing loop of criminality. On the other hand, the film potentially denounces Alfred, the gay character whose affections we have been led to assume were sincere, as an unscrupulous blackmailer, similar to the sinister extortionist Franz Bollek (Reinhold Schünzel) in Oswald's film. It is difficult to read the scene where he appears at Sommer's apartment with a bouquet of flowers merely as Alfred's naive effort to rekindle a loving relationship: Alfred, standing in the door frame in the background, is positioned between a dejected Sommer (crouched, foreground left) and a stunned Helene (standing, mid-ground right). The three characters are, for a moment, caught up in a nervous relay of glances (fig. 13.5). Cut to a medium close-up of Helene covering her eyes with her hands in horror as she realizes the nature of the relationship between the two men. Alfred is then ordered out by an angry Sommer. He stumbles out, mumbling a confused apology to Helene: "Madam . . . if I've killed your happiness . . . forgive me." Has Alfred come to understand that his effort to continue his romance with Sommer was misguided? Is he horrified by the havoc his sexual advances have wreaked upon a loving marriage? Or has he merely realized that he won't be able to go through with his projected blackmail? Significantly, the last we see of Alfred's presence in the film is the bouquet of flowers he has left on the banister in the empty staircase of Sommer's apartment building: visually, the film leaves no place for Alfred and his misplaced affections.

For the sake of the emotional appeal of the story, Dieterle's film here seems to betray and forego its enlightened, rationalistic premise and to veer into conservative territory. The recourse to contemporary "science" had enabled the film to provide "clarifying information" or "enlighten-ment" (*Aufklärung*) on sexual and political issues. It advanced a biologis-tic notion of sexual activity as a basic human need and a universal right. The melodramatic conclusion, in its refusal to acknowledge the practical necessity of renegotiation and adjustment and in the near-denunciation of Alfred the homosexual, creates the impression that the film abandons its progressivist agenda to uphold an essentializing, patriarchal notion of the trans-historical sanctity of the institution of marriage — and a restrictive view of what constitutes socially acceptable sexual activity. The supposedly inescapable melodramatic resignation of the film's end stands in marked contrast to its overall emancipatory impulse, as the discourse of human rights appears to give way to the discourse of repressive bourgeois ideology — "Enlightenment" (*Aufklärung*) as described by Theodor W. Adorno and Max Horkheimer. Oscillating between a pluralistic and a normative view of human sexuality, Dieterle's film becomes an important document that highlights the peculiar dialectic of "enlightenment" in the Weimar Republic.

The supposed inevitability of the double suicide with which the film ends leaves behind a profound sense of ambivalence. The current version of the film ends with a close-up of Sommer's left hand turning the gas lever open, followed by close-ups of the faces of Helene and Franz, filmed in soft focus through a gauzy haze that mimicks their gradual loss of con-sciousness. The left hand, the one without the wedding ring, signals the destruction of a marriage, much as the unseen right hand off-screen, which we know to be embracing Helene, reaffirms their marital relationship. Moreover, the alternation between the faces in close-up sutures the viewer into the relationship, as we take on both Sommer's and Helene's position. The final image is that of a dark blurry outline of Sommer's head tilting to the left as he dies, before the screen fades to black. The viewer is overwhelmed with the feeling of sad loss, a feeling of helplessness vis-à-vis the senseless destruction of lives.

Dieterle's *Geschlecht in Fesseln* set out to highlight the necessity of social reform, yet the overwhelming sense of inexorable fate at work seems to render any form of social activism impossible. The melodramatic mode it adopted to get its reformist message across may result in paralysis. Yet there is evidence that in its original form the film aimed at escaping this impasse: contemporary reviews indicate that the double-suicide scene was followed by a sequence showing the hustle and bustle of big city life in Berlin, with the return to a realistic mode of representation tying the story of the Sommers back into the here and now, the concrete social and political circumstances of the Weimar Republic in the late 1920s (see Anon., "Aktualität"). Life, these laconic final shots suggest, goes on, indifferent to the damage that is visited upon innocent people by an unjust and untenable political system that callously destroys some of its most valuable citizens. With all its artistic shortcomings and limitations, its ideological contradictions and ambivalences, Dieterle's interventionist film advocating a humane prison reform constitutes a remarkable gesture of civil courage: it should not come as a surprise that only a few years later, within weeks of the Nazis having taken power, *Geschlecht in Fesseln* was placed on a list of films of "communist, pacifist, or sexual tendency" to be banned by the new regime.[20]

Notes

This research was supported (in part) by a grant from the Amherst College Faculty Research Award Program, as funded by the H. Axel Schupf '57 Fund for Intellectual Life. I would like to express my gratitude to the staff at the Deutsche Kinemathek Berlin (Regina Hoffmann, Peter Latta, and Gerrit Thies) for their helpfulness in providing access to materials on Dieterle and his film, and to Beate Dannhorn of the Deutsches Filminstitut Frankfurt am Main for her help with the images. And I would like to thank Eric Rentschler for providing valuable critical feedback on an earlier, shorter version of this essay and Nona Monáhin for her help with the final version.

[1] "Fast jeder Bewohner dieser Bezirke, dessen Name im Adreßbuch zu finden ist" (Anon., "Streng vertraulich."). Unless otherwise noted, all translations from the German are my own.

[2] Lines 1–3 of Canto 3 of Dante's *Inferno*, translation by Allen Mandelbaum (1980), available online at http://www.divinecomedy.org/. The German version reads, "Ich führe Dich zur Stadt der Qualerkorenen / ich führe Dich zu unbegrenztem Leid, / ich führe Dich zur Stätte der Verlorenen" (*Spielplan*).

[3] Nor does Kracauer discuss any of the other films directed by Dieterle in Germany during the Weimar period. Dieterle is mentioned only once, as an actor, playing the lead roles in *Das Wachsfigurenkabinett* (*Waxworks*, 1924), directed by Leo Birinski and Paul Leni (Kracauer, *Caligari*, 84).

[4] An extensive website, lovingly put together, complete with a detailed plot synopsis and hundreds of screen shots, details the "gay subtext" of Dieterle's film. The question remains whether the mere presence of the theme of homosexuality is enough to turn *Geschlecht in Fesseln* into a "queer silent." See http://www.queersilents.com/film.php?id=fm474548.

[5] "Gleich vorweg sei bemerkt, daß die Autoren und der feinsinnige Regisseur Wilhelm Dieterle den Stoff äußerst dezent anpacken, ohne ihm dadurch etwas von seiner Wirksamkeit zu rauben" (Olimsky).

[6] "Ein leidenschaftlicher Tendenzfilm — aber mit einer Tendenz, der wir uns alle anschließen können: Es ist das ein Film, der für Liberalität und Menschenwürde, gegen Dickfelligkeit und Unduldsamkeit kämpft. Zudem ein Film, der ein heikles Thema mit Ernst aufwirft" (—e—, "Geschlecht in Fesseln").

[7] "Tendenz als Kunst! Tendenz zur Belebung der Materie, dabei nicht langweilen, ruhig unterhalten, zum Nachdenken anregen. Zustände schildern, warnen und bessern" (Dieterle).

[8] Anon. "Der Starfilm-Erfolg."

[9] "Gewagtestes durch einen gewissen Takt der Behandlung doch erträglich wird und dass ein ernster Stoff zwar mutig und bisweilen recht deutlich, aber nicht ohne eine gewisse Dezenz behandelt wird." Zensurgutachten Oberprüfstelle O.15 of 16 January 1929, 14; available online at http://www.deutsches-filminstitut.de.

[10] On the *Liga für Menschenrechte* during the Weimar Republic, see the section "The German League for Human Rights before 1945" in Wildenthal, 3–5.

[11] Born in 1893 in a small town in the Harz region, Karl Plättner was trained as a metal worker and became part of the industrial labor movement in Hamburg. He left the Social Democratic Party (SPD) he had joined in 1912 to protest the party's compliance with the German war effort in 1914, was drafted into the army, and released in 1915 after an injury that prevented him from taking up his former profession. Illegal underground activism was followed in 1917 by a stint in prison. In 1918, Plättner was one of the founding members of the *Kommunistische Partei Deutschlands* (KPD, German Communist Party). After his involvement with the short-lived Bremen Soviet Republic in 1919, he fled to Berlin, where he participated in militant street fights and was imprisoned for a few months. In 1920, he became the cofounder of the *Kommunistische Arbeiterpartei Deutschlands* (KAPD; German Workers' Communist Party), a splinter group to the left of the regular KPD, and began to organize armed robberies and bombing attacks, much to the abhorrence of his former party comrades (Ullrich).

[12] Franz Höllering (1896–1968) was a well-known Austrian left-wing writer and journalist based in Berlin and a member of the *Unabhängige Sozialistische Partei* (USPD, Independent Socialist Party), a splinter party to the left of the Social Democrats. A friend and colleague of prominent artists like Bertolt Brecht and

John Heartfield, Höllering was chief editor of the *Berliner Zeitung am Mittag* (of the Ullstein publishing house) and the *Arbeiter Illustrierte Zeitung* (Worker's Illustrated Magazine). His involvement in film included his editorship of *Film und Volk* (Film and People), a left-wing journal that sought to harness film for the political education of the populace (Murray, 139–42). He is also credited for providing the script for a film adaptation of Carl Zuckmayer's stage play *Katharina Knie*, directed in 1929 by Karl Grune. See www.filmportal.de.

[13] Dieterle had close contact with left-wing circles in Berlin: in November 1918 he had enthusiastically welcomed the collapse of the German monarchy and the "workers' councils" of the revolution, appearing at several meetings reciting incendiary poetry (Mierendorff, 24). For years Dieterle appeared at meetings held for political and social causes, such as a gathering on behalf of the "Künstlerhilfe für die Hungernden in Rußland" (Artists' Aid for those suffering hunger in Russia) in February 1922 (Mierendorff, 33). As late as 1928 Dieterle would publish a short prose piece reflecting on the revolutionary fervor of November 1918 ("der Jubelschrei der endlich Befreiten" — "the jubilant cries of those finally set free") and on the ensuing disillusionment ("Die Weltbefreiung erstickte" — "world liberation suffocated"; Mierendorff, 260).

[14] The first petition form letter is addressed to the "Abgeordneten deutscher Parlamente" (delegates of the German parliaments) in support of Plättner's initiative; the second one appeals to social elites and public pressure groups and solicits endorsement of Plättner's key demands; the third one is addressed to current prisoners and seeks expressions of solidarity with the incarcerated. The book also features a tear-out questionnaire on which prisoners can report their predicament to Plättner.

[15] Even the wording of Plättner's own list of practical demands leaves it unclear whether the "Besuch des Geschlechtspartners" (visit of the sexual partner) that he says should be granted every four weeks would include same-sex partners (Plättner, 221).

[16] "Nur die leiden im Gefängnis am Weibe, die auch schon in der Freiheit dieselben Sorgen gehabt haben." Quoted in part 6 (Saturday, 9 June 1928) of the 17-part anonymous series "Liebe im Gefängnis."

[17] This is one of the scenes that had to be shortened after objections by the Berlin Censorship Board (censorship record number O.15, 16 January 1929).

[18] The author of the website www.queersilents.com claims that Alfred says "I love you, Franz" (presumably in German). Yet Alfred clearly mouths more syllables than the German phrase "Ich liebe dich, Franz." This would suggest that Alfred's supposed declaration of love is embedded in a more complex syntactical structure.

[19] The casting of Dieterle himself in the main role enhances the character's unambiguous heterosexuality. Through his bulky, distinctly masculine, physical presence and his role profile as the romantic male lead in dozens of previous Weimar German movies, Dieterle's screen persona represents the very opposite of the sexually ambivalent persona of Conrad Veidt (see Elizabeth Otto's essay in this volume).

[20] Letter from "Landesfilmstelle Süd" of the NSDAP to the Bavarian Ministry of the Interior, dated 13 March 1933; available online at http://www.deutsches-filminstitut.de.

Works Cited

Anon. "Aktualität." *Montag Morgen*, 29 October 1928.

———. "Liebe im Gefängnis: Bericht eines entlassenen Sträflings." *Die Welt am Abend* 6, numbers 128 (Monday, 4 June 1928) through 144 (Friday, 22 June 1928) [17 parts].

———. "Der Starfilm-Erfolg. *Geschlecht in Fesseln* — künstlerisch wertvoll." *Film-Kurier*, 26 October 1928.

———. "Streng vertraulich." *Reichsfilmblatt* 47 (24 November 1928).

Brooks, Peter. *The Melodramatic Imagination: Balzac, Henry James, Melodrama, and the Mode of Excess.* New Haven and London: Yale UP, 1995.

Dieterle, Wilhelm. "Tendenz im Film." *Filmwoche* 2 (1929). Reprinted in Mierendorff, 260–61.

Dingeldey, Hugo. "Lebensgeschichte des Jubilars." In *Erich Wulffen: Festschrift zu seinem siebzigsten Geburtstag*, edited by Alexander Baumgarten and Hugo Dingeldey, 12–40. Berlin: Hanseatischer Rechts- und Wirtschaftsverlag, 1932.

—e—. "Geschlecht in Fesseln." *Reichsfilmblatt* 43 (27 October 1928).

Fuechtner, Veronika. "Alfred Döblin and the Berlin Psychoanalytic Institute." PhD diss., U of Chicago, 2002.

Gallwitz, Tim. "In der Falle von Triebtheorie und repressiver Moral: *Geschlecht in Fesseln.*" In *Geschlecht in Fesseln: Sexualität zwischen Aufklärung und Ausbeutung im Weimarer Kino, 1918–1933*, edited by Malte Hagener, 154–65. Munich: edition text + kritik, 2000.

"*Geschlecht in Fesseln*: Die Sexualnot der Strafgefangenen." *Illustrierter Film-Kurier* 991 (1928).

Haeberle, Erwin J. "The Jewish Contribution to the Development of Sexology." *The Journal of Sex Research* 18:4 (November 1982): 305–23.

Hirschfeld, Magnus, ed. *The Sexual History of the World War.* 3 vols in 1. New York: Panurge, 1934.

Kracauer, Siegfried. *Die Angestellten: Aus dem neuesten Deutschland.* Frankfurt am Main: Societätsdruckerei, 1930. English version, *The Salaried Masses: Duty and Distraction in Weimar.* Translated by Quintin Hoare. London: Verso, 1998.

———. *From Caligari to Hitler: A Psychological History of German Film.* Princeton, NJ: Princeton UP, 1947.

Mercer, John, and Martin Shingler. *Melodrama: Genre, Style and Sensibility.* London and New York: Wallflower, 2004.

Mierendorff, Marta. *William Dieterle: Der Plutarch von Hollywood.* Berlin: Henschel, 1993.

Murray, Bruce. *Film and the German Left in the Weimar Republic: From "Caligari" to "Kuhle Wampe."* Austin: U of Texas P, 1990.

Olimsky, Fritz. "*Geschlecht in Fesseln*: Tauentzien-Palast." *Berliner Börsen-Zeitung,* 28 October 1928.

Plättner, Karl. *Eros im Zuchthaus: Sehnsuchtsschreie gequälter Menschen nach Liebe.* Vorwort von Magnus Hirschfeld und Felix Abraham. Berlin: Mopr-Verlag, 1929.

Spielplan vom 24. bis 30. Oktober 1928. Tauentzien-Palast, Berlin. Deutsche Kinemathek Berlin, Schriftgutarchiv, Nr. 2937.

Ullrich, Volker. *Der ruhelose Rebell: Karl Plättner, 1893–1945.* Munich: Beck, 2000.

Usborne, Cornelie. *Cultures of Abortion in Weimar Germany.* Oxford and New York: Berghahn, 2007.

Wildenthal, Lora. "The Origins of the West German Human Rights Movement, 1945–1961." *Human Rights Institute Research Papers,* University of Connecticut, 2004. Available online at http://digitalcommons.uconn.edu/hri_papers/4/.

14: Babel's Business — On Ufa's Multiple Language Film Versions, 1929–1933

Chris Wahl

The Coming of (Foreign) Sound(s): *Melodie des Herzens*

ON 28 OCTOBER 1929 THE FIRST all-talking German film, *Atlantik*, loosely based on the foundering of the "unsinkable" Titanic, premiered in Berlin. Although the director, E. A. Dupont, and all the main actors were indeed of German origin (Schöning), the film had been shot in the "British Hollywood," at the Elstree studios near London (Warren). German filmmakers responded to the coming of sound film by shooting movies simultaneously in two or three languages (primarily English, German, and French) with different casts, but on identical sets, and based on the same script. *Atlantik,* shot in a German and an English version (*Atlantic*) by the same director, inaugurated the concept.[1]

In Germany and elsewhere, multiple language versions (MLVs) soon became the predominant method of adapting films for other countries. They had two important advantages over dubbing: they guaranteed unity of body and voice, important to secure the credibility of the new technology with contemporary audiences; and the stories could be adapted to the different tastes of the respective target audience. Over time, however, international audiences got used to seeing dubbed or subtitled films (Wahl, *Sprechen*, 105–20 and 139–44), and film producers increasingly decided to sell or buy the rights to remake films instead of shooting expensive multiple versions. British and American companies abandoned MLVs in the early 1930s, and only the largest European film company of the time, the German *Universum Film Aktiengesellschaft* (Ufa) based in Babelsberg near Berlin, continued to produce MLVs on a grand scale until 1936. By the end of the Weimar Republic, Ufa had produced a total of twenty-nine MLVs of its German films (seventeen in French; six in French and English; three in English; two in Hungarian; and one in French, English, and Hungarian) (fig. 14.1).

Ufa's directors had initially been extremely hesitant to switch to sound film production, although the sound-on-film system had actually been developed in Germany in the early 1920s by two engineers, Hans Vogt and

Heinz Rühmann und Lilian Harvey in der deutschen Fassung des Tonfilms „Einbrecher"

Dieselbe Szene der französischen Fassung mit französischen Darstellern in der deutschen Dekoration

Fig. 14.1. The German and French casts of Einbrecher / Burglars/ Flagrant Délit *(Hanns Schwarz, 1930), filmed on the same sound stage. Promotion still.*

Joseph Massolle, and physicist Jo Engl, who called their invention *Tri-Ergon* ("Work of the Three"). Driven by American successes, however, in February 1929 Ufa became the first German film company to stop producing silent films (Mühl-Benninghaus, 70). During June and July 1929, while *Atlantik* was being filmed in England, Ufa shot its own first talkie, also as an MLV, *Melodie des Herzens* (Melody of the Heart, directed by Hanns Schwarz), which premiered in Berlin on 16 December 1929.

Starting with *Melodie des Herzens*, producer Erich Pommer would be the decisive figure to develop and advance Ufa's strategy of MLV production until the takeover by the Nazis on 30 January 1933. Throughout, Pommer remained strictly opposed to dubbing and favoured MLVs, which in his view allowed films to better correspond to particular national mentalities (Pommer). After the financial debacle of Fritz Lang's *Metropolis* (1927), Pommer had moved to Hollywood, where he briefly worked for Paramount and MGM. By September 1927, however, he was back at Ufa as head of the Erich Pommer Production Unit (Kappelhoff, 208). From 1929 to 1932 this unit produced seventeen German films, fifteen of which were shot in foreign language versions (seven in English and French, six in French, and three in English).

It is worth noting that from *Melodie des Herzens* onwards Pommer received a share of the net profit of the films he produced for every country (he had previously only profited from the net earnings in Germany, the United States, and Canada; see Minutes of Ufa's Board of Directors = MUBD, 23 September 1929). In a list from 1955, now in the Ufa files at the Bundesarchiv, Pommer named only sixteen films, ignoring his last Ufa production, *Ich und die Kaiserin* (I and the Empress; released as *The Only Girl*, 1933, directed by Friedrich Hollaender), which was only released after the Nazi takeover, on 22 February, 1933. Strangely, he lists the film *Ihre Hoheit befiehlt* (Her Highness Commands, 1931, directed by Hanns Schwarz), which according to all available information was not produced by his unit, instead of the Pommer film *Voruntersuchung* (Preliminary Inquest, 1931, directed by Robert Siodmak). Both were shot in a German and a French version.

Pommer, like all the other high-ranking Ufa officials, had a keen business sense. Perhaps because of his Hollywood experience, he was one of the few people at Ufa who immediately understood that, in comparison to silent films, sound films would require an increased budget. *Melodie des Herzens* was shot in five versions: German, English, French, Hungarian, and silent.[2] In contrast to *Atlantik*, the same actors were used for every version and learned their lines phonetically.[3] Only afterward were their words dubbed by native speakers (Krützen, 149).[4] This method was called "optical version" (Garncarz, "Made in Germany," 257). Pommer wanted not only to avoid the multi-casting required by different language versions but also to achieve a better lip sync than an ordinary synchronization could provide.[5] Unfortunately we are not able to check the results of these efforts, because only the German version of *Melodie* has survived.[6] But anyone viewing the film is struck by how slow and unnatural the dialogues are; this had already been noted by Maurice M. Bessy, a contemporary critic, with regard to the French version. In view of these technical short-comings and the general lead Hollywood had over European sound-film production, it is not surprising that the film did not meet the tastes of the critics in New York, where the German and the English version were shown only in late 1930: "There have been many silly American productions, but none that falls as low as this" (Hall).

Early English Language Versions:
Love Waltz, The Blue Angel, The Temporary Widow

The idea of building a European alliance against Hollywood had been discussed since 1924. With the advent of sound, it finally became necessary to create a continental market, a *Film-Europa*, to be able to compete with the United States, where the large monolingual home market guaranteed profitability (see Higson, both essays). On the other hand, the American film industry suffered huge losses on the European market, even in Britain, a fact that made the directors at the Ufa convention of 1930 very confident about the future.[7] As the strongest film company in Europe, Ufa planned to win hegemony over the continent and to attack Hollywood in its own market.

In the wake of *Melodie des Herzens* three English versions were designed during the business year 1929/30 to serve this purpose. These productions reveal Pommer's uncertainty about how to proceed to obtain a satisfactory result. For *Der blaue Engel/The Blue Angel*, shot between 4 November 1929 and 22 January 1930, he imported a sophisticated director from Hollywood, Josef von Sternberg, and retrieved the first actor ever to win an Oscar (in 1928), Swiss-German Emil Jannings, who it was hoped would open the doors for Ufa's products in the United States. In contrast to the optical-version methodology applied to *Melodie des Herzens*, the German actors were not dubbed but had to speak English themselves, their accents being explained in the script (Beyer; Wahl, *Sprechen*, 175–77). The MUBD files reveal that there had been heated discussion regarding the casting of Jannings, with the head of distribution, Hermann Grieving, voicing his disapproval during a meeting of 8 May 1929, when it was still very unclear whether Ufa would seek to tackle the foreign market with its first sound films. But once it was decided to challenge Hollywood on its own turf, Jannings seemed to be the perfect star to guarantee the attention of the American public. Unfortunately, the bosses learned during the production of *The Blue Angel* how bad Jannings's foreign language skills really were. In fact, his poor knowledge of English seems to have been the real reason for his withdrawal from Hollywood simultaneously with the demise of silent-film production.

Nevertheless, even after this disappointing experience with *The Blue Angel*, Ufa continued to plan to include Jannings in another English version, this time of *Liebling der Götter* (Darling of the Gods, 1930, directed by Hanns Schwarz). Then, for a moment, the Ufa bosses considered engaging the Russian actor Ivan Mozzhukhin (MUBD, 28 March 1930). However, they soon found out that Mozzhukhin did not speak German, English, or French and was therefore unsuitable for sound-film production (MUBD, 16 April 1930). Eventually Pommer produced the film with Jannings, but only in a German version. Shooting started on 26 May 1930.

For *Love Waltz*, the English version of Wilhelm Thiele's *Liebeswalzer*, shot between 4 October 1929 and 9 January 1930, the method applied for *The Blue Angel* was slightly altered: Pommer cast Lilian Harvey, a bilingual actress, in the main female role in both versions and replaced her German partner, Willy Fritsch, with John Batten, a British actor who had already worked in Hollywood, in the English version. *Love Waltz* starts in the office of a leading American automobile manufacturer who is a German immigrant, just as were many Hollywood studio bosses of that time. His son Bobby, American by birth, is hired to serve a German aristocrat, the Archduke Ferdinand, as a kind of private secretary and follows him to a small German principality called Lauenburg, where the archduke is supposed to marry the princess. But at Lauenburg, the princess mistakes Bobby for the archduke and falls in love with him. He reciprocates her love, and in spite of the class difference they eventually are allowed to marry because Bobby's father, after all, is a "king" as well, a king of cars. Old Europe and the New World are reconciled.

As the story was built around a German immigrant to the United States and mostly set in Germany, the accents of the German actors were again easy to explain. In some cases, however, they were replaced by native speakers in the English version. Karl Etlinger, for example, who played the small part of Dr. Popper, was replaced by Charles Hooper Trask,[8] a former Broadway actor and a film critic who wrote about German cinema for the *New York Times* and *Variety*. In the latter journal he stated on 19 March 1930, without mentioning his personal involvement in the film: "To judge by the several reels of a rough cut version which I saw in the projection room, the picture [*Love Waltz*] should go big in Great Britain, and should also be pleasing to audiences in the States as a novelty." *Liebeswalzer*, touted as "the first German film operetta" (Olimsky in the *Berliner Börsen-Zeitung*), was, according to a survey among exhibitors published annually by the *Film-Kurier*, the most financially successful German sound film of the 1929/30 season (Garncarz, "Hollywood," 199). Considering the *Variety* review of *Melodie des Herzens* quoted above, it comes as a surprise that *Love Waltz* received extraordinarily good reviews even from critics who were rather less partial than Trask. A British film journal praised it thus:

> This picture is excellent light entertainment and a model of how a film can be made for both English and German consumption. The detail work is clever, the music extremely tuneful, and the acting excellent. It can be described as a comedy with music, and as such is one of the most satisfactory to date.[9]

The Temporary Widow, the English version of Gustav Ucicky's *Hokuspokus*, was shot in April and May 1930 and was the next step toward a standardized Ufa style of MLV production. To achieve higher quality, and in spite of much higher costs, Ufa would never again use German actors, whose sometimes terrible accents had to be justified in the script for foreign-language versions. Instead, the casts of MLVs would now be composed of bi- or multilingual stars, such as Lilian Harvey, and famous or promising actors from the target countries. Thus, by mid-1930, Pommer had established a very effective working method for international productions.

On 10 March 1930, three months after the shooting of the German and English versions had ended, it was decided to make a French international version. Even though, as Joseph Garncarz has noted, "the French market had become increasingly important for German film production since the mid-1920s,"[10] it seems that a nationalist attitude prevailing among the Ufa Board of Directors prevented them for a while from hiring French actors to produce French-language versions.[11] Thus the Ufa sound films of the 1929/30 season were presented to the French public in so-called international versions. Basically, this meant the suppression of the dialogue track and its replacement by intertitles, which could be exchanged from country to country just as in the silent period, to be accompanied by a permanent music score. The all-talking film *Der blaue Engel* was shown like that in France, to the disgust of many contemporary critics (Icart, 110).

Ufa Co-Produces with Itself:
The *Alliance Cinématographique Européenne* (ACE)

In the first years after the arrival of sound cinema, France lacked a technologically and institutionally competitive film industry (Bowles). Ufa's Board of Directors thus abandoned their traditional hatred toward the French and yielded to economic reason: the chance to sell German films in the neighboring country was too obvious to be disregarded. And Germany would sell: in 1930, 111 feature films were exported to France, but only thirteen imported from there (Harlé). From 1929 to 1932, 400 German films in France stood against sixty-two French pictures in Germany

(Bowles, 131). From mid-1930, Ufa's emphasis shifted, with the company now preferring to concentrate on French-language versions and to shoot English versions only in addition to a French version. By this time, the Ufa directors must have already understood the difficulties of succeeding in the American as well as the British market. When the Nazis finally took over governmental power in Germany, the production of English-language versions had already ceased.[12]

In the early 1930s, film import and export was a very delicate political affair, engendering controversial public discussions regarding quota regulations, and it was subject to annual revision. One of the sensitive issues was the definition of a maximum number of films allowed to be imported (MUBD, 17 November 1931).[13] The *Kontingentabkommen* (quota agreement) of 8 August 1930 envisioned French-language versions shot in Berlin being treated like regular French movies.[14] Ufa, on the other hand, objected to the import of five German-language versions of films produced by Paramount in France (MUBD, 1 May 1931). In spite of agitated negotiations at the highest levels of film politics,[15] France decided in 1932 to treat the language version of a film (whether dubbed or re-shot) as a film on its own. This was awkward for Germany, because the quota thereby restricted the numbers of films to be shown in the French bilingual region of Alsace-Lorraine.

On 14 May 1930 Ufa's Board of Directors initially decided, and on 11 June finally approved, the shooting of Wilhelm Thiele's *Die drei von der Tankstelle* (Three from the Gas Station) in a German *and* in a French version (fig. 14.2). The French version, *Le chemin du paradis,* premiered on 2 October 1930 in Paris to become a stunning success: by 1934, the film earned a total revenue of nearly seven million francs.[16] This fact certainly contributed to Ufa's decision to concentrate on French-language versions. The public success of the film had only been possible thanks to solid political and economic preparatory work.

According to appendix 1 to the annual report on the ACE business year 1932/33 (1 June until 31 May), Ufa had founded the *Alliance Cinématographique Européenne* (ACE) on 19 May 1926 as a French subsidiary company based in Paris. The entity consisted of five branches (Paris, Bordeaux, Marseille, Lyon, and Strasbourg) that had to take orders from headquarters, as well as of two agencies (Lille and Brussels in Belgium) that were allowed to schedule films independently.[17] Although ACE was officially a French company, Ufa always indirectly held 100 percent of the capital stock of two million francs. This move turned out to be extraordinarily profitable for Ufa, with the earnings in France and Belgium increasing from 218,000 Reichsmark in 1925/26, the last business year before the foundation of the ACE, to a peak of 17,594,817 francs (6 francs = 1 Reichsmark) in 1932/33.[18] In the annual report on Ufa's business year 1930/31, the company identified the spring of 1930, when the first MLVs

Fig. 14.2. Lilian Harvey between her German (Willy Fritsch) and French partner (Henri Garat) in Die drei von Tankstelle / Three from the Gas Station / Le chemin du paradis *(Wilhelm Thiele, 1930). Bibliothèque du Film, Paris.*

were released, as the starting point for the revival of their foreign business in general. The report of the next business year (1931/32) shows earnings from foreign countries increased by about 50 percent to 11 million Reichsmark, about two million of which stemmed from ACE (F12,694,701), at that time one of fourteen Ufa affiliates in foreign countries. By controlling ACE, Ufa sought to bypass actual coproductions with France under the French quota regulations, which stipulated that French film productions had to be carried out in France by Frenchmen (MUBD, 10 January 1928). No doubt a French subsidiary controlled from Berlin would help with lobbying the French government.

ACE's administrative board consisted of six representatives, four Frenchmen and two Germans. One of the French representatives, Louis Aubert, the owner of several cinemas and a distribution chain, had negotiated, as early as May 1924, with Ufa a voluntary association in order to form a European block against Hollywood (Sturm, 409). In the late 1920s Ufa's financial situation was precarious, and the international financial crisis in the wake of the Great Depression of 1929 did not help ameliorate the situation. Hence there was a constant search to find new resources, especially after the coming of sound,[19] and later, after the extremely expensive production of MLVs had been decided upon (MUBD, 24 June 1930). For the French business, transactions involving so-called "Repko" acceptances offered one viable solution. "Repko" stands in the MUBD for *Reparationskommission*, the committee of the Allied Forces assessing and supervising the reparations Germany had to pay after the First World War. It is difficult to exactly understand and trace these activities by means of the few surviving Ufa documents.

Nevertheless, the general idea appears to have been the following: the French Ministry of Finance was in possession of Repko acceptances in Reichsmark and thus of cashless obligations of the German government. These acceptances were lent to the ACE, which in turn used them to buy films from Ufa for the French market. With this money, Ufa could finance part of the production costs and, after 1929/30, especially the French-language versions. According to the minutes, the disposition of the French Finance Ministry in mid-1929 was very much in favor of importing feature films from Germany by means of Repko transactions, because of the public boycott of American sound movies (MUBD, 25 April 1929).[20]

But there were several restrictions: Ufa had to repay the French Ministry of Finance in francs and thus in foreign currency, a big problem at the time.[21] In addition, the ministry asked for warrantors before lending the acceptances, and especially for a French warrantor (the French major bank Crédit Lyonnais: MUBD 2 December 1930) when a larger amount was concerned (sometimes more than 12 million francs: MUBD, 29 October 1928). The German warrantor, Otto Wolff, was not only a member of Ufa's supervisory board but, since his investments in July 1927, he also belonged to a task force of five men endowed with the right and the duty to control Ufa's Board of Directors (Dahlmann, 95). Throughout the 1920s he had been a vehement advocate of a political and economic rapprochement between Germany and France (Conze, 119–20). Of course, these warrantors wanted compensation for their services; Otto Wolff, for example, claimed 1 percent (MUBD, 8 July 1927). Nevertheless, the Repko business must have been worthwhile for Ufa, because from mid-1927 to mid-1931 six consecutive Repko transactions are documented in the minutes (MUBD, 8 July 1927 and 25 March 1931). The end of this particular kind of business is likely to have been due to the termination of the reparation committee as a consequence of the Young Plan of 17 May 1930 as well as to the Hoover Moratorium of 20 July 1931, which put a de facto end to the payment of reparations.

There seem to have been two reasons, one media-related and the other political/artistic, for the economic failure of Ufa's MLVs after 1933. The first threat to the foreign-language versions was the quickly increasing number of French-dubbed American films on the market, which found rising acceptance on the part of the French public. In the business year 1932/33, 147 French-language films were screened in France, of which thirty-one had been produced outside the country, including eighteen in Germany. Aside from the original French-language films, sixty French-dubbed films were on the market, forty-nine of which were made in the US.

The second reason for the problems Ufa began to face with their foreign language versions from 1933 was the highly visible decay in quality due to the hemorrhage of talent, with thousands of people active in the German film industry forced to flee the country for racial and/or political reasons. To the French public, this loss of quality made German films, formerly appreciated for their lightness of touch, appear increasingly dull. After the takeover by the Nazis, Ufa's fortunes on the Francophone market declined rapidly, with the earnings from France and Belgium dropping from F17,594,817 to F13,187,506 in the first year of their regime.[22] It was with with *Das Hofkonzert / La chanson du souvenir* (directed by Detlef Sierck, aka Douglas Sirk), shot between September and November 1936, that Ufa's production of French-language versions, and MLVs in general, eventually came to an end.

Notes

For an extensive study on Ufa's MLVs see Wahl, *Sprachversionsfilme*. Basic contributions to the history of Ufa are Bock/Töteberg and Kreimeier, and to the question of Hollywood's MLVs, Vincendeau and Ďurovičová. Barnier and O'Brien offer more recent elaborations on the French versions produced in Hollywood and the difference between American and French filmmaking in the 1930s respectively.

[1] In March/April 1930 Jean Kemm shot in Elstree a French version on the basis of a slightly altered script by Pierre Maudru. The coproducer was Jacques Haïk, quite an important figure in the French cinema business of the time (Wahl, *Sprechen*, 78–79).

[2] The silent version was meant to supply the cinemas not yet wired for sound-film screenings. For the Hungarian version see Wahl, "Paprika."

[3] This is the same approach as applied by MGM for the MLVs with Laurel and Hardy, who could, of course, not be replaced by other actors.

[4] Irritating in this respect is the following comment in a review by Mordaunt Hall (*New York Times*, 1 Sept. 1930): "The English copy [. . .] has but one or two lines that are not uttered with a decided foreign accent."

[5] For the same reason, Roger Goupillère, who was responsible for the French dubbed version of *M* (1931, directed by Fritz Lang), re-shot the famous apology of the killer with Peter Lorre performing in French before dubbing him with another voice (Gaubel, 22). This seemed to be particularly appropriate because in this sequence Lorre keeps talking toward the camera in close-ups.

[6] Even the National Hungarian Film Archive (MNFA) holds a print of only the German, not the Hungarian version.

[7] Anon., "L'Assemblée de l'Ufa pour 1930–31," *La Cinématographie Française*, 20 September 1930, 14.

[8] Charles Hooper Trask also appeared in the English version of *Bomben auf Monte Carlo* (Bombs on Monte Carlo, released as *Monte Carlo Madness*, 1931, directed by Hanns Schwarz) as well as in the German film *Ein blonder Traum* (A Blonde Dream, 1932, directed by Paul Martin).

[9] Anon., Review of *The Love Waltz, Kinematograph Weekly*, 31 July 1930.

[10] "In 1924 the number of German films screened in France was 20; in 1926 it rose to 33, in 1928 to 122, and in 1930 it was 111" (Garncarz, "Made in Germany," 254).

[11] They even "refused to sign up Abel Gance as potential director on grounds of his nationality" (Claus/Jäckel, 77).

[12] Concerning Ufa's struggle to establish itself on the American and British market and the diverse strategies applied to reach this goal, see Wahl, "Inside."

[13] MUBD, 17 November 1931; and Anon., "Endlich Klarheit! Das französische Kontingent. Keine zahlenmäßige Importbegrenzung," *Film-Kurier*, 29 July 1932.

[14] Marcel Colin-Reval, "Grâce à la prompte intervention de M. Charles Delac, un important Accord franco-allemand a été conclu," *La Cinématographie Française*, 16 August 1930, 9.

[15] This is documented in a letter of 2 March 1932, sent by the organization representing the interests of the German film industry (Spio = Spitzenorganisation der Filmwirtschaft) to the Department of the Interior and the Department of State; Political Archive of the German Department of State, Berlin.

[16] Appendix 6 to the annual report on the ACE business year 1933/34.

[17] Annual report on the ACE business year 1932/33, 16–17.

[18] Appendix 6 to the annual report on the ACE business year 1933/34, 2.

[19] For a couple of months Ufa thought intensively about a fusion of ACE with Gaumont or Pathé, even about selling the company (MUBD, 21 October 1929). As late as 22 January 1930 the talk was about an association with Tobis.

[20] Maybe this alleged boycott refers to a few screenings with subtitles, which enraged spectators (Chirat, 10). As a matter of fact, Maurice van Moppès in late 1931 saw the reason for the massive drawback from Hollywood (to the advantage of the German film industry) in France in the fact that most American films were shown in a dubbed version. By contrast, the French-language versions produced in the United States were the only successful American films (van Moppès, 1066–68). Germany, and especially Ufa, had obviously succeeded with the strategy to focus on MLVs.

[21] MUBD, 24 August, 19 September, 4 November, 19 December 1927, as well as appendix to the MUBD, 6 October 1931.

[22] Appendix 6 to the annual report on the ACE business year 1933/34, 2.

Works Cited

Altman, Rick, ed. *Sound Theory: Sound Praxis*. New York: Routledge, 1992.

Anon. "Endlich Klarheit! Das französische Kontingent. Keine zahlenmäßige Importbegrenzung." *Film-Kurier*, 29 July 1932.

———. "L'Assemblée de l'Ufa pour 1930–31." *La Cinématographie Française*, 20 September 1930, 14.

———. Review of *The Love Waltz. Kinematograph Weekly*, 31 July 1930.

Barnier, Martin: *Des films français made in Hollywood: Les versions multiples, 1929–1935*. Paris: L'Harmattan, 2005.

Bessy, Maurice M. Review of the French version of *Melodie des Herzens. La Cinématographie Française*, 31 May 1930, 101.

Beyer, Friedemann. "A Clone, but Not Identical: The English Version of *Der blaue Engel*." In *Film and Its Multiples: IX International Film Studies Conference*, edited by Anna Antonini, 79–82. Udine, Italy: Forum, 2003.

Bock, Hans-Michael, and Michael Töteberg, eds. *Das UFA-Buch*. Frankfurt am Main: Zweitausendeins, 1992.

Bowles, Brett. "The Attempted Nazification of French Cinema, 1934–44." In *Cinema and the Swastika: The International Expansion of Third Reich Cinema*, edited by Roel Vande Winkel and David Welch, 131–32. Basingstoke, UK: Palgrave Macmillan, 2007.

Chirat, Raymond. *Le cinema français des années 30*. Rennes, France: 5 Continent, 1983.

Claus, Horst, and Anne Jäckel. "*Der Kongreß tanzt* revisited." *CINEMA & Cie* 6 (2005): 76–95.

Colin-Reval, Marcel. "Grâce à la prompte intervention de M. Charles Delac, un important accord franco-allemand a été conclu." *La Cinématographie Française*, 16 August 1930, 9.

Conze, Eckart. "Titane der modernen Wirtschaft: Otto Wolff (1881–1940)." In Danylow and Soénius, 99–151.

Dahlmann, Dittmar. "Das Unternehmen Otto Wolff: Vom Alteisenhandel zum Weltkonzern (1904–1929)." In Danylow and Soénius, 13–97.

Danylow, Peter, and Ulrich S. Soénius, eds. *Otto Wolff: Ein Unternehmen zwischen Wirtschaft und Politik.* Munich: Siedler, 2005.

Ďurovičová, Nataša. "Translating America: The Hollywood Multilinguals, 1929–1933." In Altman, 138–53.

Garncarz, Joseph. "Hollywood in Germany. Die Rolle des amerikanischen Films in Deutschland 1925–1990." In *Der deutsche Film: Aspekte seiner Geschichte von den Anfängen bis zur Gegenwart,* edited by Uli Jung, 167–213. Trier, Germany: WVT, 1993.

———. "Made in Germany: Multiple-Language Versions and the Early German Sound Cinema." In Higson and Maltby, 249–73.

Gaubel, Louis. "Comment Roger Goupilliéres a réalisé la version française du film de Fritz Lang *Le Maudit.*" *La Cinématographie Française,* 16 April 1932, 22.

Hall, Mordaunt. Review of Melody of the Heart. *New York Times,* 1 September 1930.

Harlé, P. A. "En face de l'Allemagne." *La Cinématographie Française,* 2 May 1939, 45.

Higson, Andrew. "Film Europe: Cultural Policy and Industrial Practice." In Higson and Maltby, 117–31.

———. "Polyglot Films for an International Market: E. A. Dupont, the British Film Industry, and the Idea of a European Cinema, 1926–1930." In Higson and Maltby, 274–301.

Higson, Andrew, and Richard Maltby, eds. *"Film Europe" and "Film America": Cinema, Commerce and Cultural Exchange, 1920–1939.* Exeter: U of Exeter P, 1999.

Icart, Roger. *La révolution du parlant, vue par la presse française.* Perpignan, France: Institut Jean Vigo, 1988.

Kappelhoff, Hermann. "Lebendiger Rhythmus der Welt: Die Erich-Pommer-Produktion der UFA." In Bock/Töteberg, 208–13.

Kreimeier, Klaus. *The Ufa Story: A History of Germany's Greatest Film Company, 1918–1945.* Berkeley: U of California P, 1999.

Krützen, Michaela. "Esperanto für den Tonfilm: Die Produktion von Sprachversionen für den frühen Tonfilm-Markt." In *Positionen deutscher Filmgeschichte: 100 Jahre Kinematographie; Strukturen, Diskurse, Kontexte,* edited by Michael Schaudig, 119–54, Diskurs Film 8. Munich: Schaudig & Ledig, 1996.

Minutes of Ufa's Board of Directors = MUBD, various dates. Ufa files, Bundesarchiv-Filmarchiv, Berlin.

Mühl-Benninghaus, Wolfgang. *Das Ringen um den Tonfilm: Strategien der Elektro- und der Filmindustrie in den 20er und 30er Jahren.* Düsseldorf, Germany: Droste, 1999.

O'Brien, Charles: *Cinema's Conversion to Sound: Technology and Film Style in France and the U.S.* Bloomington: Indiana UP, 2005.

Olimsky, Fritz. Review of *Liebeswalzer. Berliner Börsen-Zeitung*, 9 February 1930.

Pommer, Erich. "Einleitende Worte." In *Dramaturgie des Tonfilms*, edited by Hans Kahan, 5–6. Berlin: Mattisson, 1930.

Sturm, Georges. "UFrAnce 1940–1944. Kollaboration und Filmproduktion in Frankreich." In *Das UFA-Buch,* edited by Hans-Michael Bock and Michael Töteberg, 408–14. Frankfurt am Main, Germany: Zweitausendeins, 1992.

Trask, Charles Hooper. Review of *The Love Waltz. Variety*, 19 March 1930.

van Moppès, Maurice. "Doublage et versions polyglottes." *Le cinéma d'avant-garde* 12 (1931): 1066–68.

Vincendeau, Ginette: "Hollywood Babel." In *Screen* 2 (1988): 24–39.

Wahl, Chris. "Inside the Robots' Castle: Ufa's English Language Versions in the Early 1930s." In *Destination London: German Speaking Émigrés and British Cinema 1925–1950*, edited by Tim Bergfelder and Christian Cargnelli, 47–61. Oxford: Berghahn, 2008.

———. "'Paprika in the Blood.' On UFA's Early Sound Films Produced in/about/for/with Hungary." *Spectator* 2 (2007): 11–20.

———. *Sprachversionsfilme aus Babelsberg: Die internationale Strategie der Ufa, 1929–1939.* Munich: edition text + kritik, 2009.

———. *Das Sprechen des Spielfilms.* Trier, Germany: WVT, 2005.

Warren, Patricia. *Elstree: The British Hollywood.* London: Elm Tree Books, 1983.

15: "A New Era of Peace and Understanding": The Integration of Sound Film into German Popular Cinema, 1929–1932

Ofer Ashkenazi

IN THE LATE 1920S PASSIONATE DEBATES erupted among German artists and critics about the impact of sound on film making. Some feared that the new technology would dictate low artistic standards. Experimental filmmaker Walther Ruttmann, writing in late 1928, bemoaned the end of the era in which "serious people made serious films" (Ruttmann). Other commentators rejected such pessimism and emphasized the new horizons opened by the creative use of sound. Inventive director Ewald André Dupont, for instance, predicted that the new technology would fundamentally enrich cinematic expression and would guarantee it a prominent place among the "respectable" arts. The "appropriate" use of the new cinematic tools, he maintained, would bind the German filmmakers with the renowned national lineage of "poets and philosophers" (Dupont).

Many critics noted that the importance of sound-recording technology in film extended beyond the narrow debate on artistic values into the social and political arena. In January 1929 the film journal *Film-Kurier* rang in the New Year with a special editorial declaring sound film a symbol and a vanguard of a new, cosmopolitan stage in the progress of humanity: "The sound film is marching in and it brings along a new era of peace and understanding for all cultured nations" (Aussenberg). The ability to document reality comprehensively later prompted the *Film-Kurier* to hail sound film as a veritable "gift to humanity" (Meissner).

Germany's historical trajectory in the following years coincided, of course, with the most ominous epoch in German history, the demise of the Weimar Republic and the rise of the National Socialist regime (Blasius). The years 1929 to 1933 brought not only the implementation of sound film in German studios and theaters but also the collapse of Hermann Müller's government (March 1930), the "Prussian Coup" (July 1932), and the appointment of Adolf Hitler as the German chancellor (January 1933). The final years of the Weimar Republic were a time of "total crisis," when "the real question [. . .] was no longer whether the republican constitutional system could be saved or restored; it was what would come in its stead" (Peukert, 249).

Since the early reviews by Siegfried Kracauer, German sound films of the early 1930s have been criticized for their escapist tendencies or for their fascination with authoritarianism that supposedly predicted the rise of Nazism, or even contributed to it (Kracauer, Korte, Kreimeier). In this essay I examine several popular films that were made at the time of the incorporation of sound into the German film industry and show that they were neither "escapist" nor "proto-fascist." Instead, these films addressed the sense of pervasive crisis head-on and display a sincere, if sometimes desperate, effort to maintain a progressive-liberal society, which was to be based on a free, rational individual.

I will focus on two main issues that appear in numerous German genre films of the pre-Nazi years. The first — concerning the anxiety caused by the loss of privacy in contemporary German urban spheres — is demonstrated in the early sound films of Robert Siodmak. Siodmak's films relate this loss directly to the incompetence of certain fundamental social institutions, such as welfare services and law and order. The second theme — the question of the origins of an "authentic" identity and the ability to express it — is examined mostly through a reading of Hanns Schwarz's musical melodrama *Liebling der Götter* (Darling of the Gods, 1930). The sound films of popular filmmakers such as Siodmak and Schwarz (and others, like E. A. Dupont and G. W. Pabst), I argue, express two anxieties commonly associated with Enlightenment-based liberalism: the fear of a decrease in the freedom of the individual, and the fear of cultural homogeneity brought about by a collective identity imposed upon the individual.

In September 1929, more than a year after the *Film-Kurier* had heralded Berlin's future as a "a sound-film metropolis," only 3 percent of German film productions used sound-recording technology on the set (Anon., "Berlin"). A poll conducted in Berlin in at the time revealed that more than 60 percent of local moviegoers favored the silent version of Alfred Hitchcock's *Blackmail* (1929) over the sound-film version (Goldschmidt). Reviewers and filmmakers lamented both the "provincial mentality" of German spectators and the comparatively low quality of imported sound films (Reichenberg-Film). Yet the industry pushed ahead with the conversion to sound, eager to seek control of the European sound film market: by the fall of 1930 more than 90 percent of German productions involved sound recording (Korte, 132–33; Manvell/Frankel, 5).

The introduction of sound into German film production brought with it a certain standardization of the production and consumption of film. At a time of severe economic upheaval in the wake of the Great Depression, the considerably higher costs of the early sound film elicited a more cautious approach towards experimental or politically controversial films that were directed at a significantly limited audience (Silberman; Murray). The established studios leaned increasingly toward the reproduction of success-ful formulae, while many smaller production companies — frequently identified with anti-nationalist and anti-conservative goals — simply van-ished, reducing the range of voices and perspectives, as a critic from the Social-Democratic paper *Vorwärts* noted (F. Sch.).

From a sonic point of view, the experience of viewing silent films had been subject to extreme variations, depending on the cinema: viewers were exposed to a variety of sound effects, including the music accompaniment (ranging from a single piano to an orchestra) and, sometimes, the remarks of the announcer (Polet). By way of contrast, recorded sound offered all the spectators of the film (almost) the same experience. Alongside the increased standardization of the film-viewing experience, however, the vast transformation of film technology between 1929 and 1933 initiated a process of learning and a search for imaginative exploitation of the new medium (Carroll). The quest for new cinematic forms of expressions was promoted even by prominent German producers, who sought to deter-mine the audience's reactions to different uses of sound in films, and thus to broaden their films' spectatorship (cf. Pommer). In many ways, then, Weimar sound films offered a rearguard action for a diversified culture threatened by the radicalization of the political discourse.

The Annihilation of the Private Sphere in Robert Siodmak's Early Sound Films

Abschied (Departure), Robert Siodmak's first sound film, premiered at the end of August 1930.[1] The summer of 1930 was characterized by remark-able political and social upheaval: during that year, capital goods produc-tion in Germany sank by more than 20 percent and labor wages dropped by approximately 15 percent. Average unemployment nearly doubled, ris-ing to 14 percent, mainly among workers between the ages of eighteen and thirty. This group of young blue- and white-collar workers — many of whom were barred from receiving unemployment benefits, since they had held only temporary or short-term jobs — suffered the most from the economic depression and political instability. In March 1930 the Great Coalition, under Social Democratic Chancellor Hermann Müller, had col-lapsed, and his successor, Heinrich Brüning, had dissolved the *Reichstag*, calling for new elections in September, in which the Communists and National-Socialists both were to make significant gains. The loss of secu-rity, confidence, and hope for social mobility led many young unemployed to join radical political organizations that promised revolutionary change and encouraged violent acts to seize control of the urban public sphere.

Siodmak's film is set in a milieu profoundly affected by the loss of a sense of security during the world economic crisis triggered by the Great Depression of 1929. As he had in his first silent feature, *Menschen am Sonntag: Das Dokument der Gegenwart* (People on Sunday: The Document of Our Time; premiere 4 February 1930), Siodmak sought in *Abschied* to document the life of the petit-bourgeois urbanites "as it really is [. . . the life of] normal people in the normal city" (Feld). In contrast to his first film, *Abschied* is set entirely within a single closed space, a Berlin boardinghouse that accommodates several "normal" young people: short-term employees and job seekers. As reviewers of the film noted, Siodmak's film did not resort to "filmed theater"; instead, according to Fritz Olimsky in the *Berliner Börsen-Zeitung*, Siodmak revealed genuine "moments of truth," achieved through his experimental approach to cinematic forms of expression, in particular through his use of sound.[2]

Abschied narrates one evening filled with mistrust and misunderstanding between two young lovers. Hella (Brigitte Horney), a young saleswoman, comes to visit her boyfriend, Peter (Aribert Mog), in his "hostel for homeless bourgeois people." Before she meets him, she hears a rumor regarding Peter's planned departure the next morning. When she asks him about the surprising, upsetting rumor, Peter informs her that he has a potential job opportunity in another city. In an attempt to rationalize the situation, Hella recommends that he take the job, even though it might put an end to their relationship. This reaction determines the vague future of their affair, which is at the core of the film's narrative. Their insecurity and fear of loss promptly leads both protagonists away from rational behavior toward a series of impulsive reactions and increasing miscommunication. Confronting the unknown future by an urge to seize the moment, Hella borrows money to buy an extravagant hat for their (possibly) last night together. Disappointed and suspicious because of her too-reasonable advice to take the job, Peter gazes at Hella's diary while she is gone, and mistakenly finds in it certain "clues" of her unfaithfulness. He packs his suitcase hastily and leaves on the evening train, before she returns with the new hat. As she mourns the misunderstanding that led to his disappearance, she finds out that Peter had bought an engagement ring for her, which he forgot to take with him in his hurried departure. At this moment, when Peter has gone (forever?), the sincere love of the two protagonists is exposed.

Reviewers noted that Siodmak's realist vision originated in his "conscious rejection of familiar conventions of narration" (Olimsky), including the closure brought about by the visual depiction of a happy ending: as is the case for "normal people" — that is, not the ones in the movies — there is no promise of salvation, Hella and Peter "are mere pawns in the game of fate" (Feld). The last scene hints that the two lovers may indeed find one another sometime in the future and celebrate their love through marriage: some of the hostel's guests meet in a bar "few years later"; one of them recounts the story of Hella and Peter, suggesting that they are now happily married.

Siodmak's manipulation of time in the film also goes against cinematic conventions: not only does the story occur in a single closed space, but it also takes place in a single, continuous time frame: a film that lasts an hour and a half presents events that last approximately the same time, between 7:00 and 9:00 PM. According to Emmerich Pressburger, the scriptwriter, the "unified time-space" was constructed in order to create the impression that the camera documents an authentic "slice of life in the big city" (Pressburger). The impression of the congruence of fictional and real time depends heavily on the soundtrack: continuous piano music — played by one of the hostel's guests in an adjacent room — accompanies the protagonists throughout the film.

The constant music is integrated as "an organic part of the story," an essential element of the reality depicted in the film; according to Pressburger, this reality is exposed when "the tunes penetrate from one room to another," and show that "the four walls [of the room] are not impassable boundaries" (Pressburger). The continuous soundtrack that permeates the walls nullifies any sense of privacy within the hostel. In their most intimate moments in Peter's room, when the protagonists feel most vulnerable and struggle to save their relationship, they — along with the spectators — are reminded by the penetrating music that they are *not* alone, that their secrets and confessions are heard clearly outside of the room, just as they can hear the sounds from the outside. The piano music is the soundtrack that accompanies the unwanted break-up, the insecurity, and mistrust; it is a signifier for the complete lack of privacy and for the constant encroachment of exterior reality upon the private sphere (fig. 15.1).

Abschied, then, is a film about the absence of privacy, the lack of a genuine private sphere — a space concealed from the outside social sphere in which secrets can be kept and in which the individual can construct and express his/her identity.[3] Siodmak sought to make a realist film, at a time of devastating unemployment, immiseration, street violence, and parliamentary paralysis, and he portrayed these crises by highlighting the absence of a private sphere in the big city. The hostel itself, of course, is a poor substitute for the private home, a replacement for people who lost the means to maintain an apartment of their own. It may give an illusion of privacy, but this illusion is shattered systematically, mainly through the film's soundtrack. The film repeatedly shows the tenants eavesdropping on one another, behind their backs, or listening in on a conversation through the keyholes of locked doors. Information is quickly spread among other guests (this tendency indifferently to share the overheard secrets is introduced right away in the opening scene, when Hella is notified by the hostel waitress about Peter's possible departure). Peter and Hella's tragic separation occurs because they cannot reveal their genuine feelings to one

Fig. 15.1. Cramped spaces and eavesdropping neighbors highlight the lack of privacy in Abschied *(Robert Siodmak, 1930). Deutsche Kinemathek Berlin.*

another; naturally, this inability to express genuine feelings takes place in a reality characterized by the absence of privacy.

A similar disparity between what can be seen and what can be heard was also used by several German filmmakers of the early 1930s as an indication for the profound anxiety and helplessness that characterized soldiers' experience of the trenches in the First World War: G. W. Pabst's renowned *Westfront 1918* (1930), with its long camera movements within the trenches and inside the bunkers, complemented by the constant clamor of off-screen gunfire, shells, and grenades, is maybe the most familiar example for this employment of sound (see Jaimey Fisher's essay on the film in this volume). Likewise, in Luis Trenker's *Berge in Flammen* (Mountains in Flames, 1931), the camera is trapped, together with the German soldiers, within a bunker in the Alps, surrounded by the advancing Italian army. Here a soldier is driven insane by the constant threatening sounds of the (invisible) drilling of the advancing Italians, who seek to seize the bunker by digging a tunnel: the continuous off-screen sound calls constant attention to the omnipresence of meaningless death, while simul-

Fig. 15.2. The discovery of the dead body on the doorstep in Voruntersuchung *(Robert Siodmak, 1931). Deutsche Kinemathek Berlin.*

taneously contributing to the sense of "realism" by referring to the continuity of reality outside the visible image.

Intriguingly, the same matrix of associations that combines anxiety, insanity, and death is found also in several German films that consider the postwar annihilation of the urban private sphere.[4] One remarkable example is Robert Siodmak's second sound film, *Voruntersuchung* (Preliminary Inquest, 1931), which was hailed by the critics as "extremely realistic," a "film about the most burning [problems] of the present."[5] The destruction of the private sphere is portrayed here in a fascinating sequence, in which the continuation of sound (that is, the unbroken duration of time) is paired with a notable fragmentation of the visible space. A young woman is walking up the stairs of an apartment building and whistles an uninterrupted melody; the camera accompanies her walk, shows fragments of the stairs and the hall, and focuses mainly on her feet. The whistling stops only as she enters her friend's apartment and discovers a girl's dead body lying on the floor (fig. 15.2). At this moment the melody is replaced by a shrill scream, "Murder!" which is repeated several times. While she screams, the woman starts running down the stairs; now the camera is located on a crane outside the building, accompanying her panic-stricken run. This long-shot emphasizes that the building lacks a front wall — its interior is revealed and all the intimate secrets it might have concealed are exposed to the gaze of the spectators.

The use of the private sphere as a spatial metaphor for subjective identity, its unity and distinctiveness, has a long tradition in modern Western culture, and in the bourgeois novel in particular (Adorno; Assmann; Bachelard; Jonsson). The tension between the private and the public spheres in this tradition often indicates the struggle of the individual to maintain a unique and continuous identity in a modernized environment of advanced technology and mass culture. In *Voruntersuchung* Siodmak depicts ineffective legal institutions that have neglected a methodological, objective inquiry.[6] This neglect leads to the prosecution of an innocent man, who — under pressure from his interrogator — confesses to a murder he did not commit. Echoing contemporary liberal political commentators, Siodmak's film suggests that without a rational and objective mechanism for the investigation and punishment of crime, privacy and freedom are mere illusions, and every individual is constantly threatened by the state. Sound penetrating into the apartment from outside brings an end to the illusions of the protagonists: it destroys the fantasy of a private sphere that separates and shelters the individual from the exterior; and it negates the fantasy of a just society, in which rational inquiry leads to the capture of criminals and perverts.

Siodmak's earlier film, *Abschied*, more directly evokes a comprehensive social crisis that generates vast insecurity and despair. But in *Voruntersuchung* the protagonists actually express no yearning for a sheltered private sphere; the absence of privacy is recognized as a "normal" characteristic of their provisional way of life. By his emphasis on *absence*, rather than on *loss*, Siodmak highlights the evaporation of privacy from modern urban spheres through the use of sound: it is the conspicuously artificial division between fragmented (visible) space and continuous time (represented through sounds) that becomes the major signifier for the lack of intimacy. His films warn against the manifested indifference of contemporary young people toward the absence of privacy, which is both a result of the general insecurity and a catalyst for it.

Against a Detectable "Innate" and Homogeneous Identity: Sound and Deception

Hanns Schwarz's *Liebling der Götter* (Darling of the Gods, 1930) uses an even more radical schism between the components of the cinematic image that are seen and those that are heard: detaching the visible gestures of the protagonist from his voice, the film challenges the fundamental connection between personal identity and its expressions. The question of an authentic self, which is at the core of this film, is linked to an inquiry concerning the problem of distinguishing effectively between truth and deception.

Liebling der Götter was one of Ufa's first four sound film productions, which were intended to examine German spectators' reaction to different sound-film genres. It features Emil Jannings, the distinguished star of German silent film, who had recently returned from Hollywood, after failing to make it in American talkies. In this musical melodrama Jannings plays the role of Albert Winkelmann, a talented opera singer who resents the simple bourgeois life cherished by his wife and who seeks excitement on the stages of the world's great cities, as well as in the arms of female admirers. When he has to choose between his wife and a concert tour in America, he opts for the latter and sails away from Germany to the New World. On opening night there, however, he discovers that he is suffering from a critical heart problem: in order to survive he must stop singing. Unable to perform, Winkelmann returns to his homeland, devastated. Notably, he does not return to the city where he started in the film, but to a small village in Bavaria, the home of his wife's family. In the rural Alpine scenery, far away from the bustle of modern urban centers, he experiences the traditional, "authentic" way of life of the locals. Nevertheless, this environment does not help him discover his own genuine self. Irritated and restless, he deserts this rustic idyll and starts performing again, despite the risk. Wiser now, he takes his wife with him, and makes her an indispensable part of his new life.

Ironically, even though Jannings returned to Berlin because his thick German accent had limited possible roles in American sound films, in *Liebling der Götter* his voice was partially erased from the recorded soundtrack. In order to portray a more realistic image of the tenor opera singer, and to provide an entertainment of better quality, Jannings's singing sequences are replaced by the voice of Marcel Wittrisch, a professional singer. Even though the actual artistic value of the film was debated by the reviewers, it was unanimously agreed that the combination of Jannings's body and Wittrisch's voice promised success at the box office (Olimsky, "Jannings"). Thus the split between the appearance and the voice of the protagonist was highlighted by the distributors to attract a wide audience. The advertisement campaign for the film, which depicted it as an "Emil Jannings show," only further emphasized the uncanny presence of the dubbed singing.

Before sound film, creating a rupture in the protagonist's expressions, a division between his visible gestures and his voice, would not have been possible. In fact, the disparity between visual appearance and sound — and the ability to express, or construct, the "genuine" personal identity — intrigued filmmakers and spectators from the earliest moments in the history of sound film. It will be remembered that in the very first full-length sound film, Alan Crosland's *The Jazz Singer* (1927), the protagonist disguises himself as an African-American in order to make his own "authentic voice," that of a Jewish immigrant, heard. The manipulation of recorded sounds was thus already connected to the discourse of identity formation in the modern world with this first sound film. *Liebling der Götter* is constructed as a journey towards the "authentic" self, a journey that seems — until the final scenes — to bridge the gulf between the two attributes of the protagonist's identity, his appearance and voice.

The journey starts in a city tavern in the early 1930s. A long pan of the camera, situated on a roof overlooking the crowded street, displays the surroundings in which Albert Winkelmann thrives. The next scene is located inside the tavern, where a young woman begs Winkelmann to take her with him to America. After he kisses her — and several other admirers — on the lips, he starts singing. At this moment — as Jannings's voice is erased from the soundtrack — the impression of a break between his visible body and the singing voice is amplified by the location of the camera, outside the bar, where he cannot be seen, but only heard. The next scene is located backstage of Winkelmann's performance as Verdi's Otello. At this point Winkelmann can no longer distinguish between his stage persona and his "real" identity. Persuaded by the admiration of the audience, he arrogantly blows smoke in the face of his manager, throws the presents he has received to his dog, and accedes to the sexual advances he receives from female fans, who sneak into his room despite the threatening presence of his wife behind the door. Winkelmann's inability to distinguish between his "authentic" self and his image as a popular star is underlined by his appearance: his body is painted black, as his stage character Otello; he wears big "African" earrings and a curly black wig (fig. 15.3).[7]

This scene also constructs a distinction between the visible image and the offscreen noises. The former is coupled here with deception, with an endeavor to conceal the truth. At the middle of the frame stands Winkelmann, dressed and painted as Otello; his disguise foreshadows his later behavior in the scene. One after the other, young, attractive girls enter the room in order to seduce Winkelmann. One after the other, Winkelmann has to hide them when someone else sneaks inside — and, eventually, when his wife enters the room. By the end of this comic sequence, Winkelmann rebuffs his wife's suspicions, claiming — pointing to the supposedly empty room — that he is alone. Like Winkelmann in blackface, the "empty" room, and all that is visible on the screen, is a lie, a pretense. Only a cough — of a hidden girl — heard from behind the shower door, hints at the real state of things. Winkelmann goes on protest that he did not know of the presence of the women, but his lie is undermined by a close-up shot focusing on the back of one of the girls: a black mark of a hand, made by the painted palm of Winkelmann when he embraced her before.

Fig. 15.3. Opera singer Albert Winkelmann (Emil Jannings) in blackface as Verdi's
Otello, and his wife Agathe (Renate Müller) in Liebling der Götter (Hanns
Schwarz, 1930). Promotion still.

Intriguingly, this black signature of the sinner's hand on the back of his
lover resembles the manner in which the psychotic child-killer is branded in
Fritz Lang's celebrated M, which premiered in May 1931. Like Siodmak and
Schwarz, Lang uses the new medium of sound film in an innovative way: in
his renowned and influential thriller, the complete break between sounds
and visual images functions as the main means of identifying the killer. The
film emphasizes that the murderer looks — and appears to behave — exactly
like any "normal" bourgeois urbanite (and apparently also similar to the
police inspector who chases after him). Nevertheless, it also suggests that the
murderer has a conspicuous characteristic that differentiates him from his
middle-class surroundings and that makes it possible (for the *blind* balloon
vendor) to recognize his presence: the sound he makes, his whistling, indicates an obvious insanity, which cannot be seen but can, as it were, be heard,
testifying to his "genuine" identity. Like Schwarz's construction of
Winkelmann's adventures, Lang's treatment of the audio components followed an extensive debate regarding the "appropriate" use of sound among
German filmmakers and critics. Fears were expressed that dialogues would
replace the principal role of images, resulting in "filmed theater," and that a
shallow "realism" would be achieved by an indifferent documentation of all
actual sounds on a given scene (Kästner).

This fear stems from a traditional "realist" ethos held by many critics and filmmakers in the years of the Weimar Republic. Films, according to commentators such as critic Fritz Olimsky or film director Gerhard Lamprecht, should not merely depict the surface of reality in "naturalistic" representations; instead, they should reveal the hidden truths behind that surface.[8] Such aspirations transcended aesthetic classification ("Expressionism," "New Objectivity," and so on) and ran across the entire political spectrum (Wesse). This ethos had a profound impact on the debates concerning the "appropriate" use of sound in film; it was asserted that sound — to be considered as a device belonging to "art" and not merely a tool of "technology" — should convey the *meanings* of the visual image and thus explore an invisible component of reality (Dupont; von Sternberg). Weimar reviewers thus often expected sound to be a manifestation of psychological realism, an expression of the genuine state of mind of the protagonist that cannot be seen on the surface.[9]

While Fritz Lang's dark thriller is a skillful demonstration of the contemporary discourse, Hanns Schwarz's comic melodrama only partially follows the mandate of an "artistic" use of sound. Appearances are deceitful in this film; they are easily manipulated and serve as a veil that conceals the genuine state of affairs. The sounds, however, are not a sign for "authentic" truth, indicating the genuine thoughts and identity of the individual being shown, but merely another illusion (an illusion that was presented in the promotion of the film as an exciting attraction). Even during the backstage scene discussed above, Schwarz does not let the spectators forget the manipulative power of the audio-visual image. When Winkelmann runs out of the frame, to check on the strange voices coming from the shower, his singing is now heard from the other room, a sign of the deceptive nature of the whole scene. Whereas auditory clues reveal the truth in the urban surroundings depicted in *M* by Fritz Lang, in the reality displayed in *Liebling der Götter* there is no definite method of distinguishing truth from pretense; truths are revealed to the spectators only through the extra-filmic context, for instance through their previous knowledge of the singer who replaces Jannings's voice.

The emphasis on visual as well as aural deceptions in *Liebling der Götter*, which differs from *M*'s austere dichotomy between the deceiving visible and the "authentic" quality of sound, was not extraordinary in German film of the early 1930s. Whereas Schwarz's film relates the problem of authenticity to the question of genuine personal identity, other films used the vague connection between "essence" and "representation" to contemplate the nature of a collective, national identity. An interesting example for this tendency is E. A. Dupont's *Peter Voss, der Millionendieb* (Peter Voss, The Thief Who Stole Millions, 1932), a film about the ubiquitous presence of deception in the modern world, and about the problem of differentiating between fact and fiction.[10] Peter Voss (Willi Forst) is the trustee of a bank that is faced with bankruptcy at time of a world economic crisis. In order to save the bank, he conspires with the bank manager to give the impression that he robbed the (empty) safe, and escaped with the money. Unfortunately for the conspirators, two stubborn people chase after Voss and the alleged fortune he robbed — the police detective Bobby Dodd and the manager's daughter, Polly. The rest of the film recounts the adventurous hunt for Voss, and his continual last-minute escapes, which take him from Berlin to Marseille, and continue in colonial Morocco.

Dupont, who earlier insisted that an adventure film could be more than sheer entertainment — if it provides a "faithful and clear" representation of "life" — presents the story of Peter Voss's fraud as a series of various deceptions (Gehler). Throughout the film both Voss and Detective Dodd wear various costumes and accessories (such as fake mustaches) to perfect their impersonation.[11] This tendency to fake appearance and behavior reaches its peak when the three protagonists meet on a boat and try to find out who their companions really are. Each of them tries to get the others drunk, while they secretly spill their own wine from the glass onto the floor. Rather than using visual appearance to signal differences, however, the film seems to insinuate that the essential differences between people — that is, their belonging to a specific nation — can be determined without question by the language they speak (or do not speak). The scenes in Marseille highlight this demarcation of different identities: the city hosts people of several nationalities; each speaks his/her own language and cannot understand the other languages. Furthermore, the difference between the Europeans and the natives in Morocco is evident through the same means — the former use an intelligible language, the latter either do not speak at all (within the vicinity of the Europeans), or are situated in extremely noisy surroundings, where their words cannot be understood (at the city's "oriental" market).

This division between (the deceptive) visual appearance and (the authentic) vocal representation of national identity fits a widespread approach toward sound film in the late Weimar years. Different languages, it was repeatedly asserted in the discussion about sound film, manifested considerable cultural differences; the vernacular dialogue explores the national distinctiveness of the speaking protagonists. The identification of a genuine national distinctiveness with the national language — as part of the quest for "realist" imagery — was common even among filmmakers and critics who sought to transcend the national rivalry.

Nevertheless, Dupont — and his protagonist Voss — use this expected essential connection between national identity and language as a point of departure for yet another deception. When Detective Dobb manages to corner Voss in Marseille he calls the local police for help in his capture. Alas, when they arrive, Peter Voss explains to them, speaking French with a perfect accent, that Dobb is the famous German thief, whereas he himself is a local citizen. The policemen should choose between what is seen — Dobb captures Voss at a street corner — and what is heard; unsurprisingly, as if they were trained spectators of Weimar Cinema, the policemen choose to believe the voiced over the visible — and arrest Dobb, who cannot speak the language properly. With this short comic scene, Dupont mocks the expectations of the spectators for an "authentic" national identity, which can be recognized by an "objective" signifier, the language.

Like Dupont, in *Liebling der Götter* Hanns Schwarz seeks to challenge the spectators' expectations of an essential connection between the protagonist's "identity" and its cinematic representations. Winkelmann's journey to America and back, in which he loses his ability to sing — and remains exclusively with Jannings's own voice — seems at first to be a quest for his "authentic" self. Without the "singing voice," Jannings's appearance and vocal expressions come from a single source. The external influence disappears when his heart condition prevents him from singing, and Winkelmann — who now has no place in the world of mass entertainment — stops his international tour and returns home. The "genuine" Winkelmann has only one sphere, one *Heimat*, where he can dwell: the rural mountains of Bavaria, where the homogeneous, premodern community celebrates its traditional ceremonies wearing traditional clothes, where he can finally reunite with his wife, and be the head of a "normal" family. The search for the "authentic" self seems to reach an end when Winkelmann becomes a part of this pre-urbanized Bavarian community, after his destructive experience in the ultra-modern sphere of urban mass culture.

The duality — and tension — between the threats of the urban sphere and the "simple" communal life of the premodern village was the topic of several German films during the 1920s. The travel of the protagonist from one sphere to another enabled many German filmmakers to depict the rural community — usually with unmistakable references to the iconic nineteenth century imagery of the *Heimat* — as a therapeutic sphere, in which the genuine "self" of the protagonist is revealed, his family life is restored, and his pathological behavior (a result of urban experiences) is cured. *Liebling der Götter* seems to follow this tradition when Winkelmann "returns" to the Bavarian *Heimat* and reunites with his wife. Nevertheless, Winkelmann's story is not merely a tale of migration from the modern city to the rural community, but also a tale of migration from the homeland to the modern capitals of the Western world, and of homecoming from a foreign country.

The new "home" of Winkelmann is situated in the embodiment of a traditional visual imagery of German nationality. When Winkelmann settles in the village, the narrative pattern and visual affinities of *Liebling der Götter* and Luis Trenker's early Nazi era film *Der verlorene Sohn* (The Prodigal Son, 1934) are remarkable. Trenker's protagonist, a talented young son of a village in the Bavarian Alps, leaves his *Heimat* behind and comes to America, where he becomes a mass-culture hero, a boxer in the ring. Nonetheless, the sight of a decorative pagan mask — used in the rites of his village — draws him back to his homeland, the only place he can "really" be himself.

Schwarz's film, however, does not end with this nationalist assertion. The simple, "authentic" life in the country is revealed as another fantasy, a "lively" illusion made by ignorant city-dwellers. Unsurprisingly, the illusion is visualized through the formation of a sheltered private sphere, in which Winkelmann and his wife now reside; once again, this illusion of an ideal separation between the private and the public spheres is shattered by the penetration of sounds into the private sphere, which disturbs the impression of uninterrupted privacy. Even though a high fence detaches the Winkelmann family from its neighbors, the music played by the neighbor — a record of Winkelmann's singing — is heard inside their property and prevents him from accomplishing his routine housework. Eventually he loses control, leaves his apartment behind, and runs frantically to break the neighbor's gramophone.

The peaceful therapy of the *Heimat* invoked irrational violence; the "release" of the protagonist from the "foreign" voice that facilitated his singing career did not eliminate his essential desire, his perceived vocation — to perform his art. He realizes he must sing again, and — in a genuine triumph of the will — overcomes his heart disease, on his way back to the stage. Instead of retreating to an isolated premodern community, Winkelmann now finds his "authentic" self in the arenas of modern culture, in the modern city.[12] It is still a divided, not unified self — since it still combines the body of Jannings and the voice of Wittrisch — but it is a "genuine," functional identity.

Much like the German society of the late Weimar period, Winkelmann's identity incorporates inconsistent elements, incompatible "voices" that cannot be reduced to a single paradigm. The filmmakers of *Liebling der Götter* do not seek to construct a homogeneous identity and do not locate this kind of identity in a premodern community. They rather encourage the perception of an identity of heterogeneous voices and situate the bearer of this identity as a successful hero of modern urban culture. Contemporary reality conveys grave threats to Winkelmann's very existence (as his heart condition suggests), as it did to the urban protagonists of Siodmak's films. Nonetheless, in this more optimistic production, Winkelmann overcomes his heart condition and sings again, once he destroys the deceitful nature of his surroundings. Advancing his career in partnership with his wife, he fulfills both the bourgeois virtue of monogamy and his vocation as a mass entertainer.

In their "shallow" popular comedies and musicals, filmmakers such as Schwarz and Dupont celebrated the conspicuous richness of Weimar urban culture, in which incompatible aspirations and beliefs existed simultaneously, without a definite criterion that could establish unambiguous truth. Like Siodmak, they feared the destruction of the subject and loss of the subjective point of view. Thus the early experimental period of the use of sound enabled late Weimar filmmakers to accomplish several goals. They employed recorded sound first as a symbol for and a warning about the contemporary threats to the rational individual; second, as a reminder of the manipulation that is involved in any expression of personal or national identity; and finally, as evidence of the various "voices" that constitute the identity of an individual, or a community, in its ideal form. From this standpoint, then, late Weimar filmmaking did include a serious attempt to engage the crisis of German bourgeois society from a liberal perspective. Sebastian Haffner commented that in 1930 he and his middle-class Berlin friends anticipated the coming of a "second liberalism," an era in which the faults of classical liberalism would be overcome, along with the conservatism and radicalism of current German society (Haffner, 79). It would appear that the filmmakers discussed above shared his vision and tried to promote it through their work in sound film. The "era of peace and understanding" they envisioned never materialized; when this vision was shattered by the rise of Nazism, their endeavor was marginalized and forgotten.

Notes

[1] *Abschied* was Siodmak's second feature film. It was released a few months after the well-received *Menschen am Sonntag* (*People on Sunday*, 1930), which he codirected with Edgar Ulmer and for which he shared the scriptwriting credit with Fred Zinnemann and Billy Wilder. Between these two features Siodmak directed a short film titled *Der Kampf mit dem Drachen, oder Die Tragödie des Untermieters* (Fighting the Dragon, or Tragedy of a Tenant, 1930).

[2] All the same, Fritz Olimsky maintained that Siodmak's "limited story" eventually displayed some banalities that prevent the film from being about "thoroughly normal people [. . .] as Siodmak intended" (Olimsky, "Abschied").

[3] For the interrelations between the image of the private sphere and bourgeois identity, see Bird, 34–42; McCann, 184–186; and Shklar, 24.

[4] Pabst's *Westfront 1918* demonstrates this equivalency between the bunker and the apartment in the sequence that describes the protagonist's short leave from the front, in which offscreen sounds are heard (exclusively) when the protagonist discovers his wife in bed with the butcher.

[5] These citations appear without specific identification of the reviewers in an ad for the film in the magazine *Der Film* 16:10 (18 April 1931).

[6] The same identification of the penetration of sounds into an apartment with investigations by incompetent legal authorities appears in Georg C. Klaren's *Kinder vor Gericht* (Children Standing Trial, 1931). In this film as well, an inno-

cent man is imprisoned because authorities fail to conduct an "objective" investigation, based on facts (and not "testimonies").

[7] The white actor impersonating a black character can be read as a high-brow reminiscence of Al Jolson's blackface performance in *The Jazz Singer*. Moreover, like the story of departure and homecoming, the costume suggests the similarities between the actor Jannings and his character Winkelmann: Jannings had starred in blackface in a film adaptation of Shakespeare's *Othello* in 1922 (directed by Dimitri Buchowetzki), and the film was screened again in Berlin in 1928.

[8] Fritz Olimsky, "Zehn Jahre Film." Lamprecht's notion of film as an exposure of hidden reality is expressed in an interview that was made in 1926 and is kept in the archives of the Deutsche Kinemathek, Berlin (f-2647).

[9] See the reviews of Siodmak's *Voruntersuchung* (Anon. and Olimsky).

[10] Dupont's film is a remake of a 1920/21 series of six films, *Der Mann ohne Namen* (The Man without a Name, directed by Georg Jacoby); the reviewers tended to emphasize the "small scale" of Dupont's film in comparison with the original big-budget series and related it to the contemporary tendency to prefer reality over fantasy.

[11] One of Voss's costumes includes a Hitler-shaped moustache, suggesting that — like Voss — the leader of the Nazi party himself "is playing" a role in order to distract attention from his "real" identity.

[12] The conclusion of the search for identity within the city, through which the protagonist identifies himself/herself as a bourgeois urbanite, rather than a member of a specific nation, has its own tradition in Weimar film. This tradition is notable in films of the late 1920s that dealt with returning from the Great War, such as Joe May's *Heimkehr* (Homecoming, 1928), or Richard Oswald's *Dr. Bessels Verwandlung* (The Transformation of Dr. Bessel, 1927).

Works Cited

Adorno, Theodor W. *Kierkegaard: Konstruktion des Ästhetischen*. Frankfurt am Main: Suhrkamp, 1962.

Anon. "Berlin wird eine Tonfilm-Metropole." *Film-Kurier*, 18 August 1928.

———. "Voruntersuchung." *Der Film*, 18 April 1931.

———. "Was wir mit *Liebling der Götter* erreichen wollen." *Film-Kurier*, 13 October 1930.

Assmann, Aleida. *Erinnerungsräume: Formen und Wandlungen des kulturellen Gedächtnisses*. Munich: Beck, 1999.

Aussenberg, Julius. "Tonfilm auf dem Marsch." *Film-Kurier*, 1 January 1929.

Bachelard, Gaston. *The Poetics of Space*. Boston: Beacon, 1969.

Bird, Colin. *The Myth of Liberal Individualism*. Cambridge: Cambridge UP, 1999.

Blasius, Dirk. *Weimars Ende: Bürgerkrieg und Politik, 1930–1933*. Göttingen: Vandenhoeck & Ruprecht, 2005.

Carroll, Noël. "Lang, Pabst and Sound." *Ciné-Tract* 2 (Fall 1978): 15–23.

Dupont, Ewald André, "E. A. Dupont an seine Kritiker." *Film-Kurier*, 2 November 1929.

Feld, Hans. "Abschied." *Film-Kurier*, 26 August 1930.

Gehler, Fred. "Peter Voss, der Millionendieb." In *Deutsche Spielfilme von den Anfängen bis 1933*, edited by Günther Dahlke, 290–91. Berlin: Henschel, 1988.

Goldschmidt, Max. "Tonfilm oder stummer Film? Dir. Goldschmidt zur Frage des Tages." *Film-Kurier*, 10 September 1929.

Haffner, Sebastian. *Geschichte eines Deutschen: Die Erinnerungen, 1914–1933*. 1939. Reprint, Munich: dtv, 2002.

Jonsson, Stefan. *A Subject without Nation: Robert Musil and the History of Modern Identity*. Durham, NC, and London: Duke UP, 2000.

Kästner, Erich. "Die Ästhetik des Tonfilms." *Neue Leipziger Zeitung*, 20 August 1930.

Korte, Helmut. *Der Spielfilm und das Ende der Weimarer Republik: Ein rezeptionshistorischer Versuch*. Göttingen: Vandenhoeck & Ruprecht, 1998.

Kracauer, Siegfried. *From Caligari to Hitler: A Psychological History of the German Film*. 1947. Reprint, Princeton, NJ: Princeton UP, 1966.

Kreimeier, Klaus. *The UFA Story*. Translated by Robert Kimber and Rita Kimber. Berkeley: U of California P, 1999.

Manvell, Roger, and Heinrich Frankel. *The German Cinema*. New York: Praeger, 1971.

McCann, Charles R., Jr. *Individualism and the Social Order: The Social Element in Liberal Thought*. London: Powell, 2004.

Meissner, Reinhold. "Möglichkeiten des Tonfilms." *Film-Kurier*, 19 July 1929.

Murray, Bruce. *Film and the German Left in the Weimar Republic: From "Caligari" to "Kuhle Wampe."* Austin: U of Texas P, 1990.

Olimsky, Fritz. "Abschied." *Berliner Börsen-Zeitung*, 26 August 1930.

———. "Jannings als Liebling der Götter." *Berliner Börsen-Zeitung*, 15 October 1930.

———. "Voruntersuchung." *Berliner Börsen-Zeitung*, 19 April 1930.

———. "Zehn Jahre Film." In *75 Jahre Berliner Börsen-Zeitung*, edited by Arnold Killisch von Horn, 112–15. Berlin: Berliner Börsen-Zeitung Verlag, 1930.

Peukert, Detlev. *Weimar Republic: The Crisis of Classical Modernity.* New York: Ferrar, Strauss & Giroux, 1992.

Polet, Jacques. "Early Cinematographic Spectacles: The Role of Sound Accompaniment in the Reception of Moving Images." In *The Sound of Early Cinema*, edited by Richard Abel and Rick Altman, 192–97. Bloomington: Indiana UP, 2001.

Pommer, Erich. "Was wir mit *Liebling der Götter* erreichen wollen." *Film-Kurier*, 13 October 1930.

Pressburger, Emmerich. "Abschied." *LichtBildBühne*, 19 August 1930.

Reichenberg-Film. "Warum sollen Sie Tonfilme spielen?" *Film-Kurier*, 1 June 1929.

Ruttmann, Walther, "Prinzipielles zum Tonfilm." *Film und Volk* 2/2 (December/January 1928/29).

Sch., F. "Ein Film von der Arbeitslosigkeit: Lohnbuchhalter Kremke." *Der Abend, Spätausgabe des Vorwärts*, 5 September 1930.

Shklar Judith N. "The Liberalism of Fear." In *Liberalism and Moral Life*, edited by Nancy Rosenblum, 21–38. Cambridge, MA: Harvard UP, 1989.

Silberman, Marc. "Political Cinema as Oppositional Practice: Weimar and Beyond." In *The German Cinema Book*, edited by Tim Bergfelder, Erica Carter, and Deniz Göktürk, 165–72. London: The British Film Institute, 2002.

von Sternberg, Josef. "Mein Tonfilm." *Film-Kurier*, 3 July 1929.

Wesse, Curt. *Großmacht Film: Das Geschöpf von Kunst und Technik.* Berlin: Deutsche Buch-Gemeinschaft, 1928.

Winkler, Heinrich A. *Der lange Weg nach Westen: Deutsche Geschichte 1806–1933.* Munich: C. H. Beck, 2000.

16: Landscapes of Death: Space and the Mobilization Genre in G. W. Pabst's *Westfront 1918* (1930)

Jaimey Fisher

WHEN G. W. PABST'S ANTI-WAR FILM, *Westfront 1918*, premiered in 1930, it was greeted with extravagant praise.[1] *Der Kinematograph*, Germany's oldest weekly film journal, devoted its entire front page to an article on it, emphasizing the link between the film's importance and its authenticity: the reviewer noted the location shooting and the fact that three of the film's lead actors had actually served in the military during the war (the fourth, the actor playing "der Student," was still a child when the Versailles peace treaty was signed). Another reviewer, Hans Wollenberg in *LichtBildBühne*, likewise praises the film's ostensible realism, while adding a note of unabashedly nationalist rhetoric: the film's quality, he claims, constitutes a "victory for the independent German film producer in the international competition for quality products."[2] Such martial posturing was a political position that would come to be lamented by many at the time (viz. "Westfront 1918" from the *Kreuz-Zeitung*). But Wollenberg's reaction also underscores how the film was, upon the very first viewings, already well woven into national and transnational contexts. Not only was Wollenberg prepared to cheerfully declare the film a German watershed, but he also immediately claimed a place for it in global culture, both film culture and economies around the world.

Wollenberg's response to the film resonates, in this way, with the ideas of Stephan Schindler and Lutz Koepnick, who have recently exhorted German film studies to move toward the transnational and cosmopolitan (Schindler/Koepnick, 3–4). Their exhortation to probe the limits of the national with the transnational aligns with important theoretical developments in thinking about and through space in culture. Many authors have remarked on a recent "spatial turn" in German cultural studies, one that underscores how cultural production is always situated in the world, always presumes and builds on some imagination of place and space, especially a place of the self in a dynamically mapped world. Spatial turns in theory and culture have been recently associated with the works of French and Anglophone theorists Henri Lefebvre, David Harvey, Doreen Massey, and Edward W. Soja as well as with the US cultural critic Fredric Jameson and the Italian literary scholar Franco Moretti. But these theorists of space are often, and quite openly, indebted to the important tradition of spatial and urban studies in German culture, including especially the work of Walter Benjamin and Siegfried Kracauer. These theorists were among the first to underscore not only the importance of space for the cultural imaginary, but also to bring it into conjunction with the constellation of the city as well as with the reconfiguration of space and time in modernity.

It is this spatial context of the film that I shall emphasize in a close reading of *Westfront 1918*, a highly significant film both as Pabst's first sound film and as a German representation of war, a film that has surprisingly attracted little critical attention, given that it was one of the few Weimar auteurist films that did well commercially (Hake, 45).[3] Taking a cue from these early reviews, including one by Kracauer himself, one can appreciate the radically new technologies of sound that Pabst applied in a new context, Germany's first sound war film. The spatial turns of recent theory can elucidate how Pabst deploys the new technology of sound to manipulate on- and offscreen space in ways that also dovetail with the culture's wider spatial imaginary.

With its realism and its antiwar message, *Westfront 1918* sets itself against what I call the mobilization genre, reconfiguring that genre's typical techniques, themes, and iconography. Following the important work of Anton Kaes on military mobilization and modernity, I would argue that the genre of the mobilization film reflects the impact of modernity both on society and on cultural technologies: it deploys the frenetic new perspectives (mental as well as literal, in point-of-view shots) that technology afforded the new, moving medium in order to remap mental geographies of the nation, the foreign, and the transnational. A central aspect of this remapping was negotiating private social bonds and the threat to them that militarism and mobilization would pose: these films had to negotiate the co-constitutive linkage between family and nation in novel ways, given the direction in which it was pushing the nation, namely, aggressively outward (cf. Mosse, Stoler). Mobilization films, as I shall elaborate below, often operate via and between two mental maps: that of the private (and often local) life and that of the nation moving toward war (often via transportation technologies like trains and other troop transports). *Westfront 1918*'s main narrative features negotiate precisely this kind of double-mapping of the mobilization genre, but in altogether different ways and toward very different ends.

The 1920s sustained a pitched discursive battle about the memory of the Great War: the stakes of these memory contestations and contests, as we know in retrospect, were uncommonly high. Michael Geisler notes how Pabst's film responded to the way in which nationalistic readings of the First World War had dominated the early, crisis-ridden years of the republic; scholars of war and its aftermath such as Bernd Hüppauf have also emphasized precisely these kinds of discursive struggles that straddled both history and memory (Hüppauf, "Langemarck"). *Westfront 1918* sets out to suggest a kind of countermemory to the prevailing nationalist interpretation of the fateful (as they would say) defeat and events of 1918/19. For example, the specificity of the title (*"Westfront 1918"*) seems directed against the vague, romantic shibboleths, like the "Spirit of 1914," still assiduously rolled out in the 1920s. This countermemory was delivered above all by a kind of countermapping, through sound and the spaces such sounds help establish, of the war-genre film, performing a refiguration of the two maps (familial and national) that underpin the mobilization film.

Sound and the Double Mapping of War Films

To track the aural and spatial manipulations performed by Pabst's innovative use of sound, it is useful first to consider how the film establishes and negotiates its basic spatial aspects. The film's narrative includes three main types of space: first, quasi-private spaces behind the front; second, the eponymous (western) frontlines of trench warfare; and, finally, in the film's final sequences, the improvised field hospital in a Christian church. Narratively speaking, the first hour of the film oscillates between the first two types of space: the film opens in an interior space, a French tavern near the front where a few German infantrymen are enjoying themselves, but then quickly returns them to the front. In this first private space, the youngest ("der Student") of the "four from the infantry" ("Vier von der Infanterie," the title of the novel by Ernst Johannsen on which the film is based), falls in love with a French woman, Yvette/Jacqueline, who returns his love.[4] The film's second half hour negotiates, in deliberately parallel fashion, between the frontlines and another private terrain of desire: the home in Germany of Karl, another of the four. With the subsequent death of the student, the evacuation of Yvette/Jacqueline from her home, and the return of Karl at around one hour, the film's final half hour unfolds between the latter two of the film's three types of space: between the frontline of the film's climactic battle scene (especially the appearance of tanks on the French side) and the hospital/church.

In this way, the film traces a basic spatial trajectory from, in the film's first hour, private plus public spaces to, in the last half hour, the nationalized spaces of war (the battlefield, the field hospital). This trajectory itself suggests a narrative-spatial arc that overlaps with, though not entirely dovetailing with, the mobilization film, a genre that, above all, maps space for its characters in certain teleological ways. One of the central themes of the recent interest in spatiality in cultural studies has been the emphasis on mental mapping, that is, the emphasis, on the one hand, on how people map spaces for themselves in a kind of mental geography and how that mapped imaginary guides their behavior and, on the other hand, how thinking non-spatial concepts is itself linked to space, that is, to space that is always already mapped in the spatial imaginary.

This notion of a postwar transformation in cognitive mapping or mental geography I derive from a series of theorists and/or cultural historians, especially Jameson, Lefebvre, Wolfgang Schivelbusch, and Paul Virilio. For both Jameson and Lefebvre, and implicitly in Schivelbusch and Virilio, there is an attempt in their historicizing and contextualizing analyses to expand and deepen how scholars analyze perceptions, conceptualizations, and representations of space: they want not only to highlight the content of space by mapping it out, but also to emphasize how the very act of this mapping or the "production of space" (Lefebvre's favored term) changes historically and contextually, and how such mapping and production affect individuals epistemologically. This is, I would suggest, why Jameson calls it "cognitive mapping" rather than just mapping, and why Lefebvre writes at such great length, in analyzing the production of space, about the representation of space, and about representational space and "spatial practices" (Lefebvre, 28). Jameson's cognitive mapping is probably closest to Lefebvre's "representational space," space as conceived and conceptually lived by non-expert individuals, that is, non-specialists in architecture or planning. For Lefebvre, representational space is both space as individuals represent it and space as representation that influences individuals' conceptualizations of the world and themselves.[5] Among these writers Lefebvre is the the one most careful to distinguish among different types (and agents) of such spatial conceptualization, while Jameson may be the most explicit in describing its political consequences. For Jameson, the operations of this "geopolitical unconscious," this specifically spatial mapping, deserve a place in the ideological pantheon of categorizing by class, fantasizing events in larger mythic narratives, and allegorizing consumption "in terms of Utopian wishes and commercially programmed habits" (*Geopolitical Aesthetic*, 3–4). For the purposes of the war film, perhaps the most important such spatial concepts are the nation and its opponents as well as national borders, battlefields, and home fronts. Mobilization films involve an explicitly mental mapping of the world, both a new spatial imaginary and new spatial grounding for concepts.

Jameson encourages his readers to think through mental mapping in *Postmodernism, or The Cultural Logic of Late Capitalism* and offers an extended example of such analysis a couple of years later in *The Geopolitical Aesthetic*, in which he traces the geopolitical mental mapping of various cultural objects, especially the paranoid thrillers of 1970s New Hollywood, including works like *Three Days of the Condor* and *Parallax View*. In these films Jameson unfolds a double mapping that rests at the heart of the films' narratives and plotting: there is the map of the explicit diegesis (the film's fictional world), usually understood without much difficulty by both protagonist and audience, and then there is a second, secret map that often determines the narrative trajectory of the first map.[6] Rather atypically and in contrast to many thrillers (of, for example, Hitchcock), viewer knowledge here rarely surpasses that of the protagonist. The (metaphorical/ mental) dimensions, key landmarks, and accessible routes of this second map stay secret, or at least obscured, for both protagonist and viewer, creating an epistemological challenge for both that expresses, in its very structure, the confused paranoia of both the political context and the emerging global totality.

Mobilization films typically also manifest a kind of double mapping, one more legible but still nonetheless challenging for the character and narrative; in mobilization films, there is typically, especially toward the beginning, a map of the characters' private lives (usually desires and attachments in romance, family, and/or local community) and then there is a second map of nationalized public spaces of mobilization and war. Of course both of these maps are much more comprehensible than the inscrutable secondary mapping that Jameson describes in *Geopolitical Aesthetic*, but there are still, as in the films he analyzes, considerable tensions between them, tensions that help structure the narrative, creating narrative tension, suspense, and ultimate resolution. The satisfaction or dissonance associated with that resolution will depend on the particular film's approach to the war. Mobilization films lobbying for war usually drive toward a narrative telos that will happily balance the two: the map of private desire can only be completed by the nationalized, public project of the war, and vice versa. The national effort to raise and motivate a fighting force can only succeed if there is some happy balance reached with the terrain of private desires and attachments, but the film consistently limns the way one map can guide the behavior of characters who are on another map. As in *The Geopolitical Aesthetic*, the mental geographies of the two maps exert force on characters and the narrative, notwithstanding their momentary physical location.

Westfront 1918, I argue, offers a similar kind of double mapping between the private desires and attachments and nationalized, public commitments of its characters. Much of the film's power, its putative "realism," arises from its negotiation between these spaces, rather than from any particular narrative complexity. Even at the time of the film, a number of reviewers noted, for instance, that the film's strength was not in its plotting. With the introduction of dialogue, of course, plot and story could grow much more complex, simply for reasons of representational exposition, but in terms of the scenes and information offered as plot, *Westfront 1918* seems quite like a silent film, as one of its negative reviewers complained (Kurt Pinthus). Instead, the dramatic power of the film resides in the tension and intercutting between these two maps, a tension and intercutting that Pabst created by deploying sound. In this way he creates some of the film's most memorable effects.

In his review of *Westfront 1918*, Siegfried Kracauer focuses above all on the use of sound in the film. In fact, he dedicates two paragraphs to these aspects in a review of merely six paragraphs, so it is clear that he considers these mechanisms to be central to the film's overall effect. Kracauer remarks on two specific deployments of the new sound technology that I think are useful to keep in mind today, since they have become ubiquitous and their power and strangeness, clear to audiences whose viewing habits were conditioned by silent films, would not be very apparent to viewers today. First, he underscores the way in which the film uses sound to "explode" the "borders of the picture" ("sprengen" . . . "den Bildrahmen"), that is, he emphasizes, in dramatic rhetoric underscoring its novelty, the use of offscreen sound to expand the depicted space of the frame. This effect is central to war films, in which, to pick just one relevant instance, the whiz of gunfire or the booming of artillery are regularly out of frame but, of course, have a major dramatic impact even without being depicted visually on screen. War films, one might say, depict above all the unsettling experience of ubiquitous offscreen sound effects and the subsequent reaction to it. In this way, Pabst's choosing to make his first sound film about war seems particularly appropriate, as for maybe more than any silent film, sound would fundamentally transform the mise-en-scène of the film.

Second, Kracauer celebrates the way Pabst uses a variety of sound effects, especially matches on sound and sound bridges, to link the private space to the public space, a linkage that serves in *Westfront 1918* both to reference and to criticize the mobilization film. To take the much-cited first sequence, the film's opening seven minutes include a clever sound match that reveals an important theme of the film. The film opens with German soldiers relaxing away from the front in a French pub. Most of the dramatic action in the sequence follows the soldiers' attempts to seduce, in their coarse fashion, the Frenchwoman Yvette/Jacqueline. She cheerfully resists most of their advances, and, at one point, as one infantryman pulls her in one direction and a second in another, one soldier falls on the other, at which a third infantryman playfully slaps one of the would-be seducers on his backside. At the very instant of slapping, however, viewers hear the sound of incoming artillery, which puts the lights out and sends the soldiers scurrying for cover in the pub's cellar. Revealingly, the image track (sudden darkness) follows the cues of the offscreen sound. The sound of the soldiers' conflict over desire overlaps with, and has been overwhelmed, by the larger, offscreen war: it is an effect achievable, at least with this kind of economy of expression, only with offscreen sound. The thematic content of this effect is best illuminated by considering the two maps between which the film's off-screen sounds navigates: that of the off-duty desires of the individual infantrymen and that of the nation's war, offscreen at first but still reminding the soldiers of its presence and drawing ever closer.

This interpretation of the film's double mapping also affords a reading of another noteworthy shot in *Westfront 1918*'s opening sequence, one that

Fig. 16.1. Opening shot of Westfront 1918 *(G. W. Pabst, 1930): a soldier entering a French tavern. Screenshot.*

even more effectively foregrounds the sequence's two maps via offscreen sound. The film's very first shot frames, in long shot, the window and doors of the pub in which the film spends its opening minutes. It is a standard establishing shot of a dramatic location, and, after registering this location, viewers watch a soldier let himself in through the door (fig. 16.1). Later in the sequence, after the artillery and after the soldiers have been called to the town square to prepare to march back to the front — around eight minutes into the film and six and a half minutes after the film opens with the above shot — Pabst returns to a reverse angle of the same door, windows, and cart. Now, however, there is no one pictured in the frame (fig. 16.2). But, over this empty image referencing the film's opening, the soundtrack offers, in another important deployment of offscreen sound, the voices of the infantrymen as they report to duty, barking officiously each soldier's name and

Fig. 16.2. Reverse angle shot of the French tavern's windows and door, without a human presence. Screenshot.

"Angetreten!" These parallel shots framing the important opening sequence demonstrate how the innocuous shot of the opening has been rewritten, via offscreen sound, by the intrusive war. It is as if the space of the pub, that space associated with the map of private desires and attachments that takes up the first six minutes of the film, could actually become a pleasant memory, via an internal diegetic point-of-view shot, of the past for the soldiers as they report to duty. Perhaps it is exactly this pub of which they think, on the map of private desires, as they report to march off to the front.

The "Landscape of the Front": De-Auraticizing the Wanderer's Gaze

In his review of *Westfront 1918* Kracauer argues that the film distinguishes itself from previous war films not only by its use of sound but also by its consistent focus on a "Stacheldrahtlandschaft," a landscape of barbed wire. But as the first sequence analyzed above and Karl's trip home suggest, the film does not unfold entirely in that eerie terrain of barbed wire, collapsing trenches, and denatured trees. Rather, the film negotiates between two maps, one of the characters' private lives behind the front and one of the pock-marked battlefield of the war. But *Westfront 1918* does leave, as it did with Kracauer, the impression that this latter landscape dominates, because it is probably the key visual contribution of the film. In fact, the film foregrounds landscape in an important early sequence, also featuring the student, that invokes the cinematic tradition of travel through a remarkable natural (or here, radically denaturalized) setting.

One of cinema's most important early and conspicuous functions, as Giuliana Bruno has argued, was to offer a traveling perspective and experience to viewers, a kind of cinematic tourism that foregrounds what she calls the "panoramic gaze." Panoramas reference, of course, the pre-cinematic attraction that featured faraway places and their landscapes, brought close in a realism, as well as scale, hitherto unknown. *Westfront 1918* offers precisely this kind of traveling, panoramic gaze in the person of the student over the course of his journey from the front back to the French pub mentioned above. It is not surprising that landscape would feature centrally in the film and its reception, because the "landscape of the front" was an important aspect of the 1920s contestation of interpretations and memories I mention. But landscape also served at this historical moment to represent the kind of transformation in art and experience that a critic like Walter Benjamin was tracking. With landscape, Benjamin foregrounded both the conventional constitution of what he called "the aura" and its transformation in modernity's evolving aesthetics. In its depiction of landscape, *Westfront 1918* invokes the aura and auratic experience in the face of landscape in order to register the kinds of transformation in experience of which Benjamin was writing. Both the journey and the de-auraticized landscapes that Pabst's film offers ultimately serve to undercut the double map that the film sketches in its first hour.

The so-called "landscape" of the front had become an important locus for 1920s nationalist interpretations and memories of the war, as Benjamin suggests in his "Theories of German Fascism" of 1930. In this essay, a review of a collection edited by Ernst Jünger, Benjamin situates the soldier type sketched in the volume: "This soldier type is a reality, a surviving witness of the World War, and it was actually this 'landscape of the front,' his true home [Heimat], that was defended in the *Nachkrieg*" (Benjamin, "Theories," 318). Benjamin underscores how these "landscapes" became the *Heimat* for the soldiers in what Jünger insisted on calling the "*Nachkrieg*," a coinage signifying not the "postwar period" but the "postwar war" of the 1920s. The neologism emphasizes how belligerent nationalists and left-leaning critics were engaged in contesting the war, its interpretations, and memories of it, and how that very landscape of the front become the battlefield for these memories: "It should be said as bitterly as possible: in the face of this "landscape of total mobilization," the German feeling for nature has had an undreamed-of upsurge" (Benjamin, "Theories," 318).

Given the contemporary discourse surrounding the term "landscape of the front," it is not surprising that Pabst in his film and Kracauer in his review would foreground the landscapes of the film as its most important visual contribution. At almost exactly the moment he was writing critically of Jünger's landscapes of the front, Benjamin was giving the representation of landscape a central role in his historicization of perception via photography. In fact, the last quote, in its skepticism about nature amid the wartime landscapes, hints at how a discussion of landscape was at the core of the modernist aesthetics with which Benjamin was engaged at the time. Indeed, around this time the landscape became in his thinking the paradigmatic model for the aura and auratic experience: "What is aura, actually? A strange weave of space and time: the unique appearance or semblance of distance, no matter how close that object may be. While resting on a summer's noon, to trace the range of mountains on the horizon, or a branch that throws its shadow on the observer, until the moment or the hour become part of their appearance — that is what it means to breathe the aura of those mountains, that branch" (Benjamin, "Little History," 518–19). At the moment Benjamin was addressing its appropriation by the nationalists to set the mise-en-scène of the "Erlebnis" of the front, landscape also became the lynchpin, in his eyes, of a fundamental transformation in art remade by technologies like the camera. Then, in a revealing conceptual move for an essay on photography, Benjamin turns to "Russian film" to emphasize how this newest of media in the newest of countries was dispensing with the aura altogether. Benjamin would return to a very similar definition of the aura some five years later in his much cited "The Work of Art in the Age of Mechanical Reproduction" of 1935, in which he also cites auratic experience in "a mountain range on the horizon or a branch that casts its shadow on the beholder" (Benjamin, "The Work of Art," 255). "Little History," in traversing from landscape photography to Russian film, serves to link the destruction of the aura to the tradition of landscape representation.

It does so in a way that elucidates, as it does other aspects of the war-film genre, how *Westfront 1918* invokes but also sublates the so-called landscape of the front. The film undertakes the depiction of the destruction of auratic experience amid the landscape that is nonetheless recognizable as a landscape, which, as both perspective and experience within the journey form, should be auratic. That is to suggest, on the one hand, that the film invokes the auratic experience of landscape with the form of the journey and the flaneuristic, panoramic gaze that would accompany it; but then it works to deliberately subvert the auratic experience of this wandering figure with the radically de-naturalized, de-auraticized landscape of the front. Much as it invokes the mobilization genre's two maps to problematize their happy coexistence, the film thus works to sublate the auraticized landscapes of the past, evacuating the aura from nature as it drains humanity from the battlefield.

This invocation of the flaneuristic, panoramic gaze transpires above all in an eight-minute sequence about twenty minutes into the film, when the student volunteers to travel from the front to the regimental command post. The student, to the consternation of his comrades, volunteers because he plans to use the mission as an excuse to visit Yvette/Jacqueline back in the French village of the film's opening sequence. In line with the two maps discussed above, the student's journey is to be from one map to another, from the spaces of the battle to those of his private desire. He takes the message and starts off on an eight-minute sojourn to Yvette/Jacqueline, a filmic trip that brings him through various, often surreal, stations of the film's eponymous front.

As the student starts out, the camera cuts to a low-angle long shot that reveals more of the landscape than the low camera in the trenches has revealed up until that point. Viewers see, predictably, a desolate, naked landscape, but one that also deliberately establishes certain visual themes that recur throughout the sequence as well as later in the film. The film foregrounds the auratic in two important recurring themes, trees and their branches, and the cross, often naturally formed, sometimes deliberately deployed (fig. 16.3). Both elements of the mise-en-scène invoke important examples of the auratic — the tree branches of which Benjamin speaks as paradigmatically auratic in "Little History," and the religious artifact foregrounded in "The Work of Art" essay — only to, as Benjamin puts it when discussing Eugene Atget's photos, "suck the aura out of reality like water from a sinking ship" ("Little History," 518). The trees and cross are present in this first image; they will recur as the student reaches the command post, and then again when he encounters a workshop where they manufacture crosses with which to bury the fallen soldiers. The student's journey is, in this way, one marked not by recognizable sights and landmarks but by the quotidian seriality of death.

After this harrowing and exhausting trip through what Kracauer would later call, in his *From Caligari to Hitler*, a landscape of death, the student does reach the French pub and gets Yvette's/Jacqueline's attention. The initial shot that relocates viewers in the pub itself also emphasizes the awful seriality of war because it shows, a mere twenty-five minutes after the opening sequence here, a new group of soldiers strewn around the house; viewers might well expect that Yvette/Jacqueline herself would have another soldier in her bed, just as the pub has exchanged the student's company for a new one. But she answers the student's call, recog-

Fig. 16.3. The Student (Hans Joachim Moebis) in the desolate "landscape of the front." Screenshot.

nizing his uniqueness in a context in which viewers have seen uniqueness radically downgraded and nature de-auraticized, one last reminder of the distance between the map of private and individual desire and attachment and the serialized, denaturalized world of the battlefield. The shot of the student waiting for her to come and get him at the door revisits and rewrites the shot in the opening sequence that I emphasized above, creating a mise-en-scène with his person set into the scene of his love.

Despite the student's apparently successful journey between the two maps — fulfilling his official mission and realizing his private desire — the film spends its second half hour undercutting the balance between the private maps of the student's comrade Karl and the nationalized map of the battlefield. When Karl returns home, he learns he is the victim of another seriality allegedly common in wartime, that of infidelity: revisiting a theme as well as iconography from Pabst's *Die freudlose Gasse* (Joyless Street, 1925), Karl's wife has traded sexual favors for meat from the butcher's apprentice. Karl loses faith in his marriage; he does not forgive his wife as he leaves, saying that he only looks forward to seeing his comrades again, especially the student. His map of private desire has been ruined by his wife's infidelity, but the positive aspects of the war (camaraderie, and so on) are also already destroyed, as the viewer knows what Karl does not, that the student has just been killed in combat back amid the landscape of the front. This privileged viewer knowledge also underscores the obsolescence of the student's private map when Yvette/Jacqueline is forcibly evacuated from her home: the deliberate irony is that she is concerned with the student's locating her, literally and figuratively, on the map when he is, in fact, already dead. The private map is in utter tatters: both the scene of their love and one of the lovers are now gone; this is emphasized in a long-take of the ruined house and the offscreen sound of Yvette/Jacqueline's crying.

Conclusion: Counter Memorialization as Counter-Mapping

By the film's one-hour mark, the student has died, unbeknownst to both Karl and Yvette/Jacqueline, at the very moment that they, on their respective maps of private desires and attachments, are anxiously contemplating reunion with him. Not surprisingly, the film's remaining half hour subsequently turns to the commemoration of death, the student's as well as that of others. Karl's own end comes in the attempt to appropriately commemorate the death of the student. Upon returning to the front and learning how the student was killed the week before, Karl is in despair. When he hears eerie offscreen screaming, he thinks it is the student and, when disabused of this notion by the Bavarian, he nonetheless decides to volunteer for an advance mission in order to recover the student's body. The first two parts of the film use offscreen sound to register the suffering of war by expanding the space of the (often empty) frame: in the first part, the artillery and then sounds of being called up dominate the map of private desires and attachments; in the second half, the wailing of loved ones, of Karl's wife and Yvette/Jacqueline, register the interminable suffering of war for the civilian inhabitants of that second map. The last half hour adds a new offscreen sound to the exploded frames of *Westfront*, namely, ghostly screaming and groaning from the maimed and wounded, another sound effect emphasized by Kracauer in his review.

When Karl and the Bavarian move ahead to position themselves for what is expected to be a large-scale French attack, they come upon the student's corpse in a puddle of water. His comrades quickly, silently bury him, and the film, having denied an image of his entire body, shows his upstretched and rigid hand slowly covered with dirt. The silence with which they bury the student is revealing: there are no words of commemoration for the student, no mythologizing his death. The emphasis on silence around the death of a beloved comrade is particularly telling because of the importance of memorializing myth-making around the death of "fallen" soldiers. In the context of the First World War, such discursive mechanisms were particularly pointed in the case of the death of young, naive soldier-students: one of the most important legends to emerge during the war, for the 1920s, and then right up through the 1930s and 1940s was the myth of the slaughtered student-soldiers at Langemarck, also on the western front (Hüppauf, "Langemarck"). The myth of Langemarck mobilized discourse about the sacrifice of Germany's best and most innocent youths, who allegedly (though implausibly) went into battle singing, upon which they were mowed down by older, more experienced allied troops. This myth was fostered in part to obscure the mistakes made by the German military command in sending inexperienced troops against thoroughly battle-tested ones, but, in any case, the deaths were commemorated throughout the 1920s and became an important flashpoint of nationalist memory of the "youth of 1914."

Pabst's film, however, with its silent burial of the innocent's stiffened corpse, is explicitly directed against such commemorative myth-making. The film's mode of counter-memory is confirmed in the last of the film's spaces, the field hospital established in a church. For our purposes, it is worthwhile to recall that a Christian church is an institution built around the commemoration of death, one that foregrounds a memorialization of a death-as-sacrifice in its most important artifact (and one of the visual motifs of the film), the cross. To set the conclusion and climax of *Westfront 1918*, during which at least two of the remaining three protagonists will die and the third have a breakdown, to set these events in a Christian church confirms the kind of counter-memorialization toward which the film drives. The ubiquity of soldierly death in a church underscores the double aspects that historian Reinhart Koselleck ascribes to war commemoration: such commemoration interprets and codes death in a certain way such that those still living are charged with a legacy and mission based on that interpretation and coding (Koselleck, 297, 308).

In *Westfront 1918* the film's concluding space of the hospital invokes this kind of memorialization of wounded and dying soldiers, but it also shows how the protagonists of this film die anonymously as only a pitiable few of an overwhelming many. As with the (mis-)balance of the two maps or the auratic landscapes sketched above, the film invokes traditions of war films only to sublate them. The invocation of memorialization comes first, in another memorable tracking shot, as medics carry the lieutenant into the field hospital/church, in a clear reference to the iconography of the pieta (fig. 16.4). But the rest of the sequence undercuts the uniqueness of the deaths

Fig. 16.4. The injured lieutenant (Claus Clausen) as a Christ-like figure. Screenshot.

of those four (now three), the idea that they are different from the infantry-men with whom viewers have spent the film. At various moments in the sequence, the camera casually focuses, once again episodically or station-like, on a number of characters whom viewers do not even know, emphasizing the mass of casualties and relative meaninglessness of the characters whom viewers do know. Karl, for example, expires without any attending medical personnel, on a cot next to a French soldier viewers have never encountered, a Frenchman whose words, "pas ennemi" ("not an enemy") end the film.

Instead of inspiring commemoration or offering his comrades a charge to keep, Karl's death turns the film into a vehicle for a different kind of memory. In his last seconds, the surviving characters around Karl do not get a moving deathbed exhortation, but instead viewers see a flashback to his wife, begging him, as she did when he first departed home, for one kind word before he went back to the front. His last words to this apparition from the past are "we are all unhappy, we are all guilty." Maureen Turim has emphasized that in the flashback, films offer a model for memory and even history, and this is precisely what *Westfront 1918* offers in this sudden, unexpected flashback, the first of the film (Turim, 2): a different mode of memory, at precisely the moment of death, contravenes the nationalist discourse of memorialization, much as the film contests national discourse about the landscape of the front. If the film refuses to stage the diegetic mythologization of the death of its characters, but instead focuses on its utter futility and meaninglessness, it is directed against the culture of memorialization and mythologization that many would make of military death, as the Langemarck legend did of the students' death on the western front. The flashback offers a different kind of memory, one that eventually returns to the two maps with which I started. In Karl's last moments, the film foregrounds not the completion of the private map in the public war, but instead the unbridgeable gap between the two maps, a gap that haunts Karl in his remarkable end because the wartime map of the nationalist war has come to irreparably rend the map of private desire, attachment, and memory.

Notes

[1] *Westfront 1918* (Nero-Film, premiered May 30, 1930 in Berlin, 98 minutes long). Director: G. W. Pabst; producer: Seymour Nebenzahl; script: Ladislaus Vajda, based on the novel *Vier von der Infanterie* by Ernst Johannsen.

[2] "Ein Sieg des freien deutschen Filmproduzenten im internationalen Wettkampf der Qualitätsleistung" (Wollenberg).

[3] The relative critical neglect of Pabst's popular film has continued in two recent, important publications on Weimar Cinema, Anton Kaes's *Shell Shock Cinema: Weimar Culture and the Wounds of War* and Noah Isenberg's *Weimar Cinema: An Essential Guide to Classic Films of the Era*. The former has only one reference to *Westfront 1918*, the latter none.

[4] The French character in the film is referred to as Yvette in the opening credits, but the student addresses her, quite audibly, as Jacqueline.

[5] For Lefebvre, representational space is part of an ensemble that includes both "spatial practice" and representations of space, and this ensemble comprises what Lefebvre calls a (historicized and localized) spatial code. See Lefebvre, *The Production of Space*, 33.

[6] This notion of a character coming up on a secret second map is crucial to the cognitive mapping that Jameson traces in *The Geopolitical Aesthetic*, for example, "Archetypal journeys back beyond the surface appearance of things are also dimly reawakened, from antiquity and Dante . . . This promise of a deeper inside view is the hermeneutic content of the conspiracy thriller in general, although its spatialization in *Condor* seems somehow more alarming than the imaginary networks of the usual suspects: the representational confirmation that telephone cables and lines and their interchanges follow us everywhere, doubling the streets and build-

ings of the visible social world with a secondary secret underground world, is a vivid, if paranoid, cognitive map, redeemed for once only by the possibility of turning the tables, when the hero is able to tap into the circuits and bug the buggers, abolishing space with his own kind of simultaneity by scrambling all the symptoms and producing his messages from all corners of the map at the same time" (*Geopolitical Aesthetic,* 15), or "But the narrative by which it seeks to achieve this reality-effect remains one in which the individual subject of the protagonist somehow manages to blunder into the collective web of the hidden social order" (*Geopolitical Aesthetic,* 33).

Works Cited

Anon. "Westfront 1918: Ein bedenklicher Kriegsfilm." *Kreuz-Zeitung,* 30 May 1930.

Benjamin, Walter. "Little History of Photography." In *Selected Writings,* 2:507–30.

———. *Selected Writings.* Vol. 2: *1927–34.* Cambridge, MA: Harvard/ Belknap, 1999.

———. "Theories of German Fascism." In *Selected Writings,* 2:312–21.

———. "The Work of Art in the Age of Mechanical Reproduction." In *Selected Writings,* vol. 4: *1938–1940,* 250–83. Cambridge, MA: Harvard/ Belknap, 2003.

Bruno, Giuliana. *Streetwalking on a Ruined Map: Cultural Theory and the City Films of Elvira Notari.* Princeton, NJ: Princeton UP, 1993.

Geisler, Michael. "The Battleground of Modernity: *Westfront 1918.*" 1930. Reprinted in *The Films of G. W. Pabst: An Extraterritorial Cinema,* edited by Eric Renschler, 91–102. New Brunswick, NJ: Rutgers UP, 1990.

Hake, Sabine. *German National Cinema.* New York: Routledge, 2002.

Harvey, David. *The Condition of Postmodernity: An Enquiry into the Origins of Cultural Change.* New York: Blackwell, 1992.

———. *Spaces of Capital: Towards a Critical Geography.* New York: Routledge, 2002.

Hüppauf, Bernd. "Experiences of Modern Warfare and the Crisis of Representation." *New German Critique,* Special Issue on Ernst Jünger 59 (Spring, 1993): 41–76.

———. "Langemarck, Verdun, and the Myth of a New Man in Germany after the First World War." *War and Society* 6.2 (1988): 70–103.

Isenberg, Noah. *Weimar Cinema: An Essential Guide to Classic Films of the Era.* New York: Columbia UP, 2009.

Jameson, Fredric. *The Geopolitical Aesthetic: Cinema and Space in the World System.* Bloomington: Indiana UP, 1992.

———. *Postmodernism, or, The Cultural Logic of Late Capitalism*. Durham, NC: Duke UP, 1991.

Kaes, Anton. "The Cold Gaze: Notes on Mobilization and Modernity." *New German Critique* 59 (1993): 105–17.

———. *Shell Shock Cinema: Weimar Culture and the Wounds of War*. Princeton, NJ: Princeton UP, 2009.

Koselleck, Reinhart. "War Memorials: Identity Formation of the Survivors." In *The Practice of Conceptual History: Timing History, Spacing Concepts*, translated and edited by Todd Presner, 285–326. Stanford, CA: Stanford UP, 2002.

Kracauer, Siegfried. "Westfront 1918." *Frankfurter Zeitung*, 27 May 1930.

Lefebvre, Henri. *The Production of Space*. Translated by Donald Nicholson-Smith. Cambridge: Blackwell, 1991.

Massey, Doreen. *For Space*. London: SAGE, 2005.

———. *Space, Place, and Gender*. Minneapolis: U of Minnesota P, 1994.

Moretti, Franco. *Atlas of the European Novel, 1800–1900*. New York: Verso, 1998.

———. *Graphs, Maps, Trees: Abstract Models for a Literary History*. New York: Verso, 2005.

Mosse, George. *Nationalism and Sexuality: Respectability and Abnormal Sexuality in Modern Europe*. New York: H. Fertig, 1985.

Pinthus, Kurt. "Westfront 1918." *Das Abendblatt*, 24 May 1930.

Schindler, Stephan, and Lutz Koepnick. "Against the Wall? The Global Imaginary of German Cinema." In *The Cosmopolitan Screen: German Cinema and the Global Imaginary, 1945 to the Present*, edited by Stephan Schindler and Lutz Koepnick, 1–21. Ann Arbor: U of Michigan P, 2007.

Schivelbusch, Wolfgang. *Railway Journey: The Industrialization and Perception of Time and Space*. Berkeley: U of California P, 1986.

Soja, Edward W. *Postmodern Geographies: the Reassertion of Space in Critical Social Theory*. New York: Verso, 1989.

———. *Thirdspace: Journeys to Los Angeles and Other Real-and-Imagined Places*. Cambridge: Blackwell, 1996.

Stoler, Ann. *Race and the Education of Desire: Foucault's History of Sexuality and the Colonial Order of Things*. Durham, NC: Duke UP, 1995.

Turim, Maureen. *Flashbacks in Film: Memory and History*. New York, Routledge, 1989.

Virilio, Paul. *War and Cinema: The Logistics of Perception*. New York: Verso, 1991.

Wollenberg, Hans. "Westfront 1918 (Vier von der Infanterie)." *LichtBildBühne*, 24 May 1930.

17: Undermining Babel: Victor Trivas's *Niemandsland* (1931)

Nancy P. Nenno

CHRISTMAS 1914. Only a few months after the outbreak of hostilities in the First World War, soldiers in British, French, and German uniforms spontaneously declared a ceasefire and met in the barren strip of earth between the frontlines and trenches, neither possessed nor inhabited by either side, known as no-man's-land. Instead of launching individual guerrilla attacks against each other, for three days the soldiers buried their dead, exchanged gifts, and celebrated the holiday together (Brown/Seaton; Jürgs; Weintraub). In contrast to the familiar image of no-man's-land as a space of carnage, the story of the Christmas Truce transforms this horrifying in-between space into a haven of humanity.

One wonders whether this tale of community and cooperation in the extra-territorial space called no-man's-land inspired Victor Trivas and Leonhard Frank's pacifist 1931 film, *Niemandsland*, which depicts the chance meeting of five men of different nationalities and armies in an underground ruin between the fronts.[1] In contrast to the depictions of militarism that dominate the film's first half, the relative stability of this subterranean no-man's-land in the middle of the battleground makes it a space of sanctuary. The war among the nations continues here on the level of language, as English, French, and German contend with each other to be understood. It is only through the intervention of one of their number, the African colonial soldier, that the men come to recognize and embrace their similarities and to declare "war on war." Much as it did during the Christmas Truce 1914, no-man's-land acquires a symbolic meaning in the film as a site of humanity and international cooperation. In the film's dramatic conclusion the five men climb from the grave-like ruin. Side-by-side they march toward the camera, looming ever larger until they fill the frame. From a trench-inspired low angle, the camera records rifles and hands tearing down the barbed wire that encloses them, obstructing their path to freedom.

At its premiere on 10 December 1931 in Berlin's Mozartsaal on Nollendorfplatz, the conclusion of *Niemandsland* was greeted by thunderous applause. Although it received only a limited release, the mainstream press lauded the film for its humanistic message. Two years later, following the film's US premiere (under the title *Hell on Earth*), one critic even suggested that "the judges who award the Nobel prize for peace could do worse than consider the parents of this film for their next award" (Trask). But although the general public appears to have embraced the film, critics on both the far Right and the extreme Left were less enthusiastic. Predictably, the conservative *Deutsche Zeitung* dismissed the pacifist message of the film, particularly since it cast "a Negro in French uniform as the messenger of peace" ("ein Neger in französischer Uniform als Friedensengel"; quoted in Kester, 158). On the far Left, criticism was particularly directed at the film's lack of historical specificity and the abstract, impractical nature of its proposed solution. The critic for the Communist *Die Rote Fahne* took the film to task for neglecting to explore the imperialist roots of the war (Lutz-Kopp, 97), while others on the left wished that the film had attempted to grapple with the contemporary issues of rearmament and the remilitarization of Europe (Ihering).

Director Victor Trivas defended the film, maintaining that *Niemandsland* was intended to expose the mechanisms underlying the war rather than approach it historically or in a realistic manner:

> In *Niemandsland* I was not concerned with exposing the horror of the war but rather its dreadful senselessness. If enemies who have escaped the atmosphere of mass hysteria meet on a spot of earth between the fronts, then they will also discover the common language of simple human feelings. That would surely be the most revealing denunciation of the war.[2]

Trivas's project entails recasting the combatants of the conflict; rather than depicting the war as a result of disputes between nations, Trivas refigures the First World War as a more abstract dialectic between difference (nationality) and similarity (basic humanity), an opposition represented by the national sphere and the extra-territorial space of no-man's-land. The discovery of "the common language of simple human feeling" is mediated by the two outsider figures: the African soldier, whose experience as an international cabaret artist has given him limited command of the three languages spoken in this no-man's-land, and the shell-shocked Eastern European Jew, thereby inverting nationalism's insider-outsider paradigm to reveal its artificiality. It is particularly the sympathetic characterization of the African colonial, already an inhabitant of a political, cultural, and racial no-man's-land, and his key function as negotiator and interpreter, that elevates him to the position of the film's representative of this supranational ideal.

"This is a story of conflict!" reads the opening title (despite its being a sound film), and with this, the film declares its initial thematization of the frenzied, hysterical embrace of the war. From the opening montage of guns firing and flashes of the word "war," Trivas mobilizes both the visual and the acoustic registers to create a cinema of collision that mimics the conflict of nations. Although the nations involved in the First World War are identified — without, however, regard to the chronology of the war — the segment focuses less on the specific reasons for the declarations of war than on the similarities of militarism and nationalism across the nations. In this first part of the film, Trivas makes heavy use of silent-era, Soviet-style montage to draw associative parallels among the combatant nations as he dramatizes the simultaneous buildup to war. A rhythmically edited sequence of national symbols (German, French, Russian) and declarations of war (voice-overs and texts in their original languages) is followed by parallel images of uniformed soldiers at training camp. Shots of soldiers drilling, their nationalities marked by their uniforms and the language of the commands, are cleverly crosscut to "face" each other, prefiguring the coming battles between them. The carnivalesque atmosphere of August 1914 is represented symbolically by shots of hats being tossed jubilantly into the air. These symbols and costumes portray each nation in crude, stereotypical, and even racist caricature as the Japanese toss parasols rather than hats and a Turk is identifiable by his tightly-curled mustache. Through the use of symbolic objects and disembodied voices (as voice-over), the spectator is denied identification with any single nation, and is instead confronted with the larger paradigm of militarism and nationalism that transcends national borders. The sequence reaches its crescendo as various national anthems compete acoustically on the sound track while, on screen, national flags become animate, warring with each other until they are ultimately replaced by the single black flag symbolizing death.

Unlike other antiwar films of the late Weimar Republic that employ the new possibilities of sound film to immerse the viewer in the sounds as well as the sights of war — particularly Lewis Milestone's American film of Erich Maria Remarque's novel, *All Quiet on the Western Front* (1930) and G. W. Pabst's 1931 film, *Westfront 1918* — Trivas explicitly rejected the use of sound as a mere servant to realism. In a manifesto from January 1930 that Trivas cowrote with Russian director Fedor Ozep and screenwriter Natan Abramowitsch Sarchi, the three reject what they label "the danger of naturalism, of theatricality, of attraction."[3] Rather than attempting to reproduce reality in a mechanical way, they call for the exploitation of sound film's artistic potential: "for the utilization of sound and speech as material for montage, as material for poetic representation and revelation of the virtual world."[4] It was this formalist approach to the collaboration between sound and image that led one film critic to comment that it was clear that "Trivas ha[d] learnt some things from the Russians, but relatively little from the Americans."[5]

The use of sound in *Niemandsland* builds upon this idea of illuminating what is not conventionally seen or recognized in order to reveal the deeper mechanisms at work. On the sound register, Trivas accomplishes this through the strategic deployment of music that was scored by Hanns Eisler, a committed communist, who regularly collaborated with Bertolt Brecht and later composed the anthem of the German Democratic Republic. In line with Brechtian techniques of alienation, Eisler's score undercuts audience expectations that the film's music will complement and reinforce on-screen actions and instead uncovers the manipulative power of music. One of the most compelling scenes in *Niemandsland*, one in which editing and music work together to illuminate the seductiveness of nationalist propaganda, depicts the mobilization of the German soldier. As the sequence begins, German carpenter Köhler (Ernst Busch), his family, and their neighbors begin their slow walk to the town center, where the men are being mustered out, accompanied by dirge-like music. However, a musical shift into a jaunty march brings about a sea-change in the somber mood of the gathering. The German's wife begins to smile slightly, glancing up at her husband, who begins to walk with more purpose, twirls his Kaiser-Wilhelm mustache, and turns his hat brim up at a rakish angle. As a final visual punch line, the sequence concludes with cheering crowds waving to the soldiers from a building that houses a coffin store and a funeral home.

In the first half of *Niemandsland*, the individual figures that will meet in no-man's-land are introduced against the larger backdrop of the nation. Although they are given names, they remain primarily identified in the script by their national affiliations. The storyline of each figure — with the exception of the African colonial soldier — is entrenched in a familial context, these being predominantly scenarios of beginnings: the wedding of the Jewish tailor, Lewin, "somewhere in the world"; the birth of the Englishman's son in London; an early flirtation between the Frenchman and a girl on a tram in Paris. And although each is embedded in his individual domesticity, in some cases the nation is also clearly woven into the fabric of their lives. As the film begins, Brown (Hugh Stephen Douglas) is framed sitting in his window, awaiting word from the midwife in the next room; London's skyline (featuring the dome of St. Paul's Cathedral) is reflected onto the pane of glass that both separates and links him to that city. Trivas reveals how the nation is not merely a backdrop to individual life, but indeed that its ideology infiltrates all aspects of life. Borrowing a narrative motif from co-author Leonhard Frank's story "Der Vater" (The Father), Trivas further reveals how nationalism infuses all aspects of life, including play: the German carpenter shows his son how to play with a toy cannon, the mouth of which is then crosscut with that of a real cannon as the voice-over intones, "Cannons, cannons, cannons all over the world," while in Paris, the Frenchman and his girlfriend take aim at a caricatured Prussian in a shooting gallery.[6]

Of the five figures, only the racial others — the Eastern European Jew, Lewin, and Joe Smile, the African colonial soldier and cabaret artist — are not firmly and recognizably anchored in a national context. Although it is

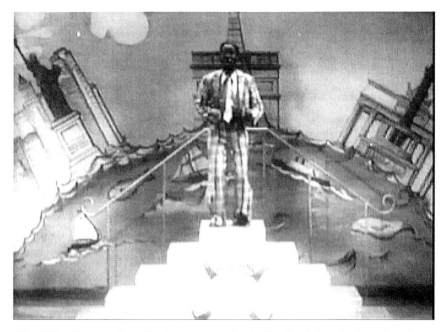

Fig. 17.1. Cosmopolitan Black entertainer Joe Smile (Louis Douglas) on the cabaret stage. Screenshot.

clear that Smile (Louis Douglas) resides in Paris, in a cabaret performance he performs his own lack of identification within the larger construct of the nation. Against the backdrop of a sparsely sketched Atlantic ocean depicting national symbols from left to right — New York's skyline and Statue of Liberty, Paris's Eiffel Tower and Arc de Triomphe, and Berlin's Brandenburg Gate and Victory Column — Joe Smile sings of his desire to "get off this boat" (fig. 17.1).[7] The only indication of any national affiliation comes as he stands stiffly at attention in the uniform of a colonial Moroccan soldier before his audience while the Marseillaise plays. Similarly, the figure of the Eastern European Jew (Vladimir Sokoloff) is not specifically located in a nation but rather in an ethnicity or race. Introduced through his wedding ceremony and feast as Jewish (the only words spoken in the sequence are Yiddish), he too is designated an outsider within the larger national paradigm. Located "somewhere in the world," as an intertitle tells us, the Jewish Lewin's departure for war is without pleasure or excitement. That Lewin's sole identification is with his personal domestic sphere rather than with a nation is evident as he packs to leave: in the background, a small, unframed, and unidentifiable picture (perhaps the

Tsar) is obscured by the close-up of Lewin's wedding photo, which he removes from its frame before leaving his grieving wife. His lack of identity is subsequently made complete when, following a shell attack, he loses not only his uniform but also his voice and his name, being thereafter simply identified as "Somewhere in the World."

The antinational and transnational focus of the film was undoubtedly informed by its screenwriters' own experiences of emigration and exile, of living and working in countries and languages that were not their own. In the mid-1920s Victor Trivas left the Soviet Union, where he had worked closely with Russian director Alexis Granowsky in Moscow's Jewish Theater as well as with an avant-garde theater troupe.[8] In Berlin, Trivas worked as a scenarist and architect in the film studios, where he met Leonhard Frank, a committed leftwing author and pacifist whose vocal disapproval of the First World War had precipitated his hasty flight to Switzerland in 1915. After coscripting Fedor Ozep's *Der Mörder Dimitri Karamasoff* (The Murderer Dimitri Karamasoff, 1931), the two collaborated again on *Niemandsland*, which was originally based on an idea by Frank. In the early 1930s both men were again forced to abandon their homes and to emigrate, first to France and then to the United States, where they ended up in Hollywood.[9] In its message and its execution, *Niemandsland* bears the marks of the early experiences of exile and emigration, but it recasts what could be construed as a tragic fate into a desirable identity, a positionality of choice rather than of convention and compulsion.

In contrast to the multiple, parallel, and abstract stories told in the film's first half, the space of the no-man's-land where the men meet invokes a *Kammerspiel* ("chamber play"): enclosed on all sides, the setting mirrors the intimacy of a theater, as well as the darkened movie theater. The film architect Trivas constructs the space as subterranean in contrast to the surface where combat takes place, rendering the opposition of surface differences and underlying commonality spatially visible. This quasi-hermetically-sealed space signifies both death and rebirth; as a tomb, it symbolizes the death of the combatants' hostility towards each other, as a womb, their rebirth as a human community.

And indeed, the men's common humanity begins to emerge with their entrance into the nation-less space of no-man's-land. As the German and the Frenchman tumble into the underground space, their mutual hostility is signaled cinematically as each appears alone in a one-shot, facing the other across the cut. After working together to free the trapped Lewin who is revealed to be both deaf and dumb from shell shock, the two enemies sit together companionably prior to resuming hostilities on the surface. The German pulls out a box containing two cigarettes, one of which he offers to the Frenchman (Georges Péclet). In a tight two-shot, the Frenchman takes a light from the German's cigarette, each eying the other warily (fig. 17.2). Despite their lack of a common language, they neverthe-

Fig. 17.2. The German (Ernst Busch) and the Frenchman (Georges Péclet) share a cigarette. Screenshot.

less understand each other, as linguistic cognates like Zigarette/cigarette, Kamerad/camarade and Wein/vin demonstrate the basic human needs and desires for sustenance and companionship that they share. The film continues to build on the idea that the men's commonalities are more important than what separates them: the Frenchman and the Englishman discover that they share a first name, the German's family photo dissolves into Lewin's wedding photo in a point-of-view shot, and each man alternately performs a verse of a melancholy war song, "Marie," in his own language, whereby the sad refrains ("I'll take you home, Mary"/"Du bist so fern, Marie") reiterate their common longing for home. Once again, it is the African soldier who facilities this meeting across national languages as he leads them into the song on his harmonica.[10]

Of all the differences among the men, language difference is the greatest hurdle and the one they are least able to discard, except in the case of Somewhere in the World, whose aphasia has transformed everyone into his friend based on the "language of simple human feeling." The choice of an African colonial to facilitate the men's communication was embraced by critic Hans Siemsen, who declared, "And it is one of the most beautiful and best ideas of this beautiful film that *this Negro*, the representative of a despised, 'uncultured,' 'inferior' race (because of his internationality as a *performer*) becomes the *interpreter and mediator* between the German, the French, the Russian Jew, and the Briton" (Goergen, *Victor Trivas*, 26–27). And while Smile's imperfect command of three languages and his nurturing role at times uncomfortably reproduce the conventions of minstrelsy, ultimately it is still this character that represents humanity, mediates the truce, and mobilizes the men to reject the war.

Given that the fierce debate surrounding the French use of African colonial soldiers to occupy the Rhine after the signing of the Treaty of Versailles was hardly a decade old, and that renewed debate about their demobilization was rekindled at the end of the 1920s, Trivas's sympathetic characterization of this figure is as remarkable as it is uncommon. In contrast to other antiwar films of this period, Joe Smile is scarcely the fearsome, depraved animal depicted by opponents of the so-called "Black Horror on the Rhine" (Nelson; Marks). Nor is he the brutal killer of Pabst's *Westfront 1918*.[11] Working against contemporary stereotypes, Trivas depicts the African *tirailleur* (infantryman), the most obvious outsider of all five because of both his racial and his continental origin, as the one rational voice in no-man's-land. As one pressed into service to a nation of which he is a citizen only in name, and forced to fight a war in which he has no stake, he recognizes and acknowledges the artifice of national identity (Rice). Further, as an African-American performer familiar to Weimar-era audiences, Louis Douglas's disenfranchised and disillusioned African soldier also invokes the situation of blacks in the United States, and particularly of the black troops that served in the First World War (Harris; Nagl). As Helmut Pankow noted, for African Americans "the Statue of Liberty is a hollow irony" (cited in Beck, 25).

In a key scene that recalls the film's opening images of the buildup to war, the Frenchman, the German, and the Englishman argue about who deserves the blame for the war. Durand claims it was not the French who wanted war, but rather the Germans. The German demands to know what the Frenchman has said, arguing that "Germany was compelled to defend itself" ("Deutschland wurde gezwungen sich zu verteidigen"). The Englishman Brown joins in, citing the German attack on Belgium as the cause of the war. Once the dialogue turns to the topic of colonies, the conversation degenerates into a multi-lingual free-for-all that is cut short only by the African's laughter. "Hooray!" he exclaims,

> Already enemies. You make a noise like the shells. And why? You all say the same thing but in a different language. That's why you don't understand each other. How stupid! You have different uniforms, different languages. I understand, but the dumb man, he has no uniform, he can't speak, we're all friends to him.

Fig. 17.3. The five new friends face a common enemy: war. Promotion still. Deutsche Kinemathek Berlin.

Familiar inhabitants of a racial and ethnic no-man's-land, the polyglot African and the silent East European Jew thus become twin figures of the film's ideal community, representatives of the supranational ideal that Trivas and Frank advocate. In his deaf and dumb state, Lewin acquires some of the animalistic qualities often attributed to Africans in this period, although in a non-threatening manner — indeed, it is thanks to his "instincts" that they are able to save themselves from a gas attack. The connection between these two figures is conveyed visually when the African strips off his uniform to join Somewhere in the World in his state-less identity, in their exchange of knowing glances and the multiple two-shots of the men. Accordingly, they are also the two figures seemingly most at home in no-man's-land, who execute the domestic chores in no-man's-land, tending this nation-less community: Smile prepares a soup and Lewin repairs a tear in the German's trousers.

Ultimately it is the act of cooking, of tending to basic human needs, that draws attention to their sanctuary and causes the guns outside to be turned against them. After the attack ends, the Englishman Brown says, "Let's get out of here," to which the German Köhler responds, "Come, comrade. Let's call it quits" ("Komm, Kamerad. Jetzt machen wir Schluß"). With this, the five help each other out of no-man's-land. The film concludes with on-screen text that reads: "What is their end? They march forward — five men. Five men who met in No Man's Land and refused to kill each other. Marching forward. Defying their common enemy — WAR" (fig. 17.3).

After 1933, the film suffered the same fate as Pabst and Milestone's films — it was banned as a threat to German honor (and imperialist aims). But unlike *Westfront 1918* and *All Quiet on the Western Front, Niemandsland* never experienced a postwar rehabilitation and reentry into the German, nor even the international, canon of antiwar films. Although revived at the Oberhausen film festival in 1968 (McKay; Patalas), it was only around the time of the fall of the Berlin Wall that German critics began to rediscover the film. After more than sixty years in the deep freeze of film archives, the film has reemerged in the consumer venues of movie theaters and video catalogs (Krautz; Goergen, "Emigrant"). One might conjecture that, in the context of the disintegration of Eastern-block Communism and the nascent integration of those who had previously been isolated behind the Iron Curtain into a larger cultural, political, and economic Western, European community, the pacifist, antiwar stance in *Niemandsland* may offer a utopian vision of a community of peoples and nations that speaks to the concerns and hopes of the present.

Notes

[1] *Niemandsland* (Trivas, 1931, b/w, 93 minutes). Produced by Anton Resch. Released 10 December 1931; banned by the Nazis on 22 April 1933. This article relies on three versions of the film: Inkwell Image's 2001 video release of Maurice Zouary's restored (but 27 minutes shorter) version under the American title, *Hell on Earth* (original release 1933), the original script, and a German film version, the latter two available at the Filmmuseum Berlin–Deutsche Kinemathek. Because the film, multilingual in all versions, is without subtitles, original dialogue will be cited and translated as necessary. Unless otherwise indicated, all translations are my own.

[2] "In *Niemandsland* ging es mir nicht darum, die Greuel des Krieges sondern seine grausame Sinnlosigkeit bloßzustellen. Wenn Feinde, der Atmosphäre des Massenwahnsinns entronnen, auf einem Fleckchen Erde zwischen den Fronten zusammentreffen werden, dann werden sie auch die gemeinsame Sprache einfacher menschlicher Gefühle finden. Das wäre doch wohl die aufschlußreichste Anprangerung des Krieges" (cited in Lutz-Kopp, 90). See also Goergen, *Victor Trivas,* for the full text of many of Trivas's texts and interviews.

[3] "die Gefahr des Naturalismus, der Theatralik, der Attraktion" (Ozep, Sarchi, Trivas).

[4] "für die Auswertung des Tons und der Sprache als Montagematerial, als Material für poetische Gestaltung und Offenbarung der visionellen Welt" (Ozep, Sarchi, Trivas).

[5] "Trivas hat manches von den Russen gelernt, verhältnismäßig wenig von den Amerikanern" (Georg, 5).

[6] Leonhard Frank's story, "Der Vater" (The Father), appeared in his collected stories of 1919, *Der Mensch ist gut* (The Human Being Is Good), and is discussed in Lutz-Kopp, 93.

[7] With his American name ("Joe Smile"), the black character blurs the distinction between African and African American. Another cabaret song, "Niggerlied," which was cut from the restored version, explicitly frames the African colonial soldier as a racial outsider: "In Afrika, da ist es heiss, / Drum bin ich schwarz — / Mein Herz ist weiss — / Die Haut, der ist das Herz egal; / Sie bleibt so schwarz! Fatal! Skandal!" (In Africa it is hot / That's why I am black / My heart is white / Skin doesn't matter to the heart / It remains so black! Awful! Scandalous!). See *Niemandsland*, file 2891, Deutsche Kinemathek, Schriftgutarchiv. On Eisler's composition, see Grabs, 129.

[8] Goergen, "Victor Trivas Biografie"; "Künstlerische Avantgarde"; *Victor Trivas*.

[9] Another Russian émigré, George Shdanoff, student and partner of Michael Chekov, reportedly also worked on *Niemandsland* but remained uncredited until the 1969 restoration of the film. Of the three, Trivas and Shdanoff had the most success in the American dream factory. Trivas worked on numerous films and received an Oscar nomination for scripting Orson Welles's *The Stranger* (1946). Shdanoff also emigrated and became one of the leading acting coaches in Hollywood. Vladimir Sokoloff, who plays Lewin, similarly ended up in Hollywood, playing character roles. Leftist singer-actor Ernst Busch (Köhler) also emigrated. Following several years fighting fascist forces in Spain, Busch was interned by the German army until 1945. After the war, he settled in the German Democratic Republic.

[10] One wonders if Trivas is also problematizing the introduction of synchronized sound, which complicated the process of international distribution and display. See Klaus Kreimeier's discussion of the silent, English, French, German, and Hungarian versions of Hanns Schwarz's 1929 film *Melodie des Herzens* (Kreimeier 215). For a more extensive discussion of multi-language versions, see Garncarz; Krützen. On early sound films, see also the essays by Chris Wahl and Ofer Ashkenazi in this volume.

[11] The positive portrayal of the African colonial soldier in Trivas's film stands in marked contrast to one of the most brutal scenes in Pabst's *Westfront 1918*: there, the student is stabbed in a puddle in no-man's-land and left to die — a scene whose graphic nature sparked much debate (Kester 131, 147–48). In *Vier von der Infanterie* (Four from the Infantry, 1929) by Ernst Johannsen, the novel on which *Westfront 1918* was based, the armed killer is described as a French-African soldier. As Montgomery notes, thousands had read Johannsen's story as a novel or in its serialized form, and even though this character in the film is not clearly distinguish-

able as black, the novel's characterization must have influenced the interpretation of the on-screen action (Montgomery, 122; Kester 131–32; Ziereis 305). On Pabst's film, see Jaimey Fisher's essay in this volume.

Works Cited

Beck, Earl R. "German Views of Negro Life in the United States, 1919–1933." *Journal of Negro History* 48.1 (January 1963): 22–32.

Brown, Malcolm, and Shirley Seaton. *The Christmas Truce*. New York: Hippocrene Books, 1984.

Garncarz, Joseph. "Die bedrohte Internationalität des Films: Fremdsprachige Versionen deutscher Tonfilme." In *Hallo? Berlin? Ici Paris! Deutsch-französische Filmbeziehungen, 1918–1939*, 127–40. Munich: edition text + kritik, 1996.

Georg, Manfred. Review of *Niemandsland*. *Tempo*, 10 December 1931, 5.

Goergen, Jeanpaul. "Emigrant im Niemandsland: Zum 100. Geburtstag von Victor Trivas." *film-dienst* 14 (1996): 4–7.

———. "Künstlerische Avantgarde, visionäre Utopie: Die Regisseure Victor Trivas und Alexis Granowsky." In *Fantasies russes: Russische Filmemacher in Berlin und Paris, 1920–1930*, edited by Jörg Schöning, 129–37. Munich: edition text + kritik, 1995.

———. "Victor Trivas Biografie." In *CineGraph: Lexikon zum deutschsprachigen Film*. Available at www.cinegraph.de/lexikon/Trivas_Viktor/biografie.html.

Goergen, Jeanpaul, ed. *Victor Trivas*. FilmMaterialien 9. Hamburg: CineGraph, 1996.

Grabs, Manfred. *Hanns Eisler: Kompositionen-Schriften-Literatur; Ein Handbuch*. Leipzig: VEB Deutscher Verlag für Musik, 1984.

Harris, Bill. *The Hellfighters of Harlem*. New York: Carroll & Graf, 2002.

Ihering, Herbert. "*Niemandsland*." *Berliner Börsen-Courier*, 10 December 1931.

Jürgs, Michael. *Der kleine Frieden im Großen Krieg*. Munich: C. Bertelsmann, 2003.

Kester, Bernadette. *Film Front Weimar: Representations of the First World War in German Films of the Weimar Period (1919–1933)*. Amsterdam: Amsterdam UP, 2003.

Krautz, Alfred. "Niemandsland." *Beiträge zur Film- und Fernsehwissenschaft* 36 (1989): 5–18.

Kreimeier, Klaus. *Die Ufa-Story: Geschichte eines Filmkonzerns*. Munich: Carl Hanser, 1992.

Krützen, Michaela. "Esperanto für den Tonfilm: Die Produktion von Sprachversionen für den frühen Tonfilm-Markt." In *Positionen deutscher Filmgeschichte: 100 Jahre Kinematographie; Strukturen, Diskurse, Kontexte,* edited by Michael Schaudig, 119–54. Munich: Schaudig & Ledig, 1996.

Lotz, Rainer. *Black People: Entertainers of African Descent in Europe and Germany.* Bonn: Birgit Lotz, 1997.

Lutz-Kopp, Elisabeth. *Mitten entzweigebrochen: Nebenprodukt und Lebensretter; Der Film in Leben und Werk Leonhard Franks.* Gerolzhofen: LAG Film Bayern, 1995.

Marks, Sally. "Black Watch on the Rhine: A Study in Propaganda, Prejudice and Prurience." *European Studies Review* 13 (1983): 297–334.

McKay, Andrew C. Research notes, 18 July 1968. Filmmuseum Berlin–Deutsche Kinemathek, Schriftgutarchiv.

Montgomery, Garth. "Realist War Films in Weimar Germany: Entertainment as Education." *Historical Journal of Film, Radio and Television* 9.2 (1989): 115–33.

Nagl, Tobias. "'Afrika spricht!' Modernismus, Jazz und 'Rasse' im Kino der Weimarer Republik." In *Singen und Tanzen im Film,* edited by Andrea Pollach, Isabella Reicher, and Tanja Widmann, 171–85. Vienna: Paul Zsolnay, 2003.

Nelson, Keith L. "The 'Black Horror on the Rhine': Race as a Factor in Post-World War I Diplomacy." *Journal of Modern History* 42.4 (1970): 606–27.

Niemandsland, file 2891. Deutsche Kinemathek, Schriftgutarchiv.

Ozep, Sarchi, Trivas. "Zum neuen Jahr: Protest!" *Film-Kurier,* 2 January 1930.

Patalas, Enno. "Einführung." *Retrospektive — X. Westdeutsche Kurzfilmtage.* Oberhausen, February 3–8, 1968.

Rice, Laura. "African Conscripts/European Conflicts." *Cultural Critique* 45 (Spring 2000): 109–49.

Trask, Charles Hooper. "A Graphic War Film Stirs Berlin." *New York Times,* 24 January 1932, X5.

Weintraub, Stanley. *Silent Night.* New York: Free Press, 2001.

Ziereis, Barbara. "Kriegsgeschichte im Spielfilmformat: Der Erste Weltkrieg im Tonspielfilm der Weimarer Republik." In *Krieg und Militär im Film des 20. Jahrhunderts,* ed. Bernhard Chiari, Matthias Rogg, and Wolfgang Schmidt, 297–318. Munich: R. Oldenbourg 2003.

18: Unmasking Brigitte Helm and Marlene Dietrich: The Vamp in German Romantic Comedies (1930–33)

Mihaela Petrescu

IN THE PAST DECADES film historians have demonstrated that in the German cinema of the early 1930s comedies were the predominant filmic genre.[1] Ulrich von Thüna notes that comedies formed 40 percent of the overall production of German films in 1930, increasing to 63 percent in 1931, and more than 64 percent in 1932 (von Thüna; see also Korte, 133–61). Von Thüna relates these high percentages to the repercussions of the Great Depression following the Wall Street stock-market crash of 24 October 1929: the German film industry sought to offer German audiences a convenient and much-needed escape from the harsh economic realities of mass unemployment, status anxieties, and increasing poverty. While von Thüna is certainly right in pointing to the escapist function of cinema in times of extreme economic distress, I wish to add a further consideration about the blossoming of film comedies during the last years of the Weimar Republic by highlighting the gender dynamics in a number of successful romantic comedies of mistaken identity from the period.

In this essay I will investigate Hanns Schwarz's film *Bomben auf Monte Carlo* (Bombs over Monte Carlo, released in the United States as *Monte Carlo Madness*, 1931), E. W. Emo's *Marion, das gehört sich nicht* (Marion, This Is Not Proper, 1932), and Karl Hartl's *Die Gräfin von Monte Christo* (The Countess of Monte Cristo, 1932). Focusing on the centrality of the figure of the vamp, a motif these films share with a host of others from the period, I will argue that these romantic comedies of mistaken identity should be read as efforts to reject and rewrite the genre of melodrama in the context of shifting gender relations. Drawing on Patrice Petro, I define melodramas as genre films that appeal to the emotions of their respective, predominantly female, audiences, by addressing the difficult life of, usually, female characters. Many times, the female protagonists resort to prostitution to make a living, and their ensuing sexual mobility tends to be depicted as a threat to society, a threat that is often controlled through their death. As historian Barbara Hales argues, the vamp is a female figure similar to the femme fatale in the sense that both present stereotypical images of women who seduce men and destroy their lives (Hales, 227; see also Müller, 259; Wager, 15; Doane, 2).

In December 1930 Richard Oswald's melodrama *Alraune* (Mandrake), a sound-film remake of Henrik Galeen's silent melodrama of 1927 (see Valerie Weinstein's essay in this volume), premiered in Berlin's movie theater Gloria-Palast. Interestingly enough, the female lead in both Galeen's and Oswald's version was Brigitte Helm, the young actress who had reached international fame overnight with her double role as robot-vamp and virgin in Fritz Lang's *Metropolis* (1927). While some film journals of the time celebrated Helm's performance and Oswald's melodrama as highly successful (Semler, 97–102), others considered both the film as well as the performance of its female lead a disappointment. One reviewer, for instance, complained that Oswald's film was monotonous and artificial, that it bordered on parody because it was unintentionally comical, and that viewers laughed throughout the entire evening.[2] The audience's laughter suggests not only that viewers perceived the acting and directing as poor but also that they were tired of melodramas. The reaction of the audience also hints that the status of the vamp, a media-creation designed to allure and frighten viewers with its intense seductiveness ever since its debut in silent film, was changing. The unexpected laughter of the audience viewing Oswald's talkie on its opening night had the effect of demythologizing the image of the vamp for the duration of that particular screening. In what follows, I will demonstrate that, in contrast to this unintended demythologization in Oswald's *Alraune*, Schwarz's comedy *Bomben auf Monte Carlo* and Emo's *Marion, das gehört sich nicht* deliberately use irony and humor to rationalize the image of the vamp, by mocking two of the most famous German femme fatale performers of the late twenties, Marlene Dietrich and Brigitte Helm. Moreover, I draw on Barbara Hales's characterization of the femme fatale as criminal and double, and on Daniela Sannwald's investigation of the use of fashion in the portrayal of vamp figures, and I argue that in Schwarz's film the criminal, the double, and the way fashion is used are thoroughly exaggerated. In fact, this exaggeration is so over-the-top that certain scenes in Schwarz's comedy indicate how not to use fashion and makeup. If understood as such, *Bomben auf Monte Carlo* parodies the fashion farce, a Weimar film genre that, as scholar Mila Ganeva argues, not only portrayed fashion as material for the narrative and as a spectacular *mise-en-scène*, but also saw itself as a source for practical fashion advice. Furthermore, I claim that Karl Hartl's comedy *Die Gräfin von Monte Christo* fails to reinvent Brigitte Helm beyond her vamp persona, because the film lacks a satirical interaction with the figure of the vamp, and because it uses visual and gestural elements that consistently codify Helm's heroine in terms of the outdated stereotype of the femme fatale.

By the time *Bomben auf Monte Carlo*, *Marion, das gehört sich nicht*, and *Die Gräfin von Monte Christo* were released, Marlene Dietrich and Brigitte Helm were well known to audiences in Germany and around the world for their vamp roles. Joseph Garncarz has shown that Marlene Dietrich was particularly popular in the late twenties for the vamps she played in films such as *Ich küsse Ihre Hand, Madame* (I Kiss Your Hand, Madam; Robert Land, 1929), *Die Frau, nach der man sich sehnt* (The Woman One Longs For; Kurt Bernhardt, 1929), *Das Schiff der verlorenen Menschen* (The Ship of Lost People; Maurice Tourneur, 1929), *Gefahren der Brautzeit* (The Dangers of the Engagement Period; Fred Sauer, 1930) and in her breakthrough success, *Der blaue Engel* (The Blue Angel; Josef von Sternberg, 1930). On 1 April 1930, when *Der blaue Engel* premiered in Berlin, Dietrich was sailing to Hollywood to start what was to become a successful international career, which was to be consistently controversial in Germany. As Gerd Gemünden and Mary Desjardins argue, many Germans viewed Dietrich's preference for vamps as untypically German because they deemed it symptomatic of the destabilizing "Americanization" that had been invading Germany since the early 1920s (Gemünden/ Desjardins, 5; see also Jelavich, 165–86). In the spirit of this argument, I would like to demonstrate that when the female protagonist in *Bomben auf Monte Carlo* masquerades as vamp, she ridicules what was perceived as the artificial and foreign, American vampness of the persona developed by Marlene Dietrich.

Brigitte Helm was only seventeen when she became instantly famous for her performance in *Metropolis*. In the following years Helm was consistently cast as a femme fatale in numerous German and European films. She performed this role in the silent *Alraune* (Henrik Galeen, 1927), *Die Jacht der sieben Sünden* (Yacht of Seven Sins; Jakob and Luise Fleck, 1928), *Abwege* (Devious Paths; G. W. Pabst, 1928), *Manolescu* (Viktor Tourjansky, 1929), *L'Argent* (Money; Marcel L'Herbier, 1929), and the talkie *Alraune* (Richard Oswald, 1930), among others. From these films Helm emerged as the European "Übervamp" (Feld) and the press often compared her to the two great screen seductresses of the time, Greta Garbo and Marlene Dietrich. According to Robert Müller, Brigitte Helm's heroines marked a fundamental shift in the iconography of the femme fatale. Unlike the dark-haired, slightly plump vamps embodied in German cinema of the early 1920s by actresses like Pola Negri and Lya de Putti, Brigitte Helm shifted the aesthetics of the femme fatale toward a new image that favored fair hair and a tall, athletic body. With the coming of talkies, Helm attempted to distance herself from her image as vamp. Although in the early 1930s she acted successfully in a number of comedies,[3] right until the end of her career (in 1935) Brigitte Helm was not able to shake the image of the robot femme fatale, the role that had made her an instant star.

Bomben auf Monte Carlo (1931)

The two protagonists of Hanns Schwarz's comedy, ship's commander Craddock (established film star Hans Albers) and Princess Yola I of Pontenero (newcomer Anna Sten) meet for the first time on the dance floor. Yola is there incognito and she seeks to punish Craddock for disobeying her orders to take her on a tour of the Mediterranean. She also seeks to seduce him because she has secretly overheard Craddock boast that the princess would not be able to compete in terms of beauty with Monte Carlo's women. It was to avoid acceding to the princess's request for a Mediterranean cruise that Craddock ordered his ship to sail to Monte Carlo for some recreation.

When Craddy, as his loyal friend and first officer Peter (Heinz Rühmann) calls him, enters Monte Carlo's casino, he does not know that his royal superior is also present in a garish disguise. Yola fails to seduce Craddock because of the artificiality of the femme fatale role she assumes, an artificiality that simultaneously satirizes what Hales considers the essential characteristics of the femme fatale, namely the criminal and the double, as well as the elaborate use of fashion accessories and makeup, which, according to Sannwald, are typical for vamp figures. Although not a criminal herself, Yola behaves in ways that are associated with criminality. For example, she does not remunerate Craddy and his crew for months and instead spends her country's finances on pleasure trips. Moreover, after she meets Craddock at the casino, she goads him into spending money at the roulette table, well aware that the cash he was betting is the sailors' salaries. Schwarz's comedy combines these negative aspects of the femme fatale with positive attributes, a combination that demonstrates the doubling typical for the vamp, albeit one with comic relief. Thus, while Yola does ask Craddy to buy her a pearl necklace, knowing both its exorbitant price and that he will make the purchase using the money meant to pay the sailors on his ship, she also attempts to undo the transaction by insisting that her request was merely a joke, that Craddy did not have the necessary cash, and by leaving the store hurriedly. The comic undertones of the scene rise from the fact that the necklace at stake had belonged to Yola, before, through a series of humorous circumstances, she sold it to ensure that Craddy and his crew would get paid. Furthermore, the humor of the situation is enhanced by the fact that Craddy does not know about Yola's royal identity and thus does not censure his ironic remarks about the princess. Thus, while for viewers Yola's comical doubling as vamp and regular woman as well as her transitions between regular woman and royalty are evident from the beginning of the film, Craddy never suspects any of this and finds out the truth only toward the end of the film, and then only because Yola herself reveals who she is.

Viewers know about Yola's royal identity and discover her presence at the casino before Craddy does. While he dances with an unknown blonde, the camera zooms in on a brunette — none other than Yola — languishing at a table, an apparition so overdone in terms of makeup, clothing, and gestures that it is utterly ridiculous. To increase her sex appeal, Yola applies the fashion advice she gleans from a book titled "How Do I Seduce Men? A Guide for Seductresses and Those Who Want to Become One" ("Wie verführe ich die Männer? Ein Leitfaden für Kokotten und solche, die es werden wollen"), which she confiscated from her chaperone. Yola follows the self-improvement book to the letter: she sheds the light brown, wavy bob, the demure makeup, and the loosely fitting dress she wears in previous scenes and transforms herself into a comically exaggerated and artificial femme fatale.

Yola's vamp performance starts with her ostentatious looks: she wears a white hat with ample, sloping black brims; a long white V-necked dress with black triangular appliqués over her breasts, and black elbow length evening gloves. Under her hat she sports a black hair strand curled up on her left cheek, hilarious in its dramatic swing. The curl on Yola's face is a visual send-up of American actress Clara Bow's trademark "kiss curls" ("Herrenwinker").[4] Bow's spectacular "Herrenwinker," made particularly popular in Germany with the release of her film *It* (Clarence C. Badger, 1927) in February 1929,[5] are used as a comic prop that hints at Yola's overdone appearance. The impression of exaggeration is reinforced by Yola's use of jewelry; she adorns her sleek gloves and alters their otherwise elegant appearance with numerous bracelets on both wrists and several rings on her fingers. The most spectacular modification towards vamp-ness happens to Yola's face, which is modeled to ridicule Marlene Dietrich. While Yola observes Craddock dancing, she assiduously studies the self-improvement booklet, and because she fails to catch his eye, she decides to optimize her sex appeal by imitating the picture featured on the manual's cover. Thus, Yola clasps a cigarette holder in her right hand and holds up her lorgnette with a pretentious gesture. Craddock's unresponsiveness amazes her. She frowns in disbelief, shrugs her shoulders, flings the boa away from her neck, consults the book and comes up with a solution: she attaches a beauty mark to her right cheek. Since this too fails to capture Craddy's attention, Yola maximizes her lure with a second beauty mark, which she places on the lower left corner of her mouth. Fashion-wise, Yola possesses all the attributes and accessories — heavy made-up eyes, large hat, boa, and cigarette holder — which, according to film historian Daniela Sannwald, define the prototypical vamp. However, the comical and exaggerated manner in which Yola employs these elements reveal her vamp performance as artificial.

Unlike Craddock, viewers have the privilege of observing the assembly of the vamp in detailed shots. The way Yola literally puts together her sex appeal by using clothes, jewelry, body posture, and makeup brings to mind associations with Fordist consumer culture. Fordism, a buzzword of the day stemming from America, promulgated, among other things, mass production based on the development of the assembly line. In Germany, Fordism was met with a variety of reactions, from approval to anxiety and repulsion (Nolan). Cultural commentator Siegfried Kracauer, for instance, asserted that the assembly line — and with it Fordism — depersonalized workers such that their bodies became governed by fragmentation and montage. *Bomben auf Monte Carlo* pokes fun at Fordist conveyor-belt practices when it presents the manner in which Yola assembles her vamp persona by combining set pieces from fashion and makeup. The image she creates is grotesque and ridiculous in its exaggeration, as emphasized by her use of not one but two beauty marks intended to enhance her appearance.

The artificiality of the persona Yola creates is further illustrated in facial details that satirize the vamps played by Marlene Dietrich. Like Dietrich's screen persona, Yola the vamp has long, curled eyelashes, her eyelids are contoured with dark liner, and she sports elongated, penciled, highly arched eyebrows. Camera angle and lighting reinforce the resemblance between Yola's appearance and Dietrich's face, from her makeup to the oval shape of her jawline. Yola further echoes Dietrich in the way she purses her lips, tucks in her chin, and tilts her forehead slightly forward, thus achieving a remarkable rendition of Dietrich's trademark elevated cheekbones (fig. 18.1). Overall, Yola's grotesque appearance curtails her power as femme fatale through the aesthetics of artificiality.[6] *Bomben auf Monte Carlo* satirizes Dietrich by showing that her vamp characters are artificial and manufactured. In addition to ridiculing and distancing itself from Dietrich, the film seeks to establish Sten as the new face to fill the space Dietrich had vacated with her departure to Hollywood.

In his discussion of the star system in Weimar Cinema, Joseph Garncarz argues that in the 1930s studios employed a two-step strategy in launching film careers. They first had newcomers imitate well-established actors, and then took steps to distinguish the new star from the original (Garncarz, 104). In this context one should consider the linguistic closeness between the name of Sten's character in *Bomben auf Monte Carlo*, Yola, and Dietrich's character in *Der blaue Engel*, Lola. Yola is so outrageously vampish à la Dietrich, so exaggerated in her Dietrich looks and gestures, that the viewer cannot help but realize that the vamp-ness is décor, constructed and artificial. Sten is Dietrich to the extent to which this association sparks laughter. In laughing at Anna Sten as a vamp look-alike of Marlene Dietrich, one laughs with Yola at Lola and with Sten at Dietrich.[7] Nowhere is this laughter harder than in the scene where Sten's masquerade of Dietrich culminates with Yola taking action against Craddock's female dance partner. After she peruses the chapter "Battling Competition" in her self-help book, Yola, unseen by others, pulls the skirt off Craddy's dance partner. As the woman leaves flustered, Yola approaches him with a big smile and places his hand on her waist, without saying a word. She points her head to the dance floor and Craddy finally realizes what she wants, and they start dancing.

Fig. 18.1. Princess Yola I of Pontenero (Anna Sten), all dolled up as a vamp, mimics Marlene Dietrich in Bomben auf Monte Carlo *(Hanns Schwarz, 1931). Screenshot.*

Here Sten adds another model to her performance of vamp-ness: in the dance scene, Yola's body language emulates the well-known dance mannerisms of Helm's femmes fatales. The vamps played by Helm dance repeatedly, and when they do, they look as if they are joined to their respective partner at the midsection, while their upper body is turned away. The result is a strangely distorted and somewhat paradoxical body posture that oscillates between desire and avoidance, a simultaneous invitation to and suspension of passion characteristic of the manner of seduction of Helm's characters (Müller, 275). As Yola and Craddock start dancing, she brings her waist and lower body closer to him, while she keeps her torso tilted backward and hence at a distance from Craddy. With eyes half closed, chin tilted inwards, by which means her forehead, her arched eyebrows, and her cheekbones are prominently displayed, Anna Sten's performance now evokes both Marlene Dietrich and Brigitte Helm, as Yola sways to the music while throwing Craddy surreptitious glances from underneath her long, fake lashes. When she talks to Craddock, she slants her head backward in an unexpected semi-circular, semi-angular motion that recalls the erratic head movements of the robot-vamp Maria in *Metropolis*.[8] During

Fig. 18.2. Dancing with Captain Craddock (Hans Albers), Yola's distorted body posture evokes Brigitte Helm's dance mannerisms as the robot-vamp Maria in Fritz Lang's Metropolis *(1927).* Bomben auf Monte Carlo *(Hanns Schwarz, 1931). Screenshot.*

the dance, Craddock is not particularly interested in Yola's conversation. In fact, he hums a tune rather than talk to her, and when he does address her, his reply is terse. Unlike the vamps played by Helm and Dietrich, who are idiosyncratically mysterious and aloof, and who never smile, when Sten performs the femme fatale, she smiles tirelessly and thus mocks the enigmatic and stereotypical aloofness of vamps.

When the music stops, Yola once again strikes a distorted pose. She turns halfway from Craddy, raises her left shoulder and arm peculiarly high, arches her back and claps her hands with large, slow motions in a posture that mimics Helm's angular gestures as the robot Maria (fig. 18.2). Little by little, Craddock tiptoes away from her. He does not find Yola appealing, but rather showy and embarrassing, as is suggested by his hurried movement away from her. The vamp-ness Yola displays during the dance, her overall artificiality, her affected head motions, her overdone facial expressions, and her relentless smile clearly put Craddock off. It is interesting to note that in this specific scene Yola's use of fashion is a humorous lesson about how not to use makeup, jewelry, and clothes, and in this sense the sequence satirizes Weimar's film genre of the fashion farce. As Ganeva asserts, the fashion farce ("Konfektionskomödie") presented audiences with the latest trends in terms of wardrobe and served as a source of inspiration alongside magazines and fashion shows. With its depiction of the grotesque use of fashion, this scene in Schwarz's comedy emerges as a parody of the fashion farce.

Yola's vamp image is finally dismantled through a process in which Craddy literally takes her persona apart. When he accidentally discovers Yola's self-help booklet and she starts crying, Craddock holds her and removes her hat. To his surprise, the hat comes off together with the dark-haired wig, and he discovers a different person under what he humorously calls Yola's "war paint" ("Kriegsbemalung"), a phrase that clearly indicates both the artificiality and the potential menace of Yola's vamp persona. From this point on, Schwarz's comedy contrasts Yola's grotesque persona as vamp with Yola's "real" personality as an elegant and sensual woman, although Craddy does not know about her royal identity until the film ends. The new Yola sports less makeup and jewelry, and the opulent and ridiculous details of her vamp persona are replaced with a more subtle physical appearance and a wardrobe that is sensual, feminine, and matter-of-factly modern. This visual change stylizes Yola into an object of admiration for Craddock and viewers alike. In the end, Schwarz's comedy uses Anna Sten's satirical performance to mock Helm's and Dietrich's vamps, without however, altogether distancing itself from the figure of the vamp. The film merely replaces the un-German and the mechanical seductiveness of a Dietrich and Helm with the more traditionally feminine seductive power of the newcomer Anna Sten. Paradoxically, only one year after the release of Schwarz's highly successful comedy and in light of her impressive performance in Erich Engel and Fedor Ozep's film *Der Mörder Dimitri Karamasoff* (The Murderer Dimitri Karamasoff, 1931), Anna Sten followed Marlene Dietrich's path: she left Berlin for Hollywood. Film mogul Sam Goldwyn was looking for a second Greta Garbo, and Sten became his pupil in this challenge.[9] However, although she appeared in some films and received good reviews from critics, Sten's Hollywood career did not take off.

Marion, das gehört sich nicht (1932)

Like Schwarz's film, E. W. Emo's[10] comedy *Marion, das gehört sich nicht* subjects the image of the vamp to rational scrutiny by mocking the archetypal detachment of the femme fatale and demythologizing her poses, and by replacing the image of the vamp with a demure model of femininity. Moreover, Emo's comedy satirizes melodramas and their preoccupation with domesticating the vamp, a theme fundamental to a number of melodramas of the time.[11] In Schwarz's comedy, the new would-be vamp Anna Sten is the central female figure. By way of contrast, Emo's film reduces the importance of the vamp at the level of the plot: Emo's vamp Gussy (Olly Gebauer) plays a supporting role as a necessary contrast figure for the main female character, Marion Satorius (newcomer Magda Schneider).

Tall, svelte, and blonde, Gussy is a young woman in search of a place to live. It is her occupation that identifies her as a vamp: like Marlene Dietrich's character Lola in *Der blaue Engel,* and Brigitte Helm's figure Alma in Richard Oswald's talkie *Alraune,* Gussy is a bar singer.[12] Her physical appearance and fashion sense also mark Gussy as a vamp. She wears a tight white dress cut low in both the front and the back, which highly eroticizes her slender figure. She flirts with great ease with men on- and offstage and enjoys being the center of attention. Gussy receives unexpected help in her search for an apartment from Brammel (Julius Falkenstein), an elderly man who works part-time as waiter at the same bar and part-time as butler to the famous but poor painter Kurt Bach (Hermann Thimig). Brammel offers Gussy a room, provided she pays rent upfront, which she does and thus moves in the same day. What follows is a short, masterful scene that mocks attempts at domesticating the vamp. By satirizing this theme, Emo's comedy responds to the fatigue with melodramas and their iconic heroine, the vamp, and introduces a new, more demure figure to replace the femme fatale. The morning after she moves in, Gussy shares a domestic moment with Brammel. While he washes dishes, she dries them and professes with a smile that she prefers house chores to being a vamp. Brammel meets this sudden affirmation of domestic life with calm and replies that she can start working for his employer at any time. Gussy laughs hard at this reply, a reaction that hints that her avowal of domesticity is casual and superficial. Furthermore, her reaction illustrates that the idea of demythologizing the image of the vamp and rationalizing it in the domestic realm is literally laughable.

Emo's film contains several scenes that invite laughter at the vamp. In one scene, for instance, Gussy assumes that Kurt Bach, Brammel's employer, follows her home because he is inescapably attracted to her. Even when Kurt tells her curtly that he lives in the same building, Gussy is certain that he is under her spell and that he cannot help but follow her. Not even Kurt's retort that he owns the apartment in which he and Brammel allow her to rent a room shakes Gussy's conviction about her seductive power over the artist. Regardless of Kurt's explanations, Gussy's confidence in her attractiveness remains unshakable; the resoluteness of this conviction, despite all logical arguments to the contrary, makes her a figure of satire. Gussy's last appearance in the film is the moment at which she is most intensely ridiculed. She is angry that Brammel has asked her to leave the house, and she storms out, shouting that she will take him to court, should he not pay back her rent. Gussy's menacing words, however, fail to yield their intended effect because of the physical humor of the situation. When she makes the threat, she is overloaded with boxes that contain her belongings. The seriousness of her utterance is satirized by the comical postures she has to assume in order to balance her boxes and prevent them from falling. Viewers are no longer invited to admire the vamp in elegant, seductive dance moves à la Helm and Dietrich. Instead, they are encouraged to laugh at the femme fatale as she is shouting and comically struggling with her packages. With Gussy, the vamp loses her status as object of desire and seduction, and literally leaves the scene as an object of laughter and ridicule.

Marion, das gehört sich nicht replaces the collapsing image of the vamp with a new model of feminity, embodied by the main female character, Marion. From her first appearance in the film, Magda Schneider's Marion is visually associated with the New Woman of the Weimar years. She wears a knee-length dress with a low waistline and a cloche hat, the typical fashion accessory of the New Woman (Hake, 188–89), and she drives her own car. The latter is a signifier of her privileged social position as the only daughter of a tycoon in the soap business. Marion is also a representation of the "automobile Amazon" ("Automobil-Amazone"), an image that, according to scholar Julia Bertschik, abounded in the Weimar German imaginary (Bertschik, 246). Bertschik argues that in the 1920s the connection between woman and technology led to images that combined the female body with technological creations such as automobiles, and these images spurred a fear of and attraction to the New Woman (von Ankum, 11). In Marion's case, her physical appearance subdues reactions of fear. She wears dresses and skirts that go to her knees, her jackets are elegant and fit loosely, and her svelte, androgynous figure strikes one as innocent, almost childlike. Magda Schneider's girl-next-door charm differs greatly from the sex appeal of a Marlene Dietrich or Brigitte Helm often presented in sensuous, form-fitting skirts and gowns. Moreover, the femininity and finesse of Marion's wardrobe are indicative of the emergence in the early 1930s of a softer and more demure female fashion, as suggested by Hake (193) and Guenther (85).

Die Gräfin von Monte Christo (1932)

With the emergence of talkies, Brigitte Helm sought to distance herself from her vamp image. In Hans Behrendt's melodrama *Gloria* (1931), for instance, Helm's performance combines images of the devoted wife with a dance scene in which she turns into a femme fatale.[13] This duality echoes her emblematic role in *Metropolis*. The similarities go beyond the name Maria and the same leading man Gustav Fröhlich, and revolve around the dual essence of the Maria characters. In both *Gloria* and *Metropolis* Helm plays a character who is half saint, half vamp, and in both films the saint wins over the seductress. Furthermore, in *Metropolis* and in *Gloria* Helm's characters are defined by the sexualizing gaze of her male audience during a dance. Interestingly, Helm herself does not recognize the twofold quality of her performance in Behrendt's film. In an interview published in 1931, she declares that her role in *Gloria* was different from her usual vamp figures, and that with it she hoped to gain distance from the femme fatale type.[14]

Like Hans Behrendt's melodrama *Gloria*, Karl Hartl's comedy *Die Gräfin von Monte Christo*, Brigitte Helm's bestgrossing talkie (Semler, 115), aims at disassociating the actress from her image as vamp. Herbert Ihering, renowned journalist and both theatre and film critic at that time, lauds the naturalness of Helm's performance in Hartl's film (quoted in Dahlke, 295). Decades later Fred Gehler and, most recently, Daniel Semler share Ihering's appreciation for Helm's artistry (quoted in Dahlke, 295; Semler, 115). I agree with Gehler and Semler that, in terms of narrative, in Hartl's film Helm is cast against the type established by her vamp roles. However, I assert that, contrary to Ihering's, Gehler's, and Semler's claims, Helm's vamp-ness lives on in the mannerisms and visual details of her performance.

In Hartl's comedy, whose title evokes Alexandre Dumas's successful adventure novel, *Le comte de Monte Cristo* (The Count of Monte Cristo, 1844), Helm plays aspiring movie starlet Jeanette Heider. Upset that her journalist boyfriend Stephan (Mathias Wieman) has broken up with her, and tired of the small parts she gets, Jeanette drives away from a movie set in the car she uses for her short role as Countess of Monte Cristo. Her best friend Mimi (Lucie Englisch), film extra and the countess's maid in the aforementioned scene, rides along. Jeanette and Mimi leave Vienna and drive until, at nightfall, they stop at the exclusive winter resort of Semmering, where their suitcases, props from the movie set, lead employees to believe the two women are indeed a countess from Monte Cristo and her maid. In the role of the countess, Jeanette meets the charming Russian nobleman Rumowski (Rudolf Forster), and they fall in love.

Jeanette is troubled by her masquerade as the countess and she decides to tell Rumowski the truth during the New Year's celebration organized at the resort. Throughout the lavish festivities, Jeanette and Rumowski enjoy their food, each other's company, and the view of the dancing couples. Although the scene is propitious for dance with its romantic atmosphere, the slow music, and couples dancing, when Rumowski asks the countess for a dance, she refuses. Narratively, the countess's refusal is explained through her fear that Baron (Gustaf Gründgens), a thief who discovered her masquerade and whose offer to work together she had refused, may notice her and alert authorities. The scene in which she declins to dance is also fundamental for understanding how the film seeks to dissociate Helm from her image as vamp. In films like *Metropolis, Alraune,* and *Gloria,* dance is the standard seduction medium of Helm's vamps. When Helm does not dance in *Die Gräfin von Monte Christo,* the film sets out to create a distance from her image as a femme fatale. However, the attempt to separate Helm from her vamp image fails due to the gestural and behavioral codification of her performance as a femme fatale throughout the entire film. For instance, Jeanette stands out visually from the beginning among the other film extras: she is the tallest and the best dressed, and the camera rests repeatedly on her face. Furthermore, there is a behavioral detachment in the way Jeanette interacts with her colleagues, her boyfriend, the film director, and Mimi. This is suggested through her large, imprecise hand gestures, and through the way she looks at people but does not always notice them. In contrast to vivacious Mimi, who has a joke and a smile for everyone and all situations, Jeanette never laughs and remains strangely detached from people and places, a detachment that harks back to Helm's vamp roles.

Helm's performance as the countess is also marked by aloofness, particularly when she appears alongside Rumowski. Despite their attraction to one another, Rumowski and the countess remain awkwardly detached and cold. They do not kiss, they do not embrace, and they do not talk about their emotions. The fact that there is no display of affection or desire between two characters supposedly enamored of each other illustrates the film's effort to sanitize Helm's vamp image and downplay her seductiveness. The viewer is to believe that Rumowski and the countess are in love, but there can be no display of their emotions, and particularly not of their erotic desire, since this would bring up associations with Helm's vamp-ness (fig. 18.3). Paradoxically, the effort to separate Helm from her image as vamp achieves the very opposite. Although plot-wise the film focuses on Jeanette, poor and innocent, impersonating a countess, and concludes with her reconciliation with her former boyfriend Stephan, in terms of performance Helm's double role is as vamp-ish as her femmes fatales ever were.

Conclusion

In early 1930s Germany, comedy was a flourishing film genre that provided more than an escape from reality. Comedies represented a creative stance against the genre of silent era melodrama and its central figure, the vamp. Hanns Schwarz's *Bomben auf Monte Carlo* and E. W. Emo's *Marion, das gehört sich nicht* are remarkable comedies, because they subject the stereotypical image of the vamp to rational scrutiny by employing humor, irony, satire, and ridicule. In these comedies Brigitte Helm and Marlene Dietrich, the German vamp icons of the late 1920s and early 1930s, are

Fig. 18.3. Love without emotional or physical closeness between the fake "Countess of Monte Cristo" (Brigitte Helm) and con-man Rumowski (Rudolf Forster) in Die Gräfin von Monte Christo *(Karl Hartl, 1932). Deutsche Kinemathek Berlin.*

thoroughly demythologized through the satirical use of makeup, fashion, dance mannerisms, and body postures. While Schwarz's comedy mocks Helm's and Dietrich's femmes fatales and introduces instead the new quasi-vamp Anna Sten, in Emo's film the vamp type finds a replacement in a figure that blends the attitudes and attributes of the emancipated New Woman and those of the sexually innocent girl next door. Emo's comedy pushes the vamp off the cinematic scene and shows that her exit is accompanied by laughter, a laughter that gains control over the destructive seductiveness of the femme fatale. Unlike Schwarz's and Emo's films, Karl Hartl's comedy *Die Gräfin von Monte Christo* does not use humor and satire in its representation of the femme fatale, and I have argued that this is part of the reasons why the film does not succeed in propelling Brigitte Helm beyond her image as a vamp.

In manifold and multilayered ways, these romantic comedies of mistaken identity seek to dismantle the outdated stereotype of the vamp and to replace it with something new. These genre films derive much of their popular appeal, and their persistent charm, from the degree to which they succeed in this enterprise. At the very least, they point to the complexities and contradictions that arose in the late Weimar Republic, as a society shaken by perpetual crisis found itself engaged in efforts to renegotiate ever-changing definitions of femininity and to reconfigure new constellations of gender relations.

Notes

The films I discuss in this essay, Hanns Schwarz's *Bomben auf Monte Carlo* (Bombs over Monte Carlo, 1931), Karl Hartl's *Die Gräfin von Monte Christo* (The Countess of Monte Cristo, 1932), and E. W. Emo's *Marion, das gehört sich nicht* (Marion, This Is Not Proper, 1932), as well as Richard Oswald's *Alraune* (Mandrake, 1930), are available for viewing at the Bundesarchiv-Filmarchiv Berlin, Fehrbelliner Platz. *Bomben auf Monte Carlo*, Henrik Galeen's *Alraune* (Mandrake, 1927), and Hans Behrendt's *Gloria* (1931) are available for rent on video from Heidelberg House: The German Language Video Center in Indianapolis, Indiana and at http://www.germanvideo.com/. More recently, *Bomben auf Monte Carlo* has become available for purchase in DVD format in the series "Deutsche Filmklassiker" produced by Black Hill Pictures GmbH, order number 9913495. Other films to which I refer, such as Fritz Lang's *Metropolis* (1927), Clarence G. Badger's *It* (1927), and G. W. Pabst's *Tagebuch einer Verlorenen* (Diary of a Lost Girl, 1929) are available for purchase at www.kino.com.

[1] Elsaesser/Wedel; Jacobsen/Bock; Elsaesser, *Weimar Cinema*; Koebner. On the development of German comedy films from the 1910s until the present, see Horak. For a thorough reevaluation of German comedies after the First World War, see Elsaesser, *Second Life*.

[2] Unknown author, unknown source, "Alraune" (5 December 1930). Folder 463 of the Bildarchiv at the Bundesarchiv-Filmarchiv Berlin.

[3] Andrea Böhm notes that in the 1930s Brigitte Helm was successful in the comedies *Eine von uns* (One of Us; Johannes Meyer, 1932), *Der Läufer von Marathon* (The Marathon Runner; E. A. Dupont, 1933), and *Inge und die Millionen* (Inge and the Millions; Erich Engel, 1933).

[4] Georg Herzberg talks about Clara Bow's "Herrenwinker" in his review of her film *It*. The German compound-noun "Herrenwinker" translates into English as "waving to gentlemen." The German noun humorously indicates the wearer's intention of attracting men's attention, a meaning that is not referenced in the English form "kiss curls."

[5] *It* tells the story of an attractive shop assistant who falls in love with and eventually gets the young millionaire she loves. The film premiered in New York on 5 February 1927, and opened in Germany two years later, on 25 February 1929.

[6] Erica Carter notes that in Germany in the late 1930s, Marlene Dietrich's vamp image was reviled for its "emptiness," "lack of meaning," and excessive visual stylization (77). Carter asserts that Dietrich was satirized for the first time in December 1937, in an article that appeared in the daily *Film-Kurier*. As I demonstrate, Dietrich was a public object of aesthetic satire as early as 31 August 1931, the day when *Bomben auf Monte Carlo* was released.

[7] In his review of the film, Herbert Ihering does not address Anna Sten's masquerade of Dietrich. This is striking, since in his article "Von Jannings bis zu einem Pseudonym" published on 23 January 1932, almost half a year after the release of *Bomben auf Monte Carlo,* Ihering clearly acknowledges that Sten's acting is linked to Dietrich's and warns that it is dangerous to train Sten as a new Dietrich.

[8] In *Metropolis* the camera focuses on Maria's zigzagging head movements in the scene in which she beguiles her all-male audience with her dancing as well as the sequence in which she incites the dancing upper class to "watch the world go to the devil," while workers bemoan what they fear is the loss of their children to invading floods.

[9] Biographical information from the special features of the DVD *Bomben auf Monte Carlo.*

[10] E. W. Emo is an abbreviated form for Emerich Walter Emo, the stage name of the Austrian director Emerich Josef Wojtek.

[11] Alexander Korda's *Madame wünscht keine Kinder* (Madame Does Not Want Children, 1927), Henrik Galeen's *Alraune* (1927), and G. W. Pabst's *Tagebuch einer Verlorenen* (Diary of a Lost Girl, 1929) are some of the melodramas of the time that present different ways of domesticating the vamp. The femme fatale dedicates herself to motherhood (*Madame wünscht keine Kinder*) or love and marriage (*Alraune*), or she helps change the life of fallen women through her kindness and altruism (*Tagebuch einer Verlorenen*).

[12] In Richard Oswald's *Alraune* Brigitte Helm played not only the vamp Alraune but also Alma, Alraune's singer-prostitute mother. Alma's onstage song-and-dance performance of the tango "When Men Cheat on Me" ("Wenn mich die Männer betrügen") strongly reminds one of Lola's performance of "Falling in Love" ("Ich bin von Kopf bis Fuss") in *Der blaue Engel.*

[13] In *Gloria*, Brigitte Helm plays Maria, wife of renowned pilot Georg Köhler (Gustav Fröhlich). Georg suspects that Maria is having an affair with his friend Jonny (Fritz Kampers); this causes him to leave his family and to embark on a dangerous flight over the ocean. Toward the end of the film, however, he finds out that Maria was faithful, and they rekindle their love.

[14] The interview appeared in *LichtBildBühne* (22 September 1931).

Works Cited

Anon. "Alraune." 5 December 1930. Folder 463, Bildarchiv of the Bundesarchiv-Filmarchiv Berlin.

Bergfelder, Tim, Erica Carter, and Deniz Göktürk, eds. *The German Cinema Book.* London: BFI, 2002.

Bertschik, Julia. *Mode und Moderne: Kleidung als Spiegel des Zeitgeistes in der deutschsprachigen Literatur (1770–1945).* Cologne: Böhlau, 2005.

Böhm, Andrea. "Brigitte Helm — Heilige und Vamp." In *Grenzgänger zwischen Theater und Kino: Schauspielerporträts aus dem Berlin der zwanziger Jahre*, edited by Knut Hickethier, 195–212. Berlin: Mythos Berlin, 1986.

Carter, Erica. "Marlene Dietrich — The Prodigal Daughter." In Bergfelder, Carter, and Göktürk, 71–80.

Dahlke, Günther, ed. *Deutsche Spielfilme von den Anfängen bis 1933: Ein Filmführer.* 2nd ed. Berlin: Henschel, 1993.

Doane, Mary Ann. *Femmes Fatales: Feminism, Film Theory, Psychoanalysis.* New York: Routledge, 1991.

Elsaesser, Thomas, ed. *A Second Life: German Cinema's First Decade.* Amsterdam: Amsterdam UP, 1996.

———. *Weimar Cinema and After: Germany's Historical Imaginary.* London: Routledge, 2000.

Elsaesser, Thomas, and Michael Wedel, eds. *The BFI Companion to German Cinema.* London: BFI, 1999.

Feld, Hans. "Manolescu." *Film-Kurier,* 23 August 1929.

Ganeva, Mila. *Women in Weimar Fashion: Discourses and Displays in German Culture, 1918–1933.* Rochester, NY: Camden House, 2008.

Garncarz, Joseph. "Playing Garbo: How Marlene Dietrich Conquered Hollywood." In Gemünden and Desjardins, 103–18.

Gemünden, Gerd, and Mary Desjardins, eds. *Dietrich Icon.* Durham, NC: Duke UP, 2007.

Guenther, Irene. *Nazi Chic? Fashioning Women in the Third Reich.* Oxford: Berg, 2004.

Hake, Sabine. "In the Mirror of Fashion." In von Ankum, 185–201.

Hales, Barbara. "Projecting Trauma: The Femme Fatale in Weimar and Hollywood Film Noir." In *Women in German Yearbook* 23 (2007): 224–43.

Herzberg, Georg. Review of *It. Film-Kurier,* 26 February 1929. Quoted in Hoeppner, 43.

Hoeppner, Klaus, ed. *City Girls: Frauenbilder im Stummfilm.* Filmheft 11. Berlin: Bertz + Fischer, 2007.

Horak, Jan-Christopher. "German Film Comedy." In Bergfelder, Carter, and Göktürk, 29–38.

Ihering, Herbert. "Von Jannings bis zu einem Pseudonym." *Von Reinhardt bis Brecht: Vier Jahrzehnte Theater und Film.* Berlin: Aufbau Verlag, 1961.

Jacobsen, Wolfgang, and Hans-Michael Bock, eds. *Der komische Kintopp.* Cinegraph Film Materialien 10. Hamburg: CineGraph, 1997.

Jatho, Gabriele, and Rainer Rother, eds. *City Girls: Frauenbilder im Stummfilm.* Berlin: Bertz + Fischer, 2007.

Jelavich, Peter. *Berlin Cabaret.* Cambridge, MA: Harvard UP, 1993.

Koebner, Thomas, ed. *Diesseits der 'Dämonischen Leinwand': Neue Perspektiven auf das späte Weimarer Kino.* Augsburg: Richard Boorberg, 2003.

Korte, Helmut. *Der Spielfilm und das Ende der Weimarer Republik: Ein rezeptionshistorischer Versuch.* Göttingen: Vandenhoeck & Ruprecht, 1998.

Kracauer, Siegfried. "Das Ornament der Masse." In *Das Ornament der Masse: Essays,* 50–64. Frankfurt am Main: Suhrkamp, 1977.

Müller, Robert. "Von der Kunst der Verführung: Der Vamp." In Koebner, 259–80.

Nolan, Mary. "The Infatuation with Fordism." In *Visions of Modernity: American Business and the Modernization of Germany,* 30–57. Oxford: Oxford UP, 1994.

Petro, Patrice. *Joyless Streets: Women and Melodramatic Representation in Weimar Germany.* Princeton, NJ: Princeton UP, 1989.

Sannwald, Daniela. "Überlebenskünstlerinnen: Frauenrollen im Film der zehner und zwanziger Jahre." In Jatho and Rother, 14–51.

Semler, Daniel. *Brigitte Helm: Der Vamp des deutschen Films.* Munich: Belleville Verlag, 2008.

von Ankum, Katharina, ed. *Women in the Metropolis: Gender and Modernity in Weimar Culture.* Berkeley: U of California P, 1997.

von Thüna, Ulrich. "Die deutsche Filmkomödie der Depressionsjahre, 1930–33." In *Photokina-Katalog,* 317–25. Cologne: Messe- und Ausstellungsgesellschaft, 1980.

Wager, Jans. *Dangerous Dames: Women and Representation in the Weimar Street Film and Film Noir.* Athens: Ohio UP, 1999.

Filmography

Abschied—So sind die Menschen (Departure—This is How People Are, 1930)
Director: Robert Siodmak.
Producer: Robert Duday, for Universum Film A.G. (Ufa).
Script: Emmerich Pressburger, Irma von Cube.
Cinematography: Eugen Schüfftan.
Art Direction: Max Knaake.
Music: Erwin Bootz.
Length: 1,991 meters (= ca. 73 minutes).
Cast: Brigitte Horney (Hella), Aribert Mog (Peter), Emilie Unda (the landlady), Vladimir Sokoloff (the baron).
Censorship record: B.26590 (14 August 1930), restricted for minors ("Jugendverbot").
Premiere: 25 August 1930, U. T. Kurfürstendamm, Berlin.
Available from Deutsche Kinemathek Museum für Film und Fernsehen, Berlin. German intertitles only.

Alraune (Mandrake; English release titles *A Daughter of Destiny/Unholy Love*, 1927)
Director: Henrik Galeen.
Producer: Ama Film GmbH, Berlin.
Script: Henrik Galeen, based on the novel by Hanns Heinz Ewers.
Cinematography: Franz Planer.
Art Direction: Max Heilbronner, Walter Reimann.
Music: Willy Schmidt-Gentner.
Length: 3,302 meters (= ca. 108 minutes).
Cast: Brigitte Helm (Alraune), Paul Wegener (Professor ten Brinken), Ivan Petrovich (Frank Braun).
Censorship record: B.17784 (16 January 1928), restricted for minors ("Jugendverbot").
Premiere: 25 January 1928, Capitol, Berlin.
Available from Bundesarchiv-Filmarchiv Berlin (German intertitles only). VHS tape (with English intertitles) available from www.facets.org. A low-quality version, in ten segments with English intertitles, can be found streamed online on www.youtube.com.

Das alte Gesetz (Ancient Law, 1923)
Director: E. A. Dupont.
Producer: Comedia Film, Berlin.
Script: Paul Reno.
Cinematography: Theodor Sparkuhl.
Art Direction: Alfred Junge, Curt Kahle.
Length: 3,028 meters (= ca. 128 minutes).
Cast: Ernst Deutsch (Baruch Mayer), Henny Porten (Archduchess Elisabeth Theresa), Hermann Vallentin (Heinrich Laube), Margarete Schlegel (Esther), Avrom Morewski (Rabbi Mayer).
Censorship record: B.07801 (18 October 1923).
Premiere: 29 October 1923, Marmorhaus, Berlin.
Available from Deutsche Kinemathek Museum für Film und Fernsehen, Berlin (35 mm print: restored version, Deutsche Kinemathek 1986). German intertitles only.

Anders als die Andern (Different from the Others, 1919)
Director: Richard Oswald.
Producer: Richard-Oswald-Film GmbH, Berlin.
Script: Richard Oswald, Magnus Hirschfeld.
Cinematography: Max Faßbender.
Art Direction: Emil Linke.
Length: 2,115 meters (ca. 90 minutes; original version).
Cast: Conrad Veidt (Paul Körner), Fritz Schulz (Kurt Sivers), Anita Berber (Else, Kurt's sister), Reinhold Schünzel (Franz Bollek), Magnus Hirschfeld (medical consultant).
Censorship record: 16 October 1920, banned for public screenings, restricted to medical/scientific/educational settings.
Premiere: 24 May 1919, Apollo-Theater, Berlin (press preview); 30 May 1919, Prinzess-Theater, Berlin.
Available on DVD (restored version of the surviving 51 minutes, with English intertitles), Edition Filmmuseum Munich, www.edition-filmmuseum.com.

Bomben auf Monte Carlo (Bombs over Monte Carlo; released in the United States as *Monte Carlo Madness*, 1931)
Director: Hanns Schwarz.
Producer: Erich Pommer, for Ufa, Berlin.
Script: Hans Müller, Franz Schulz.
Cinematography: Günther Rittau, Konstantin Tschet.
Art Direction: Erich Kettelhut.
Editor: Willy Zeyn jun.
Music: Werner Richard Heymann.
Length: 3,032 meters (= ca. 101 minutes).

Cast: Hans Albers (Captain Craddock), Anna Sten (Queen Yola I of Pontenero), Heinz Rühmann (Peter), Kurt Gerron (director of the casino), Peter Lorre (Pawlitschek), Otto Wallburg (prime minister).
Censorship record: B.29670 (24 August 1931), restricted for minors ("Jugendverbot").
Premiere: 31 August 1931, Ufa-Palast am Zoo, Berlin.
Available from Bundesarchiv-Filmarchiv, Berlin (German only). Also available from www.blackhillpictures.de (DVD; Warner Home Video, German only, no English subtitles).

Das Cabinet des Dr. Caligari (The Cabinet of Dr. Caligari, 1920)
Director: Robert Wiene.
Producer: Erich Pommer, Rudolf Meinert, Decla-Film (Berlin).
Script: Carl Mayer, Hans Janowitz.
Cinematography: Willy Hameister.
Art Direction: Hermann Warm, Walter Reimann, Walter Röhrig.
Music: Guiseppe Becce.
Length: 1,703 meters (= ca. 67 minutes).
Cast: Werner Krauß (Caligari), Conrad Veidt (Cesare), Lil Dagover (Jane), Friedrich Fehér (Francis), Hans Heinrich von Twardowski (Alan).
Censorship record: B.01498 (11 March 1921), restricted for minors ("Jugendverbot").
Premiere: 26 February 1920, Marmorhaus, Berlin.
Available from Kino International, www.kino.com (DVD with English intertitles).

Diagonalsymphonie (alternate title, *Symphonie diagonale*, Diagonal Symphony, 1924)
Director: Viking Eggeling.
Cinematography: Viking Eggeling, Erna Niemeyer.
Length: 145 meters (= ca. 7 minutes).
Censorship record: B.10335 (21 April 1925).
Premiere: 3 May 1925, U. T. Kurfürstendamm, Berlin, as part of the matinee "Der absolute Film."
Available from Kino International, www.kino.com (on *Avant-Garde: Experimental Cinema of the 1920s and 1930s*), DVD with English subtitles.

Die entfesselte Menschheit (Humanity Unleashed, 1920)
Director: Joseph Delmont.
Producer: Max Nivelli, Nivo-Film Company GmbH, Berlin.
Script: Joseph Delmont, based on a novel by Max Glass.
Cinematography: Gustave Preiss, Emil Schünemann.
Art Direction: Willi A. Hermann, Paul Lachenauer, E. A. Zirkel.

Length: 2,453 meters (= ca. 98 minutes).
Cast: Paul Hartmann (Michael Clarenbach), Eugen Klöpfer (Karenow), Carl de Vogt (Winterstein), Trude Hoffmann (Rita, Clarenbach's wife), Marion Illing (Camilla, Winterstein's lover), Hermann Bachmann (Turenius), Rosa Valetti (prostitute).
Censorship record: B.43692 (21 August 1920).
Premiere: 19 November 1920, Marmorhaus, Berlin.
The film has not survived, but large parts were reused in *Einigkeit und Recht und Freiheit* (Unity and Law and Freedom; Joseph Delmont, 1926), a nitrate copy of which is available at Bundesarchiv-Filmarchiv Berlin (German intertitles only).

Film ist Rhythmus, Film is Rhythm, 1921)
see *Rhythmus 21* (Rhythm 21, 1921)

Geschlecht in Fesseln (Fettered Sexuality; released in the United States as *Sex in Chains*, 1928)
Director: Wilhelm Dieterle.
Producer: Leo Meyer, Essem-Film & Star Film, Berlin.
Script: Herbert Juttke, Georg C. Klaren.
Cinematography: Walter Robert Lach.
Art Direction: Max Knaake, Fritz Maurischat.
Music: Pasquale Perris (orchestra), Emil Sagawe (organ).
Length: 2,654 meters (= ca. 107 minutes).
Cast: Wilhelm Dieterle (Franz Sommer), Mary Johnson (Helene Sommer), Paul Henckels (Helene's father), Hans Heinrich von Twardowski (Alfred), Gunnar Tolnaes (Steinau).
Censorship record: B.20390 (10 October 1928), restricted for minors ("Jugendverbot").
Premiere: 24 October 1928, Tauentzienpalast, Berlin.
Available from Kino International, www.kino.com (DVD with English intertitles).

Der Golem, wie er in die Welt kam (The Golem, How He Came into the World, 1920)
Director: Paul Wegener.
Producer: Paul Davidson, Projektions-A.G. "Union" (PAGU), Berlin.
Script: Paul Wegener, Henrik Galeen.
Cinematography: Karl Freund.
Art Direction: Hans Poelzig, Kurt Richter.
Music: Hans Landsberger.
Length: 1,922 meters (= ca. 86 minutes).
Cast: Paul Wegener (Golem), Albert Steinrück (Rabbi Löw), Lyda Salmonova (Mirjam, Löw's daughter), Ernst Deutsch (Famulus), Otto

Gebühr (Emperor Rudolf II), Lothar Müthel (Count Florian), Loni Nest (little girl).
Censorship record: B.00613 (21 October 1920), restricted for minors ("Jugendverbot").
Premiere: 29 October 1920, Ufa-Palast am Zoo, Berlin.
Available from Kino International, www.kino.com (DVD with English intertitles).

Die Gräfin von Monte Christo (The Countess of Monte Cristo, 1932)
Director: Karl Hartl.
Producer: Gregor Rabinowitsch, for Ufa, Berlin.
Script: Walter Reisch.
Cinematography: Franz Planer.
Art Direction: Robert Herlth, Walter Röhrig.
Editing: Rudolf Schaad.
Music: Allan Gray.
Length: 2,684 meters (= ca. 98 min).
Cast: Brigitte Helm (Jeanette Heider), Lucie Englisch (Mimi), Rudolf Forster (Rumowski), Gustaf Gründgens (the "baron"), Mathias Wieman (Stephan Riel).
Censorship record: B.31438 (21 April 1932), restricted for minors ("Jugendverbot").
Premiere: 22 April 1932, Ufa-Palast am Zoo, Berlin.
Available from Bundesarchiv-Filmarchiv, Berlin (German only).

Die Leuchte Asiens = Prem Sanyas (The Light of Asia, 1925)
Director: Franz Osten.
Producer: Emelka, Munich (Franz Osten) and Great Eastern Film Corporation, Delhi (Himansu Rai).
Script: Niranjan Pal.
Cinematography: Wilhelm Kiermeier, Josef Wirsching.
Music: Hansheinrich Dransmann.
Length: 2,121 meters (= ca. 96 minutes).
Cast: Sarada Ukil (King Suddhodana), Himansu Rai (Prince Gotama), Seeta Devi (Princess Gopa).
Premiere: 22 October 1925, Munich.
Available from Kirch Media Archive (German version); British Film Institute, London (English version); The National Film Archive of India, Pune (Anglo-Indian version).

Lichtspiel Opus 1 (Film Opus 1, 1921)
Director: Walther Ruttmann.
Producer: Ruttmann-Film GmbH, Munich.
Music: Max Butting.

Length: 243 meters (= ca. 12 minutes).
Censorship record: M.00789 (29 October 1921).
Premiere: previewed 1 April 1921 U. T. im Schwan Theater, Frankfurt/
Main; public premiere 27 April 1921, Marmorhaus, Berlin.
Available on DVD, *Berlin: Symphony of a Great City* (Image Entertainment,
1999) and on DVD, *Berlin, die Sinfonie der Großstadt* (Edition Filmmuseum
Munich, 2008), www.edition-filmmuseum.com.

Lichtspiel Opus 2 (Film Opus 2, 1922)
Director: Walther Ruttmann.
Producer: Ruttmann-Film GmbH. Munich.
Length: 78 meters (= ca. 5 minutes).
Censorship record: M.00889 (15 February 1922).
Premiere: previewed January 1922; public premiere 3 May 1925, U. T.
Kurfürstendamm, Berlin, as part of the matinee "Der absolute Film."
Available on DVD, *Berlin, die Sinfonie der Großstadt* (Edition Filmmuseum
Munich, 2008), www.edition-filmmuseum.com.

Lichtspiel Opus 3 (Film Opus 3, 1925)
Director: Walther Ruttmann.
Producer: Kunstmaler W. Ruttmann Film.
Assistant director: Lore Leudesdorff.
Length: 66 meters (= ca. 4 minutes).
Censorship record: B.10333, 21 April 1925.
Premiere: 3 May 1925, U. T. Kurfürstendamm, Berlin, as part of the
matinee "Der absolute Film."
Available on DVD, *Berlin, die Sinfonie der Großstadt* (Edition Filmmuseum
Munich, 2008), www.edition-filmmuseum.com.

Liebling der Götter (Darling of the Gods, 1930)
Producer: Erich Pommer, Universum Film A.G. (Ufa).
Script: Hans Müller, Robert Liebmann.
Cinematography: Günter Rittau, Konstantin Tschet.
Art Direction: Erich Kettelhut.
Editor: Willy Zeyn jun.
Music: Willy Schmidt-Gentner, Karl M. May.
Length: 2,993 meters (= ca. 110 minutes).
Cast: Emil Jannings (Albert Winkelmann), Renate Müller (Agathe
Winkelmann), Olga Tschechowa (Olga von Dagomirska), Hans Moser
(Kratochvil), Marcel Wittrisch (Albert's singing voice).
Censorship record: B.26982 (30 September 1930), restricted for minors

Premiere: 7 October 1930, Urania, Budapest; German premiere: 13 October 1930, Gloria-Palast, Berlin.
Available from Transit Film Verleih, http://www.transitfilm.de/en/verleih/ (16 mm. print; German only).

Marion, das gehört sich nicht (Marion, This Is Not Proper, 1932)
Director: E. W. Emo.
Producer: Itala-Film GmbH, Berlin.
Script: Kurt Siodmak.
Cinematography: Hugo von Kaweczynski.
Music: Otto Stransky.
Length: ca. 85 minutes.
Cast: Magda Schneider (Marion Satorius), Hermann Thimig (Kurt Bach), Julius Falkenstein (butler Brammel), Olly Gebauer (entertainer Gussy).
Censorship record: 12 December 1932.
Premiere: 15 February 1933.
Available from Bundesarchiv-Filmarchiv, Berlin (German only).

Nerven (Nerves, 1919)
Director: Robert Reinert.
Producer: Robert Reinert, Monumental Film-Werke GmbH, Munich.
Script: Robert Reinert.
Cinematography: Helmar Lerski.
Length: ca. 110 minutes.
Cast: Eduard von Winterstein (Roloff), Erna Morena (his sister Marja), Lya Borré (Roloff's wife Elisabeth), Paul Bender (Johannes), Lili Dominici (Johannes' blind sister).
Premiere: December 1919, Kammer-Lichtspiele Theater, Munich.
Censorship record: B.738 (15 November 1920).
Available on DVD (with English intertitles) from Edition Filmmuseum Munich, www.edition-filmmuseum.com.

Niemandsland (No Man's Land, US release title, *Hell on Earth*, 1931)
Director: Victor Trivas.
Producer: Anton Resch, Resco Filmproduktion, Berlin.
Script: Leonhard Frank, George Shdanoff (uncredited), Victor Trivas (uncredited).
Cinematography: Alexander von Lagorio, Georg Stilianudis (= Georges C. Stilly).
Art Direction: Arthur Schwarz.
Editor: Brian King, Walter S. Stern.
Music: Hanns Eisler.
Length: 2,556 m. (= ca. 93 minutes); restored English version (1969) is ca. 66 minutes.

Cast: Ernst Busch (Köhler, the German), Hugh Stephen Douglas (Brown, the Englishman), Georges Péclet (Durant, the Frenchman), Louis Douglas (Joe Smile, the black entertainer), Vladimir Sokoloff (Lewin, "Somewhere in the World"), Renée Stobrawa (the German woman), Zoe Frank (the English woman), Rose Mai (the French woman), Elisabeth Lennarz (the Jewish woman).
Censorship record: B.30455 (15 November 1931).
Premiere: 10 December 1931, Terra-Lichtspiele (Mozartsaal), Berlin.
Available from Bundesarchiv-Filmarchiv, Berlin (German version). VHS of restored English version (Inkwell Images, Maurice H. Zouary, 1969). Restored English version streamed online at http://www.archive.org/details/HellOnEarth.

Orlacs Hände (The Hands of Orlac, 1924)
Director: Robert Wiene.
Producer: Berolina Film (Berlin) and Pan Film (Vienna).
Script: Louis Nerz, based on a novel by Maurice Renard.
Cinematography: Günther Krampf, Hans Androschin.
Art Director: Stefan Wessely.
Length: 2,507 m. (= ca. 110 minutes).
Cast: Conrad Veidt (Paul Orlac), Alexandra Sorina (Yvonne Orlac), Fritz Kortner (Nera).
Censorship record: B.09074 (25 September 1924), restricted for minors ("Jugendverbot").
Premiere: 24 September 1924, Haydn-Kino, Vienna.
Available from Kino International, www.kino.com (DVD with English intertitles).

Peter Voss, der Millionendieb (Peter Voss, The Thief Who Stole Millions, 1932)
Director: E. A. Dupont.
Producer: Karl Grune, Münchner Lichtspielkunst AG (Emelka), Munich.
Script: Bruno Frank, E. A. Dupont.
Cinematography: Friedl Behn-Grund.
Art Director: Willy Reiber, Ludwig Reiber, Max Michael Oswald, I. Nowack (revue scenes).
Music: Peter Kreuder.
Length: 2,852 m. (=ca. 100 minutes).
Cast: Willi Forst (Peter Voss), Otto Wernicke (Pitt), Alice Treff (Pitt's daughter Polly), Paul Hörbiger (detective Bobby Dodd), Ida Wüst (Madame Bianca).
Censorship record: 18 March 1932.
Premiere: 23 March 1932.
Available from Bundesarchiv-Filmarchiv, Berlin (German only).

Die Prostitution (Prostitution, 1919)
Director: Richard Oswald.
Producer: Richard Oswald, Richard Oswald Film GmbH, Berlin.
Script: Robert Liebmann, Richard Oswald.
Cinematography: Karl Freund, Max Faßbender.
Art Director: Emil Linke.
Length: 2,566 m. (= ca. 115 minutes).
Cast: Anita Berber (Lona), Gussy Holl (Hedwig), Conrad Veidt (Alfred Werner), Kissa von Sievers ("Prostitution"), Reinhold Schünzel (Karl Döring), Werner Krauß (sex murderer).
Censorship record: B.42921 (6 June 1919).
Premiere: 1 May 1919, Marmorhaus, Berlin.
Alternative Titles (given by censor): *Das gelbe Haus* (The Yellow House), *Im Sumpfe der Großstadt* (In the Swamp of the Big City).
Destroyed in 1922.

Rhythmus 21 (Rhythm 21; alternate title, *Film ist Rhythmus*, Film is Rhythm, 1921)
Director: Hans Richter.
Producer: Hans Richter, for Ufa, Berlin.
Cinematography: Svend Noldan; Otto Schmalhausen.
Length: ca. 3 minutes.
Premiere: 6 July 1923, Théâtre Michel, Paris.
Available from Kino International, www.kino.com (on *Avant-Garde: Experimental Cinema of the 1920s and 1930s*), DVD with English subtitles.

Der Ritualmord (Ritual Murder, 1919); also known as *Die Geächteten* (The Ostracized)
Director: Joseph Delmont.
Producer: Max Nivelli, Nivo-Film GmbH, Berlin.
Script: Helmut Ortmann.
Cinematography: Gustave Preiss.
Art Director: Willi A. Herrmann.
Cast: Alfred Abel, Sybil Morel, Rita Clermont, Leonhard Haskel, Colette Corder.
The film has not survived.

Die Stadt ohne Juden (The City without Jews, 1924)
Director: Hans Karl Breslauer.
Producer: Hans Karl Breslauer, H. K. Breslauer Film, Vienna; Mondiale Filmindustrie AG, Vienna; Walterskirchen & Bittner, Vienna.
Script: Hans Karl Breslauer, Ida Jenbach, based on the novel by Hugo Bettauer.

Cinematography: Hugo Eywo.
Art Director: Julius von Borsody.
Length: 2,040 m. (= ca. 80 minutes).
Cast: Johannes Riemann (Leo Strakosch), Hans Moser (Councilor Bernart), Karl Thema (Councilor Linder), Anny Milety (Lotte, Linder's daughter), Eugen Neufeld (Chancellor), Ferdinand Maierhofer (Councilor Volbert), Mizzi Griebl (Volbert's wife), Hans Effenberger (Alfons Carroni).
Premiere: 5 July 1924, Haydn-Kino, Vienna.
Available from Filmarchiv Austria, Vienna, www.filmarchiv.at (VHS tape, German intertitles only). DVD (Edition *Der Standard*, 2008, German intertitles only) available from www.filmarchiv.at and www.hoanzl.at.

Der Student von Prag (The Student of Prague, 1926)
Director: Henrik Galeen.
Producer: Henry Sokal, H. R. Sokal-Film GmbH, Berlin.
Script: Henrik Galeen, Hans Heinz Ewers; a remake of Stellan Rye's film of 1913 (scripted by Stellan Rye, Hans Heinz Ewers, Paul Wegener).
Cinematography: Günther Krampf, Ernst Nitzschmann.
Art Direction: Hermann Warm.
Music: Willy Schmidt-Gentner.
Length: 2,630 meters (= ca. 101 minutes).
Cast: Conrad Veidt (Balduin), Elizza La Porta (Lyduschka), Werner Krauß (Scapinelli), Agnes Gräfin Esterhazy (Countess Margit), Fritz Aliberti (Count von Schwarzenberg).
Censorship record: B.13959 (19 October 1926, Berlin), restricted for minors ("Jugendverbot").
Premiere: 26 October 1926, Capitol, Berlin.
Available from Bundesarchiv-Filmarchiv, Berlin (German intertitles only).

Sumurun (US release title, *One Arabian Night*, 1920)
Director: Ernst Lubitsch.
Producer: Paul Davidson, PAGU (Projektions A.G. Union), Berlin.
Script: Hanns Kräly, Ernst Lubitsch, after an oriental pantomime by Friedrich Freska.
Cinematography: Theodor Sparkuhl, Fritz Arno Wagner.
Art Director: Kurt Richter, assisted by Ernö Metzner.
Music: Victor Hollaender.
Length: 2,400 m (= ca. 100 minutes).
Cast: Pola Negri (the dancer), Jenny Hasselqvist (Zuleika, called Sumurun), Aud Egede Nissen (Haidee, her servant), Margarete Kupfer (the old woman), Harry Liedtke (Nur-al-Din, the textile merchant), Ernst Lubitsch (Abdullah, the hunchback clown), Paul Wegener (the old sheik).
Premiere: 1 September 1920, Ufa-Palast am Zoo, Berlin.

Available from Kino International, www.kino.com (DVD with English intertitles).

Vormittagsspuk (Ghosts before Breakfast, 1928)
Director: Hans Richter.
Producer: Hans Richter-Gesellschaft Neuer Film (Berlin).
Length: 170 meters (= ca. 9 minutes).
Music: Paul Hindemith.
Censorship record: B.19467 (11 July 1928).
Premiere: August 1928, Kurtheater, Baden-Baden, as part of *Kammermusikfest*.
Available from Kino International, www.kino.com (on *Avant-Garde: Experimental Cinema of the 1920s and 1930s*), DVD with English subtitles.

Voruntersuchung (Preliminary Inquest, 1931)
Director: Robert Siodmak.
Producer: Erich Pommer, for Ufa, Berlin.
Script: Robert Liebmann.
Cinematography: Konstantin Tschet, Otto Baecker.
Art Director: Erich Kettelhut.
Length: 2,610 m. (=ca. 95 minutes).
Cast: Albert Bassermann (Dr. Konrad Bienert), Hans Brausewetter (Bienert's son Walter), Charlotte Ander (Bienert's daughter Gerda), Gustav Fröhlich (Fritz Bernt), Annie Markart (Erna Kabisch).
Censorship record: B.28740 (17 April 1931), restricted for minors ("Jugendverbot").
Premiere: 24 April 1931, Gloria-Palast, Berlin.
Available from Bundesarchiv-Filmarchiv, Berlin (German only).

Wege zu Kraft und Schönheit (Paths to Strength and Beauty, 1925)
Director: Wilhelm Prager.
Producer: Universum Film A.G. (Ufa), Kulturabteilung, Berlin.
Script: Wilhelm Prager, Nicholas Kaufmann.
Cinematography: Friedrich Weinmann, Eugen Hrich, Friedrich Paulmann, Kurt Neubert, Max Brink; Erich Stöcker, Jakob Schatzow (slow motion).
Art Director: Hans Söhnle, Otto Erdmann.
Scientific Consultant: Nicholas Kaufmann.
Music: Guiseppe Becce.
Length: 2,558 m. (=ca. 104 minutes).
Cast: Jenny Hasselqvist, Niddy Impekoven, Tamara Karsavina, Rudolf Kobs, La Jana.
Censorship record: B.09825 (16 February 1925). New version B.13251 (4 June 1926).

Premiere: 16 March 1925, Ufa-Palast am Zoo, Berlin.
Available from Transit Film-Verleih, www.transitfilm.de/en/verleih
(German version).

Westfront 1918 (Western Front 1918, 1930)
Director: G. W. Pabst.
Producer: Seymour Nebenzahl, Nero-Film, Berlin.
Script: Peter Martin Lampel, Ladislaus Vajda, based on a novel by Ernst
Johannsen.
Cinematography: Fritz Arno Wagner, Charles Métain.
Art Director: Ernö Metzner, Willy Reiber.
Editor: Marc Sorkin, Wolfgang Loë-Bagnier.
Music: Alexander Laszlo.
Length: 2,401 meters (= ca. 88 minutes).
Cast: Gustav Diessl (Karl), Fritz Kampers (the Bavarian), Hans Joachim
Moebis (the student), Gustav Püttjer (the man from Hamburg), Claus
Clausen (the Lieutenant), Jackie Monnier (Jacqueline/Yvette), Hanna
Hoessrich (Karl's wife).
Censorship record: B.25961 (21 May 1930), restricted for minors
("Jugendverbot").
Premiere: 23 May 1930, Capitol, Berlin.
Available from Kultur video, VHS (NTSC, with English subtitles).

Contributors

OFER ASHKENAZI is a visiting lecturer in the German Department, University of California, Berkeley, and a research fellow of the Koebner-Minerva Center for German History at the Hebrew University, Jerusalem. His publications include a book, *Making Sense of Modernity: Madness and Subjectivity in Weimar Film* (forthcoming) and several articles on historical aspects of Weimar Cinema.

JAIMEY FISHER is Associate Professor of German at the University of California, Davis. He is the author of *Disciplining German: Youth, Reeducation, and Reconstruction after the Second World War* (2007), co-editor of *Critical Theory: Current State and Future Prospects* (2001), and of two forthcoming books, *Collapse of the Conventional: German Cinema and its Politics at the Turn of the Century* and *Spatial Turns: Space, Place, and Mobility in German Literary and Visual Culture.*

VERONIKA FUECHTNER is Associate Professor of German Studies at Dartmouth College. Her book *Berlin Psychoanalytic,* about culture and psychoanalysis in Weimar Republic Germany, is forthcoming with University of California Press. She has published on Alfred Döblin, Magnus Hirschfeld, Herbert Marcuse, Zé do Rock, and on the state of German Studies in the U.S. She is currently working on racial discourses before fascism and how they still impact ideas on "race" and immigration in contemporary Germany.

JOSEPH GARNCARZ, Dr. phil., teaches Theater, Film and Television Studies at the University of Cologne, Germany. His publications include *Filmfassungen: Eine Theorie signifikanter Filmvariation* (1992), two forthcoming books, *Maßlose Unterhaltung: Zur Etablierung des Films in Deutschland, 1896–1914* and *24 Frames: The Cinema of Germany,* and numerous articles on German cinema.

BARBARA HALES is Assistant Professor of History at the University of Houston-Clear Lake. Her publications focus on film history, cultural studies, and the intellectual history of the Weimar Republic. Her current research interests include women and the occult in Weimar Germany, and dance and early German cinema.

ANJEANA HANS is Assistant Professor of German at Wellesley College, where she teaches courses on language and on literature, culture, and film of the nineteenth and twentieth centuries. Her research focuses on questions of gender, identity, and subjectivity in twentieth-century German culture. She is currently working on a book-length study of early German "horror" films — showing how such films draw on elements of the uncanny to negotiate anxieties concerning shifting gender norms and how they challenge, as well as participate in, the development of cinematic conventions.

RICHARD W. MCCORMICK teaches German film and culture at the University of Minnesota. He has published on West German film and literature of the 1970s and 1980s, on West German feminist cinema, and in general on German cinema of the Weimar and postwar eras. His main publication on Weimar film and culture is *Gender and Sexuality in Weimar Modernity: Film, Literature, and "New Objectivity"* (2001). He is currently working on a book on the German and American films of Ernst Lubitsch titled *Sex, Politics, and "Transnational" Comedy: The Films of Ernst Lubitsch from Berlin to Hollywood*.

NANCY P. NENNO is Associate Professor of German at the College of Charleston, where she teaches all levels of language, literature, culture, and film. Her publications on Weimar German culture include essays on Josephine Baker in Weimar Berlin and on the *Bergfilm* ("Mountain Film") genre. Her research interests include representations of African Americans in Germany between the wars and the transition from silent to sound film.

ELIZABETH OTTO is Assistant Professor in the Department of Visual Studies at the State University of New York at Buffalo. Her research focuses on issues of gender, visuality, and media culture in the late nineteenth and twentieth centuries. She is the co-editor of the forthcoming collection *The New Woman International: Representations in Photography and Film from the 1870s through the 1960s* and the author of *Tempo, Tempo! The Bauhaus Photomontages of Marianne Brandt* (2005) as well as essays on such topics as gender at the Bauhaus, the represented male body in film and photomontage of the Weimar Republic, and Siegfried Kracauer's art-historical writings.

MIHAELA PETRESCU is Assistant Professor of German at Hobart and William Smith Colleges. Her fields of concentration are literature and film during the Weimar Republic, multiculturalism in Germany, and German cinema. She has published on the interconnection of the "vamp" with jazz and dance melodrama in Weimar cinema. She is currently working on a book manuscript on representations of jazz dances in the Weimar Republic.

THEODORE F. RIPPEY is Associate Professor of German at Bowling Green State University. His research areas include Weimar and exile film and literature, sound, the concept of the mass, and the relationship between aesthetics and politics. His book-length study on aural experience and German modernity (in progress) focuses in part on hearing and seeing in interwar cinema and film theory.

CHRISTIAN ROGOWSKI is Professor of German at Amherst College, Amherst, Massachusetts. His publications include two books on Austrian author Robert Musil, a CD-ROM for teaching German cultural studies, and essays on German-language literature, opera, film, intellectual history, and European drama. His current research focuses on the cinema and popular culture of the Weimar Republic, especially in terms of the politics of "race" (including the legacy of German colonialism, the impact of Afro-American culture, and the German-Jewish dynamic).

JILL SUZANNE SMITH is Assistant Professor of German at Bowdoin College. Her research focuses on gender and sexuality, nineteenth- and twentieth-century German Jewish studies, and the city of Berlin from the Wilhelmine era to the present. Her publications address issues such as the conflation of white-collar working women and prostitutes in popular Weimar fiction and space and gender in an erotic travel guide to Weimar Berlin. She is currently finishing a book manuscript on literary, social, and cultural discourses on prostitution in Berlin from 1880 to 1933.

PHILIPP STIASNY, Dr.phil., is a freelance film historian based in Berlin and editor of the film historical journal *Filmblatt*. In addition to the book *Das Kino und der Krieg: Deutschland 1914–1929* (2009), he has published numerous articles on various aspects of Weimar German film culture, ranging from "Fußballspielfilme" (silent films reflecting the German obsession with soccer) to representations of traumatized men returning home from the war ("Kriegsheimkehrer").

CHRIS WAHL, Dr. phil., is a Research Fellow at the Film & Television Academy (HFF) "Konrad Wolf" in Potsdam-Babelsberg, Germany. He is the author of *Sprachversionsfilme aus Babelsberg* (2009) about Ufa's multiple language versions. Currently, he is editing two books on German film directors, on Werner Herzog (*Lektionen in Herzog,* with text + Kritik, Munich) and on Kurt Hoffmann (*Kurt Hoffmann — Der Erfinder der Pulver,* with the German Film Museum, Frankfurt am Main).

CYNTHIA WALK received her PhD from Yale University and taught in the Department of Literature at the University of California, San Diego from 1972 to 2006, when she retired. Her research has focused on German drama, theatre, and film, with several publications on Weimar cinema, including "The Debate about Stage Tradition in Weimar Cinema: Murnau's *Herr Tartüff*" (2002) and "Cross-media Exchange in Weimar Culture: *Von morgens bis mitternachts*" (2007).

VALERIE WEINSTEIN is Associate Professor of German at the University of Nevada, Reno. Her research interests include gender, ethnicity, and "race" in German culture, particularly in cinema before 1945. She has published on Ernst Lubitsch and E. A. Dupont, among others. Her most recent publications are the articles "Working Weimar Women into the National Socialist Community" (2009) and "Dance in Ethnographic Films from the Hamburg South Seas Expedition 1908–1910" (2010).

JOEL WESTERDALE is Assistant Professor of German Studies at Smith College in Northampton, Massachusetts, where he teaches courses on film, literature, and philosophy. His publications focus on Nietzsche and on Weimar Cinema. Currently he is investigating figurations of evil in early Weimar film with the support of the Alexander von Humboldt Foundation.

Index